Writing History

General Editors: Stefan Berger
Heiko Feldner
Kevin Passmore

Contents

Notes on contributors

Stefan Berger is Professor of Modern and Contemporary History at the University of Glamorgan. Most recent publications include (with Peter Lambert and Peter Schumann) *Historikerdialoge* (Göttingen, 2003), *Labour and Social History in Britain, 1990 to the Present* (Essen, 2002) and (with Hugh Compston) *Policy Concertation and Social Partnership in Western Europe* (Oxford, 2002). He is also the author of numerous publications on comparative labour history, national identity and the history of historiography.

Geoff Eley is Sylvia L. Thrupp Collegiate Professor of Comparative History at the University of Michigan. The author of *Forging Democracy: The History of the Left in Europe, 1850–2000* (New York, 2002), he has published widely on German history of the nineteenth and twentieth centuries, including books on the German Right between Bismarck and the 1920s, and the idea of the Sonderweg in German history.

Heiko Feldner is Lecturer in Modern German History in the School of European Studies at Cardiff University. He is the author of *Das Erfahrnis der Ordnung* (Frankfurt, 1999) and is currently working on a study of the history of scientific self-distancing in eighteenth-century Germany.

Glenn Jordan is Senior Lecturer in Cultural Studies at the University of Glamorgan and Director of Butetown History & Arts Centre in Cardiff. He is co-author (with Chris Weedon) of *Cultural Politics: Class, Gender, Race and the Postmodern World* (Oxford, 1995) and is currently working on two books: *Voices From Below: People's History and Cultural Democracy* and *Race* (*Routledge*, forthcoming). He also writes on photography and regularly curates exhibitions.

Peter Lambert lectures in Modern European History at the University of Wales, Aberystwyth, and has published essays and articles on German historiography. He is co-editor (with Stefan Berger and Peter Schumann) of *Historikerdialoge*, a collection of essays on Anglo-German historiographical relations (Göttingen, 2003) and (with Phillipp Schofield) of *Historians and the Making of History* (forthcoming, London, 2003).

Jon Lawrence is Senior Lecturer in History at the University of Liverpool. His major publications include *Speaking for the People: Party, Language and Popular Politics in England, 1867–1914*, (Cambridge, 1998) and (with Miles Taylor) *Party, State and Society: Electoral Behaviour in Britain since 1820* (Aldershot, 1997). He is currently working on the transformation of public politics in modern Britain and has articles forthcoming on this topic in the *Journal of Modern History* and *Historical Research*.

Laura Lee Downs is Directeur d'études at the Centre de Recherches Historiques, École des Hautes Études en Sciences Sociales. She is the author of *Manufacturing Inequality: Gender Division in the French and British Metalworking Industries, 1914–1939* (Ithaca and London, 1995) and of *Childhood in the Promised Land: Working-Class Movements and the Colonies de Vacances in France, 1880–1960* (Durham, NC, 2002). She is currently completing a book on gender and the writing of history for the series *Writing History*.

Christopher Lloyd was born in Australia and educated at the Universities of New England, Sussex and Oxford. He is currently Professor of Economic History at the University of New England, Armidale, Australia, and affiliated fellow of the Research School of Social Sciences at Australian National University, Canberra. His research interests include historical theory and methodology, historical political economy and Holocene economic history.

Matthias Middell is Acting Director of the Centre for Advanced Studies at the University of Leipzig. His recent publications include *Historische Institute im internationalen Vergleich* (Leipzig, 2001) and *Französische Geschichte 1500–1945* (Leipzig, 1999). His research interests include world history, the history of historiography in the nineteenth and twentieth centuries, and processes of cultural transfer between France and Germany.

Kevin Passmore is Lecturer in History at Cardiff University. He has published books and articles on the right and extreme right in Europe, including *Fascism* (Oxford, 2002) and (edited) *Women, Gender and Fascism in Europe* (Manchester and Rutgers, 2003). He has also edited *Europe Since 1815: Writing National Histories* with Stefan Berger and Mark Donovan.

Milla Rosenberg is an independent scholar, researcher, activist and journalist. S/he has reviewed for the *Journal of Women's History* and has a forthcoming essay on integration in the anthology *Race in Post-Integration America*. S/he is a contributing reporter to *Gay People's Chronicle*, a statewide newspaper serving lesbian, gay, bisexual and transgender people in Ohio.

Beverley Southgate is Reader Emeritus in History of Ideas at the University of Hertfordshire, and now lives in London. His recent publications include *Why Bother with History?* (Harlow, 2000), *History: What and Why?* (second edition, London, 2002) and *Postmodernism in History: Fear or Freedom?* (London, 2003).

Garthine Walker is Lecturer in History at Cardiff University. She has published *Crime, Gender and Social Order in Early Modern England* (Cambridge, 2003), edited the forthcoming volume in this series, *Approaching Early Modern History* and edited with Jenny Kermode *Women, Crime and the Courts in Early Modern England* (London, 1994).

John Warren is Director of Sixth Form at the Oscar Romero Sixth Form Centre in Telford, Shropshire. His published works include *Elizabeth I: Religion and Foreign Affairs* (second edition, London, 2001), *The Wars of the Roses and the Yorkist Kings* (London, 1995) and *The Past and its Presenters* (London, 1998). His research interests lie in the field of Victorian intellectual history, with particular reference to radical and denominational periodicals.

Thomas Welskopp is visiting professor at Göttingen University. Recent publications include *Das Banner der Brüderlichkeit. Die deutsche Sozialdemokratie vom Vormärz bis zum Sozialistengesetz* (Bonn, 2000) and (co-edited with Thomas Mergel) *Geschichte zwischen Kultur und Gesellschaft. Beiträge zur Theoriedebatte* (Munich, 1997). His present research focuses on a social and cultural history of the United States during National Prohibition, 1919–33.

Preface

Like it or not, historians cannot avoid theory. Indeed, the idea that history could and should be a separate field of academic enquiry – now taken (largely) for granted – depended, as the first chapter of this book demonstrates, upon shifts in eighteenth-century understandings of the very nature of knowledge. Even if they do not explicitly use theory themselves, the writing of historians is subtly informed by theoretical assumptions. Geoffrey Elton, the great anti-theorist, might have argued that training in the techniques of historical research, coupled with fidelity to the documentary record, would permit the accumulation of objective accounts of the past, but his own work assumed the theoretical primacy of politics, and he presented a view of history in which the development of the British state was paramount. Some contemporary historians dismiss as jargon expressions taken from literary criticism such as 'discourse', just as their early twentieth-century predecessors turned up their noses at modish psychological concepts such as 'unconscious motivations'. Soon, 'discourse' too will pass into common sense, and it will cease to be regarded as a theoretical term. Actually, none of the concepts used by historians are innocent. Each has its history.

Writing History: Theory and Practice is the first book in a series – *Writing History* – designed to introduce students of history at university level to the theoretical ideas – conscious and unconscious – that have moulded the discipline of history, largely in the West. This particular volume surveys the competing 'schools' of theoretical reflection that have underpinned the study of history, and the empirical method is treated as one among several ways of doing history. The book provides succinct critical introductions to the ideas, techniques and institutional practices that made possible the establishment of history as an autonomous discipline. It surveys the major bodies of theoretical knowledge that have been used to explain the past and explores the impact of these ideas upon real examples of historical writing and upon certain fields of historical study.

This is not a book about the 'philosophy of history'. It is not directly concerned with abstract issues relating to epistemology, causation, the question of whether history is a science or art, or the use of laws in historical explanation. Knowledge of these matters is, nevertheless, essential to the practising historian and they figure indirectly in many of the chapters of this book. The interested reader will be able to follow such themes through the book with the aid of the Index.

Neither is this book about 'historiography' or the 'history of history'. It does not provide a comprehensive survey of the development of the historical profession in its political, social, cultural and institutional context. The complete separation of theory from this context is, of course, impossible. The empirical–scientific–professional mode of historical writing, as the first three chapters in the book demonstrate, was closely tied to the establishment of history as an autonomous discipline, and the legacy of this founding moment continues to structure the discipline today – so much so that theoretical innovations often appeared to challenge the disciplinary autonomy of history and therefore even the very possibility of objective knowledge of the past. Most recently, poststructuralism seems to some like a devilish plot by literary critics to destroy the discipline, and by extension objectivity and the whole social order. Important as these issues are, they are not at the centre of this book.

The goal of this book is to explore the ways in which theory has informed *practical* historical writing. *Writing History* is based on the recognition that students often find it difficult to see how abstract discussions of the philosophy of history or histories of the discipline, relate to their own practice as historians. Each of the chapters combines explanation of essential concepts with critical discussions of the ways in which such concepts have informed works by practising historians. Students would be well advised to combine their reading of this book with sampling of the authors discussed in it.

Of course, the range of theories used by historians is too large to cover in a single volume. Our decision was to include those methods, theories and objects of enquiry that students are most likely to find in their reading for 'normal' history courses, and thus enable them to recognize the assumptions that structure individual works and fields as a whole.

The book's structure is tripartite. The three chapters in the first section examine the intellectual and institutional conditions in which professional history developed. They explain the intellectual innovations that made possible the emergence of history as a 'scientific' discipline in Germany in the late eighteenth century, the spread of Rankean historical methods from nineteenth-century Germany to the rest of the world and the diversification of method since the late twentieth century and challenges to 'western ways' of writing history.

Part Two of the book introduces approaches to history that purport to be applicable to all periods and fields of history. The Marxist, social scientific and *Annalistes* approaches dealt with in Chapters 4, 5 and 6 are all explicitly totalizing explanations of history. Their theoretical insights and concepts have been applied to all fields of historical enquiry, and each object of study is fitted into a general explanation of history or a 'metanarrative'. In recent decades all of these approaches have witnessed attempts to eliminate more teleological and determinist features. This has led to some convergence between them and to a certain loss of specificity as theories.

Although poststructuralism provided much of the force behind this critique of metanarratives, it is included in Part Two because it proposes a method of critical analysis that is meant to be applicable to all of the objects studied by historians. Likewise, psychohistory is included in Part Two because Freudian psychoanalysis provided a set of concepts that allegedly explained all aspects of human behaviour – from individual motivations to the origins and nature of wars – in terms of infant relations with parents. More recently, psychoanalysis has come under the influence of poststructuralism, and this has not reduced its broad ambitions. Finally, comparative history is treated in Part Two because it claims to be a universally applicable method, which does explicitly what all historians do implicitly.

The chapters in Part Two of *Writing History* deal with single theoretical traditions; those in Part Three consider the impact of a diverse range of theories in a single field of history. They often assume knowledge of the particular theories discussed in the previous section. Readers must, of course, bear in mind that theories are rarely applied in a 'pure' form to specific objects of study. More frequently, historians have combined elements from a range of theories.

The decision to include a given chapter in Parts Two or Three might seem somewhat arbitrary. Gender and race historians, for example, have argued that *all* history can – and must – be rewritten in accordance with their concepts, but for two reasons chapters on these topics have been included in Part Three. First, the authors of these chapters have treated gender and race as *objects of study* onto which a number of theoretical traditions have been brought to bear, rather than as *methods*. Second, much contemporary gender and race theory can be seen as methodologically derived from poststructuralism.

Indeed, Part Three of *Writing History* reflects the extent to which engagement with poststructuralism has shaped historical writing in recent years. Historians of politics, societies, ideas, gender, race and the economy have all, in differing degrees, shifted their attention from underlying causes to histories of meaning and identity. Whatever their fields, contemporary historians concern themselves increasingly with cultures.

At the time of writing, structuralism and poststructuralism have been with us for two decades or more, and their 'cutting-edge' status is somewhat attenuated. Several chapters suggest the need for reconciliation of the poststructuralist preoccupation with culture into a method that takes more account of social structure and inequality and that is able to account for change. Chapter 4 argues that the new cultural histories need to be related to 'a bigger picture of society in general'. Chapters 7, 8 and 15 suggest that Bakhtinian methods might offer a way forward, while Chapter 9 advocates the fusion of poststructuralist-influenced cultural transfer with a socially grounded method. Chapter 10 urges the fusion of cultural with elite and social approaches to political history and Chapter 13 advocates Quentin Skinner's approach to the history of ideas as a socially contextualized method that possesses the strengths but not the weaknesses of poststructuralism. Chapter 14 calls for gender historians to reconsider the relationship between language, body and psychology. Chapters 5 and 12 suggest that economic and cultural approaches have much to learn from each other. Whether these tendencies are seen as positive, or as attempts to blunt the critical edge of poststructuralism by incorporating it into established methods is an open question.

Kevin Passmore, Stefan Berger, Heiko Feldner
February 2003

Part 1

1

The new scientificity in historical writing around 1800

Heiko Feldner

'Schorske is not so foolish as to declare the death of history,' Steven Beller concedes in his review of Carl E. Schorske's *Thinking with History*:

> but Clio has certainly, in his view, fallen on hard times. The queen of the sciences in the mid-nineteenth century, she is now in much straitened circumstances, reduced, in Schorske's phrase, to going on 'dates' with any discipline that will have her. This sense of history having suffered a fall from grace is overly pessimistic. History never had quite the pre-eminence Schorske ascribes to it, except perhaps in Germany.[1]

Beller's critique refers to a number of issues that form the backdrop of the following chapter. To begin with, there is the idea that history is a science and, subsequently, the uncertainty as to what exactly that means; second, the assumption that there was a golden age of history which, if it ever existed, was in nineteenth-century Germany; and finally, the endeavour to endow the academic discipline of history, in one way or another, with a distinctive biography. Underlying these issues is the question of what constitutes historical science (French *science historique*, German *Geschichtswissenschaft*) and its claims to objectivity, validity and truth, a recurrent theme that gives rise to controversial debates, particularly in times of paradigm shift.[2]

Part and parcel of these debates is the discussion about the *emergence* of scientific order in historical writing.[3] It is obvious that historiography as a cultural practice and true representation of the past is much older than the academic discipline of history. Even so, until the eighteenth century no serious attempt was made to claim for historical writing a scientific code of practice. In fact, within the pre-modern order of knowledge, *historia* and *scientia* were mutually exclusive.

However, what had seemed a contradiction in terms to the English philosopher Thomas Hobbes (1651), the German scholar Christian Wolff (1712) and, as late as 1751, the French editors of the *Encyclopédie*, d'Alembert and Diderot – namely that historiography could be viewed in science-like terms – was to be the point of departure for Johann Gustav Droysen's theory of historical science (*Historik*) only some hundred years later, in 1857.[4] Were nineteenth-century scholars, like the historian and Hegel-pupil Droysen, more astute than their seventeenth- and eighteenth-century counterparts? Did they detect some untapped potential in the writing of history that their predecessors had overlooked?

There is no such thing as historical science, and this is a chapter about its beginnings. Asking how it became possible to conceive of history as a science, it explores the rise of the new scientificity claimed, discussed and practised in historical writing around 1800. Since, we are usually told, it was at German universities that modern historical science took off, the German case looms large in this chapter, although this will not prevent us from reflecting on developments elsewhere and drawing some broader conclusions about history writing as a whole.

1.1 *Experientia aliena*

In *Leviathan* (1651) Hobbes introduces his system of knowledge by declaring emphatically that '(t)here are of knowledge two kinds, whereof one is knowledge of fact: the other knowledge of the consequence of one affirmation to another ... The later is called Science ... The register of knowledge of fact is called History.' Whereas science relates to 'reasoning' and 'contain(s) the demonstrations of consequences of one affirmation, to another', history represents 'nothing else but sense and memory', that is 'the knowledge required in a witnesse'. History consequently does not appear in Hobbes' table of sciences.[5]

A lot of time has passed since Hobbes wrote these lines. And yet, even to the present day it is almost impossible for a historian to speak of history as a science without provoking a smile, since whenever the topic under discussion is philosophy of science, history of science or quite simply science, historians are very likely to be the only ones to assume that their discipline belongs there too. Worse still, historians themselves have made heavy weather of this and have been at issue over whether to treat history as soft science, quasi-science, science *sui generis* (of its own kind), or even not as a science at all but as an art.[6]

While this line of questioning has its merits, it is not going to concern us here. I do not want to explore whether scientificity (acting along the lines of scientific rationality) is an attainable goal for historical practitioners. Nor do I intend to ask whether scientificity and its attendant categories of objectivity and truth really exist, and if they do, whether that is something desirable. This chapter is not concerned with problems of existence and legitimacy but with those of history. In fact, what it means 'to do things scientifically' has changed quite dramatically over the past three centuries. The traces of this change can still be seen in our current usage of the word scientific. We glide, for example, with ease from ontological assertions about the ultimate structure of historical reality (the objective truth of a scientific claim) to statements about the procedures that ensure the validity of our empirical findings (scientific methods) and to claims about the scientific ethos of a true scholar (self-distancing, detachment, impartiality, self-effacement, or simply: objectivity). Our notion of scientificity, a blend of essentially different meanings, points to differing and often conflicting histories, which in turn refer to different intellectual traditions, cultural practices and social contexts of origin in which the various images and ideals of scientificity acquired their respective meanings. What I want to do here is to trace some aspects of this history and relate them to the history of historical writing.[7]

It is safe to say that from the time of the Reformation in the sixteenth century the array of diverse genres and practices we refer to as historical writing was firmly established in Germany, if not as *scientia* then nonetheless as an important part of *eruditio* (erudition or learned education). *Historia* figured prominently as a distinct discourse, with corresponding groups of practitioners, norms and institutions. The first *lectio historica* had already been established in 1504 at the University of Mainz. Constituting a fourth form of knowledge besides *scientia*, *prudentia* and *ars*, *cognitio historica* was recognized as *experientia* or *cognitio empirica* – that is, empirical knowledge. As such, historical knowledge was seen as an indispensable component of most branches of learning, to the extent that these branches were not only based on axiomatic principles but also on empirical concepts developed by process of induction. Within this context, history achieved particular significance as *experientia aliena*, as alien experience. Expanding the horizons of personal experience by drawing exemplary lessons from the past, history was valued as a store of moral and political maxims for the guidance of present conduct. For all its importance, however, within the epistemological framework of Aristotelianism, which was prevalent in Germany and indeed across Europe until far into the eighteenth century, history as a science was in principle inconceivable. How can we explain this?[8]

Roughly speaking, the Aristotelian theory of knowledge is predicated on two principles. For one thing, only the universal and abstract can be known with certainty, while the particular and concrete allow merely for statements of probability. For another, certainty can be achieved only about constant and essentially immutable entities, whereas that which keeps changing without rules permits merely probable statements. The first category includes the universal and perennial qualities of all being and nature, covered most notably by those branches of knowledge that were grounded in mathematics and logic. The second category refers to 'man and his actions'. The metaphysical prerequisite of these principles is the assumption that ontological necessity (the quality of following inevitably from logical, physical or moral laws) and epistemological truth (the quality of being a verified or indisputable fact, proposition or theory) are inseparable. Within this framework, the notion of science implies absolute certainty. It means knowing the necessity of why something is so and not otherwise, i.e. the exploration of causes, aimed at the universal and perennial qualities of what exists.

What is important with respect to our question is the fact that historians were precluded from practising science, as it were, on two grounds. On the one hand, history was incompatible with science inasmuch as it explored the concrete realities of particular facts and circumstances. On the other hand, it was incompatible with standards of science inasmuch as it sought to capture the shifting ground of human affairs, an effort conspicuously flawed by the imponderables of human agency and free will.

My argument in this chapter is a triple one. To start with, I shall argue that *cognitio historica* became conceivable as historical science in Germany in the wake of a fundamental de-hierarchization of the edifice of scholarly knowledge, a process set in motion in the sixteenth century and accelerated during the seventeenth and eighteenth centuries by the two intellectual revolutions known as the Scientific Revolution and the Enlightenment. In other words, we have no reason to assume that at a certain historical juncture historiography successfully crossed the threshold of scientificity – an immutable, monolithic ideal – by developing certain methods that were, at long last, adequate to the study of history. Scientificity (French *scientificité*, German *Wissenschaftlichkeit*) is not a transhistorical given. Like any other concept it has itself a history.

Second, the levelling of scholarly knowledge forms was accompanied by an erosion of the plausibility and acceptance of interpretative frameworks associated with Aristotelianism. This occurred in the German setting during the second half of the eighteenth century, i.e. considerably later than in Britain and France. The philosophical agenda of Aristotelianism was eclipsed and in large measure superseded by other types of scientific rationality that a range of historians embraced and put to good use in the writing of history.

Third, the background of the dwindling plausibility of some modes of scientific rationality on the one hand, and the rise of new ones on the other, consisted of broad European changes in attitude towards knowledge in general, and the relations between knowledge and social order in particular. The environment for these changes was the crisis and fundamental transformation of European societies during the century between 1750 and 1850, which has often been portrayed as a 'dual revolution'. The Industrial Revolution, however, was not only accompanied by a revolution in political practices, as embodied in the French Revolution of 1789 and its democratic legacy. The 'dual revolution' was paralleled, and in some measure reinforced, by profound changes in *epistemic* practices, i.e. practices by which knowledge was secured, assessed and communicated.[9]

The outgoing eighteenth century witnessed a particularly tense debate about historical writing and its role in securing and subverting social order. The existing debates over method assumed greater significance as the capacity of historical knowledge to ensure certain desirable values and, in consequence, right conduct was thought to have a considerable impact on the outlook of society. Historical practitioners had to address some ticklish questions. What exactly was proper historical knowledge? Who was authorized to hold it and on what conditions? What degree of certainty was it appropriate to expect of it? Could differing groups of people be made to believe the same things and, if so, how could this be achieved? The recourse to notions of scientificity was to play a key role in answering these and other questions.[10]

I want to illustrate my argument with a brief survey of the shift from Aristotelian towards experiential conceptions of knowledge during the seventeenth and eighteenth centuries, in order to establish the exact implications of this for the province of history. Of the many aspects that a more comprehensive account would include, I have selected three main elements. I first examine the rise of useful knowledge and how that changed the map of knowledge. I then turn briefly to what the Dutch historian E.J. Dijksterhuis once called 'the mechanization of the world picture', to show what impulse historical thinking derived from this. From there I take a look at the rise of the experiment as a knowledge-making practice and consider how this affected the case for empirical historical studies. Finally, I conclude with some thoughts about how the above three elements had helped change the understanding of scientific knowledge by the end of the eighteenth century. In doing so, I shall clarify the notion of scientificity in historical writing, which I want to leave diffuse at this point, allowing its sense and implications to emerge as the inquiry proceeds.

1.2 The rise of useful knowledge

Perhaps the single most astonishing feature that a medieval intellectual like Umberto Eco's Franciscan William of Baskerville would have registered in early-modern Europe was the revaluation of knowledge produced to achieve practical ends. Broadly speaking, the aspiration to shape society according to rational principles placed intellectual practices increasingly in the service of practical objectives. 'Thinking', in Hannah Arendt's words, became 'the handmaiden of doing as it had been the ... handmaiden of contemplating divine truth in medieval philosophy.' With the rise of useful or practical knowledge (of trade, for example, or production processes), the contemplation of eternally given truth was to lose its epistemological prerogative. As a result, 'scientific and philosophic truth have parted company'.[11]

The belief that knowledge ought to be useful was not a free-floating idea, however; it was an integral part of the formation of early-modern states and the concomitant politics of knowledge. In fact, the practice of government in early-modern Europe was increasingly predicated on the systematic collection of information arranged for practical purposes such as public finances (*économie politique* or, in Russia, *kameralnaja nauka*), the mapping of the state territory (cartography) and the welfare and surveillance of the governed ('political arithmetic', statistics and, in Germany, *Polizeiwissenschaft*). Not without good reason did the sociologist Max Weber describe the rise of bureaucracy, one of the key factors in the development of early-modern states, as the 'exercise of control on the basis of knowledge'.[12]

The rise of useful knowledge found a variety of expressions. The burgeoning book markets, for instance, were swamped with publications like Thomas Bray's *An Essay toward promoting all Necessary and Useful Knowledge* (1697) and Johann August Schlettwein's *Von den nützlichen Würkungen einer Universität auf den Nahrungsstand des Volkes* (1776). The Electoral Academy of Useful Sciences in Erfurt (1754), the Mining Academy in Freiberg (1765) and similar societies in Philadelphia (1758) and Virginia (1772) are but a few examples of the numerous institutions set up to promote knowledge of crafts and trades. Designed as *Staatsdienerschulen* (schools for public servants), the newly founded universities in Halle (1694) and Göttingen (1736) promoted in large measure 'useful' subjects. 'Mechanical arts' like engineering and agriculture were playing an increasingly prominent part in best-selling encyclopaedias such as Ephraim Chambers' *Cyclopaedia: or, An Universal Dictionary of Arts and Sciences* (1728) and Heinrich Zedler's *Universal-Lexicon aller Wissenschafften und Künste* (1732–54) while, a little later, the French Academy of Sciences began producing its *description des arts et des métiers* (1761–88), thus underlining the importance it had come to ascribe to the useful or practical branches of knowledge.[13]

Even the scholastic curriculum of European universities did not escape unscathed. Although the system of the four faculties remained by and large intact – the liberal arts (including philosophy) were still followed by the three higher faculties of medicine, law and theology – its order and inherent hierarchy was increasingly challenged by a growing range of new disciplines like chemistry, political economy and, not least, history. The ascent of history as an academic discipline during the eighteenth century was inextricably linked with its usefulness for the training of the growing number of lawyers, 'politicians' (to use a convenient anachronism) and administrators. Good knowledge of international history, for example, was deemed imperative for the training of diplomats at such universities as Paris and Strasbourg. The institution of the Regius chairs in history at the universities of Oxford and Cambridge at the beginning of the eighteenth century had a similar background.[14]

By the mid-eighteenth century, useful or practical knowledge had finally become respectable. The extent to which the traditional order of knowledge had been remapped can be seen in Diderot's 'Prospectus' (1750) and d'Alembert's 'Preliminary Discourse' (1751) to the *Encyclopédie*. D'Alembert, for example, gave particular prominence to mathematics whereas theology, once queen of the four faculties, was presented as but an offshoot of philosophy. That the intellectual flagship of the French *philosophes* should allocate such an important position to the trades in general and to state-of-the-art technologies indicated, moreover, the increasingly problematic ranking of scientific and hitherto non-scientific forms of knowledge. Equally important is the fact that the entries in the *Encyclopédie* were arranged in alphabetical order, which paralleled and underpinned the general trend away from traditional hierarchies of knowledge. Francis Bacon's earlier attack on the Aristotelian classification of knowledge – his *New Organon* of 1620 was meant to replace Aristotle's *Organon* once and for all – had eventually borne fruit.[15]

1.3 Making and knowing: the world as a machine

This leads me to the second element. The revaluation of useful knowledge was connected with the increasing use of mechanical metaphors for imagining the world. The 'mechanization of the world picture', to use the title of Dijksterhuis's classic, played an important part in the shift away from Aristotelian physics. Construing matter as essentially active and motion as having developmental character, Aristotelian physics ascribed design and purpose to material nature. What is important in our context is that the historically triumphant attempts to establish an alternative theoretical framework, collectively known as mechanical philosophy, modelled nature on the characteristics of a machine. 'Disenchanting the world' (Max Weber) by construing matter as inert and nature as a causally specifiable machine, mechanical philosophers as different as René Descartes, Robert Boyle and Isaac Newton were convinced that they had found an intelligible metaphor that allowed one to understand nature and its components without having to invoke such 'occult powers' as soul-like qualities (animism) and the capacities of purpose and intention (teleology). In fact, it was a widely held belief in the seventeenth and eighteenth centuries that humans could reliably know only what they had made themselves, either manually or intellectually.[16]

The mechanical metaphor and its attendant conviction that humans could know only what they constructed themselves did not remain restricted to the study of nature; it pervaded all branches of knowledge, as the following passage from Thomas Hobbes exemplifies:

Geometry therefore is demonstrable, for the lines and figures from which we reason, are drawn and described by ourselves; and civil philosophy is demonstrable, because we make the commonwealth ourselves.[17]

The epistemological implications of this for the conceivability of a historical 'science of man' become apparent in Giambattista Vico's *Scienza Nuova* (1725/44). Expecting secure knowledge exclusively from things that owed their existence to man, the Italian professor of rhetoric turned his attention away from the study of nature to history. He reasoned that since it was God who created the natural world, only God could comprehend it. Man himself, however, could expect secure knowledge only from the study of the 'civil world', for the latter was the product of human creativity in the same sense that nature was the creation of God. Although Vico's notion of a new science did not attract much attention at the time, it indicates that, on purely epistemological grounds, the historiography of human affairs could be imagined as a science.[18]

The degree to which the mechanical metaphor had penetrated the tradition of Aristotelianism by the beginning of the eighteenth century can be seen from the case of the leading German Aristotelian Christian Wolff. In his theory of knowledge from 1712 he demands that history 'be written in such a way that where men's deeds are measured against their circumstances, one can learn the rules of divine governance therefrom'. The study of history should allow us to observe the great clockmaker in the act of clockmaking, as it were, so that we can understand the mechanics of His clockwork. 'I understand the nature of a clock,' Wolff specifies, 'when I grasp clearly what kind of wheels and other accessories it is composed of, and how each is related to the other.' Employing the clock as the favourite mechanical metaphor of his era, Wolff calls for a kind of historiography that is both didactic and useful in that it reveals history's hidden causal structure (pragmatic historiography).[19]

But the use of the clock analogy has yet another side. 'One understands the nature of a thing,' Wolff's passage on clocks emphasizes, 'only when one grasps clearly how it has become what it is, or by what manner and means it is possible.'[20] At this point, Wolff's notion of determining the nature of a thing through intellectual reconstruction of its constituent parts and structure turns into a genetic explanation of its coming into being. In fact, the latter is to complement the former, as is the case in Wolff's system of knowledge where each individual discipline is divided into an abstract-rational part and an empirical-historical one. Wolff was seconded by the Erlangen theologian Johann Martin Chladenius. In his *Allgemeine Geschichtswissenschaft* of 1752 – the German counterpart of Lord Bolingbroke's *Letters on the Study and Use of History* (1752) – Chladenius claimed:

The main event of a moral being [such as a state] is the origin of the same;

which is all the more remarkable, since it supplies the reason for the subsequent events, without which these will not be understood.[21]

The search for regular configurations, developmental patterns and laws ('rules of divine governance') was a well-established theme throughout the eighteenth century. The *Ordre Naturel* of the French physiocrats, the *Staatswissenschaften* (sciences of the state) in Germany, and the rise of conjectural history in Britain are prominent examples of this.

The clock analogy thus illustrates two things. On the one hand, it shows that the emergence of a new historical consciousness in early-modern Europe owed one of its greatest impulses to the use of the mechanical metaphor and its attendant belief that humans could know securely only what they produced themselves. On the other hand, the analogy reveals the limitations of the mechanical metaphor, which confines the notion of history to the process of coming into being. Once the clockwork is in place, it is a more or less stable end product. Mechanical analogies did not lose their metaphorical appeal until the last third of the eighteenth century when they were superseded by other, mainly organicistic, metaphors.

1.4 The rise of empirical knowledge

The third element that had a profound impact on attitudes to knowledge was the rise of the experiment as a legitimate knowledge-making practice, epitomized in Francis Bacon's dictum of 'putting nature to the question'. The plausibility of the experiment as a knowledge-making activity owed much to the view discussed above that humans could comprehend only what they had made themselves. From the same view the conviction followed that, for reliable knowledge of things that were not man-made, one had to imitate or reproduce the processes through which these things had come about. Indeed, it is the nature of the experiment that it itself produces the phenomena that are to be observed. 'Give me matter,' the German philosopher Immanuel Kant exclaimed in his theory of the origin of the universe (1755), 'and I will build a world from it, that is, give me matter and I will show you how a world developed from it.'[22] Kant's words highlight the mélange of making and knowing that was so characteristic of the time. They allow us to catch a glimpse of the awareness that still existed of the link between 'fact' and 'manufacture', two words that were to become (almost) antonyms by the end of the eighteenth century as 'fact' drifted towards 'datum', i.e. something that is given rather than made.

The critical point in our context here is the belief that lay at the heart of experimental philosophy (and early-modern empiricism more generally), namely that proper knowledge was and had to be derived from direct sense experience. This was an assault on yet another pillar of the Aristotelian tradition. Robert Boyle's experimentation with the air-pump, which was arguably the most prolific fact-making machine of the era, is emblematic of this attitude. Did Aristotelians fail to grasp the importance of sensory experience? Not at all. They gave, however, a different answer to two crucial questions. What part can experience play in the constitution of reliable knowledge? And, second, what kind of experience is thus to be sought? Suspicious as it was of the reliability of our sensory experience, the Aristotelian tradition privileged a type of experience that testified to general views of the workings of nature rather than providing the basis for those insights. Experience, while deemed important, was ultimately subordinated to securing an already established knowledge of a general and indubitable nature. In the Baconian tradition of experimental philosophy, by contrast, direct sense experience was to form the foundations of proper scientific knowledge. The purpose of experimentally constituted experience was thus not to illustrate some general point; instead of serving general philosophical reasoning, it was to control it. This type of experience, however, was not to be misconstrued as the mindless collection of data that Bacon likened to the activity of the ant. Rather, it was the result of the combined efforts of both collecting and digesting, as symbolized by the bee. The proposed method of inquiry was therefore inductive and empirically grounded – that is, one was to start out from observational and experimental facts ('particulars') and then rise step by step to causal knowledge and general conclusions.

Yet the experience sought in the experiment was not that of the spontaneous senses of the uninitiated ('old wives' tales'). Experimental philosophers from Christiaan Huygens to Robert Hooke held firmly to the belief that the workings of nature could be fully understood only if the constitution of experience was guided and disciplined by correct rules of method. The 'interrogation' of nature, as it were, was to be carried out 'as if by machinery' (Bacon). To put it another way, the rise of the experiment as an acceptable knowledge-making practice went hand in hand with aspirations to mechanize the production of knowledge itself, i.e. to discipline the procedures of knowledge-making through methodological directions designed to remove or, at least, control the effects of human passions and interests.[23]

Although experimental methods of scientific inquiry could only be applied to some branches of knowledge, their triumphant advance throughout the eighteenth century gave a strong impulse to empirical studies in many fields, including history. Just as the Protestant Reformation insisted on each Christian engaging directly with scripture (without having to rely on the readings of priests), and just as experimental philosophers from Bacon to Newton urged their contemporaries to study the 'divine book of nature' for themselves (without relying on time-honoured interpretations), so late eighteenth-century historians increasingly expected of each other that the authority of secondary works should be resorted to only when experiential access to things was impossible. Historical writing was increasingly to be based on what we have come to call the study of 'primary sources' – that is, on empirically grounded research.[24]

The success story of historical empiricism was partly written in the streets of Paris, though not necessarily by historians. Just as Gutenberg's invention of printing with movable type facilitated the Protestant demand to read the Bible for oneself; and just as the use of the telescope and microscope turned the rhetoric of individualistic empiricism ('Read the book of nature for yourself!') into a practicable idea, so 'the forcible opening of some of Europe's once secret chanceries and archives'[25] in the aftermath of the French Revolution lent impetus to the historians' call for the critical study of primary sources.

The status of the historical experience that could be derived from the study of primary sources was, however, more than precarious. The epistemology of Immanuel Kant, one of the most prominent philosophers in late eighteenth-century Europe, was, for instance, incompatible with the very idea of archival records being the 'primary sources' of what we could know about the past.[26] What is more, the study of documents with the aid of historical-critical methods is skilled reading. It requires special training that teaches us what sorts of things to 'read' in a document and what to disregard. Yet lasting institutions for the professional training of historians that would enforce correct reading were nowhere in sight before 1800.[27] In fact, only in the mid-nineteenth century were the practitioners of historical writing in a position to establish what could be sifted and evaluated from the records ('historical facts') as sufficiently reliable foundations of our knowledge of the past. In this process, the historical works of Leopold Ranke came to act both as awe-inspiring accounts of the past and as gauges to discipline the historiographical practices of others.[28]

On the whole, however, Ranke's contribution to the rise of empirically grounded, critically researched and objectively written historiography should not be overrated. He was neither the originator of objectivity in historical writing, nor did he invent the historical-philological method of source evaluation.

> In order to write and present [history] in such a way that the historical truth is not distorted, the historian must be personally impartial, must portray the events without preconceived ideas of his own, must not have a preference for any form of government, or any state; likewise, he must not regard any of the existing forms of government as the best one … nor draw up an ideal one and compare the existing ones with it; rather, with self-effacement and strict neutrality he must only tell what happened and how it happened (*bloß erzählen, was und wie es geschehn ist*).[29]

Although the above is reminiscent of his famous credo, it was not Ranke who wrote this but the Prussian medievalist Karl Dietrich Hüllmann, whom posterity has taken less seriously. Ranke had just been born when, in the spring of 1796, Hüllmann published his essay on the history of the European states, which contained these rules of conduct. The ideal of impartial or impersonal knowledge, and how to achieve it, had been hotly debated throughout the eighteenth century. Codes of impartiality and disinterestedness prevailed in many areas, ranging from legal practices of testimony evaluation to natural philosophy.[30] The rhetoric of perspectival flexibility (impartiality that rises above all particular viewpoints) appears in tracts on moral philosophy as well as historical theory. Adam Smith, for example, demanded in his *Theory of Moral Sentiments* (1759) that 'the selfish and original passions of human nature' must be transcended and things be viewed 'with the eyes of a third person ... who judges with impartiality'.[31] Indeed, transcending individual points of view in deliberation and action appeared to many moral philosophers an important recipe for a harmonious and just society. Lorraine Daston has called this attitude to knowledge 'aperspectival objectivity', i.e. the attempt to 'escape from perspective' by eliminating individual and group idiosyncrasies in the name of public knowledge and universal communicability.[32]

What was symptomatic of the historiographical debates in the second half of the century was the heightened sense that viewpoint and partiality were in fact unavoidable attributes of the historian as such, which had to be dealt with effectively rather than bemoaned.[33] To try and eliminate the effects of perspectival distortions by calling on the historian's moral integrity was, however, increasingly considered inadequate. The emphasis was shifting from moral notions of personal impartiality (ethical imperatives) towards a type of aperspectivity and impartiality to be guaranteed by impersonal rules of method (methodological imperatives). In Chladenius' *Allgemeine Geschichtswissenschaft* it reads:

> Should not historical truth enjoy the same right ... of also being formulated in rules, since now almost all the motivating forces of human reason in the discovery of general truths ... lie explained before our eyes?[34]

Not only were formal methodological directions to ensure the metamorphosis of the historian into a disembodied epistemological subject that rose above all particular viewpoints; the empirical credibility of eighteenth-century historians as a whole depended increasingly on their methodological expertise. If historical writing was to be based on an inductive and empirically grounded procedure, this groundwork had to be secure. It was in this context that the historian's ability to sort out the genuine from the fabulous became paramount and considerations of textual criticism took centre stage. Finally, the triumph of inductive methods in historical writing was inextricably linked to the rise of the 'footnote'.[35] The practice of giving reference to one's sources was in many respects the equivalent of the minute report on an experiment, as it was meant to enable the reader to repeat and verify the process through which the knowledge in question was constituted. This was held to be an indispensable feature of scientific rationality. The extent to which footnoting had become entrenched practice in historical writing during the eighteenth century can be seen from the fact that, in 1758, David Hume felt obliged to apologize for the lack of proper references in his *History of England*.[36]

To sum up, the discussion of specific historiographical rules of method had been well under way before history writing became a profession in the nineteenth century. However, in practice, formal rules of method were often far less import-ant in 'sifting and evaluating' historical records than a good knowledge of what counted as acceptable and proper, i.e. the social codes of truth-telling that did not need to be spelled out. What kind of historical experience was to ground histori-cal writing? Whose experience should count as authentic historical experience that could provide the proper foundation of historical knowledge? What exactly constituted a credible primary source? Was it the oral testimony of popular tra-dition or the written testimony of the elites? Answering questions like these implied judgement about where to draw the line between the genuine and the fabulous, the historical and the philosophical, the literary and the scientific, the vulgar and the sublime. In the eighteenth, no less than in the nineteenth century, the methodicization of historical knowledge implied a map of the social order.

1.5 History as human science

The shift from Aristotelian towards experiential attitudes to knowledge had many other facets that had equally important implications for historiography and its conceivability as a science. The Newtonian conception of linear and uni-direc-tional time, for example, according to which time was an absolute, real and uni-versal entity that was experienced by everyone, everywhere, in the same way, had a dramatic impact on the convergence of historical and scientific modes of inquiry. It also facilitated the notion of time being a progressive and homogeneous con-tinuum and, by extension, the emergence of the idea of the past being and having 'history'. The idea of history (in the singular) as a distinct and coherent form of reality that could be analysed in entirely this-worldly and rational terms only finally crystallized in the discourses of the eighteenth century.

Another strong impulse to historical writing came from what – in the wake of the French historian Michel Foucault – has been called the 'anthropological turn' in the second half of the eighteenth century and the attendant rise of the 'life sci-ences' (such as anthropology, biology and psychology).[37] One can hardly overesti-mate the importance of the new paradigm of 'vitalism' for the aspirations to conceptualize history as a human science. Peter Hanns Reill, for example, has shown the particularly vigorous impact of the appearance in 1749 of the first three volumes of the French natural historian Georges Louis Leclerc de Buffon's *Histoire naturelle* (1749–1804). Buffon championed a notion of scientificity that distinguished between abstract truths (such as mathematical proofs) and real physical truths. While the former were the fruit of human invention, the latter were essentially empirical and historical in nature and required both detailed analysis and creative imagination ('divination').[38] Taking a similar line to Reill, Jörn Garber has argued that, around 1750, anthropology assumed the role of a lead discipline for various strands of historical studies. The most obvious manifestation of this was the thriving, if short-lived, genre of 'history of humanity', which construed history as the evolution of humanity in the double sense of the word: as the development of humankind in space and time, on the one hand, and the gradual realization of the potential quality of being humane, on the other. Johann Gottfried Herder's *Ideen zur Philosophie der Geschichte der Menschheit* (1782–91) is one of the most prominent examples of this. The link forged between historical writing and anthropological discourses, Garber suggests, not only facilitated the formation of a distinctive subject area (the history of 'man'), it also equipped historical practitioners with a set of strategies and methods, such as comparative analysis, analogical reasoning and intellectual intuition, that made it feasible for historical writing to acquire a scientific identity without recourse to an overall philosophical framework.[39] The fact that in this context the notions of active matter, self-generating motion and purposive development regained some of their former currency – with 'organ', 'organism' and 'organization' replacing 'machine', 'mechanism' and 'mechanization' as lead metaphors – shows that the shift from Aristotelian to experiential practices of knowledge-making was neither a clear-cut process nor one that was ever complete.

Despite this, the Aristotelian theory of knowledge had lost its intellectual predominance for good in the course of the eighteenth century. While empirical forms of discourse had superseded deductive theories as paradigms of scientific inquiry, the Aristotelian concept of *scientia* had slowly but surely been supplanted by a new concept of scientific rationality that emphasized probability rather than certainty. Conceding that absolute certainty was beyond human grasp in all but a few areas, many advocates of the new scientificity took their bearing on John Locke's *Essay Concerning Human Understanding* (1689), which distinguished between different 'degrees of ascent'.[40] In sharp contrast to the demonstrative certainty demanded by the Aristotelians – and, for that matter, the Cartesians (the followers of René Descartes) – the truth-claims of this empirical concept of scientificity rested on the purely pragmatic criterion of critically tested probability. Not unlike evidence in legal practices, historical evidence was treated as a matter of relative degrees of certainty ('beyond reasonable doubt'). In his article 'Histoire' (1764), Voltaire, one of the century's leading historical thinkers, declared with laconic brevity, 'All certainty which does not consist in mathematical demonstration is nothing more than the highest probability; there is no other historical certainty.'[41] But then again, as the French mathematician and physicist Pierre

Simon Laplace argued in his *Essai philosophique sur les probabilités* (1814): 'How few things are demonstrated? Proofs convince only the mind; custom makes our strongest proofs. Who has demonstrated that a new day will dawn tomorrow or that we die? And what is more universally believed?'[42] The passage from Laplace is indicative of probabilistic attitudes to knowledge and the intellectual confidence that went along with them.[43]

The 'probabilistic turn' is in many respects the keystone of the developments discussed in this chapter. As the eighteenth century drew to a close, it had become possible, on epistemological grounds, to construe historiography as a science. It was around 1800 that – in the German setting – *historia* departed from the edifice of the fine arts under which it had been subsumed along with poetry, rhetoric, painting and music.[44] While a growing number of textbooks, such as Johann Joachim Eschenburg's introduction to the system of knowledge of 1792, came to count history among the sciences,[45] historians themselves now referred with increasing frequency to historiography as a 'truly rational science'[46] that 'justly deserved the name of science'.[47] One of the luminaries of historical scholarship in late eighteenth-century Germany, August Ludwig Schlözer wanted history even to 'be lectured scientifically' ('*scientifisch vorgetragen werden*').[48] The idea of history being a science was, however, heterogeneous, fragile and by no means universally shared. After all, the underlying notion of scientificity was a mixed bag of differing concepts and beliefs, reflecting a fast-changing constellation in the turn-of-the-century politics of knowledge.

1.6 Some conclusions

1   The scientificity claimed, discussed and practised in historical writing around 1800 was new in two respects. First, the very linking of the historical and the scientific was novel in empirical historical writing. Second, the new scientificity differed fundamentally from the Aristotelian concept of *scientia* that had been prevalent in large parts of Europe until far into the eighteenth century.

2   It was not in opposition to the natural sciences that history developed into a human science. The dichotomy between the humanities on the one hand, and the natural sciences on the other, is essentially a progeny of the nineteenth century and its particular map of knowledge.

3   There is no reason to assume that at a particular historical juncture historiography successfully crossed the threshold of scientificity by developing certain methods that were, at long last, adequate to the study of history. As Irmline Veit-Brause has put it, 'the scientification of history' was not 'a linear process towards a fixed goal of "proper" scientific

practice'.[49] Scientificity is a moving target and so is the very nature of what is considered reliable knowledge.

4   The notion of scientificity not only changed over time; it was also contested, with different people drawing their distinctions in different places. This, in turn, had different consequences for the practical outlook of historical writing. Just as the category of history (as object of inquiry) was understood in radically different ways by different historical practitioners, so too was the concept of scientificity.

5   The idea of scientificity did not float freely in conceptual space. As a code of conduct, way of knowing and set of methodological maxims, it was inextricably linked to social institutions, discourses and practices. (For more about this, see Peter Lambert's chapter in this volume.)

6   Finally, scientific rationality should not be confused with reason. There is no substitute for thinking, not even scientificity.

Guide to further reading

Hannah Arendt, *The Human Condition* (Chicago, 1958).

Peter Burke, *A Social History of Knowledge: from Gutenberg to Diderot* (Cambridge, 2000).

William Clark, Jan Golinski and Simon Schaffer (eds), *The Sciences in Enlightened Europe* (Chicago, 1999).

Lorraine Daston, *Classical Probability in the Enlightenment* (Princeton, NJ, 1988).

Christopher Fox, Roy Porter and Robert Wokler (eds), *Inventing Human Science: Eighteenth-Century Domains* (Berkeley, 1995).

Anthony Grafton, *The Footnote: A Curious History* (London, 1997).

Bruce Haddock, *An Introduction to Historical Thought* (London, 1980).

Reinhart Koselleck, *Future's Past* (1979), trans. K. Tribe (Cambridge, 1985).

George H. Nadel, 'Philosophy of History before Historicism', *History and Theory* 3 (1964), pp. 291–315.

Steven Shapin, *A Social History of Truth: Civility and Science in Seventeenth-Century England* (Chicago, 1994).

Rolf Torstendahl and Irmline Veit Brause (eds), *History-Making: The Intellectual and Social Formation of a Discipline* (Stockholm, 1996).

Björn Wittrock, Johan Heilbron and Lars Magnusson (eds), *The Rise of the Social Sciences and the Formation of Modernity* (Dordrecht, 1998).

Notes

I would like to express my gratitude to Ute Feldner, Graeme Garrard and David Jackson whose stimulating ideas and critical comments I appreciate more than ever.

1 *Times Literary Supplement*, 30 July 1999.
2 For an introduction, see Mary Fulbrook's *Historical Theory* (London, 2002).
3 For a good overview, see Irmline Veit-Brause, 'Eine Disziplin rekonstruiert ihre Geschichte: Geschichte der Geschichtswissenschaft in den 90er Jahren', *Neue Politische Literatur* 46 (2001), pp. 67–78 and 43 (1998), pp. 36–65.
4 Hobbes, *Leviathan* (London, 1651); Wolff, *Vernünfftige Gedancken von den Kräfften des menschlichen Verstandes* (Halle, 1712), Jean le Rond d'Alembert, *Preliminary Discourse to the Encyclopedia of Diderot* (1751), ed. Richard N. Schwab (Chicago, 1995), which also includes Diderot's *Prospectus* (1750); Droysen, *Historik* (1857), ed. Peter Leyh (Stuttgart-Bad Cannstatt, 1977); Droysen, 'Die Erhebung der Geschichte zum Range einer Wissenschaft', *Historische Zeitschrift* 9 (1863), pp. 1–22.
5 Hobbes, *Leviathan*, ch. ix.
6 See Christopher Lloyd's chapter in this volume (Chapter 5).
7 I draw here heavily on Lorraine Daston's 'Objectivity and the Escape from Perspective', *Social Studies of Science* 22 (1992), pp. 597–618, esp. pp. 597–9.
8 Here and in the following, Arno Seifert, *Cognitio historica: Die Geschichte als Namengeberin frühneuzeitlicher Empirie* (Berlin, 1976) and Horst Dreitzel, 'Die Entwicklung der Historie zur Wissenschaft', *Zeitschrift für historische Forschung* 8 (1981), pp. 257–84.
9 See Björn Wittrock, Johan Heilbron, Lars Magnusson (eds), *The Rise of the Social Sciences and the Formation of Modernity* (Dordrecht, 1998).
10 For these debates and their contexts, see Christoper Fox, Roy Porter and Robert Wokler (eds), *Inventing Human Science* (Berkeley, 1995) and Daniel Fulda, *Wissenschaft aus Kunst: Die Entstehung der modernen deutschen Geschichtsschreibung 1760–1860* (Berlin, 1996).
11 Hannah Arendt, *The Human Condition* (Chicago, 1958), pp. 290, 292.
12 Max Weber, *Economy and Society* (1920), ed. G. Roth and C. Wittich, 3 vols (New York, 1968), 1, p. 339.

13 Peter Burke, *A Social History of Knowledge* (Cambridge, 2000), pp. 81–148, esp. pp. 110ff.; Thomas Ellwein, *Die deutsche Universität* (Wiesbaden, 1997), pp. 38–224, esp. pp. 42ff. and 47ff.; Robin Briggs, 'The Académie Royale des Sciences and the Pursuit of Utility', *Past and Present* 131 (1991), pp. 38–88, p. 40.

14 Burke, *History*, pp. 91f. and pp. 99ff.; Notker Hammerstein, *Jus und Historie* (Göttingen, 1972) esp. pp. 216ff.; Jürgen Voss, *Universität, Geschichtswissenschaft und Diplomatie im Zeitalter der Aufklärung* (Munich, 1979).

15 Burke, *History*, pp. 110, 115, and M. Malherbe, 'Bacon, Diderot et l'ordre encyclopédique', *Revue de Synthèse* 115 (1994), pp. 13–38.

16 The classical account on this is E.J. Dijksterhuis's *The Mechanisation of the World Picture* (1950; Princeton, 1986); more recently, Peter Dear, *Revolutionizing the Sciences* (London, 2001), esp. pp. 80–101.

17 Hobbes, 'Six lessons to the Savillian Professors of the Mathematics', in *The English Works of Thomas Hobbes*, ed. William Molesworth, 11 vols (London, 1839–45), 7, p. 184.

18 Vico, *Scienza Nuova* (final edn, Naples, 1744), esp. Section 331.

19 Wolff, *Gedancken*, ch. I, section 48 and ch. X, section 6.

20 Wolff, *Gedancken*, ch. I, section 48.

21 Chladenius, *Allgemeine Geschichtswissenschaft* (Leipzig, 1752), p. 64.

22 Kant, *Universal Natural History and Theory of the Heavens* (1755), trans. W. Hastie, ed. W. Ley (New York, 1968), p. 17.

23 See esp. Steven Shapin, *The Scientific Revolution* (Chicago, 1996), pp. 65–117; Steven Shapin and Simon Schaffer, *Leviathan and the Air-Pump: Hobbes, Boyle and the Experimental Life* (Princeton, 1985); Lorraine Daston (ed.), *Biographies of Scientific Objects* (Chicago, 2000), p. 4; Burke, *History*, pp. 16f., 204ff.; Bacon, *New Organon* (1620), Aphorisms II, XVI, XIX, XXII, XCV.

24 Here and in the following, esp. Shapin, *Scientific Revolution*, pp. 72–80.

25 Anthony Grafton, *The Footnote* (London, 1997), p. 60.

26 See Kant's 'Prolegomena to Any Future Metaphysics that will be able to come forward as a Science' (1783), in *Immanuel Kant: Philosophy of Material Nature*, trans. J.W. Ellington (Indianapolis, 1985) and 'Conjectures on the Beginning of Human History' (1786), in *Kant: Political Writings*, ed. Hans Reiss (Cambridge, 1991), pp. 221–34.

27 For the institutionalization and professionalization of history in the nineteenth and twentieth centuries, see Peter Lambert's chapter in this volume (Chapter 3).

28 On Ranke and the Rankean tradition, see John Warren's chapter in this volume (Chapter 2).

29 Karl Dietrich Hüllmann, *Entwurf einer bessern Behandlung der*

Europäischen Staatengeschichte in akademischen Vorlesungen (Warsaw, 1796), pp. 26f. On Hüllmann, see Heiko Feldner, *Karl Dietrich Hüllmann, 1765–1846* (Frankfurt on Main, forthcoming).

30 Peter Dear, 'From Truth to Disinterestedness in the Seventeenth Century', *Social Studies of Sciences* 22 (1992), pp. 619–31.

31 Adam Smith, *The Theory of Moral Sentiments* (1759), eds D.D. Raphael and A.L. Macfie (Oxford, 1976), p. 135.

32 Daston, 'Objectivity'.

33 Chladenius' concept of *Sehepunckt* (theory of viewpoint) is an early example of this; see Chladenius, *Geschichtswissenschaft*.

34 Chladenius, *Geschichtswissenschaft*, p. xiv.

35 Grafton, *Footnote*.

36 Burke, *History*, pp. 208f.

37 Foucault, *The Order of Things* (1966), (London, 1970).

38 See esp. Reill's 'Science and the Science of History in the Spätaufklärung', in Hans Erich Bödecker *et al.* (eds), *Aufklärung und Geschichte* (Göttingen, 1986), pp. 430–52 and 'History and the Life Sciences in the Early Nineteenth Century', in Georg G. Iggers and James M. Powell (eds), *Leopold Ranke and the Shaping of the Historical Discipline* (Syracuse, 1990), pp. 21–35. On Buffon and his reception, see Frank W.P. Dougherty, *Collected Essays on Themes from the Classical Period of Natural Philosophy* (Göttingen, 1996), pp. 59–70, 70–89.

39 Jörn Garber, 'Selbstreferenz und Objektivität: Organisationsmodelle von Menschheits- und Weltgeschichte in der deutschen Spätaufklärung', in Hans Erich Bödecker *et al.* (eds), *Wissenschaft als kulturelle Praxis* (Göttingen, 1999), pp. 137–87.

40 Locke, *An Essay Concerning Human Understanding* (London, 1689), Chapter xvi.

41 Voltaire, 'Histoire', in *Dictionnaire philosophique* (1764), in *Oeuvres completes de Voltaire*, 70 vols (Paris, 1785–9) 52, p. 266.

42 Quoted in Lorraine Daston, *Classical Probability in the Enlightenment* (Princeton, NJ, 1988), p. 221.

43 See esp. Daston, *Probability*; Barbara Shapiro, *Probability and Certainty in Seventeenth-Century England* (Princeton, NJ, 1983); Shapiro, *Beyond Reasonable Doubt* (Berkeley, 1991); Ian Hacking, *The Emergence of Probability* (Cambridge, 1975).

44 See Werner Strube, 'Die Geschichte des Begriffs "Schöne Wissenschaften" ', *Archiv für Begriffsgeschichte* 33 (1990), pp. 136–216.

45 Eschenburg, *Lehrbuch der Wissenschaftskunde* (Berlin, 1792), pp. 3–11, 3988

46 Jacob Dominikus, *Über Weltgeschichte und ihr Prinzip* (Erfurt, 1790), p. 29.

47 Augustin Schelle, *Abriß der Universalhistorie*, 2 vols (Salzburg, 1780–1), 1, p. 10.

48 August Ludwig Schlözer, *Vorstellung seiner Universalhistorie* (1772–3), ed. H.W. Blanke, 2 vols (Hagen, 1990) 2, p. 235.

49 Irmline Veit-Brause, 'The Disciplining of History', in Rolf Torstendahl and Irmline Veit Brause (eds), *History-Making* (Stockholm, 1996), p. 19.

2

The Rankean tradition in British historiography, 1840 to 1950

John Warren

2.1 The Lipstadt/Irving libel case

On 11 January 2000, at the High Court in London, a libel case came to trial. The defendants were the American academic Professor Deborah Lipstadt and Penguin Books, publisher of her 1993 book *Denying the Holocaust: The Growing Assault on Truth and Memory*. The plaintiff was the British writer, David Irving. The author of many books on the period of the Second World War, Irving claimed that Lipstadt had defamed him through alleging that he was a 'Holocaust-denier' and a deliberate falsifier of historical truth. Not so, said Irving: he did not, in his view, deny the Holocaust and, although he was as liable as anyone to make mistakes, he was a genuine scholar, whose work on the documentary evidence in particular was painstaking and had led to the discovery of vital, untapped sources on the Hitler era.

On the face of it, then, the trial was about a writer's reputation as a historian and the alleged damage done to his publishing career. In practice, it became a sounding-board for any number of academic and pseudo-academic positions on a startling range of issues: freedom of speech, the absolute right to challenge received opinions, the relationship between scholarly and political activity, the historicity of the Holocaust, the writing of history and the nature of history – all served up in a media-friendly adversarial format under the baleful gaze of Mr Justice Charles Gray, who had clearly hoped that any analogies between historical and legal evidence would serve to restrict, rather than fuel, the arguments. Such hopes were indeed illusory. Commentators are clear on the broader implications of the case. The journalist D.D. Guttenplan offered his account of the case under the title *The Holocaust on Trial*, and, in *Telling Lies About Hitler: The Holocaust, History and the David Irving Trial*, Richard Evans – an expert witness for the defence – chose 'History on Trial' as the title for his first chapter.

One reason why the judge's hope was illusory is that the writing of history cannot be divorced from assumptions about the nature and purpose of historiography any more than historians can be divorced from the context in which they write. Both Lipstadt and Irving voice a common view of the obligations, duties and methodology of the historian that is ultimately the product of what can be called the Rankean tradition, and Mr Justice Gray in effect decided against Irving on the basis that he had neither honoured those obligations and duties nor upheld the methodology of the historian as judged by the Rankean model of scholarship.

The purpose of this chapter is to discuss in context the nature of that tradition associated with Leopold von Ranke (1795–1886) and, in particular, to analyse its impact on the world of English-speaking historiography. Richard Evans, in attacking the calibre of Irving as a historian, defended the centrality of the Rankean legacy to the practice of history. It was fitting that he should do so, since his 1997 book *In Defence of History* amounts to a pungent critique of the various philosophical, linguistic and occasionally hermeneutic attacks on the fundamental tenets of Rankeanism. And what, then, are those fundamental tenets? Here is Irving on the subject: 'Real history is what we find in the archives, and it frightens my opponents because it takes the planks out from beneath their feet.'[1]

This emphasis on the rigorous study of historical documents, with its implication that such study should be fair-minded and as objective as possible, was precisely the rod with which the defendants sought to beat Irving. Evans was commissioned by the defence to assess Irving's claims to objective scholarship, and found them wanting. According to Evans, Irving certainly employed the appropriate scholarly apparatus of referencing and evaluation of sources uncovered by research, but did so to deceive.

> The footnotes and sometimes the text cited innumerable archival sources, documents, interviews and other material that seemed at first glance to conform to the normal canons of historical scholarship ... It was only when I subjected all of this to detailed scrutiny, when I followed Irving's claims and statements about Hitler back to the original documents on which they purported to rest, that Irving's work in this respect was revealed as a house of cards, a vast apparatus of deception and deceit.[2]

In short, Irving is not a historian wrestling with the demands and inherent difficulties of objectivity and allowing his hypotheses to be amended where necessary by the historical sources: he is a writer with a far-right agenda who is prepared to prostitute what he himself accepts as the *credo* of the historian in the service of that agenda. Mr Justice Gray concluded in judgement:

It appears to me that the correct and inevitable inference must be that for the most part the falsification of the historical record was deliberate and that Irving was motivated by a desire to present events in a manner consistent with his own ideological beliefs even if that involved distortion and manipulation of historical evidence.[3]

It is fortunate, perhaps, that the Rankean model lends itself to courtroom practice and fortunate also that, as we have seen, all the participants in the Lipstadt case were agreed on the definition of what constitutes the discipline called history. Such agreement is, of course, by no means universal. The tenets of Rankeanism – the (albeit partial) reality of objectivity, the possibility of meaningful interpretation of documentary evidence in an equally meaningful attempt to understand the past on its own terms, a rejection of the distortion of that evidence with personal and present needs in mind – have been subjected to challenges both noisome and bruising. The remaining sections of this chapter will discuss Ranke's own historical writings, as well as the use to which his legacy has been put, with reference to such challenges. This does not imply, of course, that Ranke was fully understood by those who felt his influence. Nor does it imply that those who felt his influence did so irrespective of their personal, academic, professional or political milieu. In fact, it will become clear that the tradition of historical scholarship associated with Ranke provided, and continues to provide, a defence against contemporary political and/or philosophical trends that opponents see as fraudulent or dangerous, and deserving of the fate of the Midianites and Amalekites under the sword of Gideon.

2.2 The historical writings of Leopold von Ranke

Ranke's output, over a long life, was simply enormous. He wrote the multi-volume histories of peoples who had, in his rather euro-centric terms, an impact on the history of the world: hence his *Histories of the Latin and Germanic Peoples* (1824), *The Ottomans and the Spanish Monarchy* (1827), *German History in the Age of the Reformation* (1839–47). His *History of the Popes* (1834) complemented his history of nations as the power of the supranational institution of the Roman Catholic Church inevitably made it a great player throughout Europe and beyond. Towards the end of his life, Ranke expressed his discontent with the narrowness of his subject matter (which he felt did not allow him fully to explore connections and sequences of events). And so, in 1880, he wrote his *Universal History*.

Lord Acton can be used as a convenient starting point for a discussion of Ranke's work and its reception by British historians in the nineteenth century. His admiration for Ranke was not restricted to his energy or his industry: nor was it unmixed with criticism. Even so, Acton made Ranke the foremost representative of the age which instituted the modern study of History. He taught it to be critical, to be colourless ... he has done more for us than any other man ... He decided effectually to repress the poet, the patriot, the religious or political partisan, to sustain no cause, to banish himself from his books ...[4]

Acton judged that Ranke's historical works have been superseded, but through the activities of his own disciples in the newly opened archives of Europe: in short, Ranke was the originator of the 'heroic study of records'[5] on which historical scholarship must be based. Acton's account of Ranke's fundamental position is a seductive one, and certainly has an echo in some of Ranke's comments. In his first published work, *Histories of the Latin and Teutonic Peoples*, Ranke wrote:

> To history has been given the function of judging the past, of instructing men for the profit of future years. The present attempt does not aspire to such a lofty undertaking. It merely wants to show how, essentially, things happened (wie es eigentlich gewesen).[6]

He added: 'Strict presentation of facts, no matter how conditional and unattractive they might be, is undoubtedly the supreme law.'[7] Writing about his *English History, Principally in the Seventeenth Century* (1859–68), he said that he had tried to 'extinguish my own self, as it were, to let the past speak'.[8]

This is not the place to discuss in any detail the issue of whether Ranke was indeed a Rankean in Acton's terms. But there is the danger of converting Ranke's thought into a simplistic programme with a set of slogans – 'Tell it as it happened!' 'Let the past speak for itself!' 'Each age is unique: history must not be judged by the standards of the present!' – or of turning him into a crude empiricist or even a positivist, bowing before the twin altars of the facticity of the past and the glory of inductive reasoning. Ranke the out-and-out empiricist sits very uncomfortably with Ranke the Lutheran, or with Ranke the Romantic idealist, who thought that the historian had a sanctified role in uncovering, albeit in a limited way, the 'divine idea' or hand of God behind the unfolding of human history, which Ranke felt was revealed (*pace* Herder) least opaquely in the flowering of national cultures (hence his interest in writing the histories of peoples). Similarly, Ranke's *dictum* 'wie es eigentlich gewesen' needs careful handling: 'eigentlich' has less the sense of 'actually' and more the sense of 'in essence' or 'characteristically'[9] and so need not be taken as a straightforward endorsement of history as a trawling through documents for facts but as a comment pregnant with idealism. One might suggest, with Krieger, that Ranke came to draw a distinction between the method of acquiring historical knowledge and the search for the universal, God-given truths that would emerge from the scholar's methodology. There is a tension between his writing about the history of peoples (seen in a thoroughly Romantic way as an aggregation of individuals) and the moving on from this particular to the general. Unsurprisingly, Ranke's description of the process is bathed in a tone of religious longing:

> A lofty ideal does exist: to grasp the event itself in its human comprehensiveness, its unity, and its fullness ... I know how far I am from having achieved it ... Only let no one become impatient about this failure ... our subject is mankind as it is, explicable or inexplicable, the life of the individual, of the generations, of the peoples, and at times the hand of God over them.[10]

2.3 The writing of history in nineteenth-century Britain

What matters for our present purposes, of course, is not so much what Ranke's main tenets actually – or in essence – were, but how they were interpreted and responded to by those involved in the writing of history in Britain in the time of Ranke. I have deliberately eschewed the phrase 'British historical establishment', as there was little that could be dignified with such a title. There were indeed Regius Professors of History at the universities of Oxford and Cambridge, but their posts were sinecures without teaching, let alone research, commitments. It was 1853 before a School of Jurisprudence and Modern History was set up in Oxford – history being the junior partner in the law training firm – and 1872 until it had its own School. The process was even more leisurely in Cambridge: the Historical Tripos was set up in 1875. History had previously been examined only as one of five subjects within the Moral Sciences (from 1851). The poverty of formal historical scholarship did not reflect a lack of interest in British history – at least, among the reading public. The need was largely met by a motley collection of gentleman-scholars and autodidacts, whose more messianic fringes were gifted with a whole panoply of bolt-on eccentricities. The celebration of national progress, of what he called 'physical, of moral, and of intellectual improvement',[11] was served up hot by Thomas Babington Macaulay (1800–59) with his cast of historical goodies and baddies, his caricatures, his dramatic contrasts and his tendency to assume that his seventeenth-century heroes on the side of progress had the thought processes of liberal Victorian gentlemen.

For those rocked by assaults on Protestant biblicism from the direction of Tractarianism or German biblical criticism, there was always the splenetic apocalypse that was Thomas Carlyle, son of a Dumfries stonemason and moral prophet of the Dickens generation. James Anthony Froude, for example, trying to salvage something from the wreck of his Christian faith, found an anchor of a sort in Carlyle's *The French Revolution* (1833–42), where the Terror and its aftermath were the visible revenge of God against human wickedness. Carlyle himself commented – as well he might – that it was a work written by a '*wild man*, a man disunited from the fellowship of the world he lives in'.[12] This was no narrative history. It was the French Revolution thrust into the spitting, bile-filled cauldron of Carlyle's mind, stuffed full of German idealist philosophy, despair and dyspepsia, and erupting into astonishingly vivid and downright alarming prose (written in the present tense) where Carlyle allowed his imagination to lacerate the reader with his outlandish vocabulary. Towards the end of the book, he yelled:

> IMPOSTURE is in flames, Imposture is burnt up: one red sea of Fire, wild-billowing, enwraps the World; with its fire-tongue licks at the very Stars. Thrones are hurled into it, . . . and – ha! what see I? – all the Gigs of Creation: all, all! Wo is me! . . . A King, a Queen (ah me!) were hurled in; did rustle once; flew aloft, crackling like paper-scroll.[13]

So much for the death throes of the French Revolution. Carlyle, in idealist vein, was attempting to mediate the Ideal through symbol: in this case, the 'Gigs of Creation' refer to the respectable bourgeoisie (who could afford to own a one-horse carriage) and the reference to paper builds upon Book II – 'The Paper Age' – in which paper is taken as representative of the flimsiness of French society. The croaking frenzy in which the book appears to have been written is explained (more or less) by Carlyle's desperate need to communicate his message: that the poor of eighteenth-century neo-feudal France had their parallel in the poor of nineteenth-century industrialized Britain, and that the ruling classes had to learn from the fate of their French counterparts before it was too late.

What Carlyle was doing, of course, was to use his interpretation of history to bewail the evils of his present. Carlyle saw the writing of history as the highest form of poetic expression, by which he meant the fullest exercise of the human imagination. In so doing, he was not cautiously and reverentially hoping that the footsteps of God might be glimpsed through a careful study of the past on its own terms: he was proclaiming where the trampling wrath of God had descended in the past and would descend in the future. In short, as a historian, his business was to interpret the workings of providence in a way that would force itself onto his readers. Clearly, the dispassionate evaluation of original documents and the careful suppression of the authorial voice were utterly foreign to the role of historian-seer. When, in 1845, he published his collection of Oliver Cromwell's letters and speeches, it was riddled with errors of fact, transcription and attribution. It is not likely that he was unduly concerned. The title of the first chapter of his introduction is 'Anti-Dryasdust', and he savaged those who, publishing and using records, failed to give them the shape to make them relevant to the present.

At its best (and particularly in *The French Revolution*), Carlyle's approach has the virtue of engaging the reader's imagination in the most vigorous way. Even so, he was too peremptory and dictatorial to engage in any sense in a *dialogue* with the reader's imagination, let alone with the intellect. By the later 1840s, as Carlyle's increasingly rabid denunciations of his society drew him into sympathy for real and would-be despots and his humanity became obscured under an increasingly illiberal and authoritarian world-view, he lost touch with his erstwhile disciples. Many of those former followers saw the world slowly improving: history written to teach the present-day must at least offer a recognizable vision of the present as well as the past, and history written as prophecy had to show some signs of coming true.

No picture of the history written by 'men of letters' would be complete without a discussion of the work of Henry Thomas Buckle (1821–62). A gentleman-scholar relying on his own enormous library, Buckle wished to establish laws of history akin to those applied to 'mechanics, hydrostatics, acoustics and the like'.[14] In so doing, he reflected the contemporary interest in the philosophical positivism of Auguste Comte, whose *Cours de philosophie positive* was translated by Harriet Martineau in 1853 and influenced, to varying degrees, such seminal figures as George Eliot, John Stuart Mill and Frederic Harrison. Comte's approach was relentlessly empirical and inductive, claiming to derive historical laws from accumulated fact. He further claimed to have identified a three-stage development in history (corresponding to a development of mind) that also predicted the shape of the future. Comte identified his present with the scientific-industrial, positivist epoch, which would in time culminate in a harmonious and prosperous world where women acted as the priestesses of humanity. Comte's theories were likely to appeal to those with an optimistic attitude towards the impact of scientific discoveries, who had lost a conventional religious faith and who nevertheless felt the need for an alternative moral basis to society. Comte did not provide a historiographical link with his philosophy, but Buckle did. The first volume of his *History of Civilization in England* appeared in 1857, and he died just after completing the second of what was clearly burgeoning into a multi-volume project. His scheme was markedly deterministic and scornful of any form of religion, which he regarded as a hindrance to the development of civilization. His book was the literary sensation of 1857, but its influence on British historiography was limited to the closer followers of Comte: those Comtists who wrote history, such as Frederic Harrison, or Edward Beesly (subsequently Professor of History at University College, London), are marginal figures in historiographical terms. Unsurprisingly, the reception in more mainstream historical circles was antagonistic and the pages of the periodicals – those great educators of the aspirant intelligentsia – were replete with complaints about Buckle's materialism, determinism and arrogance. The liberal Catholics Simpson and Acton, in their journal *The*

Rambler, objected on a soteriological level to the inductive process of establishing so-called historical laws, which, in denying free will, sabotaged the righteous judgement of God over the soul.[15] The Regius Professors at Oxford and Cambridge, Goldwin Smith and Charles Kingsley respectively, similarly objected to the attempt to ground a science of history on natural, rather than moral, laws. These are not what might be called fundamentally methodological objections rooted in a view of the nature of the discipline called history. Given the background of the objectors, this is no real surprise. Kingsley, of course, was best known as a polemical popular novelist, Christian socialist and clergyman, while Goldwin Smith was, to put it charitably, a man with wide-ranging intellectual and political interests (including a quarrel in print with Disraeli with distastefully anti-Semitic overtones).[16]

2.4 Acton, Stubbs and Rankeanism

In 1866, Goldwin Smith resigned, and was succeeded in the Regius chair by William Stubbs (1829–1901). It is under Stubbs that Rankean principles were first employed at the universities in a systematic manner, with the aim to professionalize the teaching and study of history. It is important to recognize and to summarize why those principles should be so appropriate and efficacious in this context. First of all, Ranke offered a methodology based on the critical use of archival material that established history as an autonomous discipline, and one that could be communicated (as Ranke did at the University of Berlin) to generations of future historians. The historicist insistence on the uniqueness of each age countered the objectionable distortion of the discipline into a mere mechanism for collecting facts from which positivists might horribly and anachronistically derive 'natural laws' of human behaviour. Indeed, the demand for objectivity and the refusal to countenance the exploitation of history for present-day purposes would give it stability and integrity. The Rankean paradigm offered, in short, a defence against Carlylean prophets, positivists, social-Darwinists and other, equally objectionable, belles-lettrists who could claim the right to pronounce on history because there was no standard by which to judge their pronouncements. There was a price to pay, of course, that the theologically inclined had to live with if they were to be entirely consistent: history could neither be exploited as a theological weapon, nor as a moral weapon with or without the theology. The most famous victim of tension between the acceptance of the need for scholarly and objective erudition and the call of moral duty was Lord Acton.

John Emerich Edward Dalberg Acton (1834–1902), a Roman Catholic, born in Naples, was fluent in English, French, Italian and German. His mentor was the pre-eminent German theologian Johann von Döllinger. Hugh Tulloch[17] ably discusses the conversion of Acton the doctrinaire Catholic to Acton the Liberal

Catholic, but we should note in particular one of the most important agents of that transformation: Acton's sojourn with Döllinger in the Vatican archives. Significantly, it was Ranke who had come to Döllinger's university of Munich in 1854 to teach his techniques of source evaluation: as Altholz puts it, 'Döllinger had to train himself in the new methods and to revise his historical outlook in the light of his new studies.'[18] It was through his archival researches with Döllinger that it became clear to Acton that Church historians had compromised with the truth in the service of orthodoxy. Acton came to consider it axiomatic that the truth could never disadvantage the Church, and, therefore, that historical truth should serve it. His opposition to the ultramontanes – the enthusiasts for papal monarchy and declaration of infallibility – was therefore buttressed by his conviction that history offered no justification for such claims. This made it all the more important – indeed, a sacred duty – for one's research to be the last word in thoroughness. Rigorous analysis of documents had to be extended to the writings of historians themselves, and there is a sense in which Acton was out-ranking Ranke (if I may) by relying less heavily on official documents and attempting to expose, without prejudice, the inner lives of his historical characters: as he put it, 'stripping off the borrowed shell, and exposing scientifically and indifferently the soul of a Vestal, a Crusader, an Anabaptist, an Inquisitor'.[19] However, once the historical truth had been ascertained by the humble, devoted, detached historian, then he had the right, the need and the obligation to apply what Acton would have thought of as God's moral judgement on the actors on the stage of history. At this point, Acton appears not only to have jumped the Rankean ship but to have torpedoed it. In a bitter controversy with Mandell Creighton over the latter's unwillingness to make moral judgements on the Renaissance popes, Acton commented: 'it is the office of historical science to maintain morality as the sole impartial criterion of men and things, and the only one on which honest minds can be made to agree'.[20]

To put it another way, Acton was afraid that the Rankean method was a form of relativism: the unwillingness to judge and the constant demand for context, for understanding, would lead to a debilitating acceptance of base – often political – motives. The problem with this approach is clear, and explains why Acton can justly be accused of lapsing into the anachronistic ways of the so-called Whig historians: assuming that human nature was constant through time, that moral absolutes were similarly unchanging and, in essence, simple, and that, as Providence acted through history, then history was essentially progressive as human beings gradually attained a more complete understanding of individual liberty and conscience.

Notoriously, Acton found it immensely difficult to put his precepts into practice. To make moral judgements without presumption would mean a depth of knowledge of frightening profundity. The result was that Acton never published a single historical work. His projected 'History of Liberty' was never written, submerged as it was under a Byzantine system of index cards and weight of reading. His influence on historical writing, and on the development of the profession of history, is correspondingly limited. He is likely to have done little to discourage the increasing influence of the scholar in the Rankean mould over history at the universities. His inaugural lecture as Regius Professor of Modern History at Cambridge in 1895 was generally supportive of Ranke, as we have seen, and he played a significant part in the founding of the *English Historical Review* in 1886 (which took some time to echo its scholarly German counterparts and eschew the veneer of the literary review). What Acton illustrates best is the strength and limitations of the appeal of Rankean methodology. For those convinced of the value of history, it offered a way of distancing the discipline from dilettantism and mere partisanship; but that was not always enough. Should history not have some deeper purpose, for the elucidation of which the Rankean approach was a preparation? Acton felt this, and so, significantly, did his predecessor in the Regius chair, Robert Seeley. Seeley thought of himself as a disciple of Ranke, but also claimed that 'history, while it should be scientific in method, should pursue a practical object'.[21] In this case, the object was political training, arrived at through appreciating (in a manner not dissimilar to Comtean positivism) the generalizations that were possible once historical data had been accumulated.

It was at Oxford, however, that the purest draughts of Rankeanism were to be drunk. William Stubbs (1829–1901), Regius Professor of Modern History from 1866 to 1884, not only aimed to set up a School of History at the university on the Rankean model, but demonstrated through his own publications how it was to be done. In 1860, he published the seminal Stubbs' *Charters (Select Charters and Other Documents Illustrative of English History)*. His three-volume *Constitutional History of Medieval England in its Origin and Development* (1873–78) was based on an extensive evaluation of the records, and his inaugural lecture made clear his credo and his programme. As for Ranke himself, Stubbs said:

> Leopold von Ranke is not only beyond all comparison the greatest historical scholar alive, but one of the very greatest historians that ever lived. Unrivalled stores of knowledge, depth of research, intimate acquaintance with the most recondite sources . . .[22]

With Ranke, Stubbs shared a distaste for the positivist-style inducing of general laws from history; with Ranke, he shared a sense of the progress of history through divine providence; and, with Ranke, he saw what Burrow has called 'the concept of an animating Individuality, or rather of Individualities, as the protagonists of history: unique historical configurations in each of which is embodied an underlying unique Idea'.[23] In other words, both saw the individuality of nations and a national spirit as God's tool for shaping history. And so, constitutional history attracted him, in part because it was intellectually strenuous (given the complexity of the data), in part because it exploited the growing accessibility of state papers, in part because it encouraged a sense of the uniqueness of the English state, in part because it reflected contemporary experience of a growing governmental machine[24] and in part because it was eminently suited to establishing the prestige of the School of Modern History.[25]

2.5 The very partial triumph of Dryasdust (I): Herbert Butterfield (1900–1979)

Herbert Butterfield, a scholar at Peterhouse, Cambridge, in 1919, was elected to a chair of modern history at Cambridge in 1944 and became Regius Professor in 1968. It is, frankly, outrageous to label Butterfield as an exponent of Dryasdustism, but his important contributions to the study of historiography essentially crystallized attitudes towards certain types of history and upheld the British version of the Rankean tradition. What is equally important is that Butterfield's stance was an ambivalent one, and at least suggests the extent to which most practitioners upholding the 'professional' or 'craftsman' model of the historian found that model ultimately rather unsatisfying but nevertheless far preferable to alternatives that would, in their view, have consequences that were unacceptable on several levels.

In *The Whig Interpretation of History* (1931), Butterfield famously castigated historians for 'present-mindedness'. The desire to *use* history for the needs of the present day was, in Butterfield's terms, not simply a methodological aberration, but also dangerous, hubristic and fundamentally blasphemous. Whig historians were those whose teleology was horribly secular and correspondingly presumptuous. History, they claimed, had a detectable sense of direction, sometimes striding, sometimes meandering, but ever progressing towards the consummation devoutly to be wished: liberal parliamentary democracy on the British model. The result was that they wrote bad history: often nationalistic, always anachronistic and distressingly optimistic. Butterfield's objections to Whig history in general were both methodological and theological, and are in this way strongly reminiscent of Ranke. The past deserved to be understood for its own sake, and so the historian was to appreciate its complexity, to eschew the generalization in favour of an appreciation of the role played by the individual, and to seek to recover the particular and the concrete without regard to the present (other than to make the past comprehensible to one's own time). Butterfield complained that the present-minded invariably wrote 'abridged' history because they sought to select from the past 'proof' of whatever political or moral goal the past was allegedly advancing towards: similarity and pattern were preferred over the dissimilar and the unique. The wide-ranging popular narrative, terminally complacent and egregiously smug, discarded the inconveniences of rigorous scholarship in favour of the simplistic and spuriously analogous.

It could be argued that fulminating against 'present-mindedness' is something of a luxury ill-suited to times of deep anxiety and turmoil, where people might look to history for reassurance and a sense of purpose. Butterfield clearly felt that, in the middle of the Second World War, he could afford to reflect on a positive contribution made by Whig historiography. In *The Englishman and his History* (1944), he accepted that the Whig interpretation, however defective it might be, had entered history itself as a positive force for patriotism and unity.

Butterfield was deeply suspicious of attempts to find answers to transcendent questions within academic history. History was in no way a guide: it could not be reduced to deterministic laws or exalted to the role of prophecy. His perspective, like Ranke, was that of the convinced Christian. Where Ranke feared the influence of the Enlightenment and its denial of the sovereignty of God, Butterfield feared the influence of secularist liberal optimism and atheistic Communism, both of which also denied the sovereignty of God. With Ranke, he would not presume to identify God's purposes in history, but he could not accept that God was in any way apart from it. To claim that God was somehow absent was to sabotage personal religion. In the appropriately titled *God in History* (1958), Butterfield commented: 'And if God cannot play a part in life, that is to say, in history, then neither can human beings have very much concern about him or very real relationships with him.'[26]

World war, cold war, Holocaust and Hiroshima: the crises and horrors through which Butterfield had lived confirmed in his mind the essential sinfulness of humankind. Small wonder that he should object to the optimism of his predecessors. In *Christianity and History* (1949), his words appear to echo, of all people, Acton:

> having in his religion the key to his conception of the whole human drama, he [the historian] can safely embark on a detailed study of mundane events, if only to learn through their inter-connections the ways of Providence.[27]

The difference between Acton and Butterfield is that Acton saw progress towards liberty as part of the ways of Providence; Butterfield saw this as unwarranted presumption, and dangerously close to using history to elicit the meaning to life itself. Such hubris was the besetting sin of the academic. Those who studied history had the absolute obligation to recover it as it really was, because only then could one glimpse those connections between events that reflected God-in-history.

Butterfield's influence over subsequent historiography was profound, but owed little to his overt Christianity *per se*. He confirmed the realist, empiricist and historicist tradition by discarding determinism and emphasizing the role of the individual. His wariness of wide-ranging narrative encouraged the narrow monograph of 'technical' history, which in turn was a mark of the 'professionalism' necessary to 'real history'. In short, Butterfield was misinterpreted. As R.H.C. Davies comments:

> Butterfield himself had never intended that his work should cause historians to stop trying to explain history. But because he had demonstrated that the Whig historians had read their own ideas into historical events, lesser historians have felt timid of expressing any ideas at all.[28]

The clear similarities between Ranke and Butterfield are reflected in the nature of their appeal to their successors. For those who hated the determinism of Marxist historiography, Rankeanism and Butterfieldery was the antidote. For those suspicious of multi-disciplinary approaches to history, they were the guards of the temple within whose Holy of Holies lay the purity of a discipline unsullied by the presumptuous neophytes of social psychology, anthropology, economics and sociology.

2.6 The very partial triumph of Dryasdust (II): Namier and Namierization

The impact of Louis Bernstein Namier (1888–1960) on the historical profession in Britain in the 1950s and 1960s was unrivalled, and not just in his chosen field of eighteenth-century English political life. To the *Oxford English Dictionary* he gave the word 'Namierization'; and, through the exact and detailed scholarship to which the term refers, he gave to his colleagues and students an example to follow or to eschew, but not to ignore. Namier's capacity for minute documentary research, which clearly complemented and reflected Rankean professionalism, was focused on an approach to parliamentary politics that emphasized individual motivation and local circumstance above ideological/party affiliation. In so doing, Namier rejected teleological approaches of any kind, and offered not only a striking confirmation of the status of the historian and of the discipline of history, but also a safe passage between the Scylla of Marxism and the Charybdis of multi-disciplinary approaches.

Like Butterfield, Namier distrusted doctrines of progress because he distrusted human reason and its potential; but, if Butterfield's distrust was theological and stemmed from his Methodist beliefs, Namier's distrust was psychological and stemmed from his sense of being an outsider. Born Ludwik Bernsztajn vel

Niemirowski in eastern Poland, his parents were of the landowning class – an unusually patrician status for Jews, albeit non-practising ones. Namier was disinherited by his father and emerged from Balliol College, Oxford, in 1915 with his conservative mind-set intact and a first-class degree in Modern History. His outstanding abilities were self-evident and should have led him to an Oxbridge chair, but he was also combative, arrogant and self-obsessed – not a man, in short, to wear his learning lightly in the manner appropriate to the English gentleman whose social éclat he admired and could not emulate. His research interests reflected his admiration and his conservatism. In 1929, he published *The Structure of Politics at the Accession of George III* and, in 1930, *England in the Age of the American Revolution.* In so doing, he undermined the orthodox Whiggish interpretation whereby the King's alleged attempts to restore absolutist rule were thwarted by the opposition of American rebels and the Whigs under Rockingham who sympathized with the colonists' principled stand against tyranny. Namier denied that the King had any such intention, that the Rockingham Whigs represented a party with any ideals beyond those of self-serving factionalism and, for good measure, that to write of MPs' adherence to party at all was to misunderstand their fundamentally personal motivations. Namier's so-called 'structural analysis' therefore rested upon an 'underview' rather than an overview, and prosopography rather than narrative exegesis. His detailed reconstruction of the lives and motives of individual MPs demanded a tireless quest for, and evaluation of, family papers. Analysis of MPs' letters led Namier to argue that they saw politics not in terms of ideals, party loyalties or principles, but as an extension of local and personal affairs. His rehabilitation of George III rested on the King's papers held at Windsor Castle. Analysis of his correspondence purportedly revealed that George III was an insecure and rather conventional man with no intention of reviving autocracy.

Namier had succeeded in restoring personalities to politics, but he had also removed political ideas from personality – the likely result, indeed, of using private correspondence and largely ignoring parliamentary debates. His corrective to the traditional Whig approach was timely, but too narrowly focused. To support the contention that party allegiance and party ideology were relatively unimportant to eighteenth-century politics required a broader time-scale than that provided by Namier. Nor did he provide the necessary evaluation of the functioning of the House of Lords. In short, Namier was entranced by the House of Commons, or rather by its members. On a professional level, collective biography appealed to Namier as a technique that guarded against overarching narratives resting on the activities of a 'great man', or analyses resting on ideologies (such as Marxism) that eschewed individual motivation in favour of impersonal determinism. On a personal level, Namier found it easy to empathize with self-obsessed landowners. And collective biography gave him the opportunity to exploit the one form of determinism of which he whole-heartedly approved (because it was personal): Freudian analysis. No stranger himself to the analyst's couch, Namier invited his historical characters to lie back and explain themselves. Predictably, as Namier crossed the no man's land between genuine insight and a historian's self-obsession, he sometimes thrust home his attack and sometimes stood on a mine. Reflecting on his own troubled relationship with his father, he was able to take seriously and to discuss the political impact of the fraught relationships between Hanoverian kings and their male heirs, and to explain something of the erratic career of Charles Townshend by reference to his problematic relationship with both parents. On the other hand, was it really best to explain in such terms, say, Townshend's actions as Chancellor of the Exchequer responsible for the bitterly resented American Import Duties Act of 1767? As Linda Colley has pointed out, we are 'left with the impression that perhaps the American Revolution broke out because Britain in the 1760s was governed by an oligarchy of neurotics'.[29]

Namier was far too astute not to make a virtue out of psychological necessity. He commented:

> Really intense research and analysis requires some correlation between the student's emotional life and experience and his subject ... As for accuracy, it is a conception that I would associate with statements rather than with views.[30]

It certainly required more than assiduity to devote, as Namier did, the last decade of his life to a project that provides at once a testimony and an epitaph to his obsessions, abilities and, perhaps, his limitations. In 1951, the History of Parliament Trust gave the go-ahead to Namier to write the appropriate institutional history. What the members of the trust got was nothing of the sort. In the three volumes of *The House of Commons 1754–1790*, published four years after Namier's death in 1960, Namier avoided the 'great men' but wrote any number of biographies of MPs – the more obscure the better – with, it seems, the aim of providing the raw material, not indeed for a political history charting the actual workings of both houses, but for a social history charting the changing class and economic structure of the Commons. In place of a valediction, there was an introduction and a work that, in its inevitable incompleteness, reflected the frustrations of a quintessential outsider.[31]

2.7 Conclusion

Namier's fate, like that of many of the historians discussed in this chapter, was to be labelled a champion of a type of history that he did not actually write and with which he had an ambiguous relationship. As a product of his time and his own troubled psyche, he wrote a history that was suspicious of ideology, effectively conservative, cynical about human nature and, it appeared, appropriately empirical and objective in the Rankean manner. That this was neither his nor the Rankean manner was not the issue. Peter Novick charts the similar impact of a misunderstood Ranke on the American historical profession.[32] In Britain, Namier's impact, like that of Butterfield, was to confirm a particular version of the Rankean tradition as the right and professional way to write history.

In the later twentieth and early twenty-first century, the Rankean tradition has been used as a weapon against encroachments on the discipline of history both methodological and epistemological. G.R. Elton disposed of the rival claims of cliometricians (to his own satisfaction) in *Which Road to the Past?* and, in *Return to Essentials*, he tackled (also to his own satisfaction) postmodernists who ventured to argue that there was no road to the past anyway.[33] Richard Evans, whose *Telling Lies About Hitler* was discussed at the start of this chapter, offered in his *In Defence of History* 'the basic Rankean spadework' as the tools of a trade which – postmodernist critiques notwithstanding – continues to deliver an interpretation of the past that reflects, albeit imperfectly, how it really happened.

> History is an empirical discipline, and it is concerned with the content of knowledge rather than its nature. Through the sources we use, and the methods with which we handle them, we can, if we are very careful and thorough, approach a reconstruction of past reality that may be partial and provisional, and certainly will not be objective, but is nevertheless true.[34]

This is not to say that opponents of the bastardized Rankean tradition in British historiography do not have several valid points to make. Of course it frequently rests on an unfortunate reluctance to consider history as an epistemology. Of course there are writers of history, like Carlyle, who have the capacity to engage the reader (for good or ill) in an imaginative pummelling that may spasmodically strike home by conveying the truth through the resources of fiction. And, of course, few avowed or unavowed followers of Ranke were content with history as methodology. Nevertheless, the tradition remains as yardstick or target: it cannot be ignored.

Guide to further reading

The most convenient collection of Ranke's writings in English translation is G.G. Iggers and K. von Moltke (eds), *The Theory and Practice of History: Leopold von Ranke* (Indianapolis, 1973). The authors' 'Introduction' offers an excellent brief analysis of Ranke's background, work and historiographical impact. These issues are further developed in G.G. Iggers and J.M. Powell (eds), *Leopold von Ranke and the Shaping of the Historical Discipline* (Syracuse, 1990). There are valuable chapters on transfers between the German and British historiographical traditions in Benedikt Stuchtey and Peter Wende (eds), *British and German Historiography 1750–1950* (Oxford, 2000).

The professionalization of history is tackled effectively by Philippa Levine, *The Amateur and the Professional: Antiquarians, Historians and Archaeologists in Victorian England, 1838–1886* (Cambridge, 1986), Peter Slee, *Learning and a Liberal Education: The Study of Modern History in the Universities of Oxford, Cambridge and Manchester 1800–1914* (Manchester, 1986) and by Doris Goldstein, 'History at Oxford and Cambridge: Professionalization and the Influence of Ranke', in Iggers and Powell. John Kenyon's *The History Men: The Historical Profession in England since the Renaissance* (London, 1993) offers a characteristically bracing critique. Rather more sympathetic in tone are the valuable books in the Weidenfeld & Nicolson series *Historians on Historians*: Hugh Tulloch's *Acton* (1988), Owen Dudley Edwards' *Macaulay* (1988) and Linda Colley's *Namier* (1989) are particularly good at contextualizing their subjects.

The continued relevance of the Rankean tradition as such is beyond the scope of this chapter, but Richard Evans' *In Defence of History* (London, 1997) makes the case. By way of contrast, Alun Munslow's *The Routledge Companion to Historical Studies* proclaims the death of Rankean empiricism at the hands of postmodernism. Some of Munslow's readers may feel that pall-bearers make odd companions.

Notes

1   R.J. Evans, *Telling Lies About Hitler* (London, 2002), p. 27.
2   Evans, *Telling Lies*, p. 110.
3   Mr Justice Charles Gray, quoted in D.D. Guttenplan, *The Holocaust on Trial* (London, 2001), p. 283.
4   J.E.E.D. Acton, *Lectures on Modern History* (London, 1960), pp. 32–3.
5   Acton, *Lectures*, p. 22.
6   Ranke, 'Preface' to the first edition of *Histories of the Latin and Teutonic Peoples*, in G.G. Iggers and K. von Moltke (eds), *The Theory and Practice of History* (Indianapolis, 1973), p. 137.
7   Ranke, 'Preface', p. 137.
8   Ranke, quoted in L. Krieger, *Ranke: The Meaning of History* (Chicago, 1977), p. 5.
9   Iggers and Moltke, *Theory and Practice*, pp. xix–xx.
10 Ranke, 'Preface', p. 138.
11 T.B. Macaulay, *The History of England from the Accession of James II* (Harmondsworth, 1979), p. 52.
12 J.A. Froude, *Thomas Carlyle: A History of his Life in London* (London, 1884), 1, p. 96.
13 Thomas Carlyle, *The French Revolution* (London, 1889), 3, pp. 273–4.
14 Buckle, quoted in John Kenyon, *The History Men* (London, 1993), p. 113.
15 Richard Simpson, 'Mr Buckle's Thesis and Method', *Rambler*, 2nd ser., X (1858), pp. 27–42; J.E.E.D. Acton, 'Mr Buckle's Philosophy of History', ibid., pp. 88–104.
16 Colin Holmes, *Anti-Semitism in Britain 1876–1939* (London, 1979), pp. 11–12.
17 Hugh Tulloch, *Acton* (London, 1988).
18 Josef L. Altholz, *The Liberal Catholic Movement in England* (London, 1962), p. 55.
19 Tulloch, *Acton*, p. 99.
20 Kenyon, *History Men*, p. 139.
21 J.R. Seeley, quoted in Doris Goldstein, 'History at Oxford and Cambridge: Professionalization and the Influence of Ranke', in G.G. Iggers and J.M. Powell (eds), *Leopold von Ranke and the Shaping of the Historical Discipline* (Syracuse, 1990), p. 146.
22 Stubbs, *Seventeen Lectures and Addresses on the Study of Mediaeval and Modern History* (Oxford, 1900), p. 65.
23 John Burrow, 'Historicism and Social Evolution', in B. Stuchtey and P. Wende (eds), *British and German Historiography 1750–1950* (Oxford, 2000), p. 252.
24 The link between constitutional history and the contemporary experience of burgeoning bureaucracy is explored in P.B.M. Blaas, *Continuity and Anachronism* (The Hague, 1978).

25 P.R.H. Slee, *Learning and a Liberal Education: The Study of Modern History in the Universities of Oxford, Cambridge and Manchester 1800–1914* (Manchester, 1986).

26 Butterfield, 'God in History', in C.T. McIntyre (ed.), *God, History and Historians: An Anthology of Modern Christian Views of History* (New York, 1977), p. 193.

27 Butterfield, *Christianity and History* (London, 1957), p. 87.

28 R.H.C. Davies, 'The Content of History', *History* LXVI (1981), p. 364.

29 Linda Colley, *Namier* (London, 1989), p. 33.

30 Namier, in John Brooke, 'Namier and Namierism', *History and Theory* 3 (1964), p. 343.

31 For a discussion of Namier as outsider, see John Warren, *The Past and its Presenters* (London, 1998), pp. 121–3. In his *Anti-Semitism in British Society 1876–1939* (London, 1979), Colin Holmes reflects on the discrimination faced by Namier and other Jews in terms of scholastic appointments; see in particular pp. 110–11.

32 Peter Novick, *That Noble Dream: The 'Objectivity Question' and the American Historical Profession* (Cambridge, 1988), pp. 21–31.

33 R.W. Fogel and G.R. Elton, *Which Road to the Past? Two Views of History* (New Haven and London, 1983); and Elton, *Return to Essentials: Some Reflections on the Present State of Historical Study* (Cambridge, 1991).

34 Richard J. Evans, *In Defence of History* (London, 1997), p. 249.

3

The professionalization and institutionalization of history

Peter Lambert

The quest for professional status was an endeavour to secure an authoritative status for 'the' historian's work. Unlike practitioners of other professions, historians never achieved a monopoly over their field: the matter of imparting knowledge of the past. But wherever the professionalization project succeeded, it entailed a shift in the balance of the power to interpret the past. Authority was inextricably linked to historians' claims to objectivity. Objectivity, in turn, was secured by the rigorous application of skills in the critical use of evidence. Palaeographic, philological and contextual, the skills and methodologies historians employed were their common property: they were taught, tested and communicated by and to one another.[1] Institutionalization furnished the settings in which this could happen and provided career structures and mechanisms of what might be called 'quality' control.

Constituting themselves as an imagined community, historians themselves set the standards of their profession, and sought to ensure that conformity to them was an entry requirement. However, even where they achieved autonomy, national historical professions scarcely ever came close to becoming the independent, entirely self-regulating bodies that sociological models of professionalization predict.

This chapter explores the creation of standards of professionalism in the pursuit of history. What conditions were necessary for the discipline to flourish and what motivated its advocates are the questions addressed in the first section. In a sequence of 'snapshots', the chapter then discusses key moments in the foundation of history as an academic discipline in 'first-' and 'second-world' countries in the course of a 'long' nineteenth century. Finally, the chapter broaches the expansion of the discipline into the 'third world' in the second half of the twentieth century.

3.1 Conditions and motives

Institutionalization was predicated on demand; the professionalization of research and writing largely presupposed the existence of career structures. Both were contingent on the broadly overlapping existences of adequate literacy rates and of a sufficiently developed middle class in a given society. They were dependent also on the presence of a university system and, crucially, on its public or private paymasters' readiness to see history established within the universities. More than any other, it was the presence or absence of a will to invest in history at a given time that constituted the variable determining the divergent chronologies of the professionalization of history.

Although historians continue to argue about the extent of its influence on later developers, nobody has disputed the fact that Germany was precocious. By the middle of the nineteenth century, many of the 'classical' features of a fully professionalized discipline were in place. First France, then an (at first sight bewildering) array of countries followed suit – the USA, Japan and Belgium foremost among them. Even in western Europe, however, the progress of the discipline was uneven. Professional Dutch historians remained few in number and woefully under-resourced until after the Second World War. In Johan Huizinga, Holland boasted a historian with a towering international reputation. But Huizinga felt isolated in his own nation, alienated by a national intellectual culture that showed disdain for academic history. In 1907, he sardonically proposed that Holland sell its entire national archival holdings to the highest bidder since – beyond the Dutch borders – there might be someone with the time and inclination to work on them. It was a suggestion Holland's paltry dozen professors of history in post three decades later might reasonably have repeated.[2] Britain's experience of the professionalization of history began relatively early. From the 1860s onward, historians battled to inaugurate degree schemes and sometimes to introduce training in research. But the reformers encountered obstacles, and in any case lacked a cohesive vision. Their successes were patchy and sometimes also transitory. Seminars made only fleeting appearances, remaining entirely individual initiatives that ended when their initiators moved on. Frederick York Powell, Regius Professor of History at Oxford, exemplified an attitude wholly antipathetic to any professional ethos. Late in arriving for his own inaugural lecture, he then contrived to get the show itself over within 20 minutes.[3]

Powell's was not an instance of anachronism in late Victorian Britain, nor was it confined to that period. In 1922, Charles Kingsley Webster thought it 'greatly to be regretted' that attempts to establish graduate schools of history at Oxford and Cambridge had been 'so very inadequate' and argued for radical rectification: both universities' effective destruction as undergraduate teaching institutions and their forced transformation into postgraduate training and research centres.[4] On the eve of the Second World War, Eric Hobsbawm found that Cambridge did next to nothing to supply would-be professional historians with appropriate training: the history faculty presented an overwhelmingly 'discouraging spectacle: self-satisfied, insular, culturally provincial, deeply prejudiced ... even against too much professionalism ... [I]n my day, what Marc Bloch called the "trade of the historian" was not taught in Britain.'[5] York Powell, then, was certainly not the last of a dying breed of British historians whose behaviour and approach to teaching and research was distinctly *un*professional.

Patterns of professionalization of history, Eckhardt Fuchs suggests, formed one part of a triad, whose other two aspects were industrialization and modernization.[6] In view of the fact that the professionalization of history was far more advanced in late nineteenth-century Belgium than in Holland, for instance, Fuchs' remark appears to require some modification. Where a literate, educated public existed at all, prospects for the development of the historical profession stood in inverse proportion to the 'modernity' (and sometimes also the degree of industrialization) experienced by a given country. The educated Dutch public and Dutch governments, confident in the power of their nation-state and in their identity, were prone to look down their noses at the Belgians in general and their historical profession in particular. That Belgium should have required a historical profession in the first place was seen by the Dutch as an index of Belgian backwardness. In such cases, the yardstick by which 'backwardness' was measured was neither economic nor even cultural. Rather, it was the level of attainment in nation-building and state-formation.

That Germany should have housed the first laboratories for experiments in the creation of modern historiography is intimately connected with Germany's want of modernity in other respects. A new ethos of *Wissenschaftlichkeit*[7] served partly as substitute for missing ingredients of modernity, partly as corrective for defects, both exposed in the Napoleonic Wars. Humboldt's reform of the Prussian universities provided at least a measure of academic liberty within the universities, whose subsequent expansion afforded market-driven openings for academic entrepreneurs.[8] These were favourable conditions for the emergence of new disciplines. Competition for students provided the motor. Young, ambitious and innovative professors, distinguished from mid-century by their propensity to move rapidly from one university to another, fuelled it. Some made a generous endowment of their discipline a condition of acceptance of posts offered them, and held the whip-hand in relation to their putative employers.[9] History enjoyed one key advantage over rival disciplines. States that had survived Napoleon's redrawing of the map of Europe – and often grown as a direct consequence – were obliged to seek out new strategies of legitimation after Napoleon's fall. They began to encourage the development of history in universities in pursuit of that quest. But relations between historians and the states that were their ultimate paymasters were frequently strained. Historians' intellectual ambitions were always inherently likely to take them beyond the narrow geographical confines of polities whose provenance was so recent. Petty principalities could be associated with the local imposition of censorship. Thus, in common with other educated bourgeois, historians forged connections with one another across state boundaries, especially through journals and through their correspondence. Long before its culmination in annual German historians' congresses (from 1892 onward), and before the creation of the German Empire in 1871, a 'guild' (*Zunft*) of historians had taken shape, and done so along national lines. At its heart lay the steadily increasing number of holders of established chairs in history – some 28 of them in 1850, rising to 185 over the next six decades.

Research on primary sources lodged in archives, their critical interpretation (*Quellenkritik*) and finally their threading into published narratives were hallmarks of the new species of engagement with history. Leopold von Ranke[10] was – as is now generally recognized – not the originator of this three-step method, but he was certainly its most effective publicist. Remembered as *the* advocate-practitioner of archival research, Ranke was in fact much more heavily dependent than he insinuated on secondary sources. He was – certainly at first – reluctant and scandalously inefficient about accurately acknowledging them, and a messy taker of notes throughout his career.[11] But then – for the simple reason that he belonged to a founder-generation of professionalizing historians – Ranke had had no training as a historian himself. As in the matter of method, in relation to training, Ranke long, and on the whole undeservedly, enjoyed a reputation for fundamental innovation. Equally, the pervasiveness and durability of Ranke's myth testifies to his abilities as a propagandist of the vital importance of training for apprentice historians.

What Ranke *did* have a training in was philology, and the skills he attained had been developed through philological seminars, which were themselves an eighteenth-century German invention. In the 1820s, historians simply applied the techniques of philological seminars to history: discursive and critical interaction between teachers and students and among the students themselves. 'Historical exercises' in which select handfuls of students would gather informally in their professors' houses were already being held in the 1820s. As private gatherings, they belong more immediately to the history of the development of civil society in Germany than to that of the institutionalization of history. But in 1833, Ranke held a series of these 'exercises' at the University of Berlin. Thereafter, they were increasingly frequently to be found across the German universities. Gradually, universities began to advertise their existence to students, then even to make attendance at them obligatory. In 1865, when Heinrich Sybel attached a single bookcase and its contents to the 'exercises' he held at Bonn, he not only began another trend – toward the creation of seminar libraries – but implied another.

Seminars began to enjoy their own dedicated space. A continuing problem was that the presence or absence of seminars at a particular university was determined by the tastes and energies of the historians who happened to be in post there, and its resolution was found in the formal institutionalization of the seminar, which now acquired recognized hierarchies of authority and governance by its own statutes. Universities and ministries frequently found the long-term financial commitments this entailed an acceptable price to pay for stability and attractiveness to potential students and staff.[12]

Their creators trumpeted the virtues of the seminar, the 'embodiment' of the new academic history. It was designed to induct all history students into an understanding not only of the arguments of the historian's polished finished article (or book or lecture), but crucially of how he had arrived at it. That comprehension was enhanced and tested by the requirement that each student undertake a piece of specialized research himself. Other nations, Heinrich von Sybel argued in 1868, might possess great historians – French historians might deliver lectures infinitely superior to any held in Germany – but masterly lectures were 'anything other than a school in scholarship'. The superiority of the German model rested on seminars precisely because they disclosed what glossy lectures concealed: the painstaking labours of the researcher. And, Sybel argued, this was something German historians' foreign admirers clearly understood. Yet the seminar was not intended to function *principally* as a training ground for professional historians. Future teachers, especially teachers in good secondary schools, were its real beneficiaries.[13] The demands and abilities of the budding historian were hard to reconcile with those of the run-of-the-mill trainee teacher. Ranke himself had found work with primary sources too much for the latter, and catered for them in a sort of lower order of seminar; Sybel, too, found parallel seminars a serviceable way out of the strains of mixed-ability teaching. But, from the turn of the century, demands for new research institutes grew in urgency and volume as historians came to note that seminars were typically addressing future teachers' needs at the expense of those of potential historians. These demands were duly met in the twentieth century.

3.2 The nationalization and internationalization of history

The establishment of a close affinity between nationalism and historiography often sounds accusatory. Historians who feel the still-conventional compartmentalization of the discipline into national blocs as a sort of intellectual blockage will inevitably be tempted to allege that rubbing shoulders with nationalism was the first and most ubiquitous act of treason on the part of a profession laying any kind of claim to objectivity. Paradoxically, where individual national historical professions proved to be largely transitory, it is now also alleged that they ran into the sand precisely because of the weak links in their relationships with nationalist movements. This charge has been levelled both against academic historians in late Imperial Russia and at Chinese historians active in the 1920s. The implication is clear: only where they forged strong alliances with 'their' respective nationalisms could national historical professions thrive in the long term. However, historians who promoted such links had argued rather that the equation worked in reverse: nationalism needed its historians. Writing in 1902, the Chinese historian Liang Qichao suggested that 'the rise of nationalism in Europe and the growth of modern European countries are owing in part to the study of history'. More particularly, Liang argued, it was *scientific* history that had contributed to nationalism. In China, it would require nothing short of a 'historiographical revolution' to replicate that healthy European condition.[14] In claiming a significant role in nation-building for the historian, Liang may simultaneously also have been trying to make a case for his discipline, advertising its wares to potential investors among nationalist politicians. Elsewhere, as we will see, historians certainly did employ comparisons with other – historiographically more 'advanced' – countries, as a strategic tool to shame or provoke governments into committing resources to institutional historical projects. Like nationalism itself, nationalist historiography was always obliged to perform a balancing act, emphasizing its distinctiveness on the one hand while borrowing from other national traditions on the other. One nationalism implied connection with other nationalisms, not least those it perceived as rivals or threats. How far, then, did attempts to establish history as a modern discipline follow Germany's lead not simply chronologically, but literally, taking the German example as a model worthy of emulation?

Direct and indirect German influences, the strategic use of transnational comparisons to promote investment in the discipline, and indigenous traditions were similarly combined in the practices of historians in the USA, France and Britain, for example.[15] To varying degrees and in different ways, these shared a capacity to co-opt and assimilate foreign techniques and ideas, which is testimony to the permeability of their respective 'national' cultures. They stand in marked contrast to Tsarist Russia, for example, where professional historians were – in spite of their best efforts – hemmed in by mass illiteracy on the one hand and, its preparedness to invest in the discipline in order to train state servitors notwithstanding, by a repressive state on the other. Their ethos, institutions and works remained 'an exotic import that could be dispensed with'.[16]

Academic history's advance through the USA was rapid in the extreme. As late as 1880, its professoriate barely scraped into double figures; just a decade and a half later, it was into three figures. The work of the early handful was lost in the mass of literature produced by clerics and lawyers, 'gentlemanly' and women amateurs. By the early 1900s, professional historians could lay claim to occupying the leading role in historiography. The signally diminished ranks of women among them aside, their social profile was very similar to that of amateur historians. University appointment conferred no particular social dignities upon them, nor did it fundamentally alter the level of their incomes. In contrast to the German example, then, the creation of the historical profession in the USA cannot be connected with the upward mobility of an entire social group. Here, stasis was the norm. But US historians sought to achieve the qualities of *Wissenschaftlichkeit* already attained in continental Europe. The expansion of the American universities provided them with ample scope to do so. In 1870, total student numbers stood at little more than 50,000. Within half a century, they had registered an almost twenty-fold expansion. In this context, the proliferation of academic disciplines and the articulation of boundaries between them belatedly followed the pattern set in Germany. Only where academic history might end and political science begin were the edges blurred. The overwhelming majority of America historians became political historians, and patriotic historians *of* America at that. As in Germany, research and seminar-teaching were pursued in order to put patriotism on a scholarly footing. History was a means of affirming or of constructing the nation, its role visually dramatized by Herbert Baxter Adams' inordinately detailed blueprint for the physical layout of an ideal, homogenized seminar and by his wall-map of the United States, pock-marked by an increasingly dense number of pinheads. Each marked the establishment of a new history seminar at another university, instituted by one of the products of Adams' own seminar, founded in 1876 at Johns Hopkins University.

The pace of change and disciplinary expansion in France was almost as breathless as in the USA. Mid- to late nineteenth-century France had a wealth of what might be called 'public' historians, but the French state was already beginning to urge the professionalization of university-based history in the years immediately preceding the Franco-Prussian War. In the wake of France's military and political humiliations of 1870–71, the state and historians collaborated in a purposeful drive aimed at remoulding history as part of a programme of national regeneration. A handful of patrons emerged: academic organizers like the founders of seminars in Germany, but with still greater powers of patronage. A new emphasis on research and a concomitant trend toward specialization were the dominant characteristics of the generations of historians moulded between 1870 and 1910.[17] By the eve of the First World War, the French historical profession was not quite so numerous as to match the German but, qualitatively, was certainly of a comparable order. French historians even enjoyed a stronger position within the universities than did their German colleagues.[18]

Both US and French historians presented themselves as importers of German practices in the furtherance of the professionalization project. Yet, as Gabriele

Lingelbach argues, they diverged from one another both in the means of transmission from Germany and, in consequence of the very different pre-existing
conditions under which German cultural goods were received, also in the final
outcomes. An impressively high proportion of America historians undertook part
of their studies in Germany, yet few works of German scholarship were translated
into English by American publishers. In France, relatively few historians studied
in Germany, but there was an impressive reception of German historical literature. In American universities, lacking obvious and central leading institutions
and funded privately or by the individual states, there was little connection
between history in the schools and in the universities, and graduate historians
went into politics and journalism sooner than into teaching. In France, the cen-
tralizing Republican state controlled the universities' expansion, confirmed the
dominance of Parisian over provincial institutions and encouraged close communication between school and university historians. Academic historians' principal task was to prepare their students for careers in teaching. Nevertheless, there
is also impressive evidence of convergence between these two cases, and not all
the 'lessons' learned from Germany were different. Each came to evince more
interest in the methods of historical scholarship than in its outcomes. Both
exhibited a confidence that the spadework of research combined with
Quellenkritik would secure a decent average standard of scholarship. A handful of
great works of history might emanate from raw talent; that plenty of new work
reaching an acceptable qualitative norm be produced mattered more. To this end,
training was vital. What Sybel had said of foreign interest in the German practice
of history in 1868 remained true for France and the USA in the 1880s and 1890s:
it was the seminar as the best means of communicating the historian's skills that
attracted the greatest interest from abroad.[19]

In Britain, by contrast with both France and the USA, the conjoining of state
with nation long appeared too smooth, too well documented, even too 'obvious'
to necessitate either an early or a comprehensive move toward history as a modern
discipline. From the middle of the nineteenth century onward, a growing number
of university-based British historians nevertheless began to feel the want of professional standards of scholarship and their own isolation both from one another
and from continental European developments. Just as in the other cases I have
discussed, the promoters of the professionalization of history in Britain were
broadly co-extensive with the publicly noisy society of admirers of German historical scholarship. Yet none of them either sought or wished to adopt German
norms and organizational forms wholesale. Indeed, in at least some individual
cases, their reservations about the pursuit of history in Germany grew in proportion to the improvement of their acquaintance with it.

According to his own account, Sir John Seeley's study of history began only in
1869 – the year he was appointed to the Regius Chair of History at Cambridge.[20]

A sympathetic observer of German nationalism, he was never to tire of holding up German universities as a 'model' and of proclaiming that 'as a rule, good books are in German',[21] and chose a German subject for his first major publication project in his new discipline. Thus, he travelled to Germany in 1873. There, shocked to discover that ministers and not faculties had the final say in determining appointments to chairs in Germany, he found German historians to be tainted by their governmental associations:

> The Prussian throne appears as surrounded by a kind of priesthood, whose creed is the deity of Caesar. He is their Constantine. And these men are regarded all over the world as oracles, as men whose knowledge is profound and whose collective judgment is almost final, as men especially whose opinions are not, as in other countries, hampered by subscriptions or influenced by any kind of bribe, but are inviolably free! [22]

This revelation was confined to Seeley's diary, which was not designed for publication. At no point did he betray to the British public a hint of his concerns. Perhaps British historians had done their work of erecting Germany as the standard for academic achievement too well. To deny German scholarship now was to risk ruining British plans to professionalize history.

Although 'Germanizers' succeeded in establishing history as a degree subject at Oxford and Cambridge, the founding generation of historians there did not evince the kind of interest in training that had been a hallmark of German, French and US professionalizers. In any case, collegiate structures and traditions of tutorial teaching militated against the introduction of the seminar at these 'old' universities. Seminars took hold in Britain only around the turn of the century, and then only in a handful of universities new enough to be unencumbered by the weight of tradition, but also sufficiently well endowed to be able to hire more than one or two historians. At Manchester, in the course of its liberation from the requirements of the London University degree, Thomas Frederick Tout made seminars a cornerstone of history teaching. Germany was still his chief point of reference when, in a lecture first delivered to a Cambridge audience in 1906, he sought to promulgate the seminar beyond Manchester, but he could now allude also to French and American exemplars.[23] Within London, it was again to be an institution of recent provenance, namely the London School of Economics (LSE), that was to prove the most innovative both in training students and in its understanding of the historian's craft itself. Here, in the course of the 1920s and 1930s, economic and social history made its most significant early breakthrough in Britain. But nothing better illustrates the paradoxical nature of history's development than the fact of the LSE's deserved reputation for experimentation in history. Maxine Berg has persuasively argued that it was precisely its pervasive *amateurishness* in the early 1920s that facilitated change. There were no disciplinary boundaries; all the academic staff concerned themselves with history; scarcely anyone taught the subjects they had themselves studied.[24]

3.3 A global discipline? Expansion and crisis after 1945

By the middle of the twentieth century, the modern discipline of history had established itself securely in most of Europe, in North America, and in such odd outposts as Japan. The remaining holes in continental Europe were rapidly plugged after 1945 – in Holland, for instance, where the discipline now 'caught up' with that of other western European countries, but also in a number of eastern bloc countries, where still recognizably German structures were imported, together with their Stalinist deformations. But if history could, at any time after the middle of the twentieth century, claim to have become *global* in either its vision or in the distribution of its practitioners, that claim rested – and still rests – on its institution in the 'third world'.

Here, there were intellectual barriers of European provenance to be overcome. Hugh Trevor Roper, addressing a television audience in 1963, found the 'unrewarding gyrations of barbarous tribes in picturesque but irrelevant corners of the globe'[25] unworthy of the historian's attention. Africa, for example, could thus have no precolonial history worthy of the name. Trevor Roper stood four-square in a tradition carried by scholars ranging from Hegel to James Mill. An array of 'Orientalists' working throughout the first half of the twentieth century certainly did not share the British historian's contempt for the exploration of tribal customs and everyday life. But they added the blinkers of their disciplines to the rest of Trevor Roper's bundle of prejudices. Thus, anthropologists may have contributed to 'first-world' knowledge of African societies, but their practice added also to a de facto denial of those societies' historicity. Thus, unless university history departments teaching colonial history in postcolonial countries may be imagined, establishing new routes toward an African history was a necessary concomitant of planting the roots of the discipline in Africa.

By the time of Trevor Roper's disparaging remarks, there was a growing community of historians prepared to answer him. History *in* and *of* Africa emerged, like both the colonization and decolonization of the continent, through the interaction of Europeans and Africans. Three impulses may be distinguished here. First, even while propagandists of Empire at home were complacently denying that tribal peoples had histories, missionaries and colonial authorities in India as in Africa were discovering that, if only in the interests of governmental efficiency, the history of the governed was indispensable. In the course of the nineteenth century, administrators of Empire had grown used to hiring literate Indians and

Africans to write down the oral traditions of their societies. Second, the phase of 'developmental colonialism' ushered in by Great Britain in the wake of the Second World War sought to re-cast colonialism as a service to the colonized. The latter were to be brought up to standards commensurate with their eventual independence, and the provision of an on-the-spot university education was conceived as integral to the strategy. This pattern was replicated across many of those parts of the British Empire with principally non-white populations.[26] At London University's School of Oriental and African Studies (SOAS), Roland Oliver was appointed in 1948 as the world's first university lecturer in 'the history of the tribal peoples of East Africa'; around the same time, under the tutelage and control of SOAS, a string of University Colleges – in Ghana, Nigeria and Uganda – were established, and history departments were created within them virtually immediately. Third, the experience of the war had promoted nationalism within both colonized and colonial societies, while enthusing a generation of young scholars in Europe and the USA for explicitly anti-racist and anti-imperialist intellectual agendas.

Under these influences, professional historical communities were born in much of tropical Africa. A founder generation of black African academic historians was trained by Europeans. The Europeans' remit upon appointment to posts in African universities was precisely to work their way out of their jobs. Once Africans were ready, they took over teaching in and running departments. But European historians learned as much as they taught. Most often by design, but sometimes by accident, they arrived to undertake research in Africa as well as to train historians. As one veteran British historian of Africa has put it, 'it is axiomatic that African History did not so much emerge in Britain as evolve from – often by the hands of the very same teachers – the needs and experience of university colleges in tropical Africa in the 1950s'.[27]

Trained as a medievalist at the Catholic University in Leuven, the young Belgian scholar Jan Vansina had re-tooled in the techniques of 'participant observation' at SOAS in preparation to work as an anthropologist in Africa, researching Kuba society in the Congo. He imagined that he had quit the intellectual world of his MA thesis – an exploration of medieval funerary praise songs, made to be sung at the gravesides of just deceased rulers. Evidently essentially oral compositions, these were nevertheless partly accessible to historical research because, at least occasionally, they had been 'written down as *probatio pennae*' – exercises in trying out new pens. What Vansina was to go on to do once in Africa, however, was not so much anthropology as *history* in the field. Within half a year of his arrival in the Congo in early 1953, he stumbled over his European and anthropologist's prejudices and his mental world underwent a second conversion, this time of Damascene proportions. The householder of a compound with whom Vansina had been conversing suddenly

interrupted the leisurely pace of his speech and exclaimed rhetorically ...
'We too we know the past, because we carry our newspapers in our heads.'
Full of enthusiasm, he recited as proof, a number of short poems ... In a
burst of insight, half-forgotten dirges such as Laxis febris, 'With loosening
strings' ... surged through my mind. Those Bushong poems were just like
these medieval dirges. They were texts, and hence just as amenable to the
canons of historical method. Once one could assess the value of a tradition,
it could be used as a source like any other.[28]

Other historians arrived at similar conclusions. In a meeting of anthropology
and history, oral traditions could open up vistas onto precolonial pasts. Of
course, historians did not place their sole reliance on one source for one tradition, any more than they concentrated on that generic species of source to
the exclusion of others. Written sources were scrupulously drawn on where
available and archaeology provided historians with further raw materials.
Where they had been written down in the nineteenth century, some versions
of oral traditions had already acquired a kind of respectability as sources, even
for technically conservative historians. Henceforth, the latter had to be per-
suaded to take the direct consultation of oral tradition through the conduct of
oral history as seriously. As un-Rankean as early professional historians of
Africa were in the mere fact of their use of oral sources, they were therefore all
the more determinedly Rankean in their critical and comparativist approaches
to those sources.

The uses to which they put their sources also echoed the practices of nineteenth-century European historians, and did so for comparable reasons. On gaining independence, African states found their own motives for continuing the
investment in history begun by Britain. The shared nationalist commitments of
politicians and historians encouraged the search for evidence of state-formation
in precolonial societies. Their fixation on the state, then, confirms that the first
academic historians in and of black Africa were Rankeans in most things other
than their use of oral sources.

Tropical Africa's version of a statist paradigm enjoyed a brief golden age. Its
first base was in the history department at the University of Ibadan in Nigeria.
The influence of its approach – researching and writing political histories that
concentrated on precolonial periods, and doing so in ways that would be acceptable to international standards of historical scholarship – radiated outward. The
Ibadan School set historians' agendas in university departments at Ife, Lagos, Port
Harcourt, Nsukka, Jos, Benin, Iloria and Calabar.[29] From the 1950s onward,
archive management flourished; historical associations developed; journals were
established. In short, tropical Africa had, with remarkable rapidity, acquired all
the characteristic institutions of modern historical professions.

The African historians' intellectual efforts dovetailed neatly, Roland Oliver proclaimed, with the work being done by an increasingly numerous body of historians of Africa in Britain. The USA was a latecomer to the field; but there, where Vansina found a long-term institutional home at Wisconsin, a burgeoning student interest in African history, matched by initially generous research funding, also shared many of the preoccupations of historians writing in tropical Africa, and from an African perspective. History, it seemed, was being decolonized. Historians who, like Vansina, were keenly aware that the health of African history in the rest of the world was finally dependent on its strength in Africa, could fleetingly allow themselves to hope that Africans would now take the lead in making their own histories, in their own institutions.

The first challenge to the singularly international paradigm of tropical African history rather added a dimension of vibrant debate, and opened new questions, than damaging the young sub-discipline. Terence Ranger contended that the Ibadan School's nationalism was complacent and elitist, and that it had adopted European concepts uncritically. In turning to the history of ordinary people, African historians would become more really African. By 1968, Ranger had inspired the emergence of a more socially aware nationalist historiography at the University of Dar es Salaam in Tanzania. The new school advocated 'African initiative' in both the writing and the subject of its version of history, and sought to provide 'useful history' for more than just the state.

From the mid-1970s, however, neither the Ibadan School nor its rival at Dar could look ahead with confidence. The further expansion of the discipline was proving patchy, and already there were signs of contraction. In Nigeria, home to several of the earliest university history departments, and to the first historical society as well as the first and most impressive of Africa's crop of historical journals, there was a sense of crisis by the close of the decade. E.A. Ayandele lambasted Nigerian governmental policy for having turned its back on history in its 'irrational, unhealthy and culturally homicidal' pursuit of economic, scientific and technological success. While history remained the most popular discipline among humanities undergraduates, a 'primrose path' leading to well-paid jobs in public administration was seducing potential postgraduates and so militating against the ability of the historical profession to reproduce itself. Harsh as his criticisms of the record of governments were, he reserved his most damning indictments for 'the glaring failure' of Nigerian historians themselves. They had overlooked the poverty of the teaching of Nigerian history in schools, allowing themselves to be ruled by 'the arrogant feeling that it is academically pedestrian ... to descend to the level of secondary school students!' Nor had the professionals compensated by producing enough research, so that white historiography continued to occupy vast territories of Nigerian history. Yet Nigerian historians had been selling themselves into 'academic slavery' since they were 'primarily concerned with impressing the white man', persuading him to accept that African 'is a legitimate branch of History Universal'. Ayandele's recipe for all these ills was a redoubled emphasis on historians' 'patriotic duties': they must write explicitly 'nationalist history'. The international historical community could have no cause for complaint. 'For where are our colleagues,' Ayandele asked, 'in the so-called developed parts of the world who are not writers of nationalist history?'[30]

Ayandele's worst fears for the future of his profession in tropical Africa were by no means unfounded. In the mid-1980s, as the IMF called in its loans to African states, funding for history and other humanities disciplines dried up. Neither the Ibadan nor the Dar School survived. The *Journal of the Historical Society of Nigeria* ceased publication, as did virtually all the other historical periodicals of tropical Africa. Dictatorships added to the woes of academia.[31] In Zaire, for instance, history teaching 'turned into the telling of tattered tales, buildings into ruins, programs and academic calendars into fiction, and morale into elegiac despair'. Mobutu forced historians into exile and, throughout the 1970s and 80s, periodically terrorized campuses until, after the murder of at least twenty students at Lubumbashi and the plunder of the university by elite troops one night in 1990, the universities 'practically ceased to exist'.[32]

As its material base fell apart, new kinds of intellectual trauma threatened to undermine the legitimacy of institutionalized history in and beyond Africa. Ayandele's position had been perched uncomfortably between rejection and emulation of European and US historiography. For historians like Abdullahi Smith, the central problem was just that: the Ibadan and Dar Schools remained trapped within professional and institutional categories that were mere manifestations of 'the terrible corruption of Western society'. Their nationalisms were consequently self-contradictory and threadbare. In 1975, Smith proposed a comprehensive refashioning of history in the universities on Islamic lines. At Zaria, in the Islamic north of Nigeria, Smith's ideas resulted in still another African school of history, this time challenging not only the intellectual and political, but also the institutional precepts of Ibadan.[33]

That challenge, albeit mounted largely in terms very different from those of Islam, was echoed well beyond tropical Africa. The cluster of historians who gathered around the *Subaltern Studies* series of occasional volumes appeared, on the face of it, to have put Indian historiography firmly on the mental map of 'western' historians. They did so by producing a species of 'history from below', and combining it with an anti-imperialism that was not nationalist. Increasingly, however, their originally Marxist-influenced perspectives gave way to an espousal of 'postcolonial', postmodern ones. And with these came a heightened consciousness of the ambiguities of their own position as professional historians. Thus, Dipesh Chakrabarty, a member of the *Subaltern*

Studies collective, rejected as 'gratifying but premature' Ronald Inden's congratulatory words to Indian historians who were 'showing signs of reappropriating the capacity to represent themselves' within an international scholarly community. Chakrabarty advanced the 'perverse proposition' that 'all histories' – including those made by *Subaltern Studies* practitioners – 'tend to become variations on a master narrative that could be called "the history of Europe"'. In this sense, '"Indian" history itself is in a position of subalternity; one can only articulate subaltern subject positions in the name of this history.' Europe is invariably 'a silent referent in historical knowledge itself … Third-world historians feel a need to refer to works in European history', which is not reciprocated. It follows that working 'within the discipline of "history" produced at the institutional site of the university' entails 'deep collusion' with European narratives of modernization. '"History" as a knowledge system is firmly embedded in institutional practices that invoke the nation-state at every step – witness the organization and politics of teaching, recruitment, promotions, and publication in history departments.' The global presence of history within education systems serves only to underscore the point: historians owe that presence to 'what European imperialism and third-world nationalism have achieved together: the universalization of the nation-state'. Even to seek to challenge that version of universalism is 'impossible within the knowledge protocols of academic history'. From secular chronologies to the rules of evidence employed by historians, Chakrabarty leaves no aspect of his discipline unchallenged.[34] Ashis Nandy has gone still further, rejecting the imposition of 'the category of history on all constructions of the past'. Historical consciousness, welcomed by Indian intellectuals on the occasion of its mid-nineteenth century arrival on the sub-continent 'as a powerful adjunct to the kit-bag of Indian civilization', now stands revealed as irredeemably European, and its 'domination' as 'a cultural and political liability'. Instead, Nandy champions strategies of forgetting.[35]

3.4 Conclusions

Nandy unconsciously rehearses a strategy of Stalinism: airbrushing out of history whatever may be inconvenient. Besides, his own denunciations of imperialism depend, as Frederick Cooper has pointed out, on historical knowledge imparted by academic historians. Furthermore, his rejection of academic history relies on a hard-and-fast line between that and other understandings of the past.[36] Though they have done so to varying degrees and with uneven success, modern professional historians have always drawn on and eclectically assimilated ideas emanating from beyond the academy. Nor are they prepared to see amateur historians, or the bearers of oral traditions, only as sources. Though he admits it took him years to do so, Jan Vansina came clearly to see that 'informants' like

Mbop Louis were also his 'confreres, historians just as I was, only community historians, not academics like me'.[37] Academic historians may (undeniably) stand too much on their professional dignity at times. They do abuse the 'scholarly apparatus' to confuse readers and to intimidate them, and sometimes in more or less paranoid endeavours to cover their own backs against potential critics among their fellow professionals. But, probably for the most part, they are also keenly aware of being engaged in a process that is essentially collective, and dependent on debate and criticism both within and beyond the discipline. Pluralism is its necessary condition.

Guide to further reading

Pim den Boer, *History as a Profession. The Study of History in France, 1818–1914* (Princeton, 1998).

Eckhardt Fuchs and Bendedikt Stuchtey (eds), *Across Cultural Borders: Historiography in Global Perspective* (Lanham, 2002).

Effi Gazi, *Scientific National History. The Greek Case in Comparative Perspective (1850–1920)* (Frankfurt am Main, 2000).

Doris S. Goldstein, 'The Organisational Development of the British Historical Profession, 1884–1921', *Bulletin of the Institute of Historical Research* 55 (1982), pp. 180–93.

Matthias Middell, Gabriele Lingelbach and Frank Hader (eds), *Historische Institute im Internationalen Vergleich* (Leipzig, 2001).

Peter Novick, *That Noble Dream. The 'Objectivity' Question and the American Historical Profession* (Cambridge, 1988).

Bonnie G. Smith, *The Gender of History: Men, Women, and Historical Practice* (Cambridge, MA., 1998).

Jan Vansina, *Living with Africa* (Madison, 1994).

Notes

1 The classic account of these relationships is Peter Novick, *That Noble Dream. The 'Objectivity' Question and the American Historical Profession* (Cambridge, 1988), esp. pp. 51–3. See also Matthias Middell, Gabriele Lingelbach and Frank Hader (eds), *Historische Institute im Internationalen Vergleich* (Leipzig, 2001) and Eckhardt Fuchs and Bendedikt Stuchtey (eds), *Across Cultural Borders: Historiography in Global Perspective* (Lanham, 2002).

2 Christoph Strupp, 'Die Organisation historischer Lehre und Forschung in den Niederlanden bis 1940', in Middell, Lingelbach and Hader, *Historische Institute*, pp. 199–220, p. 215.

3 Peter H. Slee, *Learning and a Liberal Education: the Study of Modern History in the Universities of Oxford, Cambridge and Manchester 1800–1914* (Manchester, 1986), p. 142.

4 British Library of Political and Economic Science, Webster Papers no. 1/5, 105–9: Webster's 'Memorandum on the Relations of Modern and Ancient Universities'.

5 Eric Hobsbawm, 'Old Marxist Still Sorting Out Global Fact From Fiction', *The Times Higher*, 12 July 2002, p. 18.

6 Eckhardt Fuchs, 'Introduction: Provincialising Europe: Historiography as a Transcultural Concept', in Fuchs and Stuchtey, *Cultural Borders*, pp. 1–26, 9.

7 See Heiko Feldner's contribution to this volume (Chapter 1).

8 R. Steven Turner, 'German Science, German Universities: Historiographical Perspectives from the 1980s', in Gert Schubring (ed.), *'Einsamkeit und Freiheit' neu besichtigt: Universitätsreformen und Disziplinenbildung in Preußen als Modell für Wissenschaftspolitik im Europa des 19. Jahrhunderts* (Stuttgart, 1989), pp. 24–36.

9 Sylvia Palatschek, 'Duplizität der Ereignisse: Die Gründung des Historischen Seminars 1875 an der Universität Tübingen und seine Entwicklung bis 1914', in Werner Freitag (ed.), *Halle und die deutsche Geschichtswissenschaft um 1900* (Halle, 2002), pp. 37–64.

10 See John Warren's contribution to this volume (Chapter 2).

11 Anthony Grafton, *The Footnote. A Curious History* (Cambridge, MA., 1997), esp. pp. 61 and 65–6.

12 See Markus Huttner, 'Historische Gesellschaften und die Entstehung historischer Seminare – zu den Anfängen institutionalisierter Geschichtsstudien an den deutschen Universitäten des 19. Jahrhunderts', in Middell, Lingelbach and Hader, *Historische Institute*, pp. 39–83 and Hans-Jürgen Pandel, 'Die Entwicklung der historischen Seminare in Deutschland', in Freitag (ed.), *Halle*, pp. 25–37.

13 Heinrich von Sybel, 'Die deutschen Universitäten und die auswärtigen Universitäten. Akademische Festrede, Bonn, 22. März 1868', in von Sybel,

Vorträge und Aufsätze (Berlin, 1874), pp. 38–55 (quotations, pp. 53 and 41).

14 Q. Edward Wang, 'German Historicism and Scientific History in China, 1900–1940', in Fuchs and Stuchtey, *Cultural Borders*, pp. 141–61, 142.

15 For further instances, see Stefan Tanaka, *Japan's Orient: Rendering Pasts into History* (Berkeley, 1993); Effi Gazi, *Scientific National History. The Greek Case in Comparative Perspective, 1850–1920* (Frankfurt am Main, 2000); Paul Guérin, 'La condition de l'historien et l'histoire nationale en Belgique du 19e et au début du 20e siècle', *Storia della Storiografia* 11 (1987), pp. 64–103.

16 Thomas Saunders, 'Introduction: "A Most Narrow Present"', in Saunders (ed.), *Historiography of Imperial Russia. The Profession and Writing of History in a Multinational State* (New York, 1999), pp. 3–13 (here pp. 8–9).

17 Pim den Boer, *History as a Profession. The Study of History in France, 1818–1914* (Princeton, 1998), pp. 224–308.

18 Pim den Boer, *History*, p. 223.

19 Gabriele Lingelbach, 'Erträge und Grenzen zweier Ansätze: Kulturtransfer und Vergleich am Beispiel der französischen und amerikanischen Geschichtswissenschaft während des 19. Jahrhunderts', in Christoph Conrad and Sebastian Conrad (eds), *Die Nation schreiben. Geschichtswissenschaft im internationalen Vergleich* (Göttingen, 2002), pp. 333–59 and Lingelbach, 'The Historical Discipline in the United States: Following the German Model?', in Fuchs and Stuchtey, *Cultural Borders*, pp. 183–204.

20 Senate House, London, Sir John Seeley Papers, MS903/4/3: Notebook: 'Tour of 1873', diary entry for 22 June 1873.

21 Deborah Wormell, *Sir John Seeley and the Uses of History* (Cambridge, 1980), p. 67.

22 Seeley Papers, diary entry for 21 July 1873.

23 Thomas Frederick Tout, 'Schools of History', in Tout, *Collected Papers* (Manchester, 1932), pp. 93–109.

24 Maxine Berg, *A Woman in History. Eileen Power, 1889–1940* (Cambridge, 1996), pp. 144ff.

25 Cit. after J.D. Fage, *On the Nature of African History* (Birmingham, 1965), pp. 1–2.

26 See Robin W. Winks (ed.), *The Oxford History of the British Empire*, Vol. 5: *Historiography* (Oxford, 1999), esp. B.W. Higman, 'The British West Indies', pp. 134–45 and K.M. de Silva, 'Ceylon (Sri Lanka)', pp. 243–52.

27 Anthony H.M. Greene, 'Introductory Remarks', in Greene (ed.), *The Emergence of African History at British Universities. An Autobiographical Approach* (Oxford, 1995), pp. 1–11, 1.

28 Jan Vansina, *Living with Africa* (Madison, 1994). Quotations on pp. 7, 16, 17.

29 Paul E. Lovejoy, 'The Ibadan School of Historiography and its Critics', in Toyin Falola (ed.), *African Historiography. Essays in Honour of Jacob Ade Ajahi* (Harlow and Ikeja, 1993), pp. 195–202, 199.

30 E.A. Ayandele, 'The Task Before Nigerian Historians Today', *Journal of the Historical Society of Nigeria* 9(4) (1979), pp. 1–13. Quotations on pp. 3, 5, 6, 7.

31 See Vansina, *Living*, p. 201 and Andreas Eckert, 'Dekolonisierung der Geschichte? Die Institutionalisierung der Geschichtswissenschaft in Afrika nach dem Zweiten Weltkrieg', in Middell, Lingelbach and Hader, *Historische Institute*, pp. 451–76, esp. pp. 472ff.

32 Vansina, *Living*, see pp. 175ff. for the Libyan experience and pp. 201 and 166–7 for Zaire.

33 Lovejoy, 'Ibadan School', pp. 198–9.

34 Dipesh Chakrabarty, 'Postcoloniality and the Artifice of History. Who Speaks for "Indian" Pasts?', *Representations* 37 (1992), pp. 1–26. Quotations on pp. 1, 2, 19, 22.

35 Ashis Nandy, 'History's Forgotten Doubles', *History and Theory*, Theme Issue, 34 (1995), pp. 44–66. Quotations on pp. 45, 65, 66.

36 Frederick Cooper, 'Africa's Pasts and Africa's Historians', *Canadian Journal of African Studies* 34 (2000), pp. 298–336, 300.

37 Vansina, *Living*, p. 17.

Part 2

4

Marxist historiography

Geoff Eley

Until the mid-twentieth century, Marxist approaches to history could be encountered mainly outside the academic world in the alternative intellectual and pedagogical environments of labour movements. Commitment to the 'materialist conception of history' was associated almost entirely with an oppositional culture of dissent, intellectual polemic and working-class autodidacticism. Marxist historiography only established its presence in the universities as part of the general turning to social history that captured the imagination of the profession in the 1960s. During the long pre-history of that development, the Marxist contribution is best seen as part of a much larger effort at developing the theories and methods that a comparative 'history of society' presupposed. Between the 1930s and the 1970s, a new generation of British Marxists became a principal source of innovation in that respect, joining the comparable influence of the *Annales* school in France, with whom they also entered into dialogue. Varying country by country, this convergence of interest around 'social history' or 'the history of society' grew ultimately from the late nineteenth- and early twentieth-century efforts – in politics and social thought – to master the meanings of capitalist industrialization.

4.1 Classical Marxism: the materialist conception of history

For the distinctive thinking of Marx and Engels about history, the sovereignty of the economy was fundamental. Their approach began as a general axiom of understanding: 'The mode of production of material life conditions the general process of social, political, and intellectual life. It is not the consciousness of men that determines their existence, but their social existence that determines their consciousness.' Or, in what became an equally famous statement, 'According to the materialist conception of history, the ultimately determining element in history is the production and reproduction of real life.'[1] Dating from their early collaborations of the 1840s, this robust philosophical materialism graduated during the next decade into a general theory of economics – of the capitalist mode of production and its 'laws of motion' – which was meant to be fully explicated in the serial volumes of *Capital*.

Explicitly linked to a political project of socialism, that general theory sought to bring the European revolutionary crises of 1848–49 into historical perspective, to capture the main logic of social development during a period of capitalist industrialization and to explain the possibilities of a future capitalist collapse. That theory also bequeathed Marx's most important legacy for the pre-1914 social democratic tradition, whose constituent parties were formed, country by country, during the last quarter of the nineteenth century. It became what contemporaries mainly understood by 'Marxism' – namely, the role of the 'economic factor' in history, the determining effects of material forces on human achievement, and the linking of the possibilities of political change to the underlying movements of the economy. As a general principle, it made the 'forces of production' and their dominant forms of development into the main motor of history: it made the most important political changes contingent upon the economic crises and associated social forces needed to sustain them.

Marx himself left behind few formal works of history per se, although his 'economics', the major work of theory published in the three volumes of *Capital* between 1867 and 1894, contained a high density of historical learning and a variety of sustained historical analysis around particular questions, most famously perhaps in the accounts of 'primitive accumulation' and the transition from manufacture to modern industry, or in the empirically rich discussions of the struggles over the length of the working day.[2] Similarly, if his journalism of the 1850s and 1860s always reflected dense historical investigations, including his intensive contemporaneous analyses of the political events in France, these were not treated historiographically in any sustained way until quite recently. In fact, it was Engels who produced the more extensive catalogue of formally historical writings. These began with his classic account of the development of modern industry and its social consequences, *The Condition of the Working Class in England* (1844–45), continued with *The Peasant War in Germany* (1850) and culminated in his writings of the 1870s and 1880s, the most conventionally historical of which was *The Origin of the Family, Private Property, and the State* (1884).

For Engels this was mainly about properly formalizing Marx's legacy, popularizing his thinking, and converting it into an all-purpose philosophy. A similar ambition inspired the earliest generations of Marx's followers in the new socialist parties, including above all Karl Kautsky, who quickly emerged by the 1890s as the senior disciple. In common with other pioneers like Eduard Bernstein in Germany, Victor Adler in Austria, Georgy Plekhanov in Russia and Antonio Labriola in Italy, Kautsky sought

> to systematize historical materialism as a comprehensive theory of man and nature, capable of replacing rival bourgeois disciplines and providing the workers' movement with a broad and coherent vision of the world that could be easily grasped by its militants.[3]

Such an effort often encompassed broad historical themes, including Kautsky's own *The Agrarian Question* (1899) and *Foundations of Christianity* (1923), or sought to analyse the conditions of capitalist development inside their own society, as in Vladimir Ilyich Lenin's *The Development of Capitalism in Russia* (1899) or Rosa Luxemburg's *The Industrial Development of Poland* (1898). Other works include Ernest Belfort Bax's *The Peasant War in Germany* (1899), Jean Jaurès's *Histoire socialiste de la Révolution française* (1900–09) and Prosper Olivier Lissagaray's *History of the Commune of 1871* (1886). The new socialist parties also generated growing numbers of histories of their own emergence, of which Eduard Bernstein's three volume history of the labour movement in Berlin (1907–10) remains an imposing example.

How might we summarize this 'classical' period in the life of Marxism as a body of thought relevant to historians, extending from the output of Marx and Engels themselves to the writings of their followers at the end of the nineteenth century? Beyond its underlying philosophical standpoint, four major commitments mainly characterized this approach to history: its progressivist theory of history based on ascending stages of development; its 'base and superstructure' model of social causality; its ascription of meaningful historical change to the conflicting interests and collective agency of social classes; and its sense of itself as a 'science of society'.

In the grand Marxist scheme of history, human society advanced from lower to higher stages of development, demonstrating ever-greater complexity in the forms of organization of economic life and making possible the eventual replacement of material scarcity by material abundance. The primary context for this thinking was the urban-industrial transformation of European society directly observed by Marx and Engels, which they conceptualized as the transition from feudalism to capitalism. In contrast, the social formations preceding feudalism were indistinctly defined, sometimes appearing as the 'Asiatic' and 'ancient' modes of production, at others broken down further into 'oriental', 'ancient', 'Germanic' and perhaps 'Slavonic' patterns of property holding, which grew in turn from the earliest forms of 'primitive communalism'. The engine behind this forward-moving developmental schema was the forces of production, whose dynamism would always eventually outgrow society's given framework of social relations and institutions, thereby requiring violent socio-political upheavals for any further advance to occur. Beyond the exhaustion of capitalism's own developmental capacities, socialism was conceived as the highest level of social development of all. This theory of stages gave Marxists their criteria for periodization. It delivered a template for judging the developmental status of any particular society.

Second, Marx and the earliest generations of Marxists classically reserved a first-order priority – ontologically, epistemologically, analytically – for the underlying economic structure of society in conditioning everything else, including the possible forms of politics and the law, of institutional development, and of social consciousness and belief. The commonest expression for this determining relationship was the architectural language of 'base and superstructure', in which the spatial metaphor of ascending and sequential levels also implied the end point in a logical chain of reasoning. This could be very flexibly understood, leaving room for much unevenness and autonomy, including the separate effectivity of the superstructure and its reciprocal action on the base, especially in the context of any detailed political, ideological or aesthetic analysis; but such analyses were ultimately still held accountable.

Third, for Marxists the main motor of change under capitalism was class conflict. Such conflict was considered to be structural and endemic, a permanent and irreducible feature of social life under capitalism, based in the unavoidable antagonisms of mutually incompatible, collectively organized class interests. In this understanding, social identity derived in the first instance from the unequal contest between those who owned and controlled the means of production and those who were dispossessed. This structural antagonism led to struggles over the social distribution of the economic value produced in the economy, which assigned people 'into two great hostile camps, into two great classes directly facing each other: bourgeoisie and proletariat'.[4] Workers were a class of direct producers who no longer owned the independent means of subsistence or even their own tools. Forced back for their livelihood onto the sale of labour power to a capitalist in return for a wage, workers had no resources beyond their own collectively organized strength, mobilized through trades unions and socialist parties. Under deteriorating conditions of capitalist accumulation and profitability, workers' collective mobilizations relayed pressures to the political system, which created openings for change. The most extreme form of such a breakthrough, in a crisis of particular and escalating severity, was revolution.

Finally, Marxism was scientific. In his formative intellectual indebtedness to the new natural sciences, for example, Kautsky was entirely typical. The impact of Charles Darwin and the works of Ludwig Büchner and Ernst Haeckel permeated his pre-Marxist thinking. His monthly review *Neue Zeit*, the European movement's most prestigious theoretical organ, effectively carried this dual affiliation with Marx and Darwin on its masthead. For Kautsky, the class struggle – 'the struggle of man as a social animal in the social community' – mirrored the biological struggle for existence. For August Bebel, the leader of the German Social Democratic Party (SPD), Marxism was 'science, applied with full understanding to all fields of human activity'. Engels had established this tone in his funeral oration for Marx – 'Just as Darwin discovered the law of development of organic nature, so Marx discovered the law of development of human history' and indeed spent much of the 1870s and 1880s seeking to ground this claim, particularly in the posthumously published *Dialectics of Nature*. For most conscious followers of Marx at the end of the nineteenth century, this equivalence between 'science' and 'society' was axiomatic. It bespoke a certitude in the directionality of history, an objectivist confidence in the knowledge Marxism was expected to deliver.

Fashioned into a unified approach during the several decades before 1914, this powerful combination of standpoints – a theory of societal development permitting the periodizing of history, a model of social determination proceeding upwards from material life, a theory of social change based on class struggles and their effects, and an objectivist approach to social understanding – served Marxists well for the best part of a century. Across that period, Marxist writings on history varied greatly in subtlety, evidentiary groundedness and general scholarly integrity, fluctuating partly with the climate of Socialist and Communist political life, partly with the degree of acceptance Marxists found within the academic world and other arenas of intellectual exchange. Periods of critical ferment within Marxist theory also complicated the straightforwardness of this general description. If the 1940s and early 1950s was a time of rather little creativity in all these respects, for example, then the early 1920s saw tremendous experimentation, as did the 1960s and 1970s.

4.2 Convergences and openings

After 1918, under the radicalizing impact of the war and accompanying revolutionary crises, Marxist ideas achieved markedly wider circulation across much of Europe, acquiring further impetus from the success of the Bolshevik Revolution and the strengthening of civil freedoms in the West. One consequence was the growth of a modest Marxist intellectual presence beyond the organized confines of the socialist and Communist parties themselves, enjoying greater legitimacy in the marketplace of ideas and establishing some foothold in the universities.

Indeed, a notable convergence of interest occurred in the early twentieth century around new forms of historical inquiry – namely, 'social' history in the terms now familiar since the 1960s – for which Marxism, as the 'materialist conception of history', offered the strongest programme. But given the sway exercised over university history departments by statecraft and diplomacy, warfare and high politics, and administration and the law, the earliest social histories developed beyond the walls of academia altogether, either in the labours of private individuals or in the alternative institutional settings of labour movements. The more propitious political climate after 1918 then allowed stronger potentials for social history to emerge, usually abetted from outside the discipline per se. If in Germany the main impetus was a flowering of sociology, and in France the ecumenical conception of social science crystallizing around Henri Berr's *Revue de synthèse historique* (launched in 1900) and leading to the founding of *Annales d'histoire économique et sociale* in 1929, in Britain the key was the creation of the Economic History Society and its journal, *Economic History Review*, in 1926–27.

The resulting historiography was certainly not 'Marxist' by conscious affiliation. In France, for example, the foundations of the new history were laid during the first three decades of the century by an exceptionally fertile encounter between historians and social science, occurring partly at the École Practique des Hautes Études in Paris under the influence of the economist François Simiand and Berr's *Revue*, partly among a remarkable grouping at the University of Strasbourg, including Maurice Halbwachs, Georges Lefebvre and the founders of *Annales*, Marc Bloch and Lucien Febvre.[5] Between the 1930s and the 1960s, the dispositions of *Annales* paralleled those of Marxists: a strongly objectivist idea of history as social science; quantitative methodology; long-run analysis of economic fluctuations through prices, trade flows and population; 'structural' history; and a materialist model of causation.

Across the Channel in Britain, social history was inspired partly by the grand narratives of the Industrial Revolution and the rise of national economies, partly by left-wing empathy for the social casualties of industrialization. The leading pioneers were each moved by strong political commitments. The early modern economic historian R.H. Tawney, who taught at the LSE, was a Christian Socialist, Labour Party parliamentary candidate, advocate of the Workers' Educational Association (WEA) and prominent public intellectual; G.D.H. Cole, who taught in Oxford from the 1920s and held the Chair of Social and Political Theory from 1945, was a Guild Socialist and leading non-affiliated socialist intellectual; the radical journalists John and Barbara Hammond published an epic account of the human costs of industrialization in a trilogy of works on the labouring poor; and Beatrice and Sidney Webb, who laid the foundations for a fully professionalized social history with an immense corpus of scholarship on trades unionism, local government, the Poor Law and social administration, heavily identified with the advance of the parliamentary Labour Party. In all of these cases, the distance from Marxism as such was clear. However, the commitment to studying material life, animated by various kinds of left-wing politics and identification with the 'common people', however paternalist or patronizing, adumbrated the shared ground. The work of Cole in labour history or Tawney on the sixteenth and seventeenth centuries bridged directly to social history after 1945 in its concern with ordinary people, with the broader impact of socio-economic forces like industrialization, and with the ethics of political engagement.[6]

Of course, these early works were also written against something else. In the British case that meant not just the nationalist paradigm of statecraft, constitutional evolution and the law, but also the earlier efforts at a 'popular' or 'democratic' alternative. Thus the precursor to the Hammonds had been the radical parliamentarian and Oxford economic historian Thorold Rogers, who countered the constitutional history of his day with a seven-volume *History of Agriculture and Prices in England* published between 1866 and 1902, which assembled rich materials from which the social history of the labouring poor might be written. Likewise, in his *Short History of the English People* published in 1874, Rogers' younger Oxford contemporary John Richard Green countered the Victorian celebration of a limited English constitutionalism with a popular counter-story of democratic self-government.[7] It helped establish a line of popular history outside the universities, running through the Hammonds and Green's widow Alice Stopford Green's Irish histories to the Communist Leslie Morton's *People's History of England*, published in 1938, which drew its inspiration from the anti-fascist campaigning for a Popular Front.[8]

The rise of a self-consciously Marxist grouping of historians inside the British universities was inseparable from this deeper-running history of political pedagogy. But until new generations of university students were radicalized by the threat of fascism in the 1930s, Marxist historical work remained a subcultural current outside the professional academic world, mainly confined to the political education practised through the Communist Party, the Independent Labour Party, the Plebs League, the National Council of Labour Colleges (NCLC), Ruskin College, parts of the WEA and other areas of the labour movement, often in highly localized ways. There the appeal of Marxism broadly replicated the pattern of thinking summarized in this chapter's previous section, held together by a passionate commitment to the concept of totality as an integrated or holistic approach to knowledge and the interconnectedness of the different spheres of life.[9] This was joined to a populist or democratic belief that history's proper subject should be 'society as a whole'. History should be less about 'the rise and fall of empires' than the 'steady progress of humanity and the succeeding social systems', less about 'battles' than 'the wonderful story of human control over nature', and 'less about kings . . . [than] the peoples'. Moreover, if history was a science, there was room neither for personalities nor for the banal details of ordinary life. As one ex-miner and NCLC student remembered, 'We weren't interested in whether so-and-so had sugar in his coffee or not. What interested us was how and why societies change.'[10]

Also inseparable from this holistic or totalizing approach to history was the firm conviction in history's forward movement or direction, which for both the popular milieu and the most prestigious Marxist theoreticians was borne by a self-confirming teleological optimism. As Peter Beilharz observes of Leon Trotsky's historical works on the course of the Russian Revolution written in this same period, that teleological understanding rested upon the familiar schema of historical stages, where the 'relation between feudalism, capitalism and socialism as successive modes of production remains strictly necessary and evolutionist in conception'. Regardless of any 'sensitivity to specificity and unevenness' characterizing their particular analyses, accordingly, Marxists held fast to their belief in historical materialism as 'a positive philosophy of history, where downward fluctuations or spirals modify but never overpower the dominant and upward tendency of evolution'.[11]

The necessary openings for a more creative Marxist historiography, where the hold exercised by these established rules of thinking (teleology, base-and-superstructure determinism, the idea of a cohesively interconnected totality) might all be relaxed, came mainly outside the official discourse of the Socialist and Communist parties. They occurred in the practical contexts where new generations of social historians began doing their work, whether inside the universities or out. In fact, most genealogies of Marxist, feminist and other forms of radical history presume too much importance for university history departments. For instance, while most of the British Marxist historians claimed as a distinctive cohort by the 1970s had a university education in the 1930s and eventually secured academic appointments, many either occupied a fairly marginal place until later in their careers or worked outside the historical profession altogether. The pioneer oral historian, ex-schoolteacher and writer George Ewart Evans (1909–87), likewise university-educated and then radicalized into the Communist Party during the 1930s, produced his works entirely beyond academia.[12]

These were the settings in which common recognition of the value of materialist forms of analysis energized the intellectual and political imaginations of younger scholars who baulked at the discipline's established protocols and routines of work. This was where the appeal of social and economic history, and the excitement of entering a common project of societal understanding, could allow both Marxists and the followers of *Annales* to converge, as the experience of Labrousse and Lefebvre in France itself implied.[13] Indeed, the motivating commitments for Marxist historians of this first academic generation are to be found not just in the guiding philosophical perspectives, which might seem rather prosaically orthodox when explicated, but far more in the detailed works of scholarship they produced, which might have a great deal in common with those of their non-Marxist colleagues. For this reason, arguably, strict demarcations between the British Marxist historians and the historians of *Annales* in this period really make little sense.[14]

4.3 The British Marxist historians: shaping an intellectual culture

By the 1960s, British social history had seen the gradual accrual of a scholarly tradition, for which the prestige of Tawney and Cole delivered valuable support and protection. Various strands were important in this respect, including the longer-term institutional strength of economic history, the impact of individual pioneers like Asa Briggs, the nexus of progressive social science at the LSE, the respective influence of J.H. Plumb and George Kitson Clark in Cambridge, significant regional centres in Leeds, Manchester and elsewhere, and the labour history networks solidifying around the Society for the Study of Labour History and its *Bulletin* launched in 1960.[15] But amidst this activity, the Communist Party (CPGB) Historians' Group, whose regular discussions began in 1946, came to exercise disproportionate influence on social history's subsequent expansion. Its members mostly composed a distinct generation, having come to the CPGB via the anti-fascist campaigning of the later 1930s. Most also left during Communism's crisis in 1956–57, when the group disbanded.

The collective discussions of these British Marxist historians shaped the contours of social history in Britain, with a longer-term significance whose international resonance was comparable to that of *Annales*. They included Christopher Hill (born 1910), George Rudé (1910–93), Victor Kiernan (born 1913), Rodney Hilton (1916–2002), John Saville (born 1916), Eric Hobsbawm (born 1917), Dorothy Thompson (born 1923), Edward Thompson (1924–93), Royden Harrison (1927–2002) and the younger Raphael Samuel (1938–96). Not many taught at the centre of British university life in Oxbridge or London. Some were not historians by discipline, such as the older Maurice Dobb (1900–76), the Cambridge economist, whose *Studies in the Development of Capitalism*, published in 1946, focused a large part of the group's discussions. Others held positions in adult education. Rudé and Thompson secured academic appointments only in the 1960s, Rudé by travelling to Australia. Their main impulse came from politics, a powerful sense of history's pedagogy, and broader identification with democratic values and popular history. A leading mentor was the non-academic CPGB intellectual, journalist and Marx scholar, Dona Torr (1883–1957), to whom the group paid tribute with a volume called *Democracy and the Labour Movement* in 1954.[16]

Inspired by A.L. Morton's *People's History of England*, published in 1938 at the height of the Popular Front campaign, the group's ambition was to produce a social history of Britain capable of contesting established or official accounts.

Some members specialized in British history per se – notably, Hilton on the English peasantry of the Middle Ages, Hill on the seventeenth-century English Revolution, Saville on industrialization and labour history, Dorothy Thompson on Chartism. Others displayed extraordinary international range. Hobsbawm's interests embraced British labour history, European popular movements and Latin American peasantries, plus the study of nationalism and a series of unparalleled general histories, which by their conclusion had covered the modern era from the late eighteenth century to the present in four superb volumes. Kiernan was a true polymath, publishing widely on aspects of imperialism, early modern state formation and the history of the aristocratic duel, as well as British relations with China and the Spanish Revolution of 1854, with an imposing wider bibliography of essays on an eclectic range of subjects. Rudé was a leading historian of the French Revolution and popular protest. Two other members of the group were British specialists who over the longer term came to enjoy massive international influence – Raphael Samuel as the moving genius behind the History Workshop movement and its journal, and Edward Thompson through his great works *The Making of the English Working Class*, published in 1963, *Whigs and Hunters* a decade later, and *Customs in Common*, which incorporated agenda-setting essays and lectures originally written in the 1960s and 1970s.

This British Marxist historiography was embedded in specifically British concerns. Several voices spoke the language of English history exclusively – Hill, Hilton, Saville, the Thompsons. The broader tradition was intensely focused on national themes, most famously perhaps in Edward Thompson's vigorous general essay, 'The Peculiarities of the English', published in 1965 as a counter-blast against a general interpretation of British history advanced by two younger Marxists, Tom Nairn and Perry Anderson.[17] Thompson's writing in the aftermath of leaving the Communist Party also converged with the cognate works of the literary critic Raymond Williams, whose *Culture and Society* and *The Long Revolution*, published in 1958 and 1961, proposed their own general interpretation of modern British history. Both Thompson and Williams sought to recuperate the national past in self-consciously oppositional and democratic fashion, wresting control of the national story from conservative opinion-makers of all kinds and rewriting it around the struggles of ordinary people in a still unfinished democratic project.[18]

During the 1950s, these British concerns were centred most strongly on two areas. On the one hand, the group decisively shaped the emergent phase of labour history, most obviously through Hobsbawm's foundational essays collected in 1964 in *Labouring Men*, but also via the influence of John Saville and Royden Harrison, and in the collective setting established by the founding of the Labour History Society in 1960. This rapidly burgeoning context of new scholarship became broadly organized around a chronology of specific questions about the presumed failure of the labour movement to realize the trajectory of radicalization projected by Marx's developmental model, laying out an enduring problematic whose dominance stretched well into the 1980s. Connected with this, on the other hand, the CP Historians' Group also shaped the history of capitalist industrialization in Britain, most notably through the standard of living controversy between Hobsbawm and Max Hartwell during 1957–63 over whether industrialism had improved or degraded the living standards of the working population.[19] At the same time, neither of these momentous contributions – to labour history and to the critique of capitalist industrialization – was thinkable without the prior labours of the Webbs, Cole, Tawney and the Hammonds.

But the vision of these Marxist historians was the opposite of parochial. While doing his groundbreaking research in Paris, Rudé worked with Georges Lefebvre and Albert Soboul; Kiernan practised an eclectic version of global history long before 'world history' became a recognized part of the profession's organization and teaching; Hobsbawm enjoyed incomparably diverse connections across Europe and Latin America; and another Communist, not a member of the Historians' Group, Thomas Hodgkin (1910–82), vitally influenced African history in its nascent years, again from the margins in adult education.[20] Hobsbawm's work developed in dialogue with Braudel and his colleagues, and with Labrousse, Lefebvre and Soboul. Internationally, Hobsbawm and Rudé transformed the study of popular protest in pre-industrial societies. Rudé meticulously deconstructed older stereotypes of 'the mob', using the French Revolution and eighteenth-century riots in England and France to analyse the rhythms, organization and motives behind collective action, in the process specifying a pioneering sociology of the 'faces in the crowd'. Hobsbawm analysed the transformations in popular consciousness accompanying capitalist industrialization – in studies of Luddism and pre-trades union labour protest; in his excitingly original commentaries on social banditry, millenarianism and mafia; and in essays on peasants and peasant movements in Latin America. He pioneered the conversations of history and anthropology. He helped redefine what politics could mean in societies that lacked democratic constitutions, the rule of law or a developed parliamentary system.

The biggest step the CP Historians' Group undertook was the new journal, *Past and Present* (symptomatically subtitled a 'Journal of Scientific History'), launched in 1952 in order to preserve dialogue with non-Marxist historians at a time when the Cold War was rapidly closing this down.[21] In the guiding vision brought by the Marxist historians to the intellectual project of *Past and Present*, 'social history' meant trying to understand the dynamics of whole societies. It was the ambition to connect political events to underlying social forces. During 1947–50, the CP Historians' Group had focused on the transition from feudalism to capitalism and a complex of associated questions – the rise of absolutism, the nature of bourgeois revolutions, agrarian dimensions of the rise of capitalism and the social dynamics of the Reformation. Hobsbawm's two-part article on 'The General Crisis of the Seventeenth Century' in 1954 then prompted the salient discussion of *Past and Present*'s first decade, the various contributions to which were subsequently collected under Trevor Aston's editorship as *Crisis in Europe, 1560–1660* in 1965. That debate energized historians of France, Spain, Sweden, Germany, Bohemia, Russia, Ireland and the early-modern era more generally, as well as historians of Britain. It connected the seventeenth-century political upheavals to forms of economic crisis graspable in Europe-wide terms, in what Aston called 'the last phase of the general transition from a feudal to a capitalist economy'.[22] It built a case for studying religious conflict in social terms, a more general project that also carried through a number of other early debates in the journal, including especially that on science and religion. It grasped the nettle of trying to conceptualize the histories of societies as a whole, with profound implications for their respective later historiographies, exemplified most powerfully perhaps in J.H. Elliott's far-reaching contribution on 'The Decline of Spain'. It re-emphasized the convergence between *Past and Present* and *Annales*, for Hobsbawm's initial intervention had relied extensively on scholarly work sponsored under Braudel. Above all, the debate featured the exciting and constructive possibilities of the 'comparative method'.[23]

It is impossible to exaggerate the enduring contributions to the rise of social history made by *Past and Present* during its early years. While directly sustained by the particular Marxist formation grounded in the CP Historians' Group, the Editorial Board's outlook translated into a series of commitments that shaped the most ambitious historical discussions of the succeeding decades. One of those commitments was internationalism, for the journal brought new and exciting access to European work into the English-speaking world, aided by the editors' political networks, direct exchanges with France, and the impetus provided by the 1950 International Historical Congress in Paris and its new Social History Section.

Second, like *Annales*, Hobsbawm and his comrades urged the comparative study of societies within an overall framework of arguments about historical change, posed explicitly at the level of European or global movements and systems. This commitment grew directly from the classical Marxist perspectives learned during the 1930s and 1940s; it crystallized from the working agenda of the CP Historians' Group, and recurred in the annual *Past and Present* conference themes from 1957.

Third, *Past and Present* pioneered the interdisciplinary exchange with sociologists and anthropologists, encouraged by the axiomatic Marxist recognition of the indivisibility of knowledge, and again paralleling the trajectory of *Annales*. The model of open-minded and eclectic materialism in this respect, explicitly grounded in a self-consciously cross-disciplinary (or perhaps 'adisciplinary') synthesis of 'historical sociology', was provided by Philip Abrams (1933–81), who joined Hobsbawm as an assistant editor in 1957. Educated during the 1950s in the intellectual-political universe of the first British New Left, rather than the popular-front Communism of the 1930s, Abrams brought a very different generational formation to the journal, one shaped far more by the critical sociologies of post-war Britain.[24] On the other hand, Peter Worsley (born 1924), who displayed the most free-ranging and eclectic of cross-disciplinary dispositions, and whose historical sensibility accompanied a training in anthropology, field research in the Pacific and South-East Asia, and an appointment in sociology, had also been in the Communist Party until 1956 and those formative years continued to mould his many varied publications.[25]

Fourth, for the Marxist architects of *Past and Present*, social history went together with economics – whether via the *Annaliste* master category of structures, or via Marxism and the materialist conception of history. Within history as an academic discipline, where social history became disengaged from the 'manners and morals' mode of popularizing or from projects of 'people's history', it invariably became coupled with economic history, as in the new departments of economic and social history created in some British universities in the 1960s.

Finally, the Marxist historians' commitment to dialogue and debate, to bringing Marxist approaches not only into the centre of discussions among historians in Britain, but also into much broader intellectual circulation, as an essential bridge for both international exchange and generous cross-disciplinary explorations, profoundly enriched the intellectual culture of the discipline just at the point of the great higher-education expansion of the 1960s, which produced such a notable leap forward in the volume, range and sophistication of scholarly historical research. In that sense, the conditions of take-off for the late twentieth-century growth of historical studies were not simply assembled by the creation of national research bodies, the founding of new universities and the growth of funding for research. Those conditions were also to be found in the hard and imaginative labours of the grouping around *Past and Present* and in the politics of knowledge they pursued.

4.4 Maturity and diffusion

Although shortly to join the Board in the late 1960s, one alumnus of the CP Historians' Group not involved in *Past and Present*'s initial phase was Edward Thompson. Known first for his sprawling and energetic study of William Morris and then for his leading role in the British New Left, Thompson came to inspire several generations of social historians with his *Making of the English Working Class*, published in 1963, which appeared in its Pelican edition in 1968. His work advanced an eloquent counter-narrative to gradualist versions of British history as the triumphant march of parliamentary evolution, grounding the latter in violence, inequality and exploitation instead: 'I am seeking to rescue the poor stockinger, the Luddite cropper, the "obsolete" handloom weaver, the "utopian" artisan, and even the deluded follower of Joanna Southcott, from the enormous condescension of posterity,' he declared in one of the most quoted lines by a historian in the late twentieth century. His book was also an anti-reductionist manifesto – attacking narrowly based economic history, over-deterministic Marxism and static theories of class. For Thompson, class was dynamic, eventuating through history – a relationship and a process, a common consciousness of capitalist exploitation and state repression, graspable through culture. Through *The Making*, the move from labour's institutional study to social histories of working people gained palpable momentum, embracing work, housing, nutrition, leisure and sport, drinking, crime, religion, magic and superstition, education, song, literature, childhood, courtship, sexuality, death and more.

Thompson wrote his great work outside the academy, working in adult education in Leeds, as a Communist (until 1956), New Left activist and public polemicist. He created the Centre for the Study of Social History at Warwick University in 1965, directing it until 1970, when he resigned. Beyond the networks of labour history and *Past and Present*, Thompson's *Making* was loudly attacked. But it energized younger generations. It also inspired the newly emergent and differently formed Marxisms that became so central to the developing social history wave.

Thompson's impact helped two initiatives on the margins to form, whose longer-term effects both mirrored the earlier dynamics of the Communist Historians' Group's influence and crucially surpassed its substantive range, organized forms and political intent. One of these was the Social History Group in Oxford, which convened on a weekly basis between 1965 and 1974. This seminar's organizers were a younger generation of graduate student Leftists, who included the Marxist author of *Outcast London*, Gareth Stedman Jones (born 1942), a specialist on Spanish anarchism, Joaquin Romero Maura (born 1940), and the historian of Nazism, Tim Mason (1940–90), who for a time was an assistant editor of *Past and Present*. They were inspired by a fourth member, the somewhat older Raphael Samuel (1934–96), who had been a schoolboy recruit to the CP Historians' Group, left the party in 1956 to become a key energizer of the New Left, and then took an appointment at Ruskin, the trades union college based in Oxford but not part of the university, from 1961. Linked to the ambitions of the Social History Group and conceived initially to bring Ruskin students into wider contact with other historians, Samuel's annual History Workshops became a vital engine of social history during the coming period, starting modestly but soon mushrooming into an international event. The first 13 workshops met at Ruskin itself between 1967 and 1979, before migrating around Britain. They inspired a series of pamphlets – 12 altogether between 1970 and 1974 – and an imprint of more than 30 books between 1975 and 1990. Most impressively of all, Samuel and his group crystallized a much wider movement, grounded in diverse local university and community settings, and linked to public interventions of various kinds, most substantially during the debate over the National Curriculum in the 1980s. Its flagship was *History Workshop Journal* launched in 1976. In common with *Social History,* another new journal founded in the same year, *History Workshop Journal* sought to re-energize the commitments inaugurated through *Past and Present.*[26]

The second movement was women's history. Originally via tense and often angry contention with History Workshop and older mentors like Hobsbawm and Thompson, pioneers like Sheila Rowbotham (born 1943) drew important support and inspiration from both. Future leaders of women's history emerged from History Workshop's milieu, including Anna Davin (born 1940), Sally Alexander (born 1943) and Catherine Hall (born 1945). Rowbotham's early works became markers of the future field.[27] The first National Women's Liberation Conference, which met at Ruskin in 1970, originated as a women's history meeting, and the Seventh History Workshop in 1973 took 'Women in History' as its theme. Social history's emergence, like the earlier twentieth-century movements and the Communist Party Historians' Group, was inconceivable outside these new political contexts.

Thompson's influence was international. *The Making* shaped North American, African and South Asian agendas, no less than studies of class formation in Britain and Europe. His eighteenth-century essays had perhaps even greater resonance, especially 'The Moral Economy', which influenced scholars working across national histories in diverse regions of the world and became the object of a retrospective international conference in Birmingham in 1992. The 1970s internationalized social history in the full sense envisaged by the British Marxist historians who founded *Past and Present,* through a growing proliferation of conferences, new journals, and active processes of translation. In one network of particular importance, Thompson and Hobsbawm became central participants in a series of Round Tables on Social History organized by Braudel's Maison des Science l'Homme, which brought together scholars from France, Italy, West Germany and elsewhere.

But by the 1980s, the energizing centre of innovative thinking among historians had moved elsewhere. Internationally, these dynamics varied. In Germany, for example, the challenge of *Alltagsgeschichte* (the history of everyday life) eventually compelled an opening of the discipline's mainstream toward forms of cultural history, partially shaped by an emergent dialogue with anthropology, where gender history also made significant inroads.[28] In Britain, an unexpected questioning of social history's materialist standpoints by Stedman Jones and others initiated a series of long-running debates, whose consequences converged with a variety of other powerful intellectual tendencies, feminist historical work, and the diffusion of cultural studies most notable among them, to dislodge social history from its earlier anticipated primacy.[29]

By the end of the century, a marked diversification was the result, encompassing not only the range of social histories that continued to be practised much as before, but also various redeployed and more sophisticated versions of political history and the history of ideas, distinct and self-consciously demarcated forms of the 'new cultural history', and a small but vociferous avant-garde of self-avowed 'postmodernists'. But the more partisan or self-isolating exponents of these tendencies notwithstanding, the most notable characteristic of this new period was the intermixing of standpoints: it was patently possible now to be both a social historian and a cultural historian, to combine the history of ideas with careful forms of contextualization, and to take the measure of contemporary culturalist critiques without entirely vacating the ground of structural or materialist investigation. Some proponents of a 'non-materialist' or 'linguistic' history might insist on the exclusivity of their approach, but such advocacy neither possessed some undisputed or universally acknowledged epistemological authority nor adequately described the continuing diversity of historiographical practices in and beyond the discipline.

Once this diversity is recognized, the continuing relevance of the Marxist historiography of the 1950s and 1960s should be secure. To make this point, it is worth returning to one of the programmatic statements of that period, which came in 1971 at the end of the forging time described above and at the cusp of the great social history wave by that time already under way. In a much-cited benchmark essay entitled 'From Social History to the History of Society', Hobsbawm argued that the real importance of the emergent approaches was less the advocacy of previously unrecognized subjects than the new possibilities for writing the history of society as a whole. This entailed partly the commitment to generalization and theory, to ways of keeping the overall picture in view, and partly analytical approaches aimed at situating all problems in their societal context. Certainly, for Hobsbawm, social causes possessed primacy. But taking seriously the tasks of social significance entails no necessary commitment to materialism of such a foundational kind.[30]

At the same time, the earlier totalizing ambition – the goal of writing the history of whole societies in some integral or articulated way – has gone definitely into recession. That macro-historical understanding of whole societies changing across time evinced by the founders of *Past and Present*, guided by a confident knowledge of developmental or structural models drawn from the social sciences, has become much harder to sustain. 'Society', as a confident materialist projection of social totality in that way, has become much harder to find, because the anti-reductionist pressure of contemporary social and cultural theory since the 1980s has radically de-authorized it. Originally, that anti-reductionist logic was very empowering. As the hold of the economy became loosened during the 1980s, and with it the determinative power of the social structure and its causal claims, the imaginative and epistemological space for other kinds of analysis grew. The rich multiplication of new cultural histories became the invaluable pay-off.[31] Now that much of the heat and noise surrounding the new cultural history has started to die down, and the more extreme anxieties accompanying the so-called 'linguistic turn' seem to have been allayed, it may be easier to reclaim social history in the main sense advocated by Hobsbawm and his contemporaries, which involves always trying to relate our particular subjects, complexly and subtly, to the bigger picture of society in general. Once that happens, the Marxist historiography discussed in this chapter will remain an invaluable resource.

Guide to further reading

Gerald Allan Cohen, *Karl Marx's Theory of History: A Defence* (Oxford, 1978).

Dennis Dworkin, *Cultural Marxism in Postwar Britain: History, the New Left, and the Origins of Cultural Studies* (Durham, NC, 1997).

Dick Geary, 'Karl Kautsky and "Scientific Marxism"', *Radical Science Journal* 11 (1981), pp. 130–35.

Eric J. Hobsbawm (ed.), *The History of Marxism, Vol. 1: Marxism in Marx's Day* (Bloomington, 1982).

Gregor McLennan, *Marxism and the Methodologies of History* (London, 1981).

S.H. Rigby, *Marxism and History. A Critical Introduction*, 2nd edn (Manchester, 1998).

Raphael Samuel, 'British Marxist Historians, 1880–1980: Part One', *New Left Review* 120 (March–April 1980), pp. 21–96.

John Seed, 'Marxist Interpretation of History', in Kelly Boyd (ed.), *Encyclopedia of Historians and Historical Writing* 2 (London, 1999), pp. 772 8.

Notes

1   Karl Marx, 'Preface' to *A Contribution to the Critique of Political Economy* (1859), in Marx, *Early Writings*, ed. Lucio Colletti (Harmondsworth, 1975), p. 425 and Friedrich Engels to Joseph Bloch, 21–22 September 1890, in Marx and Engels, *Selected Correspondence* (Moscow, 1965), p. 417.

2   Karl Marx, *Capital: A Critique of Political Economy*, Vol. 1, ed. David Fernbach (Harmondsworth, 1974). The discussion of primitive accumulation can be found in Chapters 26–33, the transition from manufacture to industry in Chapters 14–15, the struggle over the working day in Chapter 10.

3   Perry Anderson, *Considerations on Western Marxism* (London, 1976), p. 6.

4   Karl Marx and Friedrich Engels, *The Communist Manifesto. A Modern Edition*, with an introduction by Eric Hobsbawm (London, 1998), p. 35.

5   For the *Annales* school see Matthias Middell's contribution to this volume (Chapter 6).

6   See esp. G.D.H. Cole and Raymond Postgate, *The Common People, 1746–1938* (London, 1938); see generally David Sutton, 'Radical Liberalism, Fabianism, and Social History', in Richard Johnson, Gregor McLennan, Bill Schwarz and David Sutton (eds), *Making Histories: Studies in History-Writing and Politics* (London, 1982), pp. 15–43.

7   Anthony Brundage, *The People's Historian: John Richard Green and the Writing of History in Victorian England* (Westport, CT, 1994).

8   Sandra Holton, 'Gender Difference, National Identity and Professing History: The Case of Alice Stopford Green', *History Workshop Journal* 53 (2002), pp. 118–27 and Harvey J. Kaye, 'Our Island Story Retold: A.L. Morton and "The People" in History', in *The Education of Desire: Marxists and the Writing of History* (New York, 1992), pp. 116–24.

9   Stuart Macintyre, *A Proletarian Science. Marxism in Britain 1917–1933* (Cambridge, 1980), pp. 129–32.

10 The first quotation is from an article by Mark Starr on 'The History of History and its Uses' in the April 1926 issue of *Plebs*; the second is from an interview with an 80-year-old ex-miner named Dai Davies. See Ruskin History Workshop Students Collective, 'Worker-Historians in the 1920s', in Raphael Samuel (ed.), *People's History and Socialist Theory* (London, 1981), pp. 16, 17; John S. Clarke, *Marxism and History* (London, 1927). Clarke was a Scottish autodidact Marxist active in the NCLC movement.

11 Peter Beilharz, 'Trotsky as Historian', *History Workshop Journal* 20 (1985), p. 50.

12 Gareth Williams, *Writers of Wales: George Ewart Evans* (Cardiff, 1991).

13 See especially the testimony of Eric Hobsbawm, 'British History and the *Annales*: A Note', in *On History* (New York, 1997), pp. 178–85 and ibid., 'Marx and History', p. 187.

14 See here the reflections of a Marxist member of the *Annales* school, Pierre Vilar, 'Marxist History, a History in the Making: Towards a Dialogue with Althusser', *New Left Review* 80 (1973), pp. 65–106.

15 See Adrian Wilson, 'A Critical Portrait of Social History', in Wilson (ed.), *Rethinking Social History: English Society 1570–1920 and its Interpretation* (Manchester, 1993), pp. 1–24 and Miles Taylor, 'The Beginnings of Modern British Social History?', *History Workshop Journal* 43 (1997), pp. 155–76.

16 Eric Hobsbawm, 'The Historians' Group of the Communist Party', in Maurice Cornforth (ed.), *Rebels and Their Causes: Essays in Honour of A.L. Morton* (London, 1979), pp. 21–47; Bill Schwarz, '"The People" in History: The Communist Party Historians' Group, 1946–56', in Johnson et al. (eds), *Making Histories*, pp. 44–95; David Parker, 'The Communist Party and its Historians 1946–89', *Socialist History* 12 (1997), pp. 33–58; Harvey J. Kaye, *The British Marxist Historians: An Introductory Analysis* (Cambridge, 1984). For Dona Torr, see David Renton, 'Opening the Books: The Personal Papers of Dona Torr', *History Workshop Journal* 52 (Autumn 2001), pp. 236–45.

17 Edward Thompson, 'The Peculiarities of the English', in *The Poverty of Theory and Other Essays* (London, 1978), pp. 35–91; Perry Anderson, 'Origins of the Present Crisis', *New Left Review* 23 (1964), pp. 26–54, Tom Nairn, 'The English Working Class', *New Left Review* 24 (1964), pp. 45–57; Tom Nairn, 'The Anatomy of the Labour Party', *New Left Review* 27 (1964), pp. 38–65, and 28 (1964), pp. 33–62; Perry Anderson, 'The Myths of Edward Thompson, or Socialism and Pseudo-Empiricism', *New Left Review* 35 (1966), pp. 2–42.

18 The best introduction is through Raymond Williams, *Politics and Letters: Interviews with New Left Review* (London, 1979).

19 Arthur J. Taylor (ed.), *The Standard of Living in Britain in the Industrial Revolution* (London, 1975).

20 Anne Summers, 'Thomas Hodgkin (1910–1982)', *History Workshop Journal* 14 (1982), pp. 180–2.

21 See Christopher Hill, Rodney Hilton and Eric Hobsbawm, 'Past and Present: Origins and Early Years', *Past and Present* 100 (1983), pp. 3–14.

22 Trevor Aston (ed.), *Crisis in Europe, 1560–1660* (London, 1965), p. 5.

23 See John H. Elliott, 'The Decline of Spain', *Past and Present* 20 (1961), pp. 52–75. For the subsequent course of the general debate, see Geoffrey Parker and Lesly M. Smith (eds), *The General Crisis of the Seventeenth Century* (London, 1978)

24 See esp. Philip Abrams, *Historical Sociology* (Ithaca, 1982).

25 Worsley's first book was *The Trumpet Shall Sound: A Study of 'Cargo' Cults in Melanesia* (London, 1957), in some ways a parallel text to Hobsbawm's *Primitive Rebels*. He then published *The Third World* (London, 1964), followed two decades later by *The Three Worlds: Culture* *and Development* (London, 1984), together with a wide variety of other publications, including *Marx and Marxism* (London, 1982). He held the Chair of Sociology at Manchester from 1964 and was President of the British Sociological Association during 1971–74.

26 Stuart Hall, 'Raphael Samuel 1934–96', *New Left Review* 221 (1997), pp. 119–27 and Sheila Rowbotham, 'Some Memories of Raphael', ibid., pp. 128–32.

27 See Sheila Rowbotham, *Resistance and Revolution* (Harmondsworth, 1972); *Hidden from History: 300 Years of Women's Oppression and the Fight Against It* (London, 1973); *Women's Consciousness, Man's World* (Harmondsworth, 1973).

28 Geoff Eley, 'Labor History, Social History, *Alltagsgeschichte*: Experience, Culture, and the Politics of the Everyday – A New Direction for German Social History?', *Journal of Modern History* 61 (1989), pp. 297–343; Alf Lüdtke (ed.), *The History of Everyday Life: Reconstructing Historical Experiences and Ways of Life* (Princeton, 1995).

29 Gareth Stedman Jones, 'Introduction' and 'Rethinking Chartism', in *Languages of Class: Studies in English Working-Class History, 1832–1982* (Cambridge, 1983), pp. 1–24, 90–178.

30 Eric J. Hobsbawm, 'From Social History to the History of Society', *Daedalus* 100 (1971), pp. 20–45.

31 For these intellectual histories, see Geoff Eley, 'Is All the World a Text? From Social History to the History of Society Two Decades Later', in Terrence J. McDonald (ed.), *The Historic Turn in the Human Sciences* (Ann Arbor, 1996), pp. 193–243, and 'Between Social History and Cultural Studies: Interdisciplinarity and the Practice of the Historian at the End of the Twentieth Century', in Joep Leerssen and Ann Rigney (eds), *Historians and Social Values* (Amsterdam, 2000), pp. 93–109.

5

History and the social sciences

Christopher Lloyd

5.1 Problems in the history/social science relationship

The history–science relationship has always been contentious and often troubled. From the beginning of the rise of science to dominance in western thought and culture in the seventeenth century there began a long struggle for philosophy and humanism to come to terms with it. In the nineteenth century many historians adopted what they thought were scientific modes of enquiry. The attempt to be scientific was largely abandoned from the late nineteenth century only to be revived in the late twentieth. Social science then moved towards the adoption of historicity in the late twentieth century. Now there is a growing rapprochement between history and social science. Of course not all historical discourse, by any measure, has become scientific today and many scientists fail to see the centrality of history to all systems. The professional history discipline is now rather divided between those striving to become more social scientific and those resolutely rejecting it. The division between cultural historians and some social historians, on one hand, and sociological, geographical, economic and political historians, on the other, is where the fault-line now lies. But ahistoricism is, unfortunately, still prevalent in the social sciences. The often heated debate between history and science continues in spite of the obvious power and success of scientific methodology and theory in all realms of natural and human enquiry, and the obvious necessity for a historical approach to social (as well as natural) processes and systems because of their irreducibly historical character. Mutual misunderstandings are still common.

To be scientific involves, above all, the use of theory. A basic argument of this chapter is that we don't have a choice about whether to use general theories in

83

what should be a unified socio-historical science. We must be and indeed are theoretical. Therefore, as far as possible, it is better to be coherent, articulate and self-critical theoreticians. But when questions about the relationship of theory to history, of what are theories, and of how to theorize history are raised there seems often to be confusion. Confusion springs, as always, from a failure to make some important distinctions – most importantly between three separate but related questions about generalizations in explanation, which I'll indicate in a moment. These questions can be separated by keeping clearly in mind a more basic analytical distinction. This is between (a) history as a public discourse in various media and (b) history as a real-world process independent from knowledge and discourse. The idealist/social constructionist/pragmatist/postmodernist broad current of ideas is characterized essentially by the programme of collapsing this distinction. The enlightenment/scientific/empiricist/modernist current is characterized by the maintenance of this distinction as fundamental. Another way to describe this division is to label the two as 'social constructionist' and 'epistemological' schools. For the first there is little or no distinction between the knower and the known, for history has no objectivity outside of ways of describing and analysing it; for the second there is a distance that has to be bridged by a knowledge-generating process that mediates between the external world and the knower.

Now, of course, this simple description of the two camps is somewhat oversimplified, but understanding that there is this division helps with clarification of some of the confusion about history and theory. Now we can formulate the three questions about generalizations as follows, with the answers that will be defended in this chapter.

1   Do and should speculative and/or general theoretical presuppositions (including metanarrative concepts) play a role in the construction of topics and problems, descriptions, explanations and style of writings of historical texts about past and present social processes? I answer that everywhere they do play powerful and, indeed, unavoidable, roles but they must be articulated, criticized and refined so as to become a more precise part of the explanatory framework of a science of history.

2   Can there be constructed precise, coherent and powerful causal theories of past and ongoing processes of human behaviour, social interactions and social organizations? I answer 'yes, in principle', but we are some way from it yet although there are many existing candidates.

3   What role do and should theories of knowledge (epistemologies) play in the writing of historical and social science texts? I answer that these do play powerful but implicit and usually confusing roles. They too are necessary and have to be articulated, defended and criticized.

Thus general concepts, causal beliefs and ideas about explanation can be found tacitly informing the work of all social and historical writing. The task of philosophically informed and practically minded methodology of historical enquiry is, like the methodology of any science, to make a critical enquiry into the ways in which answers to these questions inform and influence the scope and explanations of historical writing. History should no more be a discipline resting on 'common sense' than are biochemistry, neurophysiology, astrophysics or any other empirical science. Theory must be brought out of the closet.

Discussion of why the history/science debate has been (and is still) so animated and of arguments about how the relationship should be resolved, such that history and social science become unified as a single mode of enquiry, are the themes of this chapter. I argue that the long history of separateness is indeed coming to an end. The study of humanity and society in the broadest senses (including culture and physiological evolution) is being seen increasingly as but one of a group of sciences, including biology, geology and astronomy, that are historical by nature in that their subject matters are historical phenomena, systems and evolutionary processes. But the 'historical revolution' that has been occurring in the sciences of nature in recent times has yet to take a full hold in the social sciences. This is because social historicization has been resisted from both points of view. That is, historians have often had a fear of the loss of humanism or free will if they embrace a social scientific (i.e. generalized and theoretical) and present-centric approach, and social scientists have too often derided history's concern with the past as being unworldly, subjective and irrelevant to current concerns of a practical nature. But it is now well understood in the natural sciences that their subject matter is essentially processual, which is to say, it is historical. Social enquiry, like natural enquiry, to be genuinely scientific, must also embrace history since present society is both the product of history and a dynamic, evolving, rather than static, reality. To fully adopt historicity will require a revolution in the social sciences and to adopt science will require a revolution in history. These converging revolutions are well under way. The supposedly *sui generis* character of historical enquiry, which many philosophers of history tried to establish over the past century, is no longer plausible.

Mindful of the many abuses of historical understandings, historians have rightly feared being co-opted by political movements that wish to use them for sectional and even dangerous purposes. But, of course, both historians and social scientists have always been embedded within socio-political contexts. The question should be, rather, of their capacity to transcend their location and strive for objectivity and explanatory improvement. Fortunately, there is much work that exhibits the transcendence of the pernicious divide between history and social science, and that strives to avoid any tendency towards narrow propaganda. Without commitments to intellectual independence, objectivity and explanatory improvement, genuine socio-historical enquiry would be in slavish obedience to the political and cultural contexts of its practitioners.

The present has to be understood as historically contingent, continuous and transformative. Present and past are organically connected so that in fact there is no real distinction between them. The past may be foreign to a greater or lesser extent but not because it is past, only because it is culturally and socially foreign. Past and present foreignness is a matter of distance not an ontological category. Historicity is at the very core of social reality in all its complexity and multi-dimensionality.

The debate has been confused by some wrong-headed views. One of the most pervasive has been that the basic historical method is the use of 'common sense' to 'interpret' evidence.[1] Historians, unlike scientists, supposedly cannot use general theories because humans and society are too complex, variable, individualistic and subjective to be comprehended through theories. Rather, historians must interpret evidence through the lens of empathetic, intelligent, well-informed common-sense understandings; understandings that can only be specific to particular cultures. Thus to understand Ancient Romans you either had to be a Roman or at least be so steeped in Roman culture and society as to know intimately the Roman mentality in all its specificity. Ultimately this is supposed to be impossible in any full sense so a thorough, rich account of Roman history cannot be written today. The linguistic or cultural turn that gave rise to the radical relativism of postmodernist methodology of recent decades tried to elevate this humanistic view to a philosophy of explanation that is, unfortunately, incoherent and ultimately self-denying. While of course it must be conceded that insightful and sensitive interpretation of alien cultures, whether past or present, is very difficult, historical research, like any systematic empirical mode of enquiry, only makes sense if it strives to *improve* its explanations, and improvement implies at least some degree of objectivity. Agreement about what constitutes a contribution to improved explanation must rest upon some idea about what would constitute better methods and better results. Thus the prior question is how to improve methodological foundations. A first step is to criticize common-sense understandings, for they always have within them unacknowledged generalizations about human nature, motivation and social organization, and so try to produce better theories that rest on firmer foundations. Explanation cannot do without theory. At bottom, then, the question of the relationship of history to social science boils down to the nature and use of general theory. After that, the issue becomes one of the nature and power of particular theories.

Another wrong-headed view, sometimes still held by historians but now little held by philosophers of history or science, is that science, and thus scientific history, has a 'covering law' model of explanation.[2] This positivist view claims that history is no different from other forms of explanation and explanation is essentially a matter of deduction from covering laws. General laws are asserted as axiomatic statements and then deductions are made from them to explain particular cases. This view has been undermined through the development of better accounts of scientific explanation and historians were always right to reject that model. (More on this later.)

A third wrong-headed view among historians is that a theory is a piece of untested speculation. In fact, in the sciences, theories are highly developed, well attested and accepted general explanations that are used as the most important part of the intellectual frameworks for explanations of particular domains of phenomena and structure and, therefore, as explanations for particular phenomena and processes within those domains. The Darwinian theory of biological evolution, the physical theories of relativity and quantum thermodynamics and the geological theory of plate tectonics are prime examples of general theories. In the social sciences there are less well confirmed and very controversial candidates for this kind of general theory, such as general equilibrium theory in economics, social class theory of politics and revolutions, the rational choice theory of social and political behaviour, and the neo-classical theory of economic history and development.

Philosophically speaking, it can be said that the debate over unification or separation of history and social science is essentially *ontological* because if societies are deemed to have a certain kind of unified fundamental existence at all times and places, then the task is the same whatever the behaviour or society being studied, whether past or present. There is no warranted separation of the two disciplines. And if knowledge about social relations, motivations and behaviour is generalizable through the construction of concepts and theories that are applicable to all cases, then a scientific approach is possible even if not yet realized. Those who deny this possibility make a powerful (ontological) claim about societies and humans as each being essentially unique. In other words, the humanistic denial of the possibility of socio-historical science rests on a deep claim about the nature of persons, their decisions, their actions and their socio-cultural relations, as being essentially non-generalizable and so knowable only through an empathetic approach by the individual enquirer into every personality, action and society. Free will rules out science; but, of course, nobody really believes this and it is contradictory for it asserts both uniqueness and the possibility of transcending that uniqueness by an enquirer. To have any enquiry there must be *sharing* of understandings by subjects and enquirers and this opens the door to generalization, for sharing requires general concepts.

However, the argument from ontology has to concede that the establishment of the nature of reality must come from within a particular mode of enquiry.[3] We cannot establish the nature of reality (an ontology) except through a theory of knowledge (an epistemology) and actual enquiry. Reality is never knowable a priori; neither is there a simple empirical relationship of sensory reflection of the world in the consciousness of the enquirer. Knowledge of the world is always mediated through social/cultural/philosophical/theoretical frameworks. The sociology of knowledge, stemming particularly from the work of Foucault and Bourdieu, argues that knowledge is always constructed from within a social context. Indeed, how could it be otherwise? But this does not mean that the knowledge itself is entirely relative to that social context and thus can tell us nothing objective about the world. There are two levels of processes in science, governed by different interests. On one level is the social context that determines to a significant degree what the current problems and tasks of science are, who does what tasks towards solving which problems, where the results are published, who notices and uses the results, and so on. This is a social power structure. On the other level is the practical, more or less objective, everyday activity of science that produces results and solves the partly socially generated problems, and accumulates knowledge, in a relatively sociologically disinterested process. Scientific progress occurs, then, in a complex, interactive context of ideas and social systems. Foucault made the important distinction between madness as a discursive social power construct and mental illness as a scientific problem susceptible to empirical research and possible solution. The challenge for the defenders of the veracity of science has always been to show how science is able to transcend its specific milieu to establish universal conceptual and explanatory truths. Science has to show that it truly *discovers* the deep causal structure of the world, of which humanity is a part.

In fact, there is no doubt that modern science has been successful in transcending its specific socio-cultural locations. The results of engineering in open rather than experimental situations is one recurring proof of this, although not all sciences have experimental or engineering tests of validity. The macro historical sciences of astronomy, biology and geomorphology rely upon observations to test theories. And unlike all other ways of enquiring into the workings of the world, science makes *universal* claims that transcend its milieu in a highly self-critical reflexive manner. No other general mode of enquiry – religion, magic, relativistic humanism – is so self-critical of its own foundations, methodologies and findings. Science, in its ideal form, is defined by this commitment to constant self-criticism and constant scepticism. Of course, science in practice also often has other commitments that are not always criticized, such as the control and manipulation of nature and humanity. Humanists are right to be wary of the engineering agenda inherent in much of science, which often takes it beyond explanation. Scientists, on the other hand, are rightly critical of the lack of general, testable, explanations in non-scientific discourses and the socially manipulative ideological agendas of much of social and historical enquiry. Through its strivings and power to uncover the deep causal structures of the world, science has triumphed over its philosophical critics, if not always over its moral critics. But that the morality of scientists and the users of science can be questioned is not the same as saying that science itself cannot in principle explain humanity. And that we lack good scientific explanations for much of the human domain does not mean that we cannot approach explanation in a scientific manner. It is methodology, theory construction and general explanatory commitment that define science, not the totality of its results, which can often be incomplete, or underdetermined and incorrect.

5.2 Rationalism and enlightenment

The present debate over history and social science is the outcome of several centuries of disputation, during which science has arisen to dominate the empirical discourses. In the sixteenth and seventeenth centuries European overseas imperialism, which brought a great increase in knowledge of disparate cultures, and then the beginnings of Newtonian science, formed the context for the great rationalist shift in European thought, epitomized by Descartes, Hobbes, Newton, Locke and Leibniz.[4] Together they rejected the dominance of a mystical religious worldview and emphasized human reason. In the eighteenth century Age of Enlightenment scientific rationality and systematic social enquiry placed Man and Reason at the centre of human affairs, and moved towards a rejection of all divine intervention in the world. The members of the Scottish Historical School, including Adam Smith and Adam Ferguson, were the most important developers of theory of economic and social history.[5] Of course they were driven, in part, like most Enlightenment thinkers, to extol the progressiveness of eighteenth-century socio-economic and intellectual developments. The progress of humanity was a central theme of the Enlightenment.

The Romantic movement in philosophy and culture, especially in late eighteenth- and early nineteenth-century Germany, struggled to come to terms with this new progressivist scientific mode of thought. Vico in Italy and Kant in Germany developed a distinction between scientific reason and human understanding that laid the foundation for a distinction between natural science and humanistic social enquiry, a distinction that was eclipsed for a century by the power of the scientific enterprise. While in most respects Kant was an Enlightenment thinker, his reason/understanding distinction became important in German thought and was re-emphasized by later thinkers such as Hegel, who elevated a notion of holistic teleological Reason to quasi-mystical status. The neo-Kantians in the late nineteenth century emphasized a distinction between generalized explanation of science and particular understandings of humanity.

During the Enlightenment, especially from the mid-eighteenth century and including the French Revolutionary and Napoleonic era, the constellation of European ideas was strongly influenced by the application of science to engineering, the beginnings of industrialization, and the coming into full consciousness of the concepts of human and civilizational progress. The use of abstractions and general concepts came to be used to understand social structure and the apparent universal stages of human progress. The systematic study of social and economic change with the attendant ideas of an organic link between past, present and future, and the role of socio-economic policy as a new task for statecraft in bringing about a desirable future, were brought together for the first time. For the Enlightenment rationalist thinkers, including the Romantic offshoot, the study of history became the study of the universal emancipation of humanity. The French Revolutionaries and their Napoleonic inheritors were concerned with universal social and human characteristics, and desired the establishment of a professional and theoretical science of history.

5.3 Positivism and scientism

Throughout most of the nineteenth century, western social and historical thought was dominated by a concern with universality. The scientific and rationalist impulse led to several versions of the idea that the task of history was to establish truthfully the trajectory of human societies or economies or nations or states. That history and social science were a single discourse united by this universalistic impulse to establish the science of society in one form or another was a central idea. Hegel, Saint-Simon and Comte led the way towards universalism. Positivism (Comte's term) was the broad movement that wished to expunge so-called metaphysical and mystical thinking from social enquiry and establish the indisputable principles of an objectivist scientific methodology. From the mid-nineteenth century, positivism became closely associated with the older idea of evolution, which, in its simplest form, is the concept that new, usually higher, stages emerge out of earlier stages. Classical economics from the mid-eighteenth century and later German economics from the early nineteenth century adopted this as the universal principle of human progress.[6] Darwin was strongly influenced by older socio-economic ideas in his theorizing about biological evolution, but his work contained the seed for a necessary rejection of teleological thinking in biological and social science.[7] Marx, perhaps the greatest inheritor of the Enlightenment, built upon ideas from Hegel, classical economics, the French revolutionary thinkers, and even Darwin, to build an all-encompassing science of social structural history.[8] By the late nineteenth century, evolutionism (non-Darwinian and Social-Darwinian) and positivism were the guiding concepts of the dominant schools of socio-historical thought throughout Europe. But from the 1880s a strong reaction began that led to the disintegration of this quasi-consensus and so laid the foundations for the fractured relationship of social science to history that was dominant through most of the following century.

5.4 The methodenstreit

The great debate in the closing decades of the nineteenth century, especially in Germany, regarding the proper method for social and historical enquiry pitted the evolutionary positivists against, on one hand, the neo-Kantians and all those asserting the *sui generis* nature of historical enquiry and, on the other, the new scientistic positivists, who wished to build a social science on the methodological foundations apparently being established by the new physics.[9] Henceforth, the model of the powerful sciences of nature, which were now revolutionizing industrial processes and engineering, would be the dominant mode of reasoning, in relationship to which the power of philosophy and empirical enquiry in all other areas would be judged. A polarization of thought between humanism and positivism began that lasted until late into the twentieth century.

The Neo-Kantians argued for an idiographic/nomothetic (particular/general) distinction that separated historical enquiry from science.[10] History could not attempt to discover laws, as science did, but had to describe and understand the detailed particularity of societies, events and lives. Their great contemporary, Max Weber, schooled in neo-Kantian hermeneutics as well as evolutionary and Marxist economics and positivist philosophy, strove to bridge the divide between causal theory and the interpretative understanding he believed was necessary for all social enquiry. It was important, he argued, to separate value judgements about which events and processes should be studied, general value-free concepts about objects of enquiry, causal analyses of events and processes, and the policy implications of the explanatory conclusions. The rule-governed rationality and meaning of behaviour had to be understood and was significant only as part of a wider materialist causal explanation. The social studies could therefore be scientific no less than the natural sciences, but in their own way.

The new form of positivism advocated the strong unification of science by imitating the most advanced sciences and rejecting all metaphysics. Philosophy of physics emphasized a logical and reductive structure of reasoning. This thinking culminated in the advent of the logical positivist school of philosophy, centred on the Vienna Circle of the late 1920s and early 1930s.[11] The influence of this school had a profound effect on all philosophical and methodological discussions for several generations. The Logical Positivists, somewhat in the spirit of Descartes, claimed to be solving all epistemological problems by cutting away all speculative and distracting aspects of thought and leaving only the kernel of truth. That kernel was sensory experience (that is, empiricism) and deductive

logic. Only logic was truly universal and indisputable, and only sensory observation, rather than metaphysics or introspection or hermeneutics, could be relied
upon. Socio-historical enquiry could be made scientific if it too adopted positivism in the guise of the covering law model of explanation and empiricism.

5.5 Common sense, hermeneutics, subjectivity

In the Anglo countries, the defence of the distinctiveness of historical enquiry
on common-sense empiricist principles became the dominant tradition in the
early twentieth century. The use of general theory such as evolution or historical materialism was rejected because it supposedly forced evidence into a pre-
conceived 'Procrustean bed' of preconception. The professional 'historical
method' was the insightful interpretation of empirical sources in themselves,
supposedly free from any prior judgement.[12] In Europe, idealist philosophers
emphasized hermeneutics as the only method for the social life world. That is,
both the main Anglo and Continental philosophies of the early twentieth century asserted that the social and human studies had to have a method quite different from the sciences of nature because of the fundamentally subjective and
culturally constituted nature of social life. One of the most influential defenders of this subjectivist methodology was the English historian and philosopher
R.G. Collingwood, who argued for the necessity of rethinking the thought processes of past actors in order to understand their actions.[13]

By the 1930s, then, social and historical thought was sharply riven between
positivistic and universalistic social science, on one hand, epitomized in different
ways by the logical positivists and some Marxists, and, on the other, by subjectivist historians and sociologists of Anglo and Continental kinds. But not all historians and social scientists fitted these broad categories. In particular, three
groups of scholars and researchers were seeking to find ways around these subjec-
tivist/objectivist and history/social science dichotomies. One group was the
French structuralist historians influenced by Durkheim. Another was the Anglo
economic historians. The third were Weberian sociologists. All were concerned
in one way or another with both the history and the present of socio-economic
structures. In the late twentieth century these currents began to merge together
and with other currents, such as Marxism, to become the foundations of the new
socio-historical science.

5.6 Structuralisms

The French structuralist tradition in the social sciences began largely with
Durkheim who developed the idea of the necessity for an empirical sociology that
studied complex, organic (or structural), social reality, including moral systems.

His ideas spread through French intellectual life to influence geography, demography, anthropology and linguistics. Growing out of these broad influences was the *Annales* school of history, founded in the late 1920s by Febvre and Bloch. They attempted to construct a totalizing approach to analysing and explaining socio-geographical change in the long run.[14]

The Anglo economic historians grew out of the English Historical Schools of Economics and Sociology, with their (non-Darwinian) evolutionary account of history. In the late nineteenth century they developed a resolutely quantitative approach to economic change in the long term, usually within its social and political contexts. What was later called 'Old' economic history was the counterpart of *Annales*. Both were leaders in statistical data gathering and use. The production and scholarly use of statistics became, as the twentieth century wore on, an integral part of socio-historical science. Indeed, quantification became associated with the idea of objective science so much so that the 'New' economic historians (sometimes called Cliometricians) argued that the combination of economic theory and statistical techniques (econometrics) would produce a science of history.[15]

Weber's contribution to the integrated histories of capitalism, religion, ideology and modernity, influenced by and in dialogue with Marx's work, and his profound contribution to the methodology of socio-historical science, was of the most significance and lasting influence in the development of socio-historical science in the later twentieth century.[16] The structural-functionalist sociology of Talcott Parsons in the 1950s, and later the work of historical anthropologists and sociologists, all owed much to his work.

All of these groups, as with Weber himself and also Marx and Durkheim, were vitally interested in the problem of 'modernization' as the basic transformation of society in the nineteenth and twentieth centuries. Dichotomous concepts of traditional and modern societies were employed to analyse the allegedly complete transformation in economy, society, culture and politics that gave rise to the 'modern' world, a world stripped of old, primordial affinities to reveal only individualism and naked self-interest. 'Modernity', while a useful and even perhaps essential sociological and cultural concept, became completely assimilated into the common sense of the twentieth century. Marxists and other economic historians and *Annales* structuralists have been (rightly) critical of its explanatory overuse, preferring more detailed conceptualizations of varieties of capitalist socio-economic formations.

5.7 Scientific explanation today

As fairly well established by the recent ferment of ideas in the philosophy of science, the methodology of the natural sciences has several key features.[17] First is a *policy* of critical realism, which entails an ontology that accords reality to the deep causal structure of kinds of things, and the integrated structures and systems of which they are part. The task is to *discover* these things, structures, causes and systems. This means, second, that structures and systems have emergent real properties, and that explanation has to have a combination of reductive and systemic explanation. Rather than a deductivist covering law model, science has a complex structure of reasoning that moves in a dialogical (or perhaps circular) and critical fashion between general concepts and theories to more precise theories to observations (including experiments where possible) and back again to concepts and theories.[18] A third feature is quantification and mathematics. These are the tools and the language of science but not its methodological essence, which the Cliometricians mistakenly thought they were. Fourth is the absence of teleology from the advanced sciences. The order of the world has no mystical telos, no final, supernatural cause. That some scientists have religious views does not alter the methodological presuppositions of their work.

To be considered as 'scientific', the methodology of the social studies must have a complex structure of reasoning, akin to but not necessarily the same as that in other sciences. The methodology of any science must be adequate to and capable of discovering and explaining the causal structure of its portion of the real world. That means being able to grasp the actual, multi-layered, complexities of the world. Any empirical enquiry that remains on the level of the simple appearances of the world will be unable to penetrate the (often counter-intuitive) structural levels.

5.8 Towards scientific socio-historical theory: the necessity for historicity and structurism

A central feature of thought in the late twentieth century was the dethronement of humanity. The 'Copernican revolution' in the study of humanity has resulted in humanity being seen as but a small part of the natural universe, neither as the centre of it nor as separate from it. The religious, idealistic, teleological worldview has lost much ground. It has turned out that human action and society have no special characteristics that preclude scientific explanation. But, of course, in order for the science of action and society to be appropriate to its subject matter there must be adequate theories of the nature of human motivation and action, and of social systems, which conceive of them as structured, contingent, historically continuous and historically changing. Socio-historical science must place *systemic process* at the centre of analysis. All bio-social systems, of which human society is a prime example, have within them an *agent/structure dynamic*. The agent/structure and systemic process problems are the central ones for all social theory.

Approaches that concentrate on, or overemphasize, action or structure (including social wholes) to the exclusion of the other, have bedevilled the construction of social theories. Until the rise of individualist methodology in the twentieth century, most historical methodology was holistic in the sense that it tried to explain the history of social wholes such as nations and empires by reference to the supposed features of those 'organic' entities. This resulted in teleological and idealistic histories and sociologies that lacked explanatory power. Methodological individualism, on the other hand, has an impoverished view of the social context of action and tries to explain it by reference only to aggregated patterns of individual behaviour. Against this, *methodological structurism* is in fact the framework in which socio-historical science is now being written by its leading practitioners[19] (see examples below). Such a methodology approaches the explanation of action and structure through concepts and theories of the structured reality of social relations, the social embeddedness of action, and the social constructiveness and reproductiveness (i.e. agency) of collective action.[20]

5.9 Theories in natural and social science

What is a socio-historical theory? This is the area where there is probably the most confusion among historians. For example, a few years ago there was a call for papers for a conference on history and theory, which said that the many contemporary theories available included 'critical theory, cultural studies, feminism, queer theory and postcolonial studies'. It is doubtful if any of these are actually theories at all in any acceptable scientific sense of the word 'theory'. The conference, the organizers said, could investigate such things as postcolonial theory, problems and advantages of cultural studies, public history, social control, history and memory, and narratives and counter-narratives of nationalism. This kind of statement illustrates that among socio-cultural historians there is a tendency to consider vaguely defined or non-defined general ideas and concepts that organize narratives and descriptive accounts as 'theories'. That is, general concepts such as 'colonialism', 'capitalism', 'revolution', 'nationalism', 'feminism', 'culture', etc., are sometimes taken to be theoretical propositions and explanations. In fact they usually remain as vaguely defined, often uncritically employed, general notions that might or might not be part of undeveloped or partial theories, but the extra work required to make them more precise and detailed is often not done or cannot be done, partly because data is so lacking. There is also some confusion, as that conference announcement showed, of research methods with theory, revealed with regard to such questions as the roles of narrative, hypothesis, statistical analysis, oral versus documentary evidence, and so on. It is crucial to make a distinction between theory and methodological postulates even if they often reinforce each other. Methodology does not explain, theory does.

Theory is one of three kinds of generalization prevalent across the broad spectrum of the sciences. The others are heuristic general ideas and concepts (e.g. 'modernity') and descriptive (often statistical) categories of phenomena (e.g. economic data). These both provide descriptions of that which allegedly requires explaining. Scientific causal theories are abstract understandings and precise modellings of powers, capacities, forces, properties that inhere within and between things to generate the observed complex patterning and ordering of the phenomenal world. For example, the theories of genetics, mutation and natural selection together explain, very generally, the long-run process of speciation. Structure, order, patterning, change are everywhere to be observed, and are everywhere and almost always taken to inhere in reality itself. The existence of structured order is necessary for the living of life and, ultimately, for the intellectualization of problems about the nature of order. Order is also dynamic. But it is a huge leap from such observations to the establishment of truthful knowledge about the actual nature of order, the complexities of the universe and the causes of change. If order were easily explained we would have no need of science and science would have presented no history of failure, success, progress and major shifts in its theorizing under the impact of research and discovery. And the work of science is never complete in any field.

Because in the socio-historical sciences there are in fact no well-confirmed causal theories anywhere near comparable in scope or adequacy to most natural science theories, social science has to rely in the first place upon the other two kinds of generalization – heuristic descriptive concepts, such as 'capitalism' and 'modernization', which are useful identifiers of types of general structures and processes, and observational (sometimes statistical) generalizations – the counterpart of pre-scientific natural history observation of multiple cases. These generalizations are attempts to record the commonalities of visible orders and patterns in large numbers of observed phenomena, relations and processes, and to categorize those observations. Social science, like everyday conversation, has a multitude of such categories and concepts, which often remain undeveloped and are often based in 'common sense'. We cannot survive without them in daily life for they make it possible for us to, more or less successfully, navigate through the social world and communicate about it. Science begins with such concepts and generalizations but must move well beyond and beneath them to criticize, validate or falsify them, and so discover the structural powers that generate the observed regularities.

Thus the significant differences between theories in the natural and social sciences are a product of three things. First is the greatly undeveloped character of the social sciences in the sense that they haven't been able to develop any well-confirmed theories, in spite of many attempts. Economics has many so-called 'laws', such as price being a function of supply and demand, but these are in fact vague empirical generalizations that have been elevated to the status of axioms. Second is the disjuncture between what can be called macro-static theories about social structure and micro social psychological theories about behaviour. In other words, the micro/macro disjuncture, now under attack of course, has tended to rob social science of a fundamentally important aspect of science – i.e. explanatory (but not ontological) reduction and the building of macro system-level theories out of knowledge of the operation of micro-behavioural components. Geology explanatorily relies upon but is not reducible to physics and chemistry; evolutionary biology, ethology and ecology rely upon but cannot be reduced to biochemistry. Thus social science needs firm foundations in socio-biology and psychology, but this has been resisted by many structuralists and social systems theorists. Furthermore, a third cause of the relative weakness of social science has been an uncritical assumption of uniformity in human motivation and social interaction, which has led to a neglect of the historicity of society when forming concepts and theories. It seems very clear that the historical character and contingency of all social interaction and social structure has to be central to theory building. But historical variability is far from absolute. Generality remains the bedrock.

There are and should be various forms of inference, then, in the social sciences that link putative or partial or elliptical theories to empirical evidence. Intuition, analogy, abduction, deduction, induction, modelling, all play some role, as in the natural sciences. But in some branches of social science there is a concentration upon axiomatic-deductive and individualist reasoning in the (mistaken) belief that it is the true scientific method. This belief springs from positivism. In the rational choice approach, which has spread from economics to now influence all branches of social science and some areas of historical study, human nature is axiomatically postulated to be of a certain kind of universal rationality, from which it can then be deduced how people will behave under certain circumstances. There is a prevalent use of so-called 'data sets' about aggregates of behaviour that are taken 'off the shelf' and subjected to hypotheses and statistical manipulation. Conclusions are drawn about the degree of correlation of sets of statistical indicators that are surmised as being somehow meaningful. The relationship of much of this data to actual events and structural processes is problematical but rarely questioned. Furthermore, in rational choice theory there is a lack of commitment to examining *structure* or *change* rather than just static patterns. Institutions are treated as just sets of formal rules rather than as social structures.[21] All of this has (rightly) made much of social theory unattractive to historians.

Fortunately, in many areas of social science today there is a growing understanding that the subject matter is indeed historical. Therefore we have seen the promising and important advent of historical economics, historical sociology, historical anthropology, historical geography, and so on. But for all we should welcome these developments, there is a basic problem that has to be overcome in these new historicizations of social science. That problem is that, in seeming to attempt to make their disciplines not only more historical but also thereby more scientific, they have sometimes misunderstood and misapplied the relationship between theory and history in the natural sciences. The consequence of this mis-understanding of scientific inference can be seen in the example of historical economics (or 'new' economic history), which is an attempt to use mainstream economic theory to 'explain' historical data in a 'scientific' fashion through the construction of a 'dynamic model' that fits the data. In fact historical economics is usually little more than static economics using longer time series of data. Most mainstream or neo-classical economics ideally tries to tie rational choice theory and statistical evidence together as a deductive structure capable of making pre-dictions and retrodictions. The subject matter is a set of generalized abstractions that are presumed to state the fundamental or essential relationships between variables within certain types of aggregate systems of decisions and actions. A set of precisely specified equations is the ultimate goal of a model-building and applying exercise, not a detailed description or narrative account of a real socio-economic process. Mainstream economics has an ontology of aggregationalism – economies are theoretically generated aggregates of a host of individual decisions and actions, and have no real structural existence. Human motivation is postu-lated as being universally individualistic and self-interested. Concepts of ideology, social class and culture play little or no role. The aim is to test and refine the model.

This can be contrasted with 'old' economic history and other forms of social scientific history. At their best they typically have a complex, interconnected, cir-cular structure of reasoning that ties all the explanatory moments of concepts, models, research and evidence together with a mixture of inductive, deductive and analogical inferences and intuitive leaps. There is a constant *circular* process of imagination, conceptualization, hypothesization, checking, revision, further research, incorporation of new evidence, interpretation, employment of new con-cepts and models, construction of narrative, and so on. All parts of the concep-tual, theoretical web of ideas are open to criticism. Nothing is axiomatically privileged. All the while there is the hope that the *real complexity* of the events and structural processes being studied can ultimately be revealed, not simplified. The implicit regulatory notion of truth employed by such historians is the idea of empirical adequacy to presumed complexity, which implies a non-abstract, real-ist conclusion.

A final methodological point: given the foregoing argument, it must be a fun-damental methodological imperative of socio-historical science to always be *com-parative*. In order to make descriptions and explanations of particular phenomena and processes, knowledge of the general context and range of possibilities should be known, on the grounds that people and societal structures everywhere share basic characteristics. The comparative postulate, then, shows that a framework of concepts, categories and descriptions of long-run world or global history is necessary for all local research.[22]

5.10 The examples of Geertz and Brenner

Two scholars whose works show the rich possibilities of socio-historical science are Clifford Geertz and Robert Brenner. Both are strongly interdisciplinary in the sense that they confidently and completely transcend the arbitrary history/social science and past/present divides. Theory and empirical enquiry are combined in a way strongly reminiscent of the work of Smith, Marx and Weber. Significantly, both employ at various moments explanatory narratives, comparisons and conceptual elucidation. Narrative remains, just as it does in the other historical sciences, an essential component of socio-historical science.

Geertz, from a base and training in Weberian and Durkheimian anthropology and sociology, has constructed an integrated approach to the problem of explaining structured social order via explaining the crucial role of social systems of meaning and culture in social life. His fundamental aim is to construct a macro social science around the micro hermeneutics of culture, a social science that could be called 'the social history of the moral imagination and the cultural history of socio-economic structures'.[23] The framework of his science, when reconstructed in relatively abstract terms, shows an integration of philosophy, methodological concepts, general theory, specific theory and descriptive narrative. As an anthropologist Geertz is an explicit theoretician. But theory-building is not the object of his science. Rather, explanations of particular, local socio-cultural structures and historical patterns of social life are the object of enquiry.

Brenner's work has the quite different provenance of late feudal and early-modern socio-economic history and Marxist theory. His chief concern has been to explain the long-run history of capitalism as a dynamic social, economic and political formation, beginning in twelfth-century Europe and emerging to powerful prominence in seventeenth-century England.[24] In later works he has analysed the vicissitudes of the world economy in the late twentieth century. His social class theory of socio-economic history is rooted in Marxism but is certainly not the simple adoption of an orthodoxy. Like Geertz, Brenner as a historian is a genuine social theorist in the sense of developing and employing theory in an explicit manner, in order to make detailed accounts of particular historical episodes.

The approaches of Geertz and Brenner should be seen as two contributions to a larger, varied and multi-dimensional historical science of society. Indeed, it might be thought that the supposed field is so large and complex, covering, as it does, everything from psychology to anthropology to sociology to geography to economics to politics and to world history, that there is no possibility of encompassing it all by a single integrated set, no matter how complex and sophisticated, of concepts and theoretical propositions. On the other hand, there have been proposed candidates for unified conceptualizations, including behaviourism, historical materialism, structuralism, social Darwinism and rational choice. All of these have made claims to universality for they all claim to have uncovered the fundamental building blocks of causal power within human behaviour and sociality. But all are based on a certain level of dogmatic assertion, beyond which they have not been able to penetrate to a deeper causal level. None has been able to make a good case yet for establishing the basic dynamic between the emergent level of systems and the reducing level of causal mechanisms. In order to achieve that kind of theory, strongly based scientific knowledge of human neurophysical psychology and socio-biology, and the connections of those levels with human structured or institutionalized social relations and culture is required. The micro–macro gulf has to be bridged. Today, two strands of integrated theoretical and empirical work, quite closely connected to each other, intimations of which can be found in the work of Geertz and, to a lesser extent, Brenner, are attempting to do that: historical eco-social geography and neo-Darwinian social theory.[25] Both sub-fields are trying to construct a new framework for socio-historical theory that attempts to integrate micro social causality, macro structure, contingency and systemic change. The micro mechanisms in both cases are being sought in a combination of human socio-biology and socio-natural ecological integration, and the macro mechanisms and connections of micro to macro are being sought in a Darwinian-type theory of social selection of micro innovations via institutional selection and structuration.

5.11 Conclusion

Detailed historical enquiry should dominate over theory and model building in socio-historical science. Theories and models are of value only when they are subordinate but essential parts of *historical* research, and historical research and discourse should have the dense structure of reasoning as indicated herein. That is, there must be a complex interconnection between theory and research around the central problem of explaining the *real historical processes of the world*. For the social sciences to make further progress they have to develop far stronger explanatorily reducing levels of theory and analysis – that is, sociobiological, psychological and ecological theories have to become necessary but not sufficient parts of macro historical social science. The relationship between the many levels of determination from ultimate micro to ultimate macro have to be better explored and theorized. At present there are too sharp disjunctures between the 'disciplines' of sociobiology, psychology, anthropology, historical sociology, historical economics, socio-economic history, environmental studies and world history. They have to be combined. In some places they are beginning to be so, especially in parts of archaeology, historical anthropology, historical geography and socio-economic history.[26]

Guide to further reading

M. Archer, *Realist Social Theory* (Cambridge, 1995).

E. Breisach, *Historiography: Ancient, Medieval, and Modern* (Chicago, 1983).

R. Brenner, *Merchants and Revolution* (Cambridge, 1993).

P. Burke, *History and Social Theory* (Cambridge, 1992).

C. Geertz, *The Interpretation of Cultures* (New York, 1973).

A.H. Goodman and T.L. Leatherman (eds), *Building a New Biocultural Synthesis* (Ann Arbor, 1998).

T. Honderich (ed.), *The Oxford Companion to Philosophy* (Oxford, 1995).

C. Lloyd, *Explanation in Social History* (Oxford, 1986).

C. Lloyd, *The Structures of History* (Oxford, 1993).

T.J. McDonald (ed.), *The Historic Turn in the Human Sciences* (Ann Arbor, 1996).

A. Rosenberg, *Philosophy of Science* (London, 2000).

W.G. Runciman, *A Treatise on Social Theory*, 3 vols (Cambridge, 1983–1997).

Notes

1   See S.A. Grave, 'Common Sense' in P. Edwards (ed.), *The Encyclopedia of Philosophy* (New York, 1967).
2   On the covering law model, see Rosenberg, *Philosophy of Science* (London, 2000), Chapter 2 and Lloyd, *Explanation in Social History* (Oxford, 1986), Chapter 3.
3   See 'Epistemology', in Honderich, *The Oxford Companion to Philosophy* (Oxford, 1995).
4   Philosophical terms such as 'Rationalism', 'Enlightenment' and 'Positivism' are all elucidated in Honderich, *Oxford Companion,* and their development in historiographical terms is discussed in Breisach, *Historiography* (Chicago, 1983)

5   The Scottish Historical School is examined in Meek, *Social Science and the Ignoble Savage* (Cambridge, 1976).

6   Early evolutionary thought in economics and other social sciences is discussed in several chapters by J.A. Schumpeter, *History of Economic Analysis* (Oxford, 1954).

7   On Darwin's revolutionary rejection of teleology, fully appreciated only in the late twentieth century, see S.J. Gould, *Full House* (New York, 1996).

8   A good brief summary of Marx's contribution to founding a science of socio-history is R. Bhaskar, 'Knowledge: Theory of' and 'Science' in T. Bottomore (ed.), *A Dictionary of Marxist Thought*, 2nd edn (Oxford, 1991).

9   The central issues of the nineteenth-century *methodenstriet* and of the second *methodenstreit* in the 1960s are discussed in D. Frisby, 'Introduction to the English Translation' of T.W. Adorno *et al.*, *The Positivist Dispute in German Sociology* (London, 1976).

10 On neo-Kantianism see Honderich, *Companion* and Frisby, 'Introduction'.

11 The Vienna Circle is discussed in Lloyd, *Explanation*, and in 'Logical Positivism' and 'Positivism' in Honderich, *Companion.*

12 On the professionalization of English historiography beginning with Lord Acton, see J. Kenyon, *The History Men* (Pittsburgh, 1983), Chapter 5.

13 Collingwood, *The Idea of History* (Oxford, 1946).

14 On the *Annales* School see F. Dosse, *New History in France: The Triumph of Annales* (Urbana, 1994).

15 New economic history was defended and exemplified in the collection of articles in D.K. Rowney and J.Q. Graham (eds), *Quantitative History* (Homewood, 1969).

16 See W.G. Runciman (ed.), *Weber: Selections in Translation* (Cambridge, 1978).

17 Cf. Rosenberg, *Philosophy of Science* and also M.H. Salmon, 'Explanation in the Social Sciences', in P. Kitcher and W.P. Salmon (eds), *Scientific Explanation: Minnesota Studies in the Philosophy of Science XIII* (Minneapolis, 1989).

18 An attempt to represent diagrammatically this structure of reasoning in its natural and social science variants is in Lloyd, *Structures,* pp. 120, 157.

19 Cf. Lloyd, *Structures,* Chapter 3.

20 On the structure of reasoning in social science and the place of agency see M. Archer, *Realist Social Theory* (Cambridge, 1995).

21 See the critique in D.P. Green and I. Shapiro, *Pathologies of Rational Choice Theory* (New Haven, 1994).

22 World or global history can be constructed according to many presuppositions. The world history 'movement', centring on the *Journal of World History* and the World History Association, takes a somewhat agnostic and atheoretical stance on the question of general theory, in contrast to Marxist, Darwinian and ecological approaches.

23 The work of Geertz is discussed in detail in Lloyd, *Structures,* pp. 103–16. Perhaps Geertz's most significant work is the collection of articles in *The Interpretation of Cultures* (New York, 1973).

24 See Brenner's contributions to T.H. Aston and C.H.E. Philpin (eds), *The Brenner Debate* (Cambridge, 1985), and Brenner, *Merchants and Revolution: Commercial Change, Political Conflict, and London's Overseas Traders, 1550–1653* (Cambridge, 1993).

25 For example, A.W. Johnson and T. Earle, *The Evolution of Human Societies* (Stanford, 2000) and W.G. Runciman, *A Treatise on Social Theory*, 3 vols (Cambridge, 1983–1997).

26 See the attempts at synthesis in A.H. Goodman and T.L. Leatherman (eds), *Building a New Biocultural Synthesis* (Ann Arbor, 1998).

6

The *Annales*

Matthias Middell

The *Annales* School is prominent in most surveys of twentieth-century historiography. The bibliography of works dealing with the *Annales*, with books written by *Annalistes*, with the stages of the school's development, with its authors and theoretical ideas, is virtually boundless. The *Annales'* far-reaching international influence, as well as the originality of its solutions to the fundamental problems of modern historiography, is repeatedly pointed out. There are also discussions of the *Annales'* internal controversies, like that between Lucien Febvre and Marc Bloch on the continuation of the journal during the German occupation of France, the separation of the so-called third generation of the *Annales* from Fernand Braudel at the end the 1960s, and whether the 'tournant critique' of the late 1980s and early 1990s meant that the *Annales* still existed as a homogenous school, and perhaps whether it had ever been one. There is no agreement either as to what should be included under the *Annales* heading, apart from Bloch and Febvre, the founders of the journal, and Fernand Braudel, the patriarch of the VIe Section en Sciences Sociales in Paris. And although the journal has been hugely important for the identity of the *Annales* and for the reputation of individual members, no content analysis of the journal's output during the last eight decades has ever been attempted.

These remarks are sufficient to show that for all the talk of the 'école des *Annales*', several approaches can be distinguished within it, and we must ask, rather, how the history of the *Annales* is being construed in individual cases. First there is the notion of the *Annales* as a scientific heritage that must be maintained, yet also criticized to displace the older generation. From this latter perspective, the *Annales* is like a family legend (a sort of saga), which is a permanently unfinished project, and which culminates teleologically in its current proponents. Second, processes of institutionalization may be emphasized. In this perspective the *Annales* journeys from its beginnings in the province of Strasbourg to the French and international academic establishment. This itinerary can be cast either as a story of unstoppable success, or as a critique of the concentration of power within the French system of arts and sciences. Third, a cyclical view may be presented in which the *Annales* displaced the German historiographical model at the turn of the nineteenth and twentieth centuries, went on to establish hegemony (or supremacy) within the international discipline of history, and in turn gave way to a pluralist historical field in which many of the centres were located in the USA. Finally, the history of the *Annales* can be seen as the reflection of globalization in the twentieth century. Globalization has itself been an important topic for the *Annales*. Bloch and Braudel proposed theoretical means – for example, comparative history – to accommodate the challenges posed by globalization to the historical discipline.

The first approach prevailed for a long time and, with its polemic undertones and its intentions of legitimization, has contributed to obscuring the history of the *Annales*. The latter two approaches boomed at the end of the twentieth century when a retrospective view (fired by the millennium effect) became possible and a new generation of *Annalistes* encouraged self-criticism. They were keen to overcome the crisis that characterized the development of the journal and of their institutional stronghold, the École des Hautes Études.

Following the defeat of 1870 and the foundation of the Bismarckian Empire in the Palace of Versailles, French elites sought explanations for Prussian superiority. The answer seemed to lie in the German universities and the training facilities for German elites more generally. In the Third Republic, French politicians sought to reform their own schools in the light of what they observed on the other side of the Rhine. They sent younger academics to assess the strengths and weaknesses of the various German universities, departments and disciplines. The positive features were to be integrated into, and combined with the traditions of the French academic infrastructure. The latter can be traced back to the innovations of the period of absolutism (e.g. the Collège de France) or to the Directorial and Napoleonic eras (divided into the Grandes Écoles and one single university for the whole of France and its faculties in dozens of cities).[1] This strategy helped promote both an atmosphere of international competition and an ongoing transnational cooperation with a growing sense of interdependent intellectual work transcending national boundaries.[2]

Among the young academics recruited by the French Ministry of Higher Education was a historian, born in 1886, the son of an Alsatian historian of the ancient world. He attended the elite Lycée Louis le Grand in Paris in 1896 and, in 1904, entered the École Normale Supérieure in Rue d'Ulm. There he became familiar both with French historiography and with German academic production (especially of Karl Bücher, Karl Lamprecht, Theodor Mommsen, Leopold von

Ranke and Gustav Schmoller).[3] Having passed the aggregation in 1908, he spent two semesters in Germany, visiting Berlin in 1908 and Leipzig in 1909. Together with Lucien Febvre,[4] who was born in 1878 in the Franche-Comté, studied in Paris and taught at the faculty of Dijon before 1914, Marc Bloch would become a founder of the *Annales d'histoire économique et sociale*.

Between Bloch's years as a student in the conference rooms of German universities and his subsequent career as a director of the *Annales*, the First World War changed many things. Franco-German hostility was intensified by four years of trench warfare on French territory and by intransigent nationalist rivalry that mobilized masses of people in both countries. German intellectuals were massively influential in legitimizing war objectives and in fabricating propaganda against the declared enemies, and more directly, by personal involvement in mapping the culture of occupied territories for military purposes. Patriotic feelings deepened on the other side as well, as Bloch's account of his experience in the Great War testifies.[5] Henri Pirenne, an outstanding Belgian historian, had been working with his German colleagues on a project of a comprehensive comparative socio-cultural history of European nations before 1914. After the war he refused to participate in any further discussion with people who had pleaded for the expansionist 'ideas of 1914' and who were plotting vengeance after the German capitulation and the Treaty of Versailles.

At well-equipped Strasbourg University, Bloch and Febvre had met and formulated their innovative approach to writing history. Febvre's proposed European review of economic history, with Pirenne as the leading figure, failed.[6] It was only in 1928 that Bloch (then more active in the project than Febvre) took up the idea again. However, Pirenne once again refused to assume the post of director, and so Bloch and Febvre decided to make the *Annales* their own. The first issue appeared in January 1929. In the preface, the two editors first emphasized the multi-disciplinary and international approach, with a strong focus on economic history.[7] They promised to overcome the gap between specialists on the past and scholars of current social tendencies. Third, they aimed to pull down the walls between historians researching the ancient, medieval, early-modern and contemporary societies, and between experts in European history and that of so-called primitive or exotic cultures. The ending of pointless disciplinary schisms was expected to lead to methodological innovation.[8]

This project was intended to displace Germany as leader in the historical sciences at a time when German historians had isolated themselves from the international community by their reactionary politics and their methodological shift to 'Volksgeschichte'. The latter was an ethno-centric interpretation of the people's history, which demanded congruence between national boundaries and the settlements of a particular ethnic group – like the Germans. Volksgeschichte was not only a plea for the expansion of Germany to territories where German-speaking people allegedly of the Nordic race had settled, but a call for historical and political explanations of the modern world to be based upon racial theories.[9]

Bloch and Febvre also attacked more traditional Rankean approaches, embraced at the Sorbonne above all by Charles Seignobos and Charles-Victor Langlois. Both used Ranke's 'critical method' and like him were principally concerned with political history, great men and a teleology of national communities.

Thanks to the support of Henri Pirenne, the two provincial historians – still in the 1920s far from the heart of academic influence in France – won renown in the international arena. Bloch published his groundbreaking *Les Rois thaumaturges* in 1924. The book examined the public attribution of the capacity of salvation to the kings of France at the moment of their coronation in the cathedral of Reims. Bloch developed an early psychohistory of myth, mass mentalities and the political use of representations. A stay at the newly founded Institute for Comparative Research in Human Culture in Oslo in October 1929 gave him an opportunity to resume comparative research on French agrarian history from the thirteenth to the eighteenth century. This was published a few years later in a 200-page essay on 'Les caractères originaux de l'histoire rurale française'. It is now well known as the first example of Bloch's 'regressive method'. This involved working back from recent to more distant periods, in the belief that since we know more about the present, it should be easier to start there than from speculations about historical origins. Later, in his *Apologie d'histoire ou le metier de l'historien*, Bloch systematized this method and argued openly against the 'mystification of origins'.

After his essay on agrarian history, Bloch wrote his masterpiece on *La société féodale*, an ambitious work framing the culture of feudalism. Having analysed the distribution of property, social hierarchy, and the form and functions of the state, he turned to mechanisms of personal dependence, social cohesion, collective memory and consciousness, and 'forms of feeling and thinking'. In *Feudal Society* Bloch refined his method. He combined the social history of property and power with that of the legal forms of social relationships, and with the history of cultural representations. The book's two volumes do not stand alone, but link Bloch's interest in the relation between the kings and lords of the manor and their bondsmen. Bloch began his interpretation of the feudal society with a detailed description of representative gestures, which both expressed vassal status and created subordinate position. He tried to explain the 'rhythm' of a given society through description of its customs and habits, its cultural practices and its rites. Such a rhythm, said to be typical of a particular stage of social development, is a sort of 'collective comprehension of time', which oscillates between routine and innovation.[10]

In his work on the forms used by medieval people to express social relationships, Bloch sought to explore the history of modern social gestures. In his *Rois thaumaturges*, Bloch had already underlined the great differences between the medieval period and the period of absolutism, and still more the modern state. In the first period there was a direct relationship between the healing king and the people, without any religious or secular institution between them. From the fourteenth century onwards, direct forms of social relationships were replaced with more indirect forms.

Feudal Society was a large-scale picture of medieval times from the ninth to the thirteenth century, in which Bloch concentrated on analysing micro-politics and the aesthetics of its cultural representations. He endeavoured particularly to understand the importance of liberty and serfdom in medieval society, and their social and economic histories. He advanced precise reasons for the failure of slavery at the end of the Roman Empire in Europe and looked for differences between slaves and serfs. Bloch pointed out that in the ninth century under the rule of the Carolingian dynasty the *servi* were not members of the community and not accepted as members of the people, for the latter was composed only of free men. In the thirteenth century the status of bondsmen developed in such a way that under the Capetian kingship serfs obtained a special juridical status of their own. Even if they were citizens of secondary rank, they were nevertheless members of the community called *populus Francorum*. Bloch returned to the question of serfdom and freedom in his 'Caractères originaux', and demonstrated that in the fourteenth and fifteenth centuries the authority of the landlords continued to diminish. Bloch's political ideal shines through. French history was the slow march towards an association of politically free citizens. The two volumes of *Feudal Society* consolidated Bloch's reputation as a specialist in comparative social history.

Bloch's search for structural explanations, which had been inspired to a considerable extent by Durkheim's sociology, was criticized by Febvre. The latter's book on Luther had explored the relationship between the individual and the community, and had focused on the history of mentalities in the period of the German Reformation.[11] In this biography Febvre left behind his earlier interest in the role of geography in history, and turned to the history of early-modern mentalities.[12] This field was simultaneously developed by his Strasbourg colleague Georges Lefebvre, the famous expert on the French Revolution.

At the Oslo International Congress of Historical Sciences in 1927, Bloch read a paper on methods of comparative history.[13] His choice was a calculated and symbolic act. He laid claim to Karl Lamprecht's heritage.[14] He discussed Max Weber's approach to historical sociology, and shared Weber's interest in explaining Europe's advantages in worldwide competition through comparison with the East.[15] Internationalism became a hallmark of the *Annales*, and the circle of contributors to the *Annales* was not restricted to the French historical community. Very quickly, contacts with an international group of like-minded historians provided the review with articles from north, south and central Europe.

This founding period was marked by a special *Annales* style; but there was no elaborate paradigm or even an *Annales* school. Nevertheless, correspondence between Bloch and Febvre[16] demonstrates only their commitment to the quality of their journal, understood as a common enterprise. They displayed a strategic interest in arranging the historiographical field into an opposition between 'our way of writing history' and representatives of another way. They sought allies and refused collaboration with those with whom they disagreed. This produced a potentially strong identification with the historiographical project represented by the *Annales*. Bloch and Febvre looked with displeasure upon the efforts of competing journals to develop international cooperation – especially when such rivals appeared in Germany.

In 1933 Febvre was the first of the founders to win a higher academic position when he was elected to the Collège de France after a long and painful campaign. Bloch followed only in 1936, taking over Henri Hauser's chair in economic history at the Sorbonne. Febvre 'translated' his institutional gains into the occupation of a series of powerful and prestigious positions, which allowed him to oversee a range of new projects. Thus, for example, he became president of the editorial board organizing the *Encyclopédie Française*, published from 1935.

The Second World War interrupted the success story of the *Annales*. Bloch participated in the defence of France in 1940, and described in '*L'étrange défaite*' his frustrating experiences in the French army. He had returned to Paris only briefly when, as a Jew, he was forced to retire. He became an active member of the Résistance. At this time he wrote an incomplete introduction to historical methods and theories, which became his scientific testimony. Febvre, who stayed in Paris, edited the *Annales* alone during this difficult time, and disagreed with Bloch on the question of how to deal with the restrictive conditions of occupation. Bloch never returned to work – he was killed in 1944 by the Gestapo. Febvre took sole responsibility for the review.

After liberation, Febvre arrived at the top of the French academic system. He was charged with drawing up proposals for the reform of the École Pratique des Hautes Études (EPHE), founded in 1884. In 1947 he was elected President of its newly founded VIe Section, which later incorporated the social sciences into the EPHE. Here, Febvre institutionalized the old idea he had developed together with Bloch in the 1920s. At that time the powerful Centre des Recherches Historiques (which Febvre directed for several years) had been embedded into an institute of social sciences, which concentrated on research. After 1945 Febvre, also French representative on the UNESCO commission for a conceptualization of a History of Mankind, became the key person in the institutionalization of the

Annales paradigm. He was supported by Fernand Braudel (who had been in close contact with Bloch and Febvre since 1937) in the administration of the Historical Research Centre. Charles Morazé (an expert on nineteenth-century history) and Robert Mandrou (historian of the pre-modern era and the absolutist state in Europe) supported him in the administration of the review.

The period between 1945 and Febvre's death in 1956 was a time of recovery and consolidation. The formerly heretic historiographical movement was transformed by Febvre into an established institution. This cannot be explained only by Febvre's personal qualities and interests, or by the support of a network of young and ambitious historians using the innovative image of the *Annales* to establish their academic careers. Political circumstances after the Second World War were also important.

France compensated for its decreasing political role in a world dominated by the USA and the Soviet Union, with an ambitious cultural and scientific international offensive. The Fourth Republic and, even more, de Gaulle's Fifth Republic, traded its former global political role for intellectual influence. Paris became a laboratory of social thinking on the competition of two ideological systems and political blocs, on the process of decolonization, and on the rise of an individualized, consumer-oriented civic society. American donors helped financially. For example, the Ford foundation financed the beginnings of the Maison de Sciences de l'Homme (MSH). The latter was intelligently administered by Clemens Heller – making it a nimble dinghy at the side of the great tanker of the VIe Section (better known later as the EHESS – École des Hautes Études en Sciences Sociales). The MSH offered grants to fellows from abroad and organized international conferences, projects and publications when national money was not available for such purposes. Under the same roof, and with a coordinated strategy, the EHESS and the MSH linked French academics with an international network under the patronage of Fernand Braudel.

Even before Febvre's death in 1956 Braudel became the key person in the *Annales*. Having taken over the leading positions of Febvre in the EHESS and on the review's board he became the undisputed representative of the *Annales* movement for more than a decade. The *Annales* now developed the appearance of an academic school. Acceptance as an author in the review, and/or serving as a collaborator in the vast enterprises of the EHESS, was a sort of knighthood that could potentially lead to a splendid academic career in French universities or abroad.

Braudel's worldwide reputation was founded upon his monumental *The Mediterranean and the Mediterranean World in the Age of Philip II* (1949), which was partly written during his time as a German prisoner of war. In this book Braudel developed his notion of three historical levels, each moving at a different rhythm. First, he claimed that geo-historical foundations of societies changed only over very long periods. Second, he distinguished medium-term up- and downswings in economic life and social relationships, which happened more quickly. On the third level, which held little interest for Braudel, was the merely artificial history of political incidents (*histoire événementielle*). Braudel had at first intended to write a dissertation on the foreign policy of Philip II of Spain, but having spent the period from 1923 to 1933 as a teacher in Algeria, he became sensitive to the reciprocal influences of Europe and Africa in the formation of a common Mediterranean region. In 1937, on his return from a two-year stay in Brazil, he met Febvre, who encouraged him to write about the influences of the Mediterranean world on the politics of Philip II and on Spanish society. The 1200-plus pages of *The Mediterranean World* ignored politics almost completely. The Spanish victory at Lepanto and the occupation of Tunis by Don Juan de Asturias were, in Braudel's perspective, of little importance for historical explanation. By contrast, he emphasized the huge influence of natural conditions upon communication, trade and production. Like Bloch in his analysis of the Middle Ages or Febvre in his interpretation of the Reformation era, Braudel emphasized the role of collective structures like economic systems, states and societies, which moved only in a rhythm of generations.

Braudel does link mid-range movements to the rise and fall of empires. The economic upswing of the fifteenth and sixteenth centuries was favourable to the Spanish and the Ottoman Empires. But, ultimately, the size of these empires became an obstacle to development because of the cost of communication between the various parts of the territory. The core of the book is nevertheless the slow-moving structures encapsulated in Braudel's notion of geo-history. Braudel distinguishes between people living in coastal regions, who were said to be more open to innovation, and those living in mountain areas, who reacted in a more conservative way. Braudel was aware that patterns of human mobility changed with industrialization and modern mobility. But in the sixteenth century high cultural performance was not only encouraged, but determined by geo-historical factors.

While Braudel developed a typology of different historical times, which emphasized the geo-historical *longue durée*, Ernest Labrousse and his disciples researched long-run cycles of prices and wages, and sought to calculate the economic conditions for the advance of modernity. Labrousse wrote two major books, one on the development of prices during the eighteenth century (1933) and the second on the crisis of the French economy at the end of the Ancien Régime and during the revolutionary period (1944). Teaching at the Sorbonne, he was associated, more than Braudel, with the traditional culture of the French historical profession, and so was less willing to condemn political history. One of his disciples, Michel Vovelle, would later endeavour, in his history of mentalities during the French Revolution, to overcome the old conflict between the social and the political. Labrousse and Braudel together edited a social and economic history of France, published in six volumes between 1970 and 1982.

In the 1960s social structures and economic cycles became the fundamental categories of the *Annales* movement's historiography. Most of its publications were concerned with the so-called *longue durée* and not with a short-term political conflict. *Annales* historians were convinced that the key to historical explanations could be found by an integrated analysis of structures and developments over decades or centuries. The advent of computers seemed to promise a great future to the quantification of data, and to the innovative notion of serialization of quantitative data (*histoire sérielle*). On the one hand, the disciples of Labrousse concentrated on a new cartography of the economic regions of France since the sixteenth century; on the other, Braudel and his colleagues tried to establish a framework of economic world-regions (*economies-monde*). The latter were characterized by their climate, morphology, population, economic behaviour and cultures. Historians traced the material conditions under which the region participated in a world increasingly connected by trade and technological exchange. Braudel created from the products of these investigations a vast panorama of the emerging capitalist system, in which he underlined the role of the Mediterranean region for European expansion to the Americas, Africa and Asia. His three volumes on the progress of material culture in the world from the sixteenth to the end of the eighteenth century represented an influential attempt to apply the *Annales*' method to world history. Braudel's successor in this field, Immanuel Wallerstein, established the world-system approach in historical sociology.

Under Braudel's directorship the VIe Section and the *Annales* became more hierarchically organized. For the first time there really was a group of historians working collectively in research projects, and linked to specialized and research-oriented teaching at the EHESS. The idea of *enquêtes*, proposed by Bloch and Febvre in the 1930s, was implemented in the form of systematic and cumulative analysis of individual regions and through combination of case studies. Individual approaches were integrated into the scheme developed by Braudel at the beginning of this period in the *Annales*' history.

The Braudel era was also that in which *Annales* and Marxist historians interacted most closely. Some *Annalistes* – like the specialist in the history of medieval western France, Guy Bois, or the historian of Catalan capitalism, Pierre Vilar – declared themselves to be Marxists. Braudel himself recognized that he owed something to a (rather incomplete) reading of Marx's writings on early-modern capitalist development in Europe and overseas. At the same time Braudel criticized Marxist historiography for its orthodox exaggeration of the economic causes of political conflicts and decisions.

The year 1968 changed a lot in France, not only in society but also, and perhaps above all, in the academic world. Generational conflicts were characteristic of the period. Within the *Annales* School a younger generation was looking for emancipation from the rule of the ubiquitous director. Braudel came under attack and, vexed by these conflicts, he retired from the board of the *Annales*. This moment dates the arrival in power of a third generation of *Annalistes*. Leading figures were Emmanuel Le Roy Ladurie, Jacques Le Goff, Georges Duby and François Furet. Some were former Communists, who now explicitly demonstrated their distance from Marxism.

In 1967 Le Roy Ladurie completed a magisterial thesis on the history of climate in Europe during the last 1000 years, a study based on Braudel's geo-historical assumptions. Le Roy Ladurie subsequently became well known for his story of the *Carnival of Romans* – a precise reconstruction of social and cultural tensions among people in a small French town (Montaillou) confronted with the Inquisition. Le Goff and Duby returned to Marc Bloch's globalizing interpretation of the medieval civilization in Europe, and complemented his social and cultural approach with biographical methods. Thus Le Goff tried to integrate the world of medieval representations into a biography of Louis XI. François Furet, together with Mona Ozouf, arrived on the scene with an impressive analysis of the social history of writing and reading in eighteenth-century France, and this inspired a host of studies of the history of book production and of literacy in the country. Furet, who became president of the EHESS in the 1980s, moved from the history of socio-cultural phenomena to the new political history of the French Revolution, and became well known for his attacks on Albert Soboul's classic Marxist interpretation.

This generation was more concerned with national – that is, French – history than Bloch, Febvre or Braudel had been. Its search for the 'world we have lost' and the effort to assimilate this into the national heritage, was an essential reason for the public success of this generation in the 1970s. The third generation met the demand for a new national metanarrative based upon the newly found and recognized methods in writing history. Le Roy Ladurie, Furet, Le Goff, Duby and others were not only internationally renowned historians, but became media stars in France – inciting jealousy when historians in other countries came under pressure from the rising social sciences. Le Goff and others proudly described their version of the *Annales* method as a 'new history' (*nouvelle histoire*), thereby ascribing an old-fashioned appearance to other approaches. They did not doubt their own position at the top of the international historiographical tree, yet comparative history was neglected and international interest in the work of the *Annales* was limited to methodological studies. Furet, and later Roger Chartier and others, looked for new transatlantic cooperation with American universities interested in the history of western civilization. In the heat of the bicentenary of the French Revolution in 1989, the new French–North American axis proved reliable.

It was exactly at the moment of the dramatic international political changes of 1989 that the crisis of the *Annales* movement became obvious and was recognized even by members of the school itself. A so-called fourth generation had appeared at the end of the 1970s. It transformed the history of mentalities, which was at the centre of methodological debates and had become an identifier of the 'new history' of the third generation, into a more coherent approach owing much to historical anthropology. At the same time women's history came to the fore, as did the history of extra-European territories, especially francophone Africa. In the 1980s Michelle Perrot inspired multi-volume projects on family history, women's history and the history of private life. These followed enormous collective enterprises on rural France and urban history in the 1970s. Roger Chartier, among others, continued the work of scholars like Henri-Jean Martin in the field of book history and the history of reading. Bernard Lepetit renewed the approach to urban history.

The rise of the fourth generation caused bitter polemics inside the *Annales* movement, but in public Duby, Furet and others presented it in terms of continuity. They feared the loss of the *Annales* heritage, and the associated academic prestige and worldwide influence. In contrast, the fourth generation openly expressed their criticisms of the established paradigm in 1989. They took on board the call of some marginalized French historians, voiced since the beginning of the 1980s, to put an end to the domination of a school they regarded as more and more sterile, triumphalist and unfruitful. In 1989 the editorial board of the *Annales* published a widely discussed manifesto that promised a fresh start, and announced a return to some of Bloch and Febvre's fundamental ideas. The outcome of the debate was a programmatic shift to new methods and topics. People and agency would replace structures as major explanatory factors. The significance of cultural representation for historical development was recognized and new interest was expressed in comparative history. The cooperation of historians with social scientists was to be enhanced by cooperation with disciplines like anthropology and area studies. The premature death of Bernard Lepetit, who had been at the heart of the reform movement, was a setback for change. Yet the *Annales* of the 1990s was markedly different from that of the third generation. Openness to research in other disciplines and other countries has once again become a characteristic of what is perhaps the most well-known humanities journal in the world.

The future development of the *Annales* cannot be foreseen. But one might point to three tendencies evident in the last decade. First, the enormous influence of the *Annales* School on international historiography seems to have come to an end, and a multi-polar system of innovative centres is coming into existence, partly as an effect of the rise of postcolonial and poststructuralist approaches. Second, historians unrelated to the *Annales* are engaging in interdisciplinary work, and are thus disputing the *Annales'* monopoly in that area (see especially the review *Genèse*). Third, the methodological and thematic shifts effected by members of a fourth generation of the *Annales* School or movement have given French historians an opportunity to integrate themselves into a more internationalized historical profession.

Guide to further reading

Peter Burke, *The French Historical Revolution. The 'Annales' School 1919–1989* (Cambridge, 1999).

Stuart Clark (ed.), *The 'Annales' School. Critical Assessments*, 4 vols (London, 1999).

John G. Craig, *Scholarship and Nationbuilding. The University of Strasbourg and the Alsatian Society 1870–1939* (Chicago, 1983).

Carole Fink, *Marc Bloch, A Life in History* (Cambridge, 1989).

George Huppert, The *Annales* Experiment, in Michael Bentley (ed.), *Companion to Historiography* (London and New York, 1997), pp. 873–88.

S. Kinser, 'Annalist Paradigm? The Geo-historical Structuralism of F. Braudel', *American Historical Review* 86 (1981), pp. 63–105.

Lutz Raphael, 'The Present as a Challenge for the Historian. The Contemporary World of the *Annales* E.S.C. 1929–1949', *Storia della Storiografia* 21 (1992), pp. 25–44.

Paul Ricoeur, *The Contribution of French Historiography to the Theory of History* (Oxford, 1980).

Troian Stoianovich, *French Historical Method. The 'Annales' Paradigm* (Ithaca, 1976).

Henk Wesseling, 'Fernand Braudel, Historian of the Longue Durée', *Itinerario* 5 (1981), pp. 16–29.

Notes

1 Victor Karady, 'Les universités de la Troisième République', in Jacques Verger (ed.), *Histoire des Universités en France* (Toulouse, 1986), pp. 323–65.
2 Christophe Charle, *La République des universitaires 1870–1940* (Paris, 1994).
3 See Peter Schöttler's reconstruction of Bloch's interests from the Archives of the Library of the École Normale in his essay on 'Marc Bloch und Deutschland', in Peter Schöttler (ed.), *Marc Bloch. Historiker und Widerstandskämpfer* (Frankfurt am Main, New York, 1999), p. 37.
4 There is no comprehensive biography of Febvre, but see Hans-Dieter Mann, *Lucien Febvre, la pensée vivante d'un historien* (Paris, 1971); Guy Massicotte, *L'histoire problème. La méthode de Lucien Febvre* (Paris, 1981); Bertrand Müller (ed.), *Bibliographie des travaux de Lucien Febvre* (Paris, 1990).
5 Ulrich Raulff, *Ein Historiker im 20. Jahrhundert: Marc Bloch* (Frankfurt am Main, 1995), pp. 66–180 and Etienne Bloch and Stéphane Audoin-Rouzeau (eds), *Marc Bloch. Ecrits de guerre 1914–1918* (Paris, 1997).
6 Bryce and Mary Lyon (eds), *The Birth of the Annales History: the Letters of Lucien Febvre and Marc Bloch to Henri Pirenne (1921–1935)* (Brussels, 1991).
7 The editorial board comprised the geographer Albert Demangeon, the archivist Georges Espinas, the sociologist Maurice Halbwachs, the economic historian Henri Hauser, the specialist in Roman history André Piganiol, Henri Pirenne (the only one who did not come from France), Charles Rist, professor of political economy in Paris, and André Siegfried, a disciple of the geographer Vidal de la Blache, who specialized in the analysis of political cultures.
8 Marc Bloch, Lucien Febvre, 'A nos lecteurs', *Annales d'histoire économique et sociale* 1 (1929), No. 1, pp. 1–2.
9 The 'Volksgeschichte' paradigm was not restricted to Germany, but can also be found in the Baltic Provinces and in Czechoslovakia, in Hungary and in Romania; see Matthias Middell and Ulrike Sommer (eds), *Volksgeschichte im Vergleich* (Leipzig, 2003).
10 Raulff, *Marc Bloch*, p. 150.
11 Lucien Febvre, *Un destin. Martin Luther* (Paris, 1928).
12 Lucien Febvre, *La terre et l'evolution humaine* (Paris, 1922).
13 Marc Bloch, 'Pour une histoire comparée des sociétés européennes', *Revue de synthèse historique* (1928). An English version is available in Marc Bloch, *Land and Work in Medieval Europe* (London, 1967), pp. 44–76.
14 Lutz Raphael, 'Historikerkontroversen im Spannungsfeld zwischen Berufshabitus, Fächerkonkurrenz und sozialen Deutungsmustern.

Lamprechtstreit und französischer Methodenstreit der Jahrhundertwende in vergleichender Perspektive', *Historische Zeitschrift* 251 (1990), pp. 325–63.

15 Hartmut Atsma, André Burguière (eds), *Marc Bloch aujourd'hui: Histoire comparée et Sciences sociales* (Paris, 1990), pp. 255–336.

16 Bertrand Müller (ed.), *Marc Bloch–Lucien Febvre. Correspondance*, Vol. 1, *La naissance des Annales 1928–1933* (Paris, 1994).

7

Poststructuralism and history

Kevin Passmore

Nothing enrages poststructuralist historians more than the claim that their relativism – their alleged belief that any one account of the past is as good as another – provides no position from which to refute those who claim that the Holocaust is merely a story.[1] This somewhat shocking charge, to which I shall return, is the most extreme manifestation of disputes precipitated by what Lawrence Stone called poststructuralism's challenge to 'the subject matter of history – that is events and behaviour – and [its] data – that is contemporary texts – and [its] problem – that is explanation of change over time'. Poststructuralists contended that reality, and by extension the past, were unknowable, and that only language and representations mattered.[2]

Some dismiss poststructuralism as evidence of the corruption of history by literary criticism, for there is a history of suspicion between them. When history diverged from literature in the late nineteenth century, aristocratic practitioners of literary history were as contemptuous of the 'tradesman-historian' grubbing about in public archives as were professional historians of the 'non-scientific' methods of the gentleman-scholars. Even now, some literary critics dismiss history as a 'journeyman' activity dependent on easily mastered techniques.[3] In the 1970s, social historians patronizingly – and reductively – called for the explanation of literature in terms of its historical context. Then, poststructuralists declared historical writing to be a branch of fiction, and claimed possession of the special techniques required to understand it. They effectively constituted historians as an object of study for literary critics, and for a few history became the 'Other' that legitimated the rationality of literary criticism.

Nevertheless, the rise of poststructuralism owes too much to a general cultural climate to be easily dismissed. We could also invoke the structure of the academic job market, tensions between historians in old and new universities, generational and gender conflicts. Also, as Laura Lee Downs points out in this volume (Chapter 14), historians were questioning the naturalness of class and gender identities well before poststructuralism arrived in the academy. Some deployed structuralist alternatives in their critique, particularly in the form of cultural anthropology[4] and structuralist Marxism.[5] Without underestimating the novelty of poststructuralism, we should not therefore assume too sharp an opposition between poststructuralism and 'conventional' history.

This chapter will explain, through a discussion of poststructuralist thinkers and historians, the nature of the challenge to 'conventional' historical practice. The intention is not to give a definitive account of poststructuralist theory, for like any body of thought it will support multiple interpretations (but not just any). Rather, the focus will be upon the ways in which poststructuralism has been used by historians and their critics. We shall see that in spite of categorical dismissal of history as a discipline on the part of some poststructuralists, the methods and agendas of poststructuralism have become enormously influential in historical writing. This seeming contradiction owes much to ambiguities within poststructuralist theory, particularly concerning the question of whether analysis should focus on language alone, whether language should be related to 'context', and what context means. The chapter concludes by suggesting that M.M. Bakhtin's view of language incorporates the strengths of poststructuralism, and yet offers a view of language more fruitful for historical practice.

7.1 Postmodernism and poststructuralism

Often the terms postmodernism and poststructuralism are used interchangeably, but for our purpose it is more useful to see the former as a broader category covering a range of tendencies in contemporary culture that share the conviction that the proper focus of artistic and intellectual enquiry is 'representation' rather than 'reality'. Postmodernism was first used to describe a form of art that rejected modernism. Modernism was based on the premise that the artist, a gifted individual standing outside society, could use the special skills of painting or writing to access hidden truths about the human condition. Impressionist painters, rather than merely reproducing the appearance of landscape, claimed to evoke the feeling aroused by looking it. By extension, 'conventional' history is modernist too, in that expert techniques are used to access truths not visible to the lay person.

Postmodernists do not believe it possible to uncover deep meanings. Art must remain at the surface, and cannot even reproduce that unproblematically. The duty of the artist is to draw attention to the contrived nature of art. This is why postmodernists mix up styles, combine high with popular art, and use both paintbrushes and photocopiers. Since the 1970s postmodernism has been influential in popular music (Malcolm McLaren, architect of the Sex Pistols), cinema (*Blade Runner*, Ridley Scott, 1983) and youth journalism (*The Face*, 1982–).

Sociologists and philosophers extended the term 'postmodernism' to characterize the condition of contemporary society. Jean-François Lyotard, in *The Postmodern Condition* (1976), argued that the modern phase of history had given way to postmodernity, in which the nature of capitalism was different. Modernist capitalism had produced 'useful' things, like cars and food. Postmodern capitalism produces images. Products are now sold not because they are useful, but because of their cultural meaning. Guinness was once promoted on the doubtful grounds that it did one good; now it is promised that drinking it will give one a certain image. The French philosopher Jean Baudrillard held that postmodern capitalism 'over-produces images'; reality is inaccessible and our perceptions are shaped by advertisers, television and computer screen.

Poststructuralism is one ramification of postmodernism in that it shares the conviction that we must concern ourselves with representation. Its special contribution is a theory of language, broadly defined as any form of communication, from writing and speech to gestures and computer images.

7.2 Structuralist linguistics

To understand poststructuralism we must begin by looking at structuralism, for poststructuralism was both a critique and a development of structuralism. Loosely defined, the term 'structuralism' is used in many fields. Structural-functionalism, for example, is one of the components of non-Marxist social science and modernization theory. Structuralist linguistics is of a different nature. It originated with the Swiss linguist Ferdinand de Saussure, whose *Cours de linguistique générale* appeared posthumously in 1916.

Saussure questioned the common-sense view that language mirrors or expresses pre-given objects – that words and signs directly reflect things existing in the real world. A tree is self-evidently 'there' and so we must have a concept of it and give it a name. Putting this view more technically, we could say that the 'signifier' (t-r-e-e) reflects the concept of a tree (the 'signified') and this in turn reflects the tree in the real world (the 'referent').

Saussure pointed out that there was no reason why a particular sign should refer to a particular concept or object. We could easily have used the signifiers 'cabbage' or 'frot' to designate the concept of a mouse. More problematically still, different languages do not just use different words for the same objects – otherwise translation would be straightforward. They define their signified and hence their referents differently. The French verb *aimer* can be translated as either 'love' or 'like'. The problem, Saussure said, is that the world is not self-evidently divided into predefined objects or concepts to which we can easily apply names. Reality has no intrinsic meaning. We receive a jumble of perceptions, and only language can make them meaningful. Structuralists illustrate this point with the example of the spectrum. We pick out particular points and define them as primary colours, but if we look carefully we find that the colours all merge into each other and we could have picked out other points.[6]

Language, Saussure argued, constructs meaning through a system of binary oppositions. A tree is a tree because it is not cabbage or a king; a man is a man because he is not a woman. Meaning is therefore derived from a system of *difference* within a linguistic system. We should not therefore examine what words *denote* in the 'real' world, but their *connotations* – their relationship with other signs in the system. Saussure called this structure *langue*, and privileged its study over that of more superficial daily speech – *parole*. Indeed, the latter was simply a particular effect of the structures of *langue*. Even the idea of the individual person, the self, is invented linguistically.

Saussure's concepts might seem banal applied to trees and cabbages, but if used to understand ideas about, say, masculinity, their significance is potentially immense. Male competitiveness would not be a biological necessity, but a cultural expectation produced in language. The potentially subversive power of structuralism was demonstrated in the 1950s by the cultural anthropologist Claude Lévi-Strauss (born 1908), who argued that identical cultural-linguistic structures underlay western and allegedly 'primitive' cultures. This implied rejection of the view that societies could be categorized in terms of progress towards 'modernization'. Meanwhile Roland Barthes (1915–80) applied structuralism to literary criticism, and demonstrated how meaning in literary texts depended more on binary opposites than on the authors' intentions – hence his proclamation of the death of the author.

In the 1960s and 1970s structuralism began to influence historical writing, and already we can detect disagreement as to how far to take the critique of conventional history. In 1966 the literary critic Hayden White argued that historical writings were structured by classic literary forms of plot (or tropes) – comic, tragic, satirical and romantic – and that these shaped historical writing more than evidence did. Historical writing was just like fiction. It had no relationship to the real past.[7] Here already was the sceptical position that history is 'just a story'.

In unwitting defiance of White's pessimism, the historian-philosopher Michel Foucault (1926–84) wrote more conventional historical works. The influence of structuralism lay in his contention that phenomena generally seen as natural were really 'constructed' through language. Thus in *Madness and Civilization* (1961), Foucault argued that insanity was not a self-evident fact of biology, but was conceived in different ways in different periods. Moreover, no story of improvement gave meaning to the history of psychiatry. On the contrary, the languages of psychiatry constructed mental illness as deviant, silenced it and formed part of an ever more subtle mechanism of social control. This argument was part of Foucault's attack on the notion that western history was a story of progress and reason.[8] It amounts, however, less to a challenge to the foundations of conventional history than to a brilliant reinterpretation of a particular topic using the techniques of structuralism wedded to a conventional, if occasionally lax, historical method. Foucault even attempted to recover the lost history of madness – a project akin to labour historians' restoration of the working class to history, and which assumes that the historian can recover untold true stories.

7.3 Poststructuralism: textual and worldly

These uncertainties were accentuated by the shift to poststructuralism. Some have described methodological tensions in terms of differences between Foucault and Jacques Derrida (born 1930). Derrida saw Foucault's project of writing a history of madness free from the oppression of western rationalism as flawed by its reliance upon the same language of western reason. All thought, Derrida argued, depended on the repression of alternative languages. So simply by writing about madness Foucault marginalized it. The implication might be that any historical writing is an act of oppression. Foucault retorted that Derrida was concerned with language in isolation, and perceived 'nothing outside the text'. Foucault preferred to analyse language in relation to social and institutional practices and power.[9] Alex Callinicos uses this dispute to distinguish between Derrida's 'textual poststructuralism' and Foucault's 'worldly poststructuralism'.[10] This distinction will help us to understand the way in which poststructuralism has been used by historians. But we must bear in mind that when Foucault spoke of social context he often assumed that social relations were structured like languages as binary oppositions and should therefore be analysed as such. So the difference with Derrida is not as great as it might seem. At other times Foucault adopted a more Marxist stance, seeing languages as produced in the interests of dominant groups. Rather confusingly, Foucault and Derrida shifted between all three possible relationships between language and context. This ambivalence is reproduced in much historical writing.

7.4 Derrida, deconstruction and history

Poststructuralists criticized structuralists for attempting to reduce all languages to an identical binary structure, a move that undermines structuralists' contention that meaning is produced through difference. The term *post*structuralism therefore suggests a break with the idea of structure, but this is only half true. Poststructuralists see language as an unstable system in which meaning is hard to pin down. Language (*langue*) remains the object of study, and the mechanisms of language still uniformly undermine meaning through an identical method. Structuralists and poststructuralists both also reject the notion that 'reality' can produce meaning.

Although Saussure argued that the relationship of language to the real world was problematic, he nevertheless assumed that binary structures established signs in mutual relationship so that the concepts they referred to were equally meaningful. In his *Of Grammatology* (1967), Derrida argued that the connection between words and concepts – signifiers and signifieds - is also uncertain. He advanced several reasons for this. First, each sign differs from an endless number of other signs, so that the 'complete' meaning of a word is never known. We might understand mouse in relation to elephant, but our understanding of 'mouse' changes as we relate it to other words. Second, there is no clear distinction between signifiers and signified. We can only express the meaning (signified) of the signifier t-r-e-e by using other signifiers, such as l-e-a-v-e-s and t-r-u-n-k. Third, meaning changes as we read and listen. Words at the beginning of sentences do not obtain their meaning until we get to the end of the sentence. Even then, the next sentence can change the meaning of the previous, and so on. Fourth, the meanings of signs are altered by the signs around them. 'Tree' means something different when linked to 'family' or 'snake'. Finally, because any sign is defined by things that it is not, its meaning must depend on its opposites. So while binary oppositions are essential to the operation of language, they are unstable and likely to collapse into each other. To express both his debt to and departure from Saussure, Derrida invented the neologism '*différance*', which both reminds us that language operates through difference (between binary opposites) and that meaning is deferred (*différé* in French) – incomplete, or uncertain.

The logic is that all we have is signs, and there is no essential truth. One of Derrida's purposes was to demonstrate, through the technique of 'deconstruction', a sort of close reading of texts for their 'aporias' (blind spots), how writing was based on this futile search for ultimate truth. For him any such assumption is 'metaphysical'. It follows that the past too is inaccessible, and that any attempt to write 'about' the past is doomed. What historians do write would be a linguistic construction. Some, including Derrida himself, deny that he intended to undermine the category of truth so radically. What Derrida 'really' meant to say concerns us less than the fact that many critics of history have interpreted Derrida thus, and not entirely without reason.

The essentialism of traditional historiography

The logic of Derrida's poststructuralism is that a text, or a piece of historical evidence cannot be interpreted in relation to an 'essential' principle lying outside it.

Most obviously this implies rejection of Marxist historians' search for reflections of class interest in historical documents. Poststructuralists counter that classes are not 'essential' interpretative objects outside the text, but are linguistically produced by the binary opposition of terms such as bourgeoisie/worker and proletariat/capitalist, and that their meaning is fluctuating and problematic.

If poststructuralism criticized only Marxism of the vulgar variety, it would be of little interest. Marxist historians, notably E.P. Thompson, have long since elaborated a more complex understanding of class, based upon a rejection of economic determinism. Yet it was precisely upon this sophisticated social history, and in particular upon Thompson's *The Making of the English Working Class*, that poststructuralists concentrated their fire.

To begin with, poststructuralists have argued that in spite of the concern with culture, social history left the primacy of class as an objective reality untouched. Although Thompson replaced determinism with the notion that economic conditions 'set limits', he still assumed that real changes in class relations were necessarily 'experienced' by workers and necessarily translated, albeit using pre-existing ideas about the rights of 'free-born Englishmen', into class consciousness. The idea of 'limits' begs the question of what those limits are, and implicitly restores a looser economic determinism.[11] Thompson insisted that whatever historical variations might be found, 'a generic mode of production has found roughly analogous expression within different societies and state institutions'.[12] Patrick Joyce argued that Thompson, typically of social historians, assumed that class and politics were rooted materially and that 'society' was a sort of 'explanatory sub-tissue', relating the economic to the cultural. As a poststructuralist, Joyce contends that 'social history does not innocently name the world, but creates it in its own image'.[13]

According to the feminist historian Joan Wallach Scott, Thompson's 'naming' of the working class relied on prejudices about gender roles. Thompson, says Scott, writes about the male world of demonstrations, politics and trades unions. Women, although numerous in the labour force, figure in *The Making* largely as domestic creatures. They leave the home only to listen to the millenarian preaching of Joanna Southcott. This is classic poststructuralism: the political rationality of class-conscious men is contrasted with, and defined by, the 'feminine irrationality' of religion. Class is shown to be constructed through cultural assumptions.[14]

From a different perspective again, Hayden White argued that each of the four parts of *The Making* is structured by different narrative tropes – metaphorical, metonymic, synecdochic and ironic. The nature of these tropes matters less than White's contention that they, rather than anything 'discovered' in the evidence, and by extension the past, give meaning to Thompson's narrative.[15] Meaning is a product of linguistic structures.

Other scholars extended the poststructuralist critique to embrace any attempt to write meaningful history. Robert Berkhofer, for whom 'contemporary literary theory defies the very intellectual foundations of current professional historical practice', is exemplary. He recognizes that historians are aware of their bias, and that they usually assume a two-way relationship between facts and interpretation. So provisional hypotheses are modified by evidence, and new evidence is sought out in the light of modified hypotheses. Nevertheless, Berkhofer argues, the historian's synthesis still rests on the fantasy of a *reconstructed* past. Historians accept that their monographs represent partial views of history, but nevertheless see them as part of a real past, reconstructed through the interconnections of the whole body of historical writing. This unified past is falsely believed to be inherently structured like a narrative, just as the historian's own writing is organized as a narrative.

For Berkhofer, all historical writing is based on the mirage of metanarrative – not just that which explicitly posits a metanarrative. The methods historians use to guarantee that their accounts 'represent' the past are useless. Historians resolve disputes between competing interpretations by appealing to evidence. Yet, says Berkhofer, facts can arbitrate disagreement only if we assume that they derive from an intrinsically coherent, narratively structured, past. In fact the past has no such meaning. Worse, the past is absent: one cannot point to it as one does a tree. We might have leftovers from the past in the form of evidence, but the past about which historians write is much larger than the evidence will allow. Historians have no idea about how the evidence fitted together. They merely refer to the equally problematic works of other historians.[16]

History as postmodern art

Perhaps surprisingly, Berkhofer does not abandon the possibility of writing history. He echoes Hayden White's calls for 'the historian to tell many different kinds of "stories" from various viewpoints, with many voices, emplotted diversely'. Such histories, like postmodern art, would frankly admit their constructed nature. Such histories would no longer use the 'meta-story' to legitimate their own discourse and disqualify others.[17]

Many of the contributions to the journal *Re-Thinking History*, established in 1997, challenge 'modernist' history. A typical sample is Robin Bisha's article on Russian noblewomen in the time of Peter the Great. The nature of the sources, Bisha argues, means that it is impossible to know much about what Russian noblewomen thought or felt, and she criticizes other historians for basing their interpretations on present-day prejudices. So Bisha resorts to literature. She writes a pseudo-autobiography of the noblewoman in question – the first-person authorial voice calls attention to the article as a story.[18] Simon Schama's compelling *Dead Certainties (Unwarranted speculations)* (1997) also adopts a postmodern manner, mixing the genres of historical writing, art history and detective fiction (but he is careful to reaffirm the authority of sources).

It is hard to see the novelty of this way of doing history. If we accept, as many 'normal' historians do, that art and literature can tell equally valid but different truths about the past from those offered by history, then recasting history in the form of art merely gives us more of what we have already. Sadly, most historians are not blessed with Schama's literary gifts. All we get is moderate art.

In any case, the idea of 'multiple perspectives' concedes too much to the authority of a past that has supposedly been demolished. Simply by claiming that a given story is one angle on a particular event, an event is defined and invested with properties that disqualify some accounts as being perspectives upon it. Some postmodern histories will be perspectives on the Russian Revolution and others on the French. This re-establishes the right of the real past (not evidence, ironically) to distinguish between interpretations.

The logic of textual poststructuralism really is that *nothing* of any value can be written about the past. No standard exists by which any perspective can be ruled out, so all are equally interesting (or uninteresting). There are no pre-defined events in the past that can be used to distinguish between stories. Keith Jenkins might be thought to be in tune with this logic when he declares that postmodern society can do without the 'knackered old horse that answers to the name of history'. But even this dismissive statement relies on the essentialist assumption that a given historical period should be characterized by the dominance of particular philosophies.[19]

7.5 Worldly poststructuralism and historical writing

These difficulties might explain why poststructuralist historians generally confine their use of textualism to deconstructing the work of other historians whilst using a more Foucauldian poststructuralism in their own writing. Their histories are poststructuralist in the sense that they examine the ways in which the past has been constructed. They write about the ways in which people in the past constructed their worlds, about how historians have constructed the past, and about the concepts used to construct the meaning in the world – class, society, the individual, truth, nation or race. Derrida called for a history of truth, but such histories are largely inspired by Foucault, who wrote brilliant historical works himself. In the last quarter-century an immense body of imaginative historical work has demonstrated the fertility of this agenda, and we shall see in subsequent chapters that poststructuralism has transformed each of the fields under discussion. However, since it is difficult to write history at all without departing from some of the major tenets of textual poststructuralism, certain tensions can be found in this work.

Discipline and punish

Foucault examined language in relation to social and institutional practices and power. He used the term 'discourse' to mean the study of language in context and in relation to power. Thus in *Discipline and Punish* (1975) Foucault described the way in which the intermittent but violent punishment of the early-modern period, exemplified in 'the spectacle of the scaffold', gave way to the regular, systematic punishment of the nineteenth-century prison. Once again, he denied that this change was the fruit of progress. Rather the prison was a more effective use of 'disciplinary' power. Moreover, the prison consti-tuted a model for surveillance in schools, factories and hospitals. Through dis-courses of education, medicine and criminality, these institutions assigned people to particular positions – pupil, worker and patient – and deprived them of power. Language, particularly professional knowledge, is intrinsically related to power.

Often Foucault's method is close to Derridean textual deconstruction, in that social relations are assumed to be structured like the languages and can be analysed, like languages, as binary oppositions in which one term is dominant (doctor/patient, for example). The focus is on the equivalent of Saussure's *langue*, and society is examined independently of the intentions of historical actors. For Foucault disciplinary power is not localized in a particular institution, state or ideology. It is 'not', he said, 'the "privilege" acquired or preserved, of the domi-nant class, but the overall effect of its strategic positions'. Power is 'diffuse' and intrinsic to all social relations.[20] It is independent of the activities or 'agency' of human beings, and must be examined as a system.

Alongside this view of language and power there is endorsement of the more familiar contention that changes in languages reflect social changes and serve the interests of the dominant class. Languages are used intentionally by particular social categories, or they somehow arise from the 'needs of the system' (a func-tionalist argument). Either way, for Foucault the shift towards punishment in prisons was a consequence of the needs of developing capitalism. Prison and army became models for the disciplined workforce and society required by capitalism. One can easily recognize the Marxist idea that institutions and ideas serve the interests of capitalism, even if they are not directly controlled by capitalists. Here Foucault's conclusions could be seen as essentialist, for the economic purposes of capitalists give meaning to the texts he studies.

Patrick Joyce's *Democratic Subjects*

In *Democratic Subjects* (1995), Patrick Joyce explains how nineteenth-century English working-class and bourgeois radicals made sense of the world through language. This fascinating book inevitably irritated social historians, for it argued for the constructed nature of class consciousness, and contended that the autonomous, self-knowing, agent – another of the sacred cows of social history – was a linguistic construction too.

In the first part of the book Joyce discusses the self-conceptions of the artisan-autodidact Edwin Waugh. Work figures in Waugh's self-identity only as the myth of the golden age of the morally dignified handloom weaver. Real work he found bothersome. His ideal was less a product of class than of a Protestant and bourgeois discourse of self-improvement transferred from organized religion to 'humanity'. Waugh dreamed of concord among men rather than social reform, let alone class conflict. Joyce then shows that John Bright, from a completely different class background, shared this religion of humanity. He details the mix of a Quaker myth of persecution, evangelical Christianity, paternalism and romanticism out of which Bright constructed his persona. Waugh and Bright both depicted themselves as romantic heroes able to transcend the world of experience, and triumph over evil – an example of the romantic narrative as defined by White.

In some of the most interesting passages Joyce shows how radicalism was constructed by music-hall motifs. Melodramas depicted the poor as victims – usually female and passive – of evil capitalists. The victim was conventionally saved by a high-minded upper-class hero. Virtue triumphed over vice, and the socially low became morally high. The outcome is a cross-class alliance between enlightened workers and bourgeois, rather than class struggle (note the binary oppositions and the interdependence of opposites). Joyce argues melodrama's combination of sensation and moralism was transposed into the reforming press and informed Gladstone's speeches. Thus liberalism was not an expression of bourgeois class interest, but is constructed through language.

In a number of apparently minor turns, Joyce uses a more conventional view of the relationship between language and context. The multiple class positions of those attending the Manchester Atheneaum prove that it was a non-class institution (*Democratic Subjects*, p. 173). The degree of bitterness of political conflict in France, Britain and America is read off from the degree of consensus around the constitution (*Democratic Subjects*, p. 195). Other examples could be given. In all cases something external to the text – an intrinsic property of social relations – explains the nature of the languages used by historical actors. In both *Discipline and Punish* and *Democratic Subjects* two views of language and its relationship to context vie for supremacy. Ironically, both sometimes unwittingly reproduce an essentialism that is justifiably criticized in 'conventional' historiography.

Postmodernism and modernization

Likewise, poststructuralist historians have found it difficult to free themselves entirely from reliance upon metanarratives. It is often remarked that Foucault's vision of a tendency in the history of punishment towards rationalization, surveillance, efficiency and control recalls the macro-historical teleology of modernization theory. The only difference is that Foucault viewed this teleology pessimistically. Joyce does not explicitly use metatheories, but the same assumption that history moves in a particular direction is present more subtly in *Democratic Subjects*, which is framed by the idea that the nineteenth century saw a shift from individual to social modes of thinking. Waugh and Bright are positioned (as so often in modernization-based accounts) in the 'transition'. Joyce is evidently uncomfortable, for he comments that this periodization 'can distort the picture by presenting change as a linear process of stages'. Nonetheless, he says, 'this very rough sketch has its uses' (*Democratic Subjects*, p. 15).

The disadvantages of teleologies are well known. Particularly relevant is that poststructuralists share the modernization theorist's tendency to characterize historical periods in terms of a 'spirit of the age', be it traditional, modern, postmodern or transitional, and to interpret their particular objects of study in the light of this spirit. Hayden White bases his account of the 'burden of history' on the alleged 'strangeness' of the present, by which he means that rapid change associated with modernization has a disorientating effect. Again we are reminded of modernization theory, which often explained revolutions as a product of the 'disorientation' supposedly caused by 'rapid change'. In situating his subject in a period of 'transition' White is typical. New Historicist literary critics prefer to study the Renaissance because it is supposedly a transition, a 'gap in history', which gave rise to the same feelings of exhilaration and fearfulness.[21] Such generalizations detract from the complexity of views in any given period, and underestimate the extent to which allegedly general characteristics are actually contested. In any case, there is no law which dictates that people living in a period of transition – even if such a blanket term could really be applied to a period – should feel disorientated.

This recourse to metanarrative and essentialism derives largely from discomfort with the idea of causes. Poststructuralist denial of the knowability of the past implies that causes are merely narrative structures gratuitously imposed on an inaccessible past. Yet the assumption that language is a system in itself, independent of human agency, raises the question of why one language should give way to another. The same problem is evident in Foucault's assumption that social relations are structured like languages. Therefore to explain the rise of the prison he resorts to the notion that a mysterious force outside history produce changes – i.e. the rise of capitalism. Large-scale inhuman forces drive history on, just as they give meaning to particular periods.

Agency

It should follow from this predilection for blind forces and from the contention that language is a system independent of human will, that the agency and choices of individual human beings or social groups mean little. No individual or group should be able to modify the system – albeit shifting and uncertain – which defines them. For poststructuralists the idea of the 'self' is merely a product of language.

Yet in *Discipline and Punish* Foucault argues that resistance to the strategies of power is possible – at least before the emergence of modern systems of surveillance. He uses two kinds of argument, each hard to reconcile with poststructuralist theory. Sometimes he claims that there is a spontaneous and unruly agency of the people, which dominant discourses endeavour to control though prisons, hospitals and schools. This implies that popular agency exists independently of language. Elsewhere Foucault suggests that because social relations are constantly in tension (an essentialist assumption, which is not necessarily true) each exercise of power carries a risk of inversion of power relations. Thus public execution fell out of favour because it brought people together in crowds and enabled them to mock the authorities.[22] This idea is familiar. Marx argued that by concentrating workers in large factories, capitalists sowed the seeds of their own downfall. Foucault's idea of resistance poses conceptual difficulties from a poststructuralist perspective, however, for if agency is constructed through language, how can it take on a life of its own outside the linguistic system? This is an odd kind of alchemy.

Similar uncertainties can be found in *Democratic Subjects*. Joyce argues that in the late nineteenth century new political narratives necessarily created 'new political subjectivities [i.e. conceptions of the self as a person able to act in the world] which *created* agency and legitimacy' (my emphasis). Identities were 'created *for* leaders and led that ensured the former's control over politics' (*Democratic Subjects*, p. 192, my emphasis). Sometimes this idea that language creates individual identities is reinforced by recourse to the notion of social control, in which beliefs are inculcated in the masses from above. Thus Bright's oratory is said to operate on the 'political unconscious', giving the people the sense – the illusion – of being active agents in the story of progress (*Democratic Subjects*, p. 201).

Joyce is too good a historian to rely upon generalizations of this sort in his practical analysis. He argues that Bright's self-conception was not just 'given to him but actively created by him out of his religion. His Quakerism was 'a resource that might be used in different ways to create different kinds of self' (*Democratic Subjects*, p. 105). All this is convincing, but it sits uneasily with Joyce's use of Derrida's vocabulary. It represents a break with poststructuralism, in that rather than being created by language, agency and language are inseparable. Joyce implicitly accepts that language cannot exist without people to speak and write it. From this it would follow that groups and individuals *could* adapt and use language, within limits, for their own purposes.

Method

Both *Discipline and Punish* and *Democratic Subjects* belong to the genre of narrative historical writing. Not for them the experimentation of postmodern histories. Both advance hypotheses designed to improve upon earlier interpretations of the past. Both cite evidence in support of their contentions and use footnotes. Both see their own interpretations as superior – more powerful? – than those of rival historians. Joyce regrets that one of his secondary sources fails to footnote adequately (*Democratic Subjects*, p. 38); the invented nature of Bright's view of the democratic impulses in Quakerism is demonstrated by showing the 'real' nature of mid-century Quakerism (*Democratic Subjects*, p. 107). Many more examples could be given. Suffice it to add that the idea of recovery of the lost past is at the heart of *Democratic Subjects* just as Foucault once sought to recover the voices of the insane. Joyce shows how historical protagonists *really* made sense of the world. Social historians are berated for imposing their conception of class on the past, when nineteenth-century contemporaries *really* understood class in moral terms (*Democratic Subjects*, p. 17). We are at the heart of the difficulty of writing poststructuralist history. Poststructuralists write histories of how meaning was constructed in the past. But it is not clear how such histories can be differentiated methodologically from 'conventional' histories.

It would, however, be unfair to charge Joyce, any more than any 'conventional historian', with advocating 'naïve' reconstructionism – the notion that the historian's narrative actually 'reconstructs' the past. In fact, the method used in *Democratic Subjects*, and by many other historians, cannot easily be pigeonholed as either reconstructionist or relativist. Joyce explains that while there is no position from which we can assess the 'correspondence or non-correspondence between our discourse and the real' (i.e. between historical writing and the past) this does not mean that we are unable to discriminate between true and false data or tenable and untenable arguments (*Democratic Subjects*, p. 9). The historians' usual protocols for deciding these issues can be used so long as we remember that these protocols are 'the product of history'. Joyce leaves it at that, perhaps because further elucidation would be difficult to reconcile with poststructuralist theory. This cryptic formula must be unpacked.

7.6 Objectivity from a point of view

The great contribution of poststructuralism to historical writing is the demonstration that nothing can be known independently of language, and that the past has no 'essential' meaning. No longer is it possible to regard men as naturally aggressive, women as naturally maternal, workers as naturally socialist, or Celts as naturally wild. No longer can historians assume that people living through periods of rapid change naturally felt disoriented. Earlier philosophers of history, such as Karl Popper (1902–94), criticized essentialism from a different starting point, and in many respects their methods are sounder. But their arguments were generally misconceived by historians. Essentialism, in so far as it has been weakened, has been weakened by poststructuralism.

As poststructuralists argue, the external world impinges upon humans in the form of sensory perceptions that have no inherent meaning. Only through language can we make sense of these perceptions, and the meanings so created could vary infinitely, especially in the case of human constructions such as classes, markets or states. The question is whether the meanings historians purport to find in, or attribute to, the past are all equally valid, as Berkhofer argues.

Berkhofer's critique rests on two contentions. The first, that historical knowledge is unverifiable because we cannot 'point to the past', is a red herring. The problem of knowing the past is no greater than that of knowing the present, and rests on the naïve reconstructionist view that only direct confrontation of an object can guarantee truth. Indeed, we cannot be certain that our favourite pub has not been destroyed by fire since we last nipped in for a drink. But there is a strong probability that it has not, and so we probably won't ring the pub and check that it's still there before setting off for our evening pint. We could, one might object, go at any moment to check the pub's existence. But even then we would need to be certain that our eyes were not playing tricks upon us, and we could not continually travel around the world to verify the existence of various places. Generally, we rely on the *strong probability* and on *indirect confirmation* that something exists. The same is true of history. We cannot go to the past to confirm that the First World War took place, but we do have plenty of evidence, ranging from memoirs to the presence of the debris of war in the soil of the battlefields. It is theoretically possible that this evidence could have been fabricated, but more *probably* it was not. Berkhofer assumes that only that which can directly be seen is verifiable; but like people in daily life, historians deal in *probabilities*, not truths.[23]

Second, Berkhofer argues that historians' claim to 'reconstruct' the past rests on the false assumption that the past is already structured like a narrative. In fact, conventional historiography needs neither to assume an intrinsically meaningful past nor attempt to reconstruct it. True, it is sometimes claimed that historians do reconstruct the past – Richard Evans writes that 'the truth about patterns and linkages of facts in history is in the end discovered not invented, found, not made' but even he adopts a nuanced probablistic view in his more recent work.[24] Poststructuralist critics have generally concentrated their fire upon 'constructionists' because they present an easier target.[25] Reconstruction of the past genuinely is impossible. Yet the method of hypothesis formulation and testing – the hypothetic-deductive method – favoured by many equally conventional historians actually combines acceptance of the unlimited interpretative possibilities open to historians with the recognition that all interpretations are not equally valid. Interestingly one of the foremost proponents of this method was Popper (especially as modified by Imre Lakatos) whose critique of positivistic model building and use of probablist method was recommended to historians by no less than Hayden White.[26]

The historian begins with an initial hypothesis or question derived from his/her own interests, in turn dependent upon the existing state of historiography and the contemporary cultural milieu. The historian starts with bias. Dependence on questions means that the resulting account will only be one possible perspective on a problem, since others might have asked different questions. Furthermore, since we cannot know what viewpoints historians will have in the future, we cannot know what questions they will ask and what results they will produce. We cannot say how much, or how little, of the past we have made sense of, or whether our knowledge will be superseded.

Questions also determine the relevance of evidence. In effect, a hypothesis is a prediction concerning the type of evidence we should find. If we hypothesize that notions of medieval kingship were influenced by contemporary ideas about masculinity, then we predict, for example, that certain gendered metaphors will be found in texts concerning kingship. The evidence is itself debatable. But it is treated according to accepted rules of evidence, which determine what is admissible (hearsay, for example, might be treated as a lower form of evidence than direct testimony). Some questions might be deemed unanswerable because of lack of evidence.

If a hypothesis appears to match the evidence, we do not claim to have told the 'truth' about medieval kingship – meaning, we can agree with Derrida, is always deferred. We have simply suggested a provisional answer to a precise question and established one possible way in which what is available to us of the past – the evidence – might be conceptualized. Our answer might be modified not only by further research and reassessment of the evidence but by redefinition of the question. Historians attempt to answer properly formulated questions in accordance with rules of evidence, just as a court of law seeks to establish whether a particular law has been broken, not the entire history of an event 'in itself'.[27] The past of the historians is the product of the historians' own protocols for making sense of part of what is reasonably believed to derive from the past – the evidence.

Historians' answers are usually presented in the form of narratives. Poststructuralist critics, perhaps fooled by the everyday language favoured by many historians, attribute to them the view that narratives are 'neutral containers for facts' and that they permit reconstruction of past reality.[28] Many historians know very well that narratives are not innocent, and it is not unknown for them to debate the implication of narrative structures in interpretations. More explicit exploration of the problems raised by White would certainly help make historians more aware of the constructed nature of their accounts, and there is no reason why the use of genre in historical writing should not itself be a subject of research – so long as other perspectives are not disallowed.

Berkhofer is right that historians assume that their particular accounts are compatible with the wider body of historical knowledge. More precisely, the historian assumes compatibility with those accounts that s/he sees as valid, for the method of hypothesis testing entails a critical approach to the work of others. This dependence of a single work upon a wide body of knowledge is not, however, peculiar to history. Presumably Berkhofer himself assumes compatibility of his own work with a corpus of critical knowledge about the writing of history. He does not – I think – claim to have reconstructed the reality of the historical discipline, only to have improved upon previous understandings of it.

The use of narratives is one of several *useful* ways of making sense of evidence – including artistic ones – each with its own rules of representation. The fact that historical writing has a narrative structure does not imply belief that the past itself has a like structure. On the contrary, the historian's account represents one possible way of making sense of a past that has no pre-given meaning, and of which there is an unknowable range of interpretations.[29] The historians' account is not a 'reflection' of the past, but, as Perez Zagorin puts it, 'reflective of process selection based on relevance to the problems and questions that the historian poses with respect to his or her subject'.[30]

Historians, poststructuralism and the Holocaust

The controversy over the relationship between poststructuralism and the question of the Holocaust draws together the points made above. There is no space here to enter into the details of the dispute. Suffice it to say that there are two strands to the debate that impinge upon the application of poststructuralism to history.

First, Richard Evans, among others, argues that poststructuralism provides no position from which Holocaust denial literature can be refuted, for all interpretations are held to be equally valid. Evans' charge has *prima facie* substance, at least for textual poststructuralists. Why should the Holocaust be exempt from Berkhofer's rule that historians have no way of distinguishing between the truth claims of different accounts of the past? But we must note that while deniers sometimes profit from the vaguely postmodern notion that all views must be granted a hearing, they are just as likely to resort to a hyperbolic constructionism in which nothing is proved without absolute verification: since the Holocaust cannot be proven beyond *all* doubt – because there are *some* discrepancies in the evidence – it cannot be proven at all. Deniers exploit both relativism and reconstructionism.[31]

Interestingly, in defending themselves against the charge of unwittingly aiding the deniers, poststructuralists abandon the strongest elements of their own position and resort to reconstructionism. They usually accept the provability of 'individual facts', while maintaining the possibility of multiple emplotments and interpretations.[32] The same Hayden White, who claims that 'no other discipline is more informed by the illusion that "facts" are found in research rather than constructed by modes of representation and techniques of discoursivization than is history', argues that the Holocaust can be considered as a 'factual statement', which he describes as a 'singular existential proposition'.[33]

This concedes too much to the notion of a reconstructable past, and indeed to the positivist notion that fact and interpretation can be separated. Interpretation and indeed emplotment are already involved in the contention that the Holocaust is a fact. As poststructuralists insist, we have used language to make sense of the world, for the term 'Holocaust' makes sense only in language. Indeed, without in any way denying mass murder, some perfectly respectable historians doubt that the term is the best way of making sense of the evidence. Furthermore, establishment of the fact is not simple. The question of when the Holocaust began has produced much complex debate among historians. And the 'simple' fact of the Holocaust actually consists of many other facts: the remains of gas chambers, memories of torture, memoirs, court records, administrative documents, political programmes, murders, anti-Semitic tracts, intentions, and so on, all of which are themselves subject to debate, but have been arranged in accordance with historians' hypotheses about the past. If it is legitimate to use the concept of the Holocaust to organize these phenomena, why is it illegitimate to attempt to relate the 'fact' of the Holocaust to other 'facts', from the rise of Nazism to the development of the war in the east? The result, of course, would be a historical narrative.

It does not follow that *any* interpretation is acceptable. Deniers' and 'conventional' views of the Holocaust are indeed both stories. Both are attempts to make sense of a past that can be construed in infinite ways. Denial is illegitimate, however, because its historical method is a sham. Historians' questions predict that if a hypothesis is true, then certain types of evidence will be found. In effect, deniers predict that *no* evidence of the systematic murder of the Jews can be found. When such evidence *is* found – in plenty – they resort to the classic response of the conspiracy theorist: the evidence has been planted. In other words, the deniers' case cannot be falsified; nothing could contradict their hypothesis. Evidence, of course, *could* be fabricated. But here another of the rules of historical method comes into play: probability. The evidence for the Holocaust is so overwhelming that the possibility that all the evidence has been manufactured is quite simply improbable. It is so unlikely that the deniers' narrative can only be maintained in ignorance or bad faith. In sum, we can never reconstruct the past, still less the Holocaust, in some transcendent sense. There is always, as postmodernists put it, an 'excess'. Neither can it be denied that literature and film can tell different kinds of truths about the Holocaust. But historians can decide between two answers to a specific question. Returning to court, the denier is convicted not just on the 'balance of probabilities', but 'beyond reasonable doubt'.

Historians cannot usually be so categorical. There is a continuum from facts established as fully as possible, in the sense that all reasonable historians agree upon them, including the Holocaust, world wars, the Crusades, and so on, to more debatable issues such as peasant mentalities in the early medieval period where there is some agreement and much debate. In any event historians do not reconstruct the event, but advance more or less probable ways of making sense of what is left over from the past. The question of objectivity cannot be resolved by recourse to the binary opposites of relativism and reconstruction – just because truth claims cannot be established absolutely, does not mean that they cannot be established at all.

The second question can be disposed of more briefly. Once it is accepted that the Holocaust is a fact, do historians and others have a free choice of how to represent it? Wulf Kansteiner feels that factually correct histories can be turned to almost any political purpose. One could have racist, Fascist, Stalinist or democratic views of any given event, each of which would be factually correct. One could distinguish between them only on moral or political grounds, not on the basis of their truth claims.[34] In a sense Kansteiner is right. The statement that the Nazis systematically murdered six million Jews cannot be refuted historically, but it can be interpreted either as a tragedy or, sadly, by anti-Semites as rightful vengeance. It is also true that the historian has little control over the moral conclusions that will be drawn from his/her work – even if a historian begins with a question prompted by a particular moral concern, there is no guarantee that the reader will interpret his/her findings in the manner expected. Morality has to be fought for socially and politically.

It remains possible to distinguish analytically between historical and moral statements. The very fact that we are able to show that the meaning of historical writing varies according to context depends on our ability to distinguish these two kinds of statement. Historians, as citizens, have the right, perhaps even a duty, to discuss the moral implications of their work, but they cannot claim special expertise in morality. Morality is a question for society as a whole. It does not derive automatically from historical work, but is *ascribed* to it by a cultural context. Even though moral lessons will inevitably be drawn, they are not, in analytical terms, the same as interpretative issues, such as why and how the Holocaust happened and who or what was responsible. Here the historian can claim some special skill.

7.7 Agency and language

Binary oppositions, such as that between objectivity and relativism, are no more helpful in understanding the problem of structure and agency. We saw in our discussion of *Democratic Subjects* that the idea that human agency is constructed through language is problematic. Languages cannot *do* anything. Only people and natural forces can act upon the world and change it. Without people and their physical capabilities there would be no language. Yet it is equally true that without language human action would be random and meaningless. Human activity is more effective and meaningful when it is organized intellectually, institutionally and socially. Language and agency are actually inseparable. Joyce recognized this in depicting Bright as simultaneously shaped by linguistic and cultural conditions, and as using these conditions to modify his world. Joyce restores the mutuality of language and agency, but at the cost of abandoning the tenet that the binary structures of language give the world all the meaning it has.

Some historians – including Joyce in later work – have seen the linguistic theory of the Russian M.M. Bakhtin (1895–1975) as a more convincing alternative to poststructuralism (although it must be born in mind that he wrote as a critic of structuralism, and that poststructuralism was unknown to him). Whereas the followers of Saussure argued that the formal structures of language produced meaning, Bakhtin argued that language should be analysed as a dynamic system in which the writer, the reader and the context all work together to produce meaning. In other words, meaning arises from *dialogue* between people – it is *dialogic*. Language is dialogic in the double sense that the writer draws upon and modifies, consciously and unconsciously, all sorts of pre-existing ideas (just as Bright did). The speaker also tries to anticipate the reactions of the listener, and thereby incorporates something of their views into the work. Any given text is *multi-vocal* or *heteroglossic* in that it contains alongside the voices of the author, those of his/her sources and unconscious influences, and the voices of the audience, all cast in terms of narrative structures. Thus John Arnold argues that records of interrogations by the Inquisition should be treated as heteroglossic. They contain the voices of interrogator and interrogated as well as competing discourses of heresy, confession, crime and sexuality. In these texts there is no voice, only *voices*, which cannot be completely separated from each other.[35]

The Bakhtinian approach also allows for the listener's ability to use and modify dominant voices, and not necessarily in ways foreseen by the speaker. Bakhtin regarded *parole* (spoken language) and *langue* (rules of language) as inseparable, so listeners could modify rules and meanings. Thus the historian Evelyn Brookes Higginbotham argued that racism in the southern states of America was a 'metalanguage', in that it ascribed negative characteristics to African-American people and legitimated discrimination against them. But the idea of race was also taken over by black nationalists, invested with positive characteristics, and used as a force for liberation.[35]

Bakhtin's approach retains the advantages of poststructuralism: the close analysis of texts, the rejection of the idea that a primary category, such as class or biology, enables us to explain the nature of our sources or of the course of history (essentialism). But also it is stronger than poststructuralism in that it allows both for human agency (not necessarily individual or conscious agency) *and* for social and linguistic structure, without claiming that one is primary.[36]

7.8 Conclusion

History has survived poststructuralism. Many historians continue to write as if poststructuralism, indeed theory of any kind, did not exist. Yet the subtle influence of poststructuralism has spread through the profession, shifting the object of historians' attention from social structures to culture. Historians have become somewhat more wary of essentialist simplifications, and are somewhat less inclined to claim that they can reconstruct the past. Poststructuralists meanwhile have largely retreated from the radical scepticism espoused by Berkhofer and others, though a few have embraced a dead-end relativism. Both sides are less likely than in the past to think in polarized terms of objectivity versus relativism or structure versus agency. History has settled back into a routine. New research tells us more of what we already know. Poststructuralism was productive as much, if not more, because it provoked new questions, than because of its methodological innovation. The time may be ripe for new questions.

Guide to further reading

Catherine Belsey, *Poststructuralism: A Very Short Introduction* (Oxford, 2002).

Richard Evans, *In Defence of History* (London, 1997).

Mary Fulbrook, *Historical Theory* (London, 2002).

Michael Holquist (ed.), M.M. Bakhtin, *The Dialogic Imagination*, trans. Caryl Emerson and Michael Holquist (Austin, Texas, 1981).

Keith Jenkins, *On 'What is History'* (London, 1995).

Keith Jenkins (ed.), *The Postmodern History Reader* (London, 1997).

Alan Munslow, *Deconstructing History* (London, 1997).

Bernard Williams, *Truth and Truthfulness* (Princeton, NJ, 2002).

Notes

1   See the exchange between Richard Evans, *In Defence of History* (London, 1997), p. 252 and Diane Purkiss, IHR website, http://www.ihrinfo.ac.uk/reviews/discourse/dianne1.html (2002).

2   Lawrence Stone, 'History and Postmodernism' *Past and Present* 131 (1991), pp. 217–18.

3   Hayden V. White, 'The Burden of History', *History and Theory* 5(2) (1966), pp. 111–34, 124.

4   Natalie Zemon Davis, 'The Reasons of Misrule: Youth Groups and Charivaris in Sixteenth-Century France', *Past and Present* 50 (1971), pp. 41–75 and 'The Rites of Violence: Religious Riot in Sixteenth-Century France', *Past and Present* 59 (1973), pp. 51–91; Alan MacFarlane, *Witchcraft in Tudor and Stuart England: A Regional and Comparative Study* (London, 1970).

5   Richard Johnson, 'Edward Thompson, Eugene Genovese, and Socialist-Humanist History, *History Workshop Journal* 6 (1978), pp. 79–100.

6   Note, however, that other analogies work less well. Colours might merge, but do the sensations of a blow on the head and reading Barthes?

7   White, 'The Burden of History'.

8   Michel Foucault, *Madness and Civilization: A History of Insanity in the Age of Reason* (London, 1967).

9   Jacques Derrida, 'Cogito and the History of Madness', in *Writing and Difference* (London, 1978; first published 1967), pp. 31–63 and Michel Foucault, 'My Body, this Paper, this Fire', *Oxford Literary review* 4(1) (1979; first published 1972), pp. 9–28.

10   Alex Callinicos, *Against Postmodernism: A Marxist critique* (Cambridge, 1989).

11   Patrick Joyce, *Democratic Subjects: The Self and the Social in Nineteenth-Century England* (Cambridge, 1994), pp. 3–4.

12   E.P. Thompson, *The Poverty of Theory and Other Essays* (London, 1978), pp. 289, 350–1.

13   Patrick Joyce, 'The End of Social History', *Social History* 20(1) (1995), pp. 73–91.

14   Joan Wallach Scott, 'Women in *The Making of the English Working Class*', in Joan Wallach Scott, *Gender and the Politics of History* (New York, 1988), pp. 68–90.

15   Hayden White, *The Tropics of Discourse: Essays in Cultural Criticism* (Baltimore, 1978), pp. 15–17.

16   Robert Berkhofer, 'The Challenge of Poetics to (Normal) Historical Practice', *Poetics Today* (1988).

17   Berkhofer, 'The Challenge of Poetics'.

18   Robin Bisha, 'Reconstructing the Voice of a Noblewoman of the Time of

Peter the Great: Daria Mikhailovna Menshikova', *Re-thinking History* 2 (1998), pp. 51–63.

19 Jenkins, '*The Postmodern History Reader*, p. 28; Keith Jenkins, 'A Postmodern Reply to Perez Zagorin', *History and Theory* 39(2) (2000), pp. 199–200.

20 Michel Foucault, *Discipline and Punish: The Birth of the Prison* (London, 1977; first published 1975), pp. 26–8.

21 H. Aram Veseer, 'The New Historicism', in H. Aram Veseer (ed.), *The New Historicism Reader* (London, 1994), p. 13.

22 Foucault, *Discipline and Punish*, pp. 27, 52.

23 R.F. Atkinson, *Knowledge and Explanation in History: An Introduction to the Philosophy of History* (London, 1978), pp. 45–51.

24 Evans, *In Defence*, p. 252; Richard Evans, *Telling Lies About Hitler* (London, 2003); Perez Zagorin's 'History, the Referent, and Narrative: Reflections on Postmodernism Now', *History and Theory* 38(1) (1999), pp. 1–21 also leans towards reconstructionism.

25 See, for example, Alun Munslow, *Deconstructing History* (London, 1997), pp. 1–9 for a remarkably simplistic view of the nature of historical writing.

26 White, 'The Burden of History', pp. 129–30.

27 Tony Bennet, *Outside Literature* (London, 1990).

28 Hayden White, 'Historical Emplotment and the Problem of Truth', in Saul Friedlander (ed.), *Probing the Limits of Representation: Nazism and the Final Solution* (Cambridge, MA and London, 1992), p. 37.

29 Karl Popper, *The Open Society and its Enemies*, 2 vols (London and Chicago, 1943), Vol. 2, Chapter 25.

30 Zagorin, 'History, the Referent, and Narrative', p. 21.

31 Dominick LaCapra, *History and Memory after Auschwitz* (London and New York, 1999), p. 12.

32 Hayden White, *The Content of the Form*, pp. 78–80.

33 Hayden White, 'Afterword', in Victoria E. Bonnel and Lynn Hunt (eds), *Beyond the Cultural Turn: New Directions in the Study of Society and Culture* (Berkeley, Los Angeles and London, 1999), pp. 315–24, esp. 322 and 'Historical Emplotment and the Problem of Truth', in Friedlander, *Probing the Limits*, pp. 37–8.

34 Wulf Kansteiner, 'Mad History Disease Contained: Postmodern Excess Management Advice from the UK', *History and Theory* 39(2) (1999), pp. 218–29, esp. 225–6.

35 John H. Arnold, 'The Historian as Inquisitor', *Re-thinking History*, 2, 3 (1998), pp. 379–86.

36 Evelyn Brookes Higginbotham, 'African-American Women's History and the Metalanguage of Race', *Signs* 17(2) (1992), pp. 251–74.

37 For a lucid example of the use of Bakhtin's theory see S.H. Rigby, *Chaucer in Context* (Manchester, 1996).

8

Psychoanalysis and history

Garthine Walker

Sigmund Freud (1856–1939) coined the term 'psychoanalysis' in 1896. Freud was one of several thinkers who questioned the idea, popular in some quarters in the nineteenth century, that human beings were rational creatures who always acted in full knowledge of what they were doing. He suggested that unconscious impulses influenced people's behaviour. Freud's ideas, like those of Darwin and Marx, have profoundly impacted on human beings' idea of themselves. His concept of the unconscious, use of free association and emphasis on the importance of dreams informed movements like Dadaism and Surrealism in the visual arts, and works of fiction such as Virginia Woolf's novel *The Waves*. His ideas also influenced historical writing. Biographers began to explain personality traits by referring to their subjects' pasts. Historians became more interested in causation. Before Freud, historians were not much concerned with the causes or origins of historical phenomena, being more interested in judging how great certain individuals were. After Freud, historians were more likely to consider that people might have been unconsciously influenced by causes of which they were unaware.

Explicit psychoanalytic theory enjoys a somewhat uncertain intellectual status. Despite many adherents in literary and cultural criticism, and in therapeutic practice, it tends to be dismissed by academic psychologists. Its reception by historians has been mixed. In 1958, William L. Langer, then President of the American Historical Association, proclaimed that incorporating 'psychoanalysis and its developments and variations' into historical research was the way forward for the discipline.[1] The decades since then, although witnessing no paradigm shift of the sort envisaged by Langer, have heard several such clarion calls.[2] Psychoanalytic theory has made a particular contribution to the fields of historical biography, early modern witchcraft and Holocaust studies. It is attractive to biographers because it provides a useful – some would say facile – way of giving unity to a life.

In the two latter cases, the behaviour to be studied is seen as 'irrational' or the product of 'trauma', and is thus anchored in the unconscious.[3] Psychoanalytic ideas and vocabulary have also permeated historical writing in the form of popular 'common sense' assumptions about human behaviour. There is, however, no consensus. Whereas some argue that the historian's and the psychoanalyst's tasks are similar,[4] others maintain their distinctiveness and incompatibility.[5] Overall, explicit psychoanalysis has remained on the margins of the historical project.[6]

Various reasons have been given for this state of affairs: 'the overwhelming majority' of historians 'have not been analyzed', so they fail to understand psychoanalysis and their objections 'probably ... spring from deep emotional sources'; they have a 'narrow, empirical outlook', and fail 'to come to grips with theoretical challenges'; they fear that psychoanalysis undermines the humanistic tradition of historical explanation.[7] These may all be valid criticisms in that they may apply to certain individuals. But the historical profession is extremely diverse. Psychoanalytic theory fails to appeal to many historians because it seems to assume historical constants and essentialism. According to Freud, 'unconscious mental processes are ... "timeless"': they 'are not ordered temporally', 'time does not change them in any way', and 'the idea of time cannot be applied to them'.[8] Many historians favour theoretical traditions that stress anti-essentialism. An anti-essentialist position denies that particular responses universally arise from given causes: one cannot interpret ambiguous feelings towards one's child as *inevitably* arising from the condition of childbirth and motherhood, for instance. Even when things have appeared constant, it does not follow that they *must* be constant – *pace* the oppression of women. The apparent essentialism of psychoanalytic theory that seems to render it ahistorical goes some way to explaining its little impact among historians.

However, psychoanalysis has been a far from stagnant field. During the past century, myriad theoretical positions have emerged. Some theorists have challenged the importance of essentialism. Others have explored the relationship between biological drives and culture. Certain scholars have claimed that particular versions of psychoanalysis *are* historical and quite compatible with historical change, arguing that they may investigate the 'varied expression in different times and places' of universal drives and fantasies.[9]

In this chapter, I shall outline some salient points for historians of certain types of psychoanalytic theory, and examine and evaluate examples of their influence in actual historical writing. I have distinguished between three bodies of thought: first, Freudian psychoanalysis and ego psychology; second, object-relations theory as developed by Melanie Klein; third, Julia Kristeva's modification of Lacanian psychoanalysis. There exist many more variants than this, and I do not attempt to summarize all the main concerns of even these three. Rather, I introduce in brief and therefore simplified terms certain of their characteristics in order to consider their use by historians. Whereas critics of psychoanalytic theory have conventionally focused on the fragility of its truth-claims or have engaged in _ad hominem_ attacks on Freud, I examine the mechanics of the arguments of practical historical writing informed by psychoanalytic ideas.[10]

8.1 Some Freudian concepts

Like Marxism and Darwinism, Freud's theory is a structural one. Although it deals with the individual psyche, it does not privilege individual agency or choice. Freudian psychoanalysis emphasizes the tripartite structure of the personality. First, _id_, the unconscious, where mental activities occur without the individual's awareness but that affect his or her behaviour. The unconscious contains universal human drives and impulses, the primitive biological instincts of sex and aggression. Dreams, free association, slips of the tongue, art and comments made under hypnosis all provide access to the unconscious. Second, _ego_, the conscious mind, involving perception, understanding and decision-making. We experience this part of the personality as 'I', or 'self'. Third, _superego_, the ideals and values derived from the familial and cultural environment, such as social mores and taboos. Of these three, the unconscious is the key concept. Freud did not invent the idea of unconscious motivation — that feelings or impulses of which we are unaware influence our behaviour. In the seventeenth century, Pascal, for instance, observed, 'The heart has its reasons of which reason knows nothing.'[11] But Freud developed the notion that a mental entity called the unconscious actually exists and contains real truths about ourselves. Hence, the term 'Freudian slip', whereby a person consciously means to say one thing, but their unconscious breaks through with a slip of the tongue to reveal their 'true' feelings. Freud also adapted pre-existing concepts of 'repression' – the idea that painful experiences are kept out of conscious awareness – and 'projection' – that people project feelings of anxiety and guilt onto others and lash out defensively, so that these hostile feelings are experienced as part of the external world rather than internally. These psychological phenomena are recognized both within and beyond psychoanalysis.

Freud stated that all individuals pass through certain stages – oral, anal, phallic and genital – of personality development. A pivotal moment in this journey is termed the Oedipus complex, after the Greek mythical hero who unknowingly killed his father and married his mother. Within Freudian theory, boys experience the Oedipus complex during the phallic stage of development, between the ages of three and five. The little boy has an instinctual sexual desire for his mother. He therefore begins to see his father as a rival for his mother's love, whence arises the desire to remove his father by murdering or castrating him. But the little boy fears reprisals, especially being castrated himself. A conflict emerges between, on the one hand, loving his mother and hating his father and, on the other, self-preservation. The latter wins and the little boy represses his feelings of sexual love and hate towards his parents. The Oedipal stage ends with the boy entering the genital stage. Having recognized his father's masculine superiority, he identifies with him rather than with his mother. Freud termed a roughly comparable process for girls the Electra complex, after the mythological female who killed her mother to avenge the mother's murder of her father. In Greek myth, Electra lures her mother to her death by appealing to her maternal instincts, and after killing her is overwhelmed with remorse. Freud did not clearly theorize the female complex. Feminist psychoanalytic theorists have since developed versions of the female unconscious.[12]

In addition to emphasizing structure, Freudian psychoanalysis stresses conflict rather than consensus. Conflict occurs between the three parts of the personality. For instance, a little boy's conscious fears of reprisal conflict with his instinctive sexual desire for his mother and so repress that impulse within the unconscious. In turn, repressed sexual urges produce anxiety, along with the fear, guilt and shame associated with sexual and aggressive fantasies. The unconscious conflict arising from these infant experiences determines behaviour in adulthood. Indeed, all variants of human activity are caused by the unconscious interaction of and conflict between the two instinctive drives: sexual urges, which are associated with constructive behaviour, and the death instinct, the source of all destructive urges. This places a question mark over how much room for individual or collective choice there is within the theory. Overall, Freudian psychoanalysis is an essentialist, structural theory based in biology. Where a Marxist would look for the underlying economic interest, a Freudian might try to explain history in terms of the historical subject's unresolved unconscious conflicts.

Ego psychology, pioneered by Anna Freud (Freud's daughter) and developed by Heinz Hartmann and Erik Erikson, follows the parameters of Freudian psychoanalysis, retaining a concern with the significance of biological drives. Personality is seen to develop from the dominance of the unconscious in infanthood to the adult's conscious control over the internal and external world. In Erikson's formulation, society and culture (in the form, for instance, of economic opportunities as well as child-rearing methods) influence how adults behave and make sense of their experiences. Individuals absorb and internalize cultural values so that their ego functions appropriately within their particular society. On the surface, there is less biological determinism in ego psychology than there is in classic Freudianism. Yet the theory depends upon the premise that humans are biologically programmed to adapt to their culture as part of the struggle for survival. Ego psychology was developed within a framework of functionalism and shares characteristics with modernization theory. Consensus is seen as positive and conflict negative, for example. A failure to conform is the result of a lack of desirable adaptation to the social environment. Ego psychology assumes a necessary historical direction towards greater ego stability and more successful adaptation to the environment.

Application in historical writing of Freudianism

We find Freudian psychoanalytic theory particularly informing historical biographies, such as Erik Erikson's *Young Man Luther* (1958) and E. Victor Wolfenstein's study of Lenin, *The Revolutionary Personality* (1973).[13] Freud himself published a psychobiography of Leonardo da Vinci (1910). The example I discuss here is an examination of Bismarck by Otto Pflanze.[14] Otto von Bismarck was Prime Minister of Prussia, and is largely held responsible for the unification of Germany in 1871, after which he became the first Chancellor of the German Empire.

Psychoanalytic theory allows Pflanze to reconcile two contradictory statements made by Bismarck. In 1838, aged 23, Bismarck wrote in a letter that he was not motivated to be a great statesman by patriotism but by 'ambition, the wish to command, to be admired, and to become famous'. In 1874, aged 59, Bismarck contrarily described himself to the Prussian parliament as 'a disciplined statesman who subordinates himself to the total needs and requirements of the state in the interests of peace and the welfare of my country'.[15] Pflanze explains the difference between these two pronouncements not in terms of their different contexts and audiences but in psychoanalytic terms:

> ... the Bismarck of 1874 was still the Bismarck of 1838. What occurred may be understood in terms of a common psychic process ... Instinctual impulses that the conscience cannot tolerate are either repressed (i.e., 'thrust back into the id') or projected (i.e., 'displaced into the outside world'). Bismarck projected his quest for power and renown onto the Prussian state. Goals that would have been intolerable if conceived as personal, could, when conceived as in the interests of the state or public welfare, be sought without a sense of guilt ... [and] therefore acceptable to his conscience.[16]

The reason Bismarck experienced this conflict was that between these two dates he had undergone a religious conversion, and so was compelled to 'protect his ego from the sting of conscience'. Bismarck's ambition of 1838 has been repressed by 1874. This demonstrates how psychoanalytic theory can perpetuate sameness and fails to allow for historical change. Psychoanalysis allows evidence that conflicts to be interpreted as having the same meaning. A theory that allows for evidence and lack of evidence to lead to the same conclusion is obviously highly problematic.

Pflanze also draws on psychoanalysis in arguing that Bismarck was a 'phallic-narcissistic' character, drawing on Wilhelm Riech's 1933 descriptions of Freudian personality types. 'Phallic-narcissistic' types are 'self-confident, often arrogant, elastic, vigorous, and often impressive . . . The facial expression usually shows hard, sharp masculine features'; they have an aggressive manner; the 'outspoken types tend to achieve leading positions in life', and so on. Such types have 'an identification of the total ego with the phallus', 'serious disappointments' at the genital stage in the relationship to the mother, and a home in which the mother was the stronger parent. Pflanze superimposes this on to Bismarck's character and past. (He claims that psychoanalytic theory provides 'character suits' in which to dress and tailor to fit historical characters.) Pflanze writes that Bismarck 'undoubtedly' displayed 'a rather exaggerated masculinity'. As a student, Bismarck had fought 25 duels in three semesters. He boasted of his ability to drink six bottles of wine without getting drunk or vomiting. He had exhibitionist tendencies, quaffing an entire bottle of wine in one gulp to impress assembled officers.[17]

Pflanze views events from Bismarck's early life in the light of the Oedipal situation associated with the phallic-narcissistic character type. He quotes a letter in which Bismarck remembered his childhood feelings towards his parents: 'it often appeared to me that [my mother] was hard, cold toward me. As a small child I hated her.' In contrast, Bismarck wrote that he 'really loved' his father, but felt remorseful because at times, 'I made a pretence of loving him . . . when innerly I felt hard and unloving because of his apparent weaknesses.' The letter seems to conform to Freudian theory only where the father is concerned. Bismarck feels an Oedipal ambivalence towards his father, feeling sometimes loving and sometimes unloving. This ambivalence is caused by a mixture of respect for his father's authority, and jealousy over his possession of Bismarck's mother. According to the theory, Bismarck should have felt love for his mother, not hate. But here, Pflanze operates a remarkable shift of perspective typical of psychoanalysis. 'Toward his mother he expressed a sense of guilt, but no ambivalence and no love. Yet appearances deceive, and here too Bismarck conforms to the pattern.' The evidence that conflicts with psychoanalytic theory – that Bismarck hated rather than loved his mother – is made to fit the theory after all. For

> it is a common phenomenon within psychoanalysis that strong negative feelings towards the parent of the opposite sex turn out to be . . . concealing the opposite of what they purport to be. Interpreted in this way, Bismarck's attitude toward his mother has to be read as love rather than hatred.[18]

Effectively, the theory is confirmed whether evidence is present or absent. Freudian psychoanalysis would thus seem to be incompatible with the historical method because its self-confirming nature means that it cannot be tested against evidence. Pflanze exemplifies how psychohistorians may come to the past with their explanation already in hand. Psychoanalytic theory is treated as if it constitutes a body of universal laws. The past is applied to the model rather than the model or hypothesis being tested against evidence.

While this sort of psychohistory was produced primarily in the 1960s and 1970s, Freudian assumptions continue to lead historians to treat historical documents as if they allow us to 'reconstruct the mental life of an individual', to identify 'the themes of [that individual's] psychology', and to see into 'the well-springs of . . . personality, motives and emotions'.[19] The problem of reading texts in this way is, of course, a non-problem for Freudian psychoanalysis. It is irrelevant whether the subject describes responses to 'real' external or imagined internal events because what matters is the individual's construction of reality, which is based on the need to contain the expression of the libido and death drive.[20] But psychoanalytic theory also allows for anxiety to arise from external factors, and the historian has no way of determining whether the origins are internal or external in any particular case. Moreover, psychoanalysts have acknowledged that theirs is not a predictive theory and have warned against 'transposing back', reducing human situations to the 'earliest, simplest, and most infantile precursor which is assumed to be its "origin"'.[21] Yet this is precisely what Freudian psychohistories attempt, thereby producing arguments that are essentialist, circular and unfalsifiable.

8.2 Object-relations theory and Melanie Klein

Object-relations theory is a development of Freudian psychoanalysis, so labelled because it focuses on the first year of life when the infant learns to distinguish its self (subject), from 'objects' with which it comes into contact. The objects in question are people (primarily the mother) or parts of people (the mother's breast). The infant initially experiences all 'good' things, such as the mother's breast, as parts of itself, and 'bad' things, such as pain, as external. Although the concept of the unconscious remains central, the experience of individuals is explained in psychosocial terms. Instead of the primary impulse being a biological need to express the sexual and aggressive drives, it is social: a need to form relationships with other humans. The desire for personal relationships explains the sex drive (the need to express intimacy) and aggression (the need to express frustration). In an ideal, romanticized mother–infant relationship, the infant's psyche is not conflicted or split. However, psychological conflict and splits originate in frustrating experiences with the maternal object. By paying particular attention to the early mother–infant relationship in the pre-Oedipal period, object-relations theorists move maternality to the fore, and play down the father-centred Oedipus complex. This has been attractive to some feminists. Problematic from certain feminist perspectives is object-relations theory's naturalization of mothering, which might imply that mothering is biologically determined rather than socially constructed. Feminist object-relations theorists have drawn attention to the way that discourses of motherhood are constructed ideologically. As the individual is interpreted in a social context and social relations are central to the construction of the self, object-relations theory is perhaps more compatible with historical analysis than is Freudian psychoanalysis. However, the defining characteristic of human existence remains biologically rooted in the impulse to form relationships with others.

Unlike later object-relations theorists who posited an idealized pre-Oedipal stage and a rosy picture of mother–infant relations, Melanie Klein, whose works were published between 1919 and 1961, emphasized the aggressive anxieties, frustrations and splitting that the infant experiences in relation to the breast.[22] Klein was the first to argue that babies initially relate to parts, such as the breast, rather than to the mother as such. This mode of identification ('paranoid-schizoid position') is eventually replaced by the infant's ability to relate to whole objects, such as the mother (the 'depressive position'). Klein also believed that the infant psyche is experienced in the inner world of 'phantasy'. Freud's instinctual drives of desire and aggression, and the negative emotions of envy, greed and loss, are dealt with within this phantasy realm. The child experiences in phantasy the mother's breast as split into good (gratifying) and bad (frustrating). The infant aims to incorporate and identify with the good breast, which represents the life instinct, and projects the anxiety provoked by the death instinct onto the bad breast.

Whereas other object-relations theorists came to stress the fundamental unity of the infant psyche, Klein's internal infant world is never unified. Although the infant's ego develops towards integration, it tends to fragment and split into good and bad as a way of dealing with anxiety. The anxiety itself is a defensive action to protect the ego from the death drive's destructiveness. Gradually, a more integrated psyche emerges and the infant begins to fear that his or her own destructive impulses might have destroyed the mother or the breast. This introduces feelings of ambivalence – rage, and afterwards, guilt, and loss for the phantasized destruction of the bad object, as well as love – towards the mother, who now becomes seen as a whole that embodies both bad and good. This 'depressive position' heralds a process of 'reparation', wherein the infant experiences restorative phantasies in which harm done to objects is undone. While the mother is now phantasized as a whole object, the infant still does not fully differentiate the mother from the father. This lack of differentiation is possible because the infant does not identify a whole 'real' mother. For Klein, the mother is a fluid construction of the infant's desires and anxieties.

Klein identified envy as a key emotion imbuing this early stage of infanthood. Envy involves the desire to be as good as the envied object (the good breast), and when this is felt to be impossible, the object is attacked in order to remove the source of envious feelings. But the infant hates and envies the bad breast too. This envy is usually dealt with in the process of resolving Oedipal feelings of rivalry; if it remains powerful, the Oedipal stage is not successfully resolved.

The problem for historians is not that this body of theory is 'wrong', as critics often assert. Rather, object-relations theory, like classical Freudianism, is based on imaginative constructions that cannot be falsified, disproved. We have no means by which to discriminate between interpretations. This makes it incompatible with a historical method that rests upon relative probabilities.

An example of Melanie Klein's object-relations theory informing historical writing

In 'Witchcraft and Fantasy in Early Modern Germany', Lyndal Roper argues that to understand witchcraft we must attend to the 'imaginative themes' of the cases.[23] These themes are maternal. The motifs in witchcraft narratives were suckling, giving birth, food and feeding, childcare. Several accused witches were lying-in maids; their accusers were newly delivered mothers; witnesses were other women for whom the lying-in maids had worked. Roper asks why witchcraft accusations took this form and why some accused lying-in maids confessed to their crimes. She contends that psychic conflicts provide the answers to both questions. Psychoanalytic concepts are central to this conclusion.

With regard to the mothers who accused lying-in maids of witchcraft, Roper stresses the biological significance of childbirth. A baby's first weeks were a period of anxiety for mothers, not only because of high infant mortality, but because this time might invoke memories of the mother's own pre-Oedipal stage when she 'may have experienced unadmitted, intolerable feelings of hatred as well as love' towards her own mother.[24] If things went wrong – if the child fell ill or died – these pre-Oedipal residues formed a psychic dramatic script that allowed her to project her anxiety and guilt onto the lying-in maid whom she duly accused of witchcraft.[25] Whereas the modern woman might internalize feelings of guilt, and experience postnatal depression, the early modern mother used the Kleinian mechanism of 'splitting' to project these feelings onto someone else. Thus, for Roper, the early modern psyche is regulated by the same psychically induced states as the modern one. Lying-in maids were also marked by ambiguous pre-Oedipal feelings, especially envy, for they had no hope of having young families of their own. Drawing again on Klein, Roper states that it is in the pre-Oedipal phase that envy develops. The lying-in maid's admission of envy could lead to a full confession of witchcraft in the context of early modern understandings that associated envy of a woman with a wish to harm her.

There is much brilliant analysis in this. Roper's identification of conflicts between women seems incontrovertible, and her contribution to understanding the nature of these conflicts is very important. The *questions* she asks and the areas she explores owe much to her knowledge of psychoanalysis and, on this score, its use has clearly been productive. But when we look at the mechanics of her argument, psychoanalysis plays a lesser and sometimes redundant role.

Critics of psychohistory are fond of denouncing it for its circular arguments. Following Karl Popper's claim that psychoanalytic propositions are unfalsifiable – that because they are self-affirming no statement can refute them – they have argued that historians cannot legitimately use psychoanalytic ideas.[26] Roper concedes that her argument may seem circular. Indeed, she seems positively to embrace circularity: 'this conceptual difficulty,' she says, 'is inherent in the productive use of ideas'.[27] One example of circularity is Roper's explanation for why envy marks witchcraft cases. Envy, psychoanalytic theory informs us, is pre-Oedipal in origin, therefore the explanation for the presence of this envy is pre-Oedipal conflict. This is a perfect circle, in that the conclusion is contained in the premise. The primary problem with circularity, however, is that it is *un*productive. It reproduces the same knowledge whatever the sources or evidence. Roper is far too good a historian not to see this. She immediately qualifies her apparent commitment to circularity by rejecting reductive readings in which 'everything speaks of phallologocentrism, or betrays the Oedipal complex'. In fact, she offers a means for psychoanalysis to break out of circularity. On the one hand, she argues that 'there are some primary areas of attachment and conflict – between those in maternal positions and children – which are pretty fundamental to human existence'. This is an unfalsifiable statement: it is difficult to conceive of any kind of evidence about motherhood that would not confirm the presence of either attachment or conflict or both. On the other hand, she says, 'the *form* those conflicts may take and the attitudes societies adopt to them may change. This ... is the territory of the historian.'[28] In other words, historians can investigate the varying forms taken by unvarying emotions. The fact of multiple forms renders any common root academic, or makes it merely one influence among many. Roper has effectively constrained the reach of psychoanalysis in that she has admitted that all aspects of human behaviour cannot be reduced to basic psychic mechanisms. This concession – that psychoanalysis should be used alongside other forms of investigation for it alone cannot provide an explanation – is undoubtedly a theoretical gain.

Nevertheless, the explanatory status of psychoanalysis is reduced more than Roper would seem to realize. Roper's explanation for why early modern women sometimes projected their guilt in witchcraft accusations, whereas modern mothers are more likely to be labelled as depressive, is a range of historically rooted cultural assumptions about childbirth, the body and women. The argument is very convincing. The psychological predisposition towards guilt and envy enters the explanation only at the level of a *potential* – a potential that rules nothing out. Who knows what 'forms' psychic conflict will take in the future? Moreover, the postnatal period often passed without incident, as Roper points out, and presumably, even when things went wrong, a witchcraft accusation did not always follow. In effect, a confluence of historical factors explains the response to a psychological conflict that *might* result from something going wrong in the postpartum period. These are serious qualifications upon the explanatory power of psychoanalysis. The cost of getting around the problem of circularity has been conceptually to remove psychic conflicts from the centre of the analysis.

Underlying this is a logical issue. Roper actually classifies her two types of causation hierarchically. Historical circumstances explain the 'form' taken by psychic conflicts, which implies that the latter is a sort of base. Psychology is primary and history secondary. But this hierarchy is difficult to maintain. Since a given behavioural outcome (the witchcraft accusation) depends on two sets of causation – (a) psychic conflicts rooted in the pre-Oedipal phase, and (b) a range of historical circumstances and phenomena[29] if either (a) or (b) were removed, the accusation of witchcraft would no longer follow. As both (a) and (b) are necessary to the explanation, we cannot say which is the more important.

Psychoanalytic theory pervades Roper's argument. Yet she also operates a form of analysis in which, if I understand it correctly, it was 'the social organization of motherhood' that made possible ambivalent feelings of mother towards child, so that, 'a certain kind of psychic dramatic script was available should things go wrong'.[30] The idea of 'available scripts' might imply that other scripts could be used as well or instead and that the women concerned had a degree of agency in terms of their response to adversity.[31] So, here too, although a *claim* is made for the primacy of psychoanalytic explanation, the actual analysis is multi-causal.

In sum, although in theory, and sometimes in practice, Roper applies psychoanalytic theory in a way that suggests biological essentialism, circularity and unfalsifiability, she also integrates it into a more historical and fruitful analysis. It seems entirely possible to answer those who advocate the wholesale rejection of psychoanalytic theory with evidence that, in *practical* historical writing, a belief in psychic causality need not lead to historical determinism.[32]

8.3 Lacanian psychoanalysis and Julia Kristeva

Like Klein, Jacque Lacan denied that the ego is a unified and coherent structure, and posited that splitting is the fundamental developmental process. Also like object-relations theory, Lacan's psychoanalysis was based on imaginative constructions that cannot be disproved. However, Lacanian psychoanalysis, heavily influenced by poststructuralist linguistic theory, offers a rigorous critique of object-relations theory. For Lacan, there is no 'true' or 'real' biological self, and no separation between self and society. Rather, like language, the self is produced by binary relationships. Lacan is concerned with how the subject becomes formed in 'otherness'.

The infant is initially a non-subject, having no concept of the self. This changes in two major splits. First is the 'mirror phase', which occurs in the pre-verbal and pre-Oedipal 'Imaginary' realm between six and eighteen months of life. The mirror phase invokes the binary opposites of poststructuralism. The gaze of whomever the infant interacts with provides, as it were, a mirror in which the infant perceives him- or herself as a unified self. This wholeness is illusory. The second split comes when the child enters the 'Symbolic' realm of language; with the appropriation of language, the child becomes social. The Symbolic is a set of external meanings embedded in language, which structure and define the social and cultural order. These meanings saturate the unconscious. Linguistic determinism has thus replaced Freud's biological determinism. However, the poststructuralist tenets that the meanings of language are never fixed and that words convey multiple meanings have led to some allowing for the theoretical possibility of change. For Lacan, human behaviour cannot be predicted.

Lacan's work appeals to some feminists because it challenges biological explanations of sexual difference: culture imposes meaning on anatomy, nature is mediated through language. Lacan also deals directly with patriarchy. Within the Symbolic realm of language, a specific law, the Law of the Father, structures culture. All interpersonal experiences, including mother–infant interaction, are organized according to this patriarchal law and its symbolism. The Oedipus complex, for instance, is resolved by the acceptance of the Symbolic Law of the Father. For Lacan, the Oedipus complex occurs not literally but as a linguistic transaction. He writes about the phallus rather than the penis as Freud does. The phallus is an attribute of power within the Symbolic realm of language, not the anatomical property of males. The phallus also signifies the desire for wholeness. Desire is thus not a sexual force as it is for Freud but an unconscious compulsion to strive towards (unattainable) wholeness. Because the unconscious is structured like language, unconscious desires reflect not the individual subject but the patriarchal power structure of society. In the patriarchal Symbolic order, the man is self and the woman 'Other'. Hence, female existence is given meaning only in relation to the male. Lacan has been criticized for this eternal repression of the feminine and for defining femininity in patriarchal terms of lack. Yet some feminist theorists have developed Lacan's idea of woman as lack or 'Other'.

Julia Kristeva (born 1941), like Hélène Cixous and Luce Irigaray, has developed the idea of femininity as marginal and rejected. For Kristeva, femininity's position in the pre-Oedipal, unconscious, Imaginary realm allows it to challenge and refuse dominant meanings imposed by the Symbolic. It thus offers an authentic expression of the self for women (and indeed for men) beyond the Law of the Father's grasp. However, by speaking from the Imaginary, there is a risk of being engulfed by a terrifying infantile realm characterized by abjection.[33] Kristeva's concept of the 'abject' is a shapeless, boundless, damp, monstrous realm outside culture that threatens to bring culture to chaos. Abjection is associated, above all, with the body fluids and bodily processes of the adult female body, which are similarly perceived in terms of the dissolution of boundaries and certainties, and permeability, a blurring between inside and outside, exemplified in menstruation, conception, pregnancy, childbirth, lactation and menopause. Abjection 'is the body's acknowledgement that the boundaries and limits imposed on it are really social projections – effects of desire, not nature'.[34]

It has been argued that Kristeva takes an anti-essentialist view of femininity in which feminine identity is produced culturally rather than biologically.[35] Actually, while eschewing biological determinism, in for instance seeing the pre-Oedipal mother encompassing both masculinity and femininity, Kristeva evokes a kind of cultural determinism. For example, the infant experiences the mother as all-powerful and therefore as phallic. This is essentialist. But Kristeva offers more than this. She argues that 'there is no essential womanhood, not even a repressed one' that can be revealed or recovered by cultural critics or historians. Instead, she analyses feminine and masculine modes of language.[36] Moreover, much of her formulation could be rephrased to allow for the availability of potential discourses of femininity and the body that women and men could utilize in various ways. The abject's association with the female body itself may be viewed as a cultural discourse. In an argument compatible with Bakhtin's view of language, Kristeva suggests that the marginality of abjection means that it can be appropriated and used positively by women. Nor does she relegate femininity absolutely to Lacan's pre-Oedipal Imaginary realm. Women can speak from the positions of both the Symbolic and the Imaginary. The former prevents women's identity being subsumed into that of the mother, while the latter allows women to challenge and resist what the Law of the Father presents as rigid patriarchal certainties. It is the job of analysis to say which they do speak in particular circumstances. Crucially, Kristeva also acknowledges the historical and social aspects of how we understand the world and ourselves. Language for Kristeva is productive; it does not merely reflect social relations. Kristeva's theoretical formulation allows for a greater degree of historicization and agency than does Lacan's. Arguably, this too aligns her as much, if not more, with Bakhtin as it does with Lacan or Derrida.[37]

Application in historical writing of Kristeva's modification of Lacanian psychoanalysis

Kristevan psychoanalysis partly informs Diane Purkiss's analysis of English witch-craft. In general, Purkiss owes more to Lacan's critique of biological essentialism than she does to Freud, and to Lacan's emphasis on the social and collective aspects of subjectivity, which dissolve conventional distinctions between the individual and the social. More specifically, Purkiss draws on Kristeva (and others of the French feminist psychoanalytic school). In 'The house, the body, the child', Purkiss identifies and explores similar themes – food and feeding, the breast, transformation, the transgression of boundaries – in women's stories of witchcraft to those dealt with by Roper.[38] Purkiss borrows what she terms a 'quasi-psychoanalytic' notion of fantasy: a story in which people express and relieve unconscious and conscious fears, conflicts and anxieties. She argues that the fantasy of the witch as antimother and antihousewife enabled early modern women to 'negotiate the fears and anxieties of housekeeping and motherhood'.[39] For Purkiss, these fears and anxieties are historically and culturally constructed. They do not necessarily exist for all time but in particular contexts. There is nothing essentialist about her analysis.

Purkiss seems to perceive this to be a radical break with the methods of historians. She characterizes historians as torn between explanatory grand narratives and a simple-minded empiricist rejection of theory. She sets herself apart from what she sees as historians' questions, stressing her interest in the *meanings* of witchcraft narratives but expressly not 'in what "natural" events underlay them'.[40] This appears to be a response to historical accounts that have tried to explain away witchcraft by understanding it predominantly in terms of something else. Witchcraft accusations are understood in terms of pre-Oedipal residues in Roper's work, discussed above, for example, and other historians have interpreted witch beliefs in terms of illness, political tools, and social categories.[41] However, Purkiss's analysis is much more conventionally historical than she seems prepared to accept.

To start with, Purkiss uses the same binary opposition between psychologically generated constants and historical variability that we find in Roper. In 'No Limit, the Body of the Witch', Purkiss says that the fantasy-image of the boundless maternal body, and its associations with dirt and disorder, is one of the constants of western civilization. Drawing on Kristeva (and Cixous), Purkiss argues that this image is 'intrinsically' threatening and powerful for women. However, like Roper, she immediately qualifies this essentialist idea with the contention that this constant can only be understood 'in relation to specific historical circumstances'. She says that the maternal body does not inevitably represent particular forms of disorder or uncleanliness. Rather, it is culture – in the early modern period, a 'confluence of medical discourses and social factors' – that produces such links. Furthermore, Purkiss's formulation is less open to criticism than Roper's. Purkiss does not attempt to reduce her evidence to psychic conflicts. Whereas Roper states that ambiguous maternal feelings towards the infant are inevitable, Purkiss's formulation of the boundless female body is much more precisely specified, and is therefore perfectly falsifiable. Although it remains arguable whether this fantasy of the body has been a *constant* of western civilization, Purkiss shows convincingly and productively that it is a useful way of understanding the discourses she examines. The claim that this fantasy is a pre-given, in western culture at least, does not really affect the practical analysis.

Purkiss aims to show that women's desires, fears and anxieties about maternity and the household 'reflected and reproduced a very specific fantasy' of the witch. She demonstrates brilliantly that the witch's deeds could be imagined in terms of a 'fantasy-image of the huge, controlling, scattered, polluted, leaky fantasy of the maternal body'. She shows how this was made possible by a range of elite and popular discourses of the body, household, transformation and femininity, and by social practices surrounding women and childcare, the maintenance of household order, the dispersal of dirt and pollution, and more.[42] Therefore, this particular figure of the witch is a social and cultural construct, and not caused by biology at all. Moreover, because Purkiss stresses the cultural construction of subjectivity, she rejects the essentialist idea that a particular effect must 'naturally' follow a particular event. She uses the notion of psychic conflicts non-essentially in that they do not necessarily lead in a particular direction. Thus she argues that it is not inevitable that a woman should feel threatened in any particular way by a woman speaking to her in a certain way or entering her home. She points instead to a combination of discourses and social practices, which vary greatly.

Purkiss's method is a critical one that would be acceptable to many historians. Despite Purkiss's claim that psychoanalysis 'offers the richest, most rewarding and most serious ways of reading texts concerned with the supernatural',[43] her approach is not distinctively psychoanalytic.[44] Does psychoanalysis cease to be psychoanalysis, or even quasi-psychoanalysis, when the primacy of psychic conflicts is sidelined to such an extent?

In sum, although Purkiss seems at first sight to privilege psychoanalytic over other modes of explanation, in practice she employs it alongside other forms of analysis, and produces a non-essentializing historical account of witchcraft. She does evoke the binary opposition between psychoanalysis and historical circumstances in the same way that Roper does, but this primarily appears to be a method of positioning within and between disciplines. As pieces of historical writing, Purkiss's chapters exemplify an excellent historical method.

8.4 Conclusion

What does all this mean for the status of psychoanalysis as a historical theory? To some extent, the debate over whether psychoanalysis can inform historical work is based on misunderstanding. Purkiss characterizes historians as believers in realism, in a correspondence view of truth in which fears of witches must represent 'real' fears. Actually, many historians work within an entirely different method, a critical method that goes beyond the false opposition between reality and relativism, truth and fiction, just as she does. Purkiss's mode of analysis would be perfectly acceptable to certain types of historian. Historians in this tradition – perhaps a conceptually informed empiricism – do not attack psychoanalysis in the name of realism, but ignore it on the grounds that it cannot deal with change, because they see it as an essentializing metanarrative. This, too, is based on a misconception. Historians who dismiss psychoanalysis have missed the extent to which psychoanalytically informed historians *have* grappled with change and essentialism. One reason why historians make this mistake is that psychoanalytically inclined historians tend to make a *claim* for the theoretical primacy of psychoanalysis. However, while this claim sometimes undermines the analysis, it does not always do so – even in work like Roper's, the entire analysis is not characterized by essentialism and circularity – and in Purkiss's case it hardly is at all. In both literary criticism and history there are antitheorists, those who believe in Theory, and those like myself, and, I would guess, Purkiss, who engage with theory in the lower case: in other words, those who favour a conceptually informed history that does not have the answers in advance.

Guide to further reading

Sally Alexander, 'Feminist History and Psychoanalysis', *History Workshop Journal* 32 (1991), pp. 128–33.

T.G. Ashplant, 'Psychoanalysis in Historical Writing', *History Workshop Journal* 26 (1988), pp. 102–19.

Stephen Frosh, *The Politics of Psychoanalysis: An Introduction to Freudian and Post-Freudian Theory*, 2nd edn (Basingstoke and London, 1999).

Peter Gay, *Freud for Historians* (New York, 1985).

Rosalind Minsky (ed.), *Psychoanalysis and Gender: An Introductory Reader* (London and New York, 1996).

Toril Moi (ed.), *The Kristeva Reader* (Oxford, 1986).

Fred Weinstein, 'Psychohistory and the Crisis of the Social Sciences', *History and Theory* 34(4) (1995), pp. 219–319.

Notes

1 William L. Langer, 'The Next Assignment', *American Historical Review* 63 (1958), pp. 284–5.

2 Tim Ashplant, 'Psychoanalysis in Historical Writing', *History Workshop Journal* 26 (1988), pp. 102–19; Tim Ashplant, 'Fantasy, Narrative, Event: Psychoanalysis and History', *History Workshop Journal* 23 (1987), pp. 165–73; Karl Figlio, 'Historical Imagination/Psychoanalytic Imagination', *History Workshop Journal* 45 (1998), pp. 199–221; Peter Loewenberg, 'Why Psychoanalysis Needs the Social Scientist and the Historian', in Geoffrey Cocks and Travis L. Crosby (eds), *Psycho/History: Readings in the Method of Psychology, Psychoanalysis and History* (New Haven and London, 1987), pp. 17–29; Hans Meyerhoff, 'On Psychoanalysis as History', in Cocks and Crosby (eds), *Psycho/History*, pp. 30–44. Two journals dedicated to psychoanalytic history are *The Journal of Psychohistory* (formerly *The History of Childhood Quarterly*) and *The Psychohistory Review*.

3 Works of historical biography and about witchcraft are mentioned below. For an example of psychoanalysis in the field of Holocaust studies, see Dominick LaCapra, *History and Memory after Auschwitz* (Ithaca and London, 1998).

4 Thomas A. Kohut, 'Psychohistory as History', *American Historical Review* 91(2) (1986), p. 337.

5 Fred Weinstein and Gerald M. Platt, 'The Coming Crisis in Psychohistory', *Journal of Modern History* 47(2) (1975), p. 212.

6 Peter Burke, *History and Social Theory* (Oxford, 1992), p. 114.

7 David E. Stannard, *Shrinking History: On Freud and the Failure of Psychohistory* (New York and Oxford, 1980), p. ix; Peter Gay, *Freud for Historians* (Oxford, 1985), p. 52; Diane Purkiss, *The Witch in History: Early Modern and Twentieth-Century Representations* (London and New York, 1996), pp. 60, 69; Paul Robinson, *Freud and his Critics* (Berkeley, Los Angeles and Oxford, 1993), p. 10.

8 Cited in Peter Loewenberg, 'Psychohistorical Perspectives on Modern German History', *Journal of Modern History* 47(2) (1975), p. 261.

9 Loewenberg, 'Psychohistorical Perspectives', p. 262.

10 Frederick Crews *et al.*, *The Memory Wars: Freud's Legacy in Dispute* (London, 1997); H.J. Eysenck, 'What is Wrong with Psychoanalysis?', in Cocks and Crosby (eds), *Psycho/History*, pp. 3–16; Adolph Grünbaum, *The Foundations of Psychoanalysis: A Philosophical Critique* (Berkeley, 1984); Stannard, *Shrinking History*; Frank J. Sulloway, 'Reassessing Freud's Case Histories: the Social Construction of Psychoanalysis', *Isis* 82 (1991), pp. 245–75.

11 Cited in Richard Webster, *Why Freud Was Wrong: Sin, Science and Psychoanalysis*, new edn (London, 1996), p. xii. See also George Frankl, *The Social History of the Unconscious* (London, 1989).

12 See the work of Hélène Cixous, Luce Irigary and Julia Kristeva.

13 See also the case studies in Bruce Mazlish (ed.), *Psychoanalysis and History*, revised edn (New York, 1971).

14 Otto Pflanze, 'Toward a Psychoanalytic Interpretation of Bismarck', *American Historical Review* 77(2) (1972), pp. 419–44.

15 Pflanze, 'Psychoanalytic Interpretation of Bismarck', pp. 420–1.

16 Pflanze, 'Psychoanalytic Interpretation of Bismarck', p. 423.

17 Pflanze, 'Psychoanalytic Interpretation of Bismarck', pp. 420, 426–7.

18 Pflanze, 'Psychoanalytic Interpretation of Bismarck', pp. 429–30.

19 Lyndal Roper, 'Oedipus and the Devil' in her *Oedipus and the Devil: Witchcraft, Sexuality and Religion in Early Modern Europe* (London and New York, 1994), pp. 229, 230, 234.

20 Weinstein and Platt, 'Coming Crisis', p. 204.

21 Weinstein and Platt, 'Coming Crisis', pp. 217–18; Kohut, 'Psychohistory', pp. 342–3; Peter Blos, 'The Epigenesis of the Adult Neurosis', *Psychoanalytic Study of the Child* 27 (1972), pp. 107–8; Fred Weinstein, 'Psychohistory and the Crisis of the Social Sciences', *History and Theory* 34(4) (1995), p. 304.

22 Janice Doane and Devon Hodges, *From Klein to Kristeva: Psychoanalytic Feminism and the Search for the 'Good Enough' Mother* (Ann Arbor, 1992), p. 8.

23 Lyndal Roper, 'Witchcraft and Fantasy in Early Modern Germany', *History Workshop Journal* 32 (1991), pp. 19–33; reprinted in her *Oedipus and the Devil: Witchcraft, Sexuality and Religion in Early Modern Europe* (London and New York, 1994), pp. 199–225. Further page references are to the latter.

24 Roper, *Oedipus*, p. 211.

25 Roper, *Oedipus*, p. 215.

26 Stannard, *Shrinking History*, pp. 24–5; Karl Popper, *Conjections and Refutations*, p. 37; Robinson, *Freud and His Critics*, p. 208.

27 Roper, *Oedipus*, p. 218.

28 Roper, *Oedipus*, p. 218.

29 For slippage between psychic and historical causation in another of her essays, see Roper, *Oedipus*, p. 240.

30 Roper, *Oedipus*, pp. 210, 215.

31 See also her comments in the essay 'Oedipus and the Devil', *Oedipus*, pp. 229, 230. She writes, 'The psychic conflicts attendant on the feminine position – whether Oedipal or related to motherhood – provided the substance of the psychic drama of the witchcraft interrogation'; 'most women', however, managed these psychic conflicts 'without falling prey to morbid diabolic temptation ... nor did all witches produce witch fantasies'; but when they did, it was 'the possibilities present in [the] culture' that 'enabled' the 'combustion of interests to occur' that produced stories of witchcraft.

32 Cf. Edwin R. Wallace IV, *Historiography and Causation in Psychoanalysis* (Hillsdale, New Jersey and London, 1985), p. 177.

33 Feminist object-relations theorists such as Nancy Chodorow have also developed the role of the mother in the pre-Oedipal phase, stressing that the mother, in being both gratifying and frustrating, is experienced by the infant as both all-powerful and all-engulfing. This intense relationship between mother and infant leads to both sexes maintaining a terrifying maternal image in the unconscious, and a rejection of the mother that works to perpetuate patriarchal dominance.

34 Elizabeth Grosz, 'The Body of Signification', in John Fletcher and Andrew Benjamin (eds), *Abjection, Melancholia and Love: The Work of Julia Kristeva* (London and New York, 1990), p. 90.

35 Rosalind Minsky (ed.), *Psychoanalysis and Gender: An Introductory Reader* (London and New York, 1996), pp. 181–2. For an opposing view, see Hoane and Hodges, *From Klein to Kristeva*, Chapter 3.

36 Chris Weedon, *Feminist Practice and Poststructuralist Theory* (Oxford, 1987), p. 69.

37 On the relative merits and demerits of alternative views of language, see Chapter 7 in this volume.

38 Purkiss, *Witch in History*, pp. 91–118.

39 Purkiss, *Witch in History*, p. 93.

40 Purkiss, *Witch in History*, pp. 3–4, 93.

41 Purkiss, *Witch in History*, p. 79.

42 Purkiss, *Witch in History*, pp. 119–21.

43 Purkiss, *Witch in History*, p. 76.

44 Similarly, Robin Briggs insists that historians neglect at their peril pre-Oedipal and Oedipal conflicts within the human psyche, yet he argues for a method that incorporates psychoanalytic concepts into a general, multi-factoral interpretation of witchcraft. Robin Briggs, ' "Many Reasons Why": Witchcraft and the Problem of Multiple Explanation', in Jonathan Barry, Marianne Hester and Gareth Roberts (eds), *Witchcraft in Early Modern Europe: Studies in Culture and Belief* (Cambridge, 1996),

p. 63; Robin Briggs, *Witches and Neighbours: the Social and Cultural Context of European Witchcraft* (London: HarperCollins, 1996), esp. Chapter 10.

9

Comparative history

Stefan Berger

Historians compare. They cannot avoid it, unless they restrict themselves to listing dates and events. If history is more than chronology, any attempt to explain and interpret what has been going on in a particular place and at a particular time involves comparing it with what has been going on before or later, or at other places at the same time. Take, for example, explanations of the rise to power of the National Socialists in Germany. If we say that the weakness of democratic traditions in Germany contributed to the Nazis' success, we also say that the strength of democratic traditions elsewhere, say in Britain, helped prevent the rise of Fascism. Narrative structures depend on comparison but these comparisons are often implicit rather than explicit.

Calls for explicit comparative history are old, and attempts to formulate a specific theory are usually traced back to John Stuart Mill.[1] In the first half of the twentieth century, eminent theoreticians and practitioners of the comparative method included Marc Bloch, Max Weber, Otto Hintze, Henri Pirenne and Emile Durkheim. These pioneers were archipelagos in a sea of nationally constituted histories, in which the vast majority of historians found it difficult to transcend the study of the societies in which they had grown up. Yet, over the last twenty years, the practice of comparative history has taken off in many societies and cultures.[2] Scholarly exchange programmes have increased international contacts after 1945, and scholars now work in national contexts different to those in which they were raised. Globalization has also directed the historians' attention to past interlinkages and comparisons between different parts of the world.[3] If comparative history is practised more frequently today than ever before, it is not done to the same extent everywhere. One of its foremost practitioners in Britain, Geoffrey Crossick, argues that comparative history has had relatively little influence on historiographical research in Britain.[4] In the Cannadine debate about

British history, Neil Evans was one of the few contributors to demand more 'rigorous and empirically grounded' comparisons to deconstruct British history into 'the building blocks of regional and national distinctiveness within the British state' and to 'see it within the perspective of Europe and the whole Atlantic world'.[5] In America, by contrast, the comparative method has made a real difference.[6] Yet comparative history courses are also taught in British undergraduate programmes (e.g. on Fascism, particular decades, revolutions, labour movements and nationalism), and students are encouraged to write comparative essays. This chapter sets out to assist students taking courses in comparative history and to encourage them to work comparatively. For comparative history to succeed, it is essential, as Thomas Welskopp points out, to make it an integral part of a theoretically aware analytical history, rather than a specialist sub-discipline that stands apart from other forms of history writing and is only practised by the initiated few.[7] To widen the appeal of comparative history this chapter will, first, discuss different kinds of comparison. Second, it will summarize some of the benefits of comparative history. Third, it will analyse problems and pitfalls of the comparative method. Fourth, it will discuss the relationship between comparative studies and cultural transfer studies, and finally it will introduce an example of comparative history to demonstrate how comparisons work.

9.1 Different kinds of comparison

Comparisons often involve nation-states. The rise of professional history writing in the nineteenth century coincided with the rise of the nation-state. Historians looking to legitimate their nation-state[8] did so by comparing it – implicitly rather than explicitly – to other nation-states, identifying allegedly unique characteristics of their own which distinguished them from and made them superior to others. The legacy of transnational comparisons is so strong that we often forget that nations do not have to be our units of comparison. In fact, as economic historians particularly point out, regions might constitute better units of comparison.[9] Since they are less heterogeneous than larger nations, regional comparisons are possibly less vulnerable to reductionism. A micro-comparison can take account of the totality of structures, experiences and values in a way that is impossible for a macro-comparison. Yet total comparisons of social contexts are still rare. The larger the comparison, the more necessary it is to select particular aspects for comparison. In fact, some historians have attempted to compare across whole civilizations and cultures.[10] Some themes can indeed best be discussed in transcultural perspectives, e.g. multi-culturalism or cosmopolitanism. Max Weber famously compared diverse world religions and their impact on the evolution of specific economic orders.[11] As we can see from these brief remarks, comparisons have an important spatial dimension. We need to reflect on which geographical units we wish to compare as it will influence the whole set-up of the comparison.

It is not only geography that matters. We also need to think about the purpose of the comparison. Most comparisons can be divided into two categories: individualizing and universalizing. Individualizing comparisons set out to demonstrate the uniqueness of one particular case by comparing it with others. They tend to be asymmetrical in that they use a variety of cases only to shed light on the one case that the comparison seeks to understand better. If one wants to examine 'American exceptionalism' or the German *Sonderweg*, or ask whether Britain really was 'the first industrial nation', then only comparison can establish what was specific about the particular history. Universalizing comparisons aim to identify similarities between cases. They are usually symmetrical in that they give equal weight to all cases compared. Jack Goody's comparison of family structures in Europe and Asia found similar domestic structures in this vast area.[12] Between these two ideal types of comparison are a range of hybrids. Charles Tilly has usefully distinguished between four types of comparison.[13] Encompassing comparisons are related to individualizing comparisons. They are primarily concerned with explaining differences between cases that share an overarching commonality. Nationalism studies, for example, are often concerned with delineating different ideas and types of nationalism while recognizing at the same time that all nationalisms are connected to one another.[14] Variation-finding comparisons are closer to universalizing comparisons. Here different cases are understood as variations of one particular phenomenon. Comparative Fascism studies often fall into this category. They assume that there is one phenomenon called Fascism, and proceed to discuss its variations through place and time. Barrington Moore's classic study on the origins of dictatorship and democracy started from the observation that agricultural societies seemed particularly vulnerable to Fascism, and set out to explore variations within this pattern.[15]

Individualizing comparisons and their variants are more common among historians, as they are more concerned with questions of the uniqueness of a particular time and place. Their strong historist, positivist and empiricist assumptions make historians partial towards complex analysis, which allows detailed understanding of particular contexts. They approach the evidence in as unbiased a manner as possible, and seek to reconstruct the past from the evidence that remains. Historical sociologists and geographers, in contrast, are happier with universalizing comparisons and their variants, as they habitually work at greater levels of abstraction. They are more willing to reduce historical complexity in order to answer specific questions for diverse societal contexts. However, as disciplinary barriers have fallen over the past decades, those differences have become less marked. On a basic level, one could say that comparativists are always interested in establishing both differences and similarities between cases.

The intention of the comparative historian is important for other reasons.[16] Historians undertake comparisons because they want to question national explanations, build typologies, stress historical diversity, encourage scepticism vis-à-vis global explanatory models, or contextualize and enrich research traditions of one society by exploring and contrasting them with research traditions of different societies. Many comparisons are concerned with highlighting the constructedness of historical identities. Often they endeavour to relativize notions of exceptionalism by demonstrating that identity is situational. A multiplicity of identities exists at any one given time: which one is foregrounded largely depends on the specific historical context. The emphasis in these cases is on the detachment of scholars from their object of enquiry. Yet other comparativists explicitly seek to teach the lessons of history. They may want to explain what went wrong in one particular society by contrasting its development with that of other societies. Or they may be concerned with highlighting the pioneering and model function of particular societies. This kind of comparative history is often informed by moral judgements. Their practitioners reject the assumption – still widespread among historians – that it is not the task of the historian to act as judge. Instead they point out that moral judgements cannot be avoided in the writing of history, as the nature of all knowledge is perspectival. A fact is only ever a fact within a specific framework of description. This not only allows for a plurality of true statements, it also means that the realm of facts cannot neatly be separated from the realm of values and hence morality. Factual statements already presuppose normative choices. They can be hidden (as is usually the case with historists) or they can be brought out in the open. Whichever is the case, knowledge is only possible within particular moral–normative–ideological 'horizons of expectation'.[17]

9.2 The promises of comparative history

Most historians have been drawn to comparative history because they want to obtain a better knowledge of their own society through comparison. Even where historians engaged in comparative history in order to understand other societies better, their interest was frequently motivated by a desire to learn from the experiences of others and to encourage adaptation of positive features of other societies. Having studied a problem or theme in different social contexts, they could draw up typologies of how different societies dealt with the same problem. They might also ask whether the same problem was present in different societies to a similar degree. Such an observation might have escaped the attention of historians who focused on one particular society. For example, the focus on national histories in Europe in the nineteenth and twentieth centuries hid from sight the fact that, beyond the boundaries of national states, something like a European experience in economic, social, political and cultural life was developing.[18] The comparative method also allows for the identification of problems not evident from observation of a single societal context. Thus only through comparison with other countries have historians asked why there was no significant Marxism in the USA and Britain.[19]

Many comparativists have argued that there is no better test in history than comparison. As far back as 1895 Emile Durkheim saw comparison as the equivalent to the natural scientist's experiment, in which variables were isolated and causal relationships proven.[20] Even if we are today more sceptical than Durkheim about the 'scientificity' of history,[21] comparison does allow us to differentiate good causal explanations from bad ones. It has, for example, been fashionable to argue that it was, above all, the economic slump of the early 1930s that caused the rise of Nazism in Germany. Yet, the slump was just as severe in the USA, which did not face a serious Fascist challenge. But the USA did have a republic, established in 1776, with a much revered constitution from 1787/8. Germany, by contrast, was a republic only after 1918/19 and its constitution was at best tolerated. The slump is therefore unlikely to have been the only explanation for why Hitler came to power. Take another example: Comparisons allow linkage of the strong reception of Marxism in European working-class parties with the degree of state repression that these parties faced. The more repression they faced, the more likely it was that they would turn to Marxism as an explanatory framework for social and political developments.[22] Comparisons are able to test existing models and explanations, but they are equally capable of developing new models. Miroslav Hroch, for instance, compared the emergence of small-nation nationalism in central Europe and developed a model that can now be tested by further comparison.[23]

Comparisons may draw attention to the fact that similar outcomes, such as strikes, sometimes have different causes and follow different patterns.[24] Inversely, comparisons may account for how similar developments produced different results. Thus, in a classic of the genre, Alexander Gerschenkron explored the impact of industrialization on different societies. He found that late industrializers such as Germany, in which a belated take-off was followed by a sprint, experienced significant social and political problems. Similarly, John Breuilly demonstrated the initial appearance of liberal labour movements in Britain and Germany, and went on to explain why in Britain a liberal labour movement succeeded, whereas in Germany it soon lost out to a rising socialist movement.[25] Overall, developments in one country can be explained better by comparing them with developments in others. No other historical method is so adept at testing, modifying and falsifying historical explanation than comparison. No other method demonstrates so effectively the range of developmental possibilities. It allows historians to gain a vantage point outside one particular regional or national history, and makes history a less provincial undertaking.

9.3 Problems and pitfalls in comparative history

If the promises of comparative history are manifold, so are the problems connected with its practice. Four preconditions need to be fulfilled before successful comparisons can be made. First, the historian needs close familiarity with more than one social context. Second, comparativists need to reflect on spatial and time constraints. Third, they have to consider theoretical and conceptual frameworks for their comparison. Finally, they have to have a feeling for linguistic pitfalls in transnational comparisons involving more than one language. In the following I would like to expand on those four potential stumbling blocks.

The first point might seem obvious, but it is nevertheless important, as it forces us to recognize the immense work involved in gaining knowledge of archival sources and secondary literature in two or more social contexts. There is a particular problem with archival sources: rarely do we find comparable sources that exist in different societal contexts. Even if we deal with secondary literature alone, we must be aware of different research traditions. Historians have asked different questions in different societies. Different questions might produce different views of developments, structures, organizations and mentalities. So a comparison of historiographies must precede any historical comparison. Take, for example, the coalfields of the Ruhr and South Wales, where historians face the problem of a much more diverse and richer historiographical tradition for the former. The impression of greater diversity of experiences in the Ruhr might, after all, be the result of different historiographical traditions rather than of actual lived experience.[26] We also need to keep in mind that familiarity with more than one social context often cannot be achieved by reading about it. It is necessary to experience a different social context at first hand, which involves extended stays in other regions or countries. Looking at two social contexts we might find similar events and institutions in one context, but their mere existence might not tell us very much about their functioning, their relevance and their wider meaning in society. We might, for example, find that most nation-states have myths of origin. But that tells us little about their impact or function in different nation-states at different times. Careful contextualization of any phenomenon to be compared is necessary.

Contexts are provided in time and space, which brings us to the second precondition for comparative history: we need to be clear about our geographical and time boundaries. We need to justify our choice of geographical comparisons. Geographical boundaries are somewhat arbitrary; they have been defined in different contexts for different purposes. Borders must be treated with extreme caution; they do not define 'natural' units of comparison. Look again at the Ruhr and South Wales. The former has been divided into three zones of industrial development that, in several respects, had very different histories. South Wales includes both the coalfield and the coastal strip with the important coal ports of Cardiff and Barry and cities such as Swansea and Newport. Even within the coalfield, the anthracite coalfield in the west differed significantly from the rest of the coalfield.[27] To presume that the geographical boundaries of the Ruhr and South Wales were fixed and self-evident is a dangerous illusion.

If geographical boundaries are rarely straightforward, we also need to attend to why the beginning and end points of our comparison are chosen. Time can be particularly tricky, as similar structures, institutions and ideas might develop at different times in different social contexts. Possible time-lags need to be taken into account in comparative studies. We must justify comparison of similar (synchronic comparisons) or different (diachronic comparisons) times for different social contexts. Synchronic comparisons are more usual, but not always the most appropriate. If labour movements, for example, are seen as reactions against rapid industrialization, it follows that since industrialization happens at different times in different social contexts, labour movements must be compared diachronically rather than synchronically.[28] The use of particular time caesuras and geographical boundaries influences the way in which particular events or structures are seen.

The next question to ask is: 'Which units of comparison do we choose for which end?' Theoretically, anything can be compared with anything. Everything depends on which theoretical and conceptual framework we choose for the comparison. This brings us to our third precondition. We must choose the cases that fit the question(s) we want to ask. The research question(s) might well be modified in light of our increasing knowledge about the units of comparison, but they form the basis of the theoretical and conceptual framework that structures all comparative work. Concepts are often interrelated. Comparisons that are concerned with establishing causal relationships between particular variables have to be aware of such dependencies. If, for example, we want to explain different degrees of nationalism in different countries, we cannot use notions such as enmity towards foreigners and willingness to defend one's country against foreign invasion as explanations, as they are related forms of nationalism. They can be used to indicate different degrees of nationalism but they do not explain the existence of nationalism.

Historical theories and concepts structure comparisons but are not free from agendas. Many comparative labour historians, for example, have assumed that the emergence and development of labour movements was tightly related to the industrialization process and to working-class formation.[29] In this they borrowed heavily from Marxist and Weberian theories of industrialization and the evolution of capitalism. The usefulness of such grand social theories for historical analyses has been questioned by postmodernism.[30] Postcolonial and subaltern perspectives have been wary of western developmental concepts and their imperialist ambitions.[31] Edward Said's analysis of 'orientalism' has been immensely influential in explicating the West's construction of an image of the other (in his case, the Orient) by defining the terms of the debate through the use of concepts such as development or modernization.[32] For comparative history, these interventions constitute a serious warning: concepts, terminologies and theories must be used self-reflexively. Comparative historians need to consider the origins and politics of their concepts. No longer must they pretend that concepts can be used within a value-free scientific paradigm. Yet, comparativists need not be disheartened by postcolonial scepticism about western concepts. As Jürgen Osterhammel has pointed out, many western concepts and terms had already been transferred to non-western contexts before European colonization from the sixteenth century onwards, and this makes it almost impossible to draw a neat line between western and non-western concepts and terminologies.[33] What is ultimately important is not the origins of concepts and terminologies but their usefulness and appropriateness for the research question(s) we want to pursue comparatively.

Some famous large-scale comparisons have paid inadequate attention to conceptual problems. One example is Samuel P. Huntington's book about the alleged clash of civilizations, which predicts major conflicts between the West and the Islamic world.[34] Both units of comparison are set up in such a way that mutually incompatible cultural entities were confronted and the many differences within each ignored. Huntington's and other similar studies ignore postcolonialism's concern with 'hybridity', 'alterity' and the differences of experiences in different social context at their own peril. Arguably grand comparisons based on universal social theories work best where they first ask about processes of diffusion, communication and exchange that took place between different cultures. Only in a second step can specific research questions be formulated and specific conceptual and terminological frameworks be developed, which then guide the comparative practice.[35]

Comparative historians should be suspicious about theories and concepts, yet every comparison requires specific research questions in conjunction with larger theoretical and conceptual frameworks.[36] If we do not approach the material with specific questions in mind, we will face the problem of excess information (this problem is obviously more serious the larger the comparison) and will run the risk of merely narrating parallel stories rather than comparing. Furthermore, the method of investigation has to fit the questions that are being asked. For example, a statistical analysis of strikes in a particular industry across various nations does not yet tell us anything about the radicalism of workers employed in that industry. Only a qualitative assessment of motivations for strikes, the workings of different systems of industrial relations and the potential variations in the meanings of strike activity will permit assessment of degrees of radicalism of the workers in question.[37]

All qualitative analysis is based on texts and language; and language is a veritable minefield for comparative historians. There is often little correspondence between the meanings of historical terms in different languages. Words that seem similar may carry different meanings in different languages. The word functionary, for example, in English carries with it a whole host of negative connotations involving bureaucracy, pig-headedness and stupid application of the rule book. In German, the very similar *Funktionär* did not carry such negativity – at least before 1933. Even key concepts and terms are difficult to translate and carry different meanings. Jörn Leonhard, for example, has argued persuasively that the genesis of the word 'liberal' in Germany is quite different from that of the word 'liberal' in Britain. In Germany, it was a French conception of the word and its meanings, carrying positive connotations, that was imported. In Britain, the word was conveyed from Spanish and carried markedly negative connotations.[38] Similar difficulties of translation arise with terms such as 'middle class' and 'gentry'. The English university was different in many respects from the German *Universität* in the nineteenth century, which in turn was something altogether different from the French *Université*. Concepts and terms often do not travel well from one society to another; linguistic and conceptual worlds are often different, and clarity concerning these differences is a very important precondition for any comparison.

Another problem with language concerns the need to find common terminology for related phenomena. Terms such as working-class parties, socialist parties and labour parties all carry different meanings, even within a single historiographical tradition let alone multiple ones. One needs to tread carefully in choosing, and comparative historians are usually well advised to start by exploring the meanings of terms and concepts in different social contexts.[39]

9.4 Cultural transfer studies and comparison

Comparative history is a difficult and labour-intensive affair. Despite its potential pitfalls, a growing number of scholars have been convinced of its merits. More recently, French and German scholars have questioned the value of comparative history, and prefer the history of cultural transfer. Since these debates have not been prominent in English-speaking countries, I will introduce the history of cultural transfers. I will then examine its challenge to comparative history.

Michael Werner's and Michel Espagne's studies of Franco-German cultural transfers have been particularly influential in generating interest in cultural transfer studies.[40] They break up the picture of homogenous and internally stable national cultures by demonstrating that these cultures depend on a dialectical process through which indigenous and foreign elements are selectively appropriated. Cultural transfer historians call into question national modes of argumentation, relativize national yardsticks and break up national explanatory frameworks. National identity appears as a process of cultural appropriation and mediation, and what is imagined as 'one's own' is bound up with what is conceived of, whether in negative or in positive terms, as 'the Other'. That 'Other' can often appear, at once and in equal measure, attractive and dangerous. As a rule, therefore, appropriation and rejection are two sides of the same coin. Research on cultural transfers thus contributes to exposing the absurdity of notions of the national character and of national cultures composed of national essences. In this way, the process of creation and evolution of plurally constituted national cultures is made visible. National memory comprises innumerable fragments of cultural assets, a goodly proportion of which are imported and adapted.

The reception of imports can take very different forms, ranging from total adoption through selective appropriation to conscious rejection. Cultural transfer research focuses on those groups most suited to the role of mediators – authors, publishers, journalists, cultural tourists, exiles, migrants, spies, translators, artists, musicians, diplomats, academics and teachers of foreign languages. These groups share the opportunity for contact with other national contexts and they settle, as it were, at the crossroads of two or more cultures. They are often able to develop or to exploit new and interconnected spheres of activity. But certain preconditions – such as linguistic competence, opportunities to travel or the availability of translations or of press reports – must be met for a cultural transfer to be rendered possible. Work on cultural transfers typically asks how newspapers and periodicals reported on the other country considered. Which books were imported or exported, and translated? What migratory movements were there? Which authorities, agencies and people knew something of the other country, and from what sources? What problems and misunderstandings arose in conveying terms and concepts from one language into the other? In what discursive and agential connections was the 'Other' used, and in pursuit of what interests? What preconditions had to be fulfilled for transfers to be completed successfully? How do selection, transportation and integration occur in different national contexts? Is an instance of integration effective over the long term, or is it temporary, its success contingent on particular circumstances?

Borders are of particular importance for research on transfers. On the one hand, a border can mean demarcation, putting off limits that which is defined as not belonging. On the other hand, however, borders can indicate preparedness for exchange and appropriation – a transmission belt of 'the other' on the way to its adoption as one's own. Border territories may variously be understood as sites of confrontation, intolerance and the collision of fundamentally incompatible 'national' values and normative horizons;[41] but they can also be terrains of an altogether different kind. Thus, delineations between 'national cultures' are blurred, for there is exchange between the mutually 'Other' and foreign.

Not every transfer is immediately recognizable as such. Once the foreign has been embedded in indigenous discursive and agential contexts, its foreign-ness tends to disappear. The archaeological capacities of the historian are required to bring the connections to light once more. The transmitters and the means of transmission must first be identified. Transmitters shared a transnational consciousness that permitted them to raise their sights above and beyond the merely national. This kind of international orientation was facilitated by personal contacts, lengthy stays abroad, and by opportunities for institutional cooperation. The cultural transfer approach, is for example, particularly promising for work on the history of scholarship, since scholarly communities evinced particularly pronounced processes of internationalization in the nineteenth and twentieth centuries.[42] However, cultural transfer studies are also being employed fruitfully in a wide range of other areas, e.g. in the history of social reform.[43]

There has been considerable tension between comparative historians and historians of cultural transfer. The former have sometimes drawn strict demarcation lines, arguing that cultural transfer studies are different from comparisons, in that they do not look for similarities and differences between social contexts.[44] The latter have replied that comparativists single out artificial units of comparison, which are then contrasted without any consideration of the transfers taking place between them. Comparisons thus construct homogenous entities, contrast them with one another, and thereby re-enforce homogeneous identities. Cultural transfer, by contrast, is about hybridity, breaking up constructed entities and undermining homogeneous identities.[45]

Historians of cultural transfer have indeed identified a potential weakness of comparative history, and comparativists have been unnecessarily exclusionary in their treatment of cultural transfer studies. Comparisons should take account of those mutual dependencies and relations, but there is no necessary methodological reason why they should not do so.[46] In fact the analysis of transfers would sharpen understanding of similarities and differences. Indeed, it was one of the founding fathers of comparative history, Marc Bloch, who pointed out that transfers need to be considered in any comparison.[47]

9.5 The practice of comparative history

Finally, I would like to demonstrate how comparative history works in practice. I have chosen an article written by Eric Hobsbawm and Joan Scott on 'political shoemakers'.[48] Like every good comparison, it starts with a specific question: 'Why did nineteenth-century shoemakers have such a reputation for political radicalism and for being worker-intellectuals?' In many national historiographies we find the observation that shoemakers were radicals, but rarely do we find any explanation for this phenomenon. In fact it is almost taken for granted. It is only by looking at shoemakers comparatively that, first of all, the universality of their radicalism comes into view. Hence only the comparative method allows the authors to identify the problem they subsequently seek to explain.

The spatial breadth of the argument is truly breathtaking. Although British, French and German shoemakers are arguably at the core of the authors' argument, there are references to at least a dozen other European countries and a range of non-European ones, including Australia, Argentina, Brazil, India and Japan. We are clearly not dealing with a totalizing comparison here. Rather, the article chooses to concentrate on a very specific theme or aspect, i.e. explaining the political radicalism of shoemakers. It comes very close to a universalizing comparison in that it is not concerned with specific national characteristics of shoemakers but looks for evidence from shoemakers around the world to explain what it identifies as a universal phenomenon, i.e. the political radicalization of shoemakers and their prominence among worker-intellectuals.

While the comparison aspires to geographical universality, its chronological framework is specific. Three time zones are evoked. First, a time before the Industrial Revolution – the golden age for the radical shoemaker; in this period they established their credentials as radical spokespersons for the people. Second, the article explores the fortunes of craft radicalism during the Industrial Revolution. Finally, it asks why the once-radical shoemakers were less prominent among the mass socialist movements of the more advanced capitalist age. Although the article includes references to dates for these distinct time periods, they are not too specific, and arguably they cannot be too specific, for the Industrial Revolution happened at different times for different social contexts. The article has to compare diachronically as well as synchronically, and this makes the specific dating of the three time zones impossible.

Hobsbawm and Scott's theoretical framework is not spelt out, but the reader soon encounters assumptions about the development of capitalism derived from a broadly Marxist understanding of history. Capitalism impacts on the organization of work, which in turn has repercussions for cultural expressions – in this case the artisanal culture of shoemakers. This materialist conception of history assumes that work forms the basis of people's social existence and out of it grows a particular culture. Hobsbawm and Scott carefully avoid the determinist implications of Marxist theory. They argue that shoemaker radicalism cannot be seen exclusively in terms of a response to early industrial capitalism, for it precedes the Industrial Revolution. Nevertheless, their basic theoretical framework remains historical materialism. Both authors, as theoretically aware Marxists, had also been influenced by Gramscian notions of the development of 'organic intellectuals' – intellectuals who emerge from the working class. Hobsbawm and Scott's shoemakers are the very epitome of organic intellectuals.

The authors' method of investigation is varied and always fits the questions that are being asked. We have much qualitative analysis of literature, poems, autobiography, social and political commentary, and dictionaries. Where appropriate, they resort to quantitative analysis – for example, to establish that cobblers often could not live by shoemaking and shoe-repairing alone, or to document the vast size of the shoemaking trade in the nineteenth century, or to demonstrate the numbers of shoemakers among socialist deputies in the German Reichstag.

Hobsbawm and Scott's comparison is noteworthy for its careful treatment of language and concepts. The key analytical concept of radicalism is not taken for granted, but carefully examined for its contextually varied meanings. The authors carefully demonstrate that words that signify the profession of shoemakers in different languages, such as 'cobbler', 'cordonnier' and 'Schuster', actually are comparable and mean the same thing. They point out that the proverb 'Shoemaker stick to your last' exists in a great variety of languages, and suggest that this indicates shoemakers' readiness to be involved in intellectual debates more usually perceived as the preserve of the educated classes.

Comparisons are about establishing similarities and differences, and this is clearly what this article does. It compares shoemakers' militancy with that of other artisanal groups. It discusses carpenters, tailors, construction workers, printers, metalworkers and many other craft groups, always delineating what they had in common with shoemakers and what made shoemakers distinctive. What was it about the shoemakers' trade that fostered their strong intellectual interests? The answers, mostly related to the world of work, are complex and varied, but they are laid out before the reader with wonderful clarity and a superb command of the literature on the worlds of artisans in very different social contexts. The intention of the comparison is analytical: the authors analyse the shoemakers' socialization, their values, institutions, work practices and mentalities. The article is an excellent example of how even the most wide-ranging comparison can avoid reductionism and improve our understanding of artisanal culture, which transcended diverse social contexts. If we are specialists on one particular social context, say a particular country such as Britain, we learn about artisans in other countries and through this we learn to rethink our knowledge of British artisans.

By raising the problem of universal artisan cultures, Hobsbawm and Scott make it possible for other authors to follow up their comparison with a more detailed typology of artisan radicalism. Sure enough, their article was the inspiration for a host of articles and monographs that examined artisanal cultures as defences of their independence and expression against an encroaching capitalist system.[49] The article is thus a pioneer and at the same time a model for subsequent comparisons of artisanal cultures from the pre-industrial to the industrial ages.

A masterpiece of comparative historical investigation, this article is also not blind to the importance of cultural transfers. It discusses the English conviction that French shoemakers were instrumental in the French Revolution of 1789. English shoemakers received and appropriated an image of the 'Other' in order to underline their own love of liberty. The authors specifically discuss the importance of travel for the socialization of shoemakers. During their journeymen days, shoemakers would visit different regions and countries, and familiarize themselves with diverse experiences in a variety of contexts. As transmitters of different social contexts they were able to transplant their own politicization (as journeymen) wherever they eventually settled. In the context of changes brought about by agricultural capitalism, shoemakers often voiced discontent among the rural population. They could do this only because they had the intellectual means to appropriate, adapt and mediate experiences from different contexts. Few comparative historians can aspire to the heights reached by Hobsbawm and Scott. Yet their article serves as a reminder of the power of comparative history and an enduring inspiration to future generations of comparative historians.

Guide to further reading

A.A. van den Braembussche, 'Historical Explanation and Comparative Method: Towards a Theory of the History of Society', *History and Theory* 28 (1989), pp. 2–24.

John Breuilly, 'Introduction: Making Comparisons in History', in Breuilly, *Labour and Liberalism in Nineteenth-Century Europe: Essays in Comparative History* (Manchester, 1992).

George Frederickson, 'From Exceptionalism to Variability: Recent Developments in Cross-National Comparative History', *The Journal of American History* 82 (1995), pp. 587–604.

Heinz-Gerhard Haupt, 'Comparative History', in Neil J. Smelser and Paul B. Baltes (eds), *International Encyclopedia of the Social and Behavioural Sciences* (Amsterdam, 2001), pp. 2397–403.

Jürgen Kocka, 'Asymmetrical Historical Comparison: The Case of the German "Sonderweg"', *History and Theory* 38 (1999), pp. 40–50.

Chris Lorenz, 'Comparative Historiography: Problems and Perspectives', *History and Theory* 38 (1999), pp. 25–39.

Charles Ragin, *The Comparative Method: Moving Beyond Quantitative and Qualitative Strategies* (Berkeley, 1987).

Jörn Rüsen, 'Some Theoretical Approaches to Intercultural Comparative Historiography', *History and Theory* 35 (1996), pp. 5–22.

W.H. Sewell, 'Marc Bloch and the Logic of Comparative History', *History and Theory* 6 (1967), pp. 208–18.

Theda Skocpol and Margaret Somers, 'The Uses of Comparative History', *Comparative Studies in Society and History* 22 (1978), pp. 174–97.

Notes

1   John Stuart Mill, *Philosophy of Scientific Method* (New York, 1950), pp. 211–33.
2   See Hartmut Kaelble, 'Vergleichende Sozialgeschichte im 19. und 20. Jahrhundert. Forschungen europäischer Historiker', *Jahrbuch für Wirtschaftsgeschichte* Part 1 (1993), pp. 173–200, for an attempt to provide a survey of the rise of comparative history in Europe from around 1980.
3   Roland Axtman, 'Society, Globalization and the Comparative Method', *History of the Human Sciences* 6 (1993), pp. 53–74.
4   Geoffrey Crossick, 'And What Should They Know of England? Die vergleichende Geschichtsschreibung im heutigen Großbritannien', in Heinz-Gerhard Haupt and Jürgen Kocka (eds), *Geschichte und Vergleich. Ansätze und Ergebnisse international vergleichender Geschichtsschreibung* (Frankfurt am Main, 1996), pp. 61–76.
5   Neil Evans, 'Debate: British History: Past, Present – and Future?', *Past and Present* 119 (1988), pp. 194–203.
6   An early marker was C. Vann Woodward, *The Comparative Approach to American History* (1968; reprinted Oxford, 1997). Studies of slavery, race relations and the frontier have been transformed by comparisons. See, for example, Carl N. Degler, *Neither Black nor White. Slavery and Race Relations in Brazil and the United States* (New York, 1971). On frontier history see Howard Lamar and Leonard Thompson (eds), *The Frontier in History: North America and Southern Africa Compared* (New Haven, 1981).
7   Thomas Welskopp, 'Stolpersteine auf dem Königsweg. Methodenkritische Anmerkungen zum internationalen Vergleich in der Gesellschaftsgeschichte', *Archiv für Sozialgeschichte* 35 (1995), pp. 339–67, esp. pp. 342f.

8 On the close relationship between nationalism and historiography, see Stefan Berger, Mark Donovan and Kevin Passmore (eds), *Writing National Histories. Western Europe Since 1800* (London, 1999).

9 Sidney Pollard, 'Industrialization and the European Economy', *Economic History Review* 26 (1973), pp. 636–48. See also Pollard, *Peaceful Conquests. The Industrialisation of Europe 1760–1970* (Oxford, 1981). On the long tradition of comparative economic history see Rondo Cameron, 'Comparative Economic History', *Research in Economic History*, Supplement 1 (1977), pp. 287–305.

10 On the theory and practice of comparative transcultural history, see Jürgen Osterhammel, *Geschichtswissenschaft jenseits des Nationalstaats. Studien zu Beziehungsgeschichte und Zivilisationsvergleich* (Göttingen, 2001).

11 On Weber see Helmut Schmidt-Glintzer, 'The Economic Ethic of World Religions', in Hartmut Lehmann and Günther Roth (eds), *Weber's 'Protestant Ethic': Origins, Evidence, Contexts* (Cambridge, 1993), pp. 347–55.

12 Jack Goody, *The Oriental, the Ancient and the Primitive. Systems of Marriage and the Family in Pre-Industrial Societies of Eurasia* (Cambridge, 1990).

13 Charles Tilly, *Big Structures, Large Processes, Huge Comparisons* (New York, 1985), pp. 81–143.

14 Liah Greenfeld, *Nationalism: Five Roads to Modernity* (Cambridge, MA, 1992).

15 Barrington Moore, *Social Origins of Dictatorship and Democracy. Lord and Peasant in the Making of the Modern World* (Boston, 1966).

16 Hartmut Kaelble, *Der historische Vergleich. Eine Einführung zum 19. und 20. Jahrhundert* (Frankfurt/Main, 1999), pp. 48–92.

17 There is insufficient space here to explicate the complex relationship between facts/science and values/morals. For a recent up-to-date and succinct introduction to these issues see Chris Lorenz, *Konstruktion der Vergangenheit. Eine Einführung in die Geschichtstheorie* (Cologne, 1997), especially pp. 400–14, 422–36; Lorenz, 'The View from Anywhere (or: On Facts, Fiction, Football and an Indian). Some Reflections on the (Im)Possibility of the Writing of History', in Jan Denolf and Barbara Simons (eds), *(Re)Constructing the Past* (Brussels, 2000), pp. 411–41; Lorenz, 'Historical Knowledge and Historical Reality: A Plea for "Internal Realism"', *History and Theory* 33 (1994), pp. 297–327. An English-language version of Lorenz's seminal book is currently being prepared by Princeton University Press.

18 Hartmut Kaelble, 'Social History of European Integration', in Clemens Wurm (ed.), *Western Europe and Germany. The Beginnings of European Integration 1945–1960* (Oxford, 1995), pp. 219–47.

19 Werner Sombart, *Why is There No Socialism in the United States?*

(London, 1976; first published in German in 1906) and Ross McKibbin, 'Why was There no Marxism in Great Britain?', *English Historical Review* 99 (1984), pp. 297–331.

20 Emile Durkheim, *The Rules of Sociological Method and Selected Texts on Sociology and its Method* (London, 1982 [1895]).

21 See Heiko Feldner's contribution to this volume (Chapter 1).

22 Stefan Berger, 'European Labour Movements and the European Working Class in Comparative Perspective', in Berger and David Broughton (eds), *The Force of Labour* (Oxford, 1995), pp. 245–62.

23 Miroslav Hroch, *Social Preconditions of National Revival in Europe: A Comparative Analysis of the Social Composition of Patriotic Groups among the Smaller European Nations* (Cambridge, 1985).

24 Friedrich Boll, 'Changing Forms of Labour Conflict: Secular Development or Strike Waves', in H.L. Haimson and Charles Tilly (eds), *Strikes, Wars and Revolutions in an International Perspective* (Cambridge, 1989).

25 John Breuilly, *Labour and Liberalism in Nineteenth-Century Europe: Essays in Comparative History* (Manchester, 1992), Chapters 6 and 7.

26 Stefan Berger and Neil Evans, 'Two Faces of King Coal: The Impact of Historiographical Traditions in the Ruhr and South Wales on Comparative History', in Stefan Berger, Andy Croll and Norman LaPorte (eds), *Towards a Comparative History of Coalfield Societies* (London, 2004).

27 Stefan Berger, 'Working-Class Culture and the Labour Movement in the South Wales and the Ruhr Coalfields, 1850–2000: a Comparison', *Llafur. Journal of Welsh Labour History* 8(2) (2001), pp. 5–40, esp. p. 7.

28 This point was first made by Lujo Brentano, 'Die englische Chartistenbewegung', *Preußische Jahrbücher* 33 (1874), pp. 431–47 and 531–50. On Brentano, see also Christiane Eisenberg, 'The Comparative View in Labour History: Old and New Interpretations of the English and German Labour Movements before 1914', *International Review of Social History* 34 (1989), pp. 411f.

29 One example among many is Ira Katznelson and Aristide R. Zolberg (eds), *Working-Class Formation: Nineteenth Century Patterns in Western Europe and the United States* (Princeton, 1986).

30 See Chapter 7. Compare also Andy Croll, 'The Impact of Postmodernism on Modern British Social History', in Stefan Berger (ed.), *Labour and Social History in the United Kingdom: Historiographical Reviews and Agendas 1990 to the Present*, special edition of the *Mitteilungsblatt des Instituts für soziale Bewegungen* 28 (2002), pp. 137–52.

31 Gregory Castle, *Postcolonial Discourses. An Anthology* (Oxford, 2001).

32 Edward Said, *Orientalism* (London, 1978)

33 Osterhammel, *Geschichtswissenschaft*, p. 72.

34 Samuel P. Huntington, *The Clash of Civilisations and the Remaking of World Order* (New York, 1996).

35 A prime example of such universal history is the work of William H. McNeill.

Among his many publications see, for example, *Keeping Together in Time. Dance and Drill in Human History* (Cambridge, MA, 1996).

36 Edgar Kiser and Michael Hechter, 'The Role of General Theory in Comparative-Historical Sociology', *American Journal of Sociology* 97 (1991), pp. 1–30.

37 An excellent example of this type of comparison is provided by Dick Geary, 'The Myth of the Radical Miner', in Berger, Croll and LaPorte (eds), *Towards*.

38 Jörn Leonhard, '"An Odious but Intelligible Phrase . . .". "Liberal" im politischen Diskurs Deutschlands und Englands bis 1830/32', *Jahrbuch zur Liberalismus-Forschung* 8 (1996), pp. 11–41.

39 Ian Hampsher-Monk, Karin Tilmans and Frank van Vree (eds), *History of Concepts: Comparative Perspectives* (Amsterdam, 1999) and Melvin Richter, '"Begriffsgeschichte" and the History of Ideas', *Journal of the History of Ideas* 48 (1987), pp. 247–63.

40 Michel Espagne and Michael Werner, *Transferts. Les Relations Interculturelles dans L'Espace Franco-Allemand* (Paris, 1988).

41 There are many studies on border territories. See, for example, Peter Schöttler, 'Le Rhin Comme Enjeu Historiographique dans l'Entre-Deux-Guerres. Vers une Histoire des Mentalités Frontalières', *Genèses* 14 (1994) pp. 63–82 and Sharif Gemie, 'France and the Val d'Aran: Politics and Nationhood on the Pyrenean Border, 1800–25', *European History Quarterly* 28 (1998), pp. 311–43.

42 On processes of cultural transfer between Britain and Germany in historical scholarship see Peter Wende and Benedikt Stuchtey (eds), *British and German Historiography 1750–1950. Traditions, Perceptions and Transfers* (Oxford, 2000) and Stefan Berger, Peter Lambert and Peter Schumann (eds), *Historikerdialoge. Geschichte, Mythos und Gedächtnis im deutsch-britischen kulturellen Austausch 1750–2000* (Göttingen, 2003).

43 A. Mitchell, *The Divided Path. The German Influence on Social Reform in France after 1870* (Chapel Hill, 1991); E.P. Hennock, British Social Reform and German Precedents. *The Case of Social Insurance, 1880–1914* (Oxford, 1987); Daniel T. Rodgers, *Atlantic Crossings. Social Politics in a Progressive Age* (Cambridge, MA, 1998).

44 Heinz-Gerhard Haupt and Jürgen Kocka, 'Historischer Vergleich: Methoden, Aufgaben, Probleme. Eine Einleitung', in Haupt and Kocka (eds), *Geschichte und Vergleich*, p. 11.

45 Michel Espagne, 'Sur les limites du comparatisme en histoire culturelle', *Genèse* 17 (1994), pp. 112–21.

46 Johannes Paulmann, 'Internationaler Vergleich und interkultureller Transfer. Zwei Forschungsansätze zur europäischen Geschichte des 18. bis 20. Jahrhunderts', *Historische Zeitschrift* 267(3) (1998), pp. 649–85 and Matthias Middell, 'Kulturtransfer und historische Komparatistik – Thesen zu ihrem Verhältnis', *Comparativ* 10(1) (2000), pp. 7–41.

47 Marc Bloch, 'Toward a Comparative History of European Societies', in Jelle C. Riemersma and Frederic C. Lane (eds), *Enterprise and Secular Change: Readings in Economic History* (London, 1953). Bloch's article was originally published in *Revue de synthèse historique* in 1928. An attempt to integrate cultural transfer and comparative approaches can be found in Fernand Braudel's masterpiece about the Ottoman and Hapsburg Empires: *The Mediterranean and the Mediterranean World in the Age of Philip II*, 2 vols (London, 1972 [1966]).

48 Eric Hobsbawm and Joan W. Scott, 'Political Shoemakers', in *Past and Present* 89 (1980), reprinted in Eric Hobsbawm, *Worlds of Labour* (London, 1984), pp. 103–30.

49 An impressive attempt to synthesize the vast literature on artisans in Europe can be found in James R. Farr, *Artisans in Europe 1300–1914* (Cambridge, 2000).

Part 3

10

Political history

Jon Lawrence

It would be an exaggeration to say that there are as many conceptions of 'political history' as there are political historians – but only just. Certainly, historians of politics disagree not just about the usual issues of theory and method, but also, more fundamentally, about what their basic subject matter should be. For some, 'true politics' is a rarefied thing – the preserve of policy-makers and administrators at the heart of government, for others it is the stuff of everyday life – the driving force behind both individual and collective aspirations in a mass society. Moreover, within both traditions there are many conflicting notions of how politics should be studied, and how (or indeed whether) the worlds of state policy and mass politics should be combined.

To understand why 'political history' represents such a fractured field of intellectual enquiry we must first examine its development as a subject during the nineteenth and twentieth centuries. For the most part I will tell this story through the prism of British historiography, partly because this is the field I know best, but also because political history has long enjoyed an unusually privileged position within British academe. At the end of the nineteenth century few historians in any country would have dissented from Sir John Seeley's famous borrowed aphorism that 'history is past politics, and politics present history' (*The Growth of British Policy*, 1895), and most would have assumed that 'politics' here meant statecraft and its impact on the long-term development of constitutional government. Indeed, throughout the nineteenth century there had been a strong tendency across Europe to understand present politics through a historical framework, and to assume that history followed a linear and progressive course. Famously true of Marx, following as he did in the Hegelian tradition of seeing history as the necessary unfolding of the inner logic that shapes human destiny, this 'teleological' approach (i.e. one assuming a known ultimate purpose) was also characteristic of nineteenth-century liberal thinking. Profoundly influenced by the legacy of the Scottish Enlightenment and eighteenth-century Whig constitutionalism, nineteenth-century liberals placed the evolution, and gradual perfection, of political institutions at the heart of their understanding of history. Nowhere was the influence of this thinking stronger than in Britain, where the Whig tradition of gradual political reform had its roots, and where political history written in the Whig tradition in consequence assumed an especially triumphalist tone. The model for such work was set by Thomas Macaulay's brilliant multi-volume *History of England* (1848–61), and was continued in the work of men such as W.E.H. Lecky and George Otto Trevelyan.

However, the influence of Whig constitutionalism was already in decline before the First World War. Historians had begun to turn their backs on grand narrative in favour of the meticulous archival work long championed in Germany by historians such as Leopold von Ranke, while political scientists passed increasingly harsh judgements about the ability of political systems to deliver rational government as democratic pressures grew. But if liberal optimism was fading in the Edwardian era, it was all but destroyed by the traumas of war and post-war transition between 1914 and the early 1920s. Even in Britain, 'Whig history' had become an object of ridicule long before the publication of Herbert Butterfield's scathing critique of its English, Protestant prejudices in *The Whig Interpretation of History* (1931). By the time Butterfield had pronounced the death of Whig history, a new school of political history was emerging in Britain – a school that focused not on the evolution of political systems, and the grand ideals they were supposed to embody, but rather on how individuals manoeuvred for advantage within more or less stable political systems. The key figure here was Lewis Namier, whose *Structure of Politics at the Accession of George III* (1929) essentially founded a new school of political history that ultimately found institutional expression in the official 'History of Parliament' project. Namier's method focused on reconstructing the motivations, not just of the 'great men' of politics, but of all the political actors that made up the system of their day. This exercise in 'collective biography' (often termed 'prosopography') tended to downplay ideology and belief as motivating factors in politics, and to stress instead the preeminent influence of psychological, personal and material factors. Strongly influenced by Freudian psychoanalytic thinking, Namier placed the individual at the centre of his historical analysis, and insisted that historians should explore the hidden, unconscious and often dark forces that frequently determined individual action. In this respect the charge that his method called on historians to 'psychoanalyse the dead' was not misplaced, though it was undoubtedly only one element to the intensive, biographical approach he advocated.[1]

10.1 High politics and the history of ideas

The modern 'high political' approach to political history has its roots in this shift from grand constitutional narratives to the micro-level analysis of political conflict within the state. However, the advocates of the 'high politics' approach, such as Maurice Cowling and Michael Bentley, generally insist that historians should focus only on 'the politicians that mattered', as Cowling described them in his 1971 study *The Impact of Labour*. In this work Cowling explained that he would treat 'back-benchers and party opinion' as off-stage 'malignant or beneficent forces . . . with unknown natures and unpredictable wills'.[2] Advocates of the 'high political' approach also show a much greater scepticism towards the virtues of biography as a key to understanding political action. Emphasis is placed less on individual psychology than on 'situational necessity' – on the imperatives generated by mutual suspicion and rivalry within the closed world of a small political elite. According to Cowling, after the First World War '[t]he political system consisted of fifty or sixty politicians in conscious tension with one another whose accepted authority constituted political leadership'.[3] In essence, 'high political' historians argue that politics should be understood as a self-contained game, with its own elaborate and well understood rules. Politicians play to win, and they adopt policy initiatives and rhetorical strategies as gambits to this end – fully aware that their rivals are playing for the same high stakes. In this sense the 'high political' approach represents one of the most thorough applications of social science 'game theory' in the historical field – though this pedigree is no more trumpeted than is the Namierite legacy.

In its most cynical form the 'high politics' approach assumes that politicians play only to win, and that consequently belief and principle play little part in the policy initiatives and rhetorical strategies they adopt. However, this bastardized version of the method is rarely adopted by those most directly influenced by Cowling and his Cambridge associates. Cowling himself tends to take the agnostic line that one can only penetrate so far into a politician's thought world, and that one can therefore never know whether he or she really *believed* what they said; one can merely reconstruct the interconnections between public utterances and actions. But 'high political' historians have always placed a strong emphasis on ideas, and in recent years many have stressed that politicians are motivated first and foremost by belief. For instance, in *British Politics and the Great War* (1992), John Turner argues that supporters of Lloyd George's wartime coalition were united by the belief that party rivalries must be suspended in the national interest – calculations of party advantage, he insists, were very definitely secondary. Similarly, in his recent study *Stanley Baldwin: Conservative Leadership and National Values* (1999), Philip Williamson explores the underlying values and beliefs that shaped both his subject's approach to politics and the ends he sought to pursue when playing the 'party game'. In *Lord Salisbury's World: Conservative Environments in Late-Victorian Britain* (2001), Michael Bentley does something similar for Salisbury a generation earlier. Both works deliberately eschew the narrative structure adopted in conventional political biographies in favour of a thematic approach that is much better suited to the exploration of a mind in the context of its times.

All these works appear to reflect a loosening of the narrow, self-limiting ordinances that shaped many early works in the 'high political' tradition. For instance, Turner is happy to explore the impact of constituency politics and intricacies of electoral sociology alongside his blow-by-blow account of intrigues within the political elite, while the studies by Williamson and Bentley are indicative of a growing openness to intellectual history among practitioners of the 'high political' approach (though as the author of *The Liberal Mind, 1914–1929* (1977) it must be acknowledged that Bentley has always been interested in the relationship between thought and political action).[4] Such works retain a central emphasis on 'situation' – on reconstructing the context within which elite politicians operated – but they also register developments in other fields of political history writing, notably the history of ideas and the history of popular politics. It is to these two fields that we must now turn.

There can be little doubt that much of the best political history writing of the last few decades has been informed by an interest in the history of ideas, and, in consequence, by a determination to make sense of the intellectual context in which political struggles were played out. Many historians approaching politics in this way have been influenced, more or less explicitly, by the approach to intellectual history championed by J.G.A. Pocock, Quentin Skinner and J.W. Burrow, with its emphasis on reconstructing the political discourse of an epoch through the systematic analysis of speech acts (i.e. texts and utterances anchored in their discursive and social context). It is an approach that allows the historical focus to shift away from the world and the actions of elite politicians by focusing on the wider debates that shaped their political world, and defined what politics itself was thought to be about at any given moment. Over the past 20 years, the historiography of nineteenth-century Britain in particular has been greatly enriched by studies of this kind. For instance, in *The Age of Atonement* (1988), Boyd Hilton traces the influence of Evangelical Christianity on the understanding of social and economic change in early nineteenth-century Britain, and demonstrates its crucial role in shaping the politics of liberal Tories from Pitt, through Peel, to Gladstone. Similarly, in *Democracy and Religion: Gladstone and the Liberal Party* (1986), Jon Parry emphasizes the essentially religious dimension of mid-Victorian political discourse and demonstrates that religious differences within the Liberal Party, both at Westminster and in the country, raised fundamental questions about the meaning of 'Liberalism', as well as culminating in the electoral debacle of 1874. Finally, in *The Decline of British Radicalism* (1995) Miles Taylor charts the growing Radical disillusionment with purely parliamentary conceptions of sovereignty from the later 1850s, and shows how this helped create the political space for a new, constituency-based popular Liberalism in the 1860s. Each is offering much more than a study in the history of ideas – these are studies acutely aware of the need to understand ideas within their social and political context, especially the shifting context of practical political conflict – but their sophisticated reconstruction of the ideas that informed political practice and defined what was, and was not, 'politics' remains a particular virtue. In effect they are broadening the method of the 'high political' tradition, reconstructing the world of public politics as a whole in order better to understand the forces that help to define the 'situational necessities' confronting 'the politicians who really mattered'.

Case study: protection and politics

Unlike many of the works discussed above, Anna Gambles' *Protection and Politics: Conservative Economic Discourse, 1815–1852* (Woodbridge, 1999) is concerned almost solely with reconstructing the world of public political debate – hence its choice as a case study here. Rejecting what she sees as the residual 'Whiggism' of recent British political and intellectual history, Gambles sets out to rehabilitate early nineteenth-century Tory protectionism as a vigorous and coherent alternative to Free Trade economics, both before and after the Repeal of the Corn Laws in 1846. In essence, she argues that historical hindsight, the knowledge that free trade rather than protectionism emerged as the dominant political creed of Victorian Britain, has led historians to play down the significance of Tory protectionism, to misunderstand its critique of liberal economics, and to dismiss its advocates as little more than an early nineteenth-century 'stupid party', unable to grasp the inevitability of 'progress'. Moreover, the logic of her position is that if we fail to understand one side of a political debate, then we fail to understand the debate itself, and hence the political context that helped inform the actions of leading politicians. Gambles' technique is to reconstruct the parameters of public political debate from a range of sources including not only parliamentary debates and politicians' speeches, but also the periodical press and pamphlet literature. Gambles insists that these latter sources, far from being peripheral to the world of 'real politics' at Westminster, represented an active and influential component of the early nineteenth-century political world. From this range of sources Gambles seeks to reconstruct public discourse on political economy as it unfolded for contemporaries – what she terms 'inhabiting contemporary intellectual debate' (*Protection and Politics*, p. 191). In doing so she demonstrates that economic arguments for protection should not be studied in isolation, but should rather be understood as part of a broader, interlocking Tory political and social world-view in the first half of the nineteenth century. Protection was championed, she argues, not primarily from narrow economic self-interest, nor from instinctual fear of the unknown, but because most Tories believed that it alone could preserve the social and economic stability upon which rested the twin pillars of Britain's greatness: her constitution and her worldwide empire. In consequence, Tory protectionists favoured the development of more secure domestic and colonial markets, fearing the inherent uncertainties of relying on free trade in foreign markets.

So far so good, but there are also limitations imposed by Gambles' methodology. By sticking much more strictly to a 'history of ideas' approach than Hilton, Parry or Taylor, Gambles finds it difficult to move beyond the reconstruction of the public discourse on protectionism. In contrast to Taylor, who combines a broad range of historical techniques to chart the rise and fall of parliamentary radicalism as a political strategy between 1832 and 1860, Gambles is able to tell us relatively little about the ultimate failure of Tory protectionism during broadly the same era. The reader remains unclear why protectionist claims that free trade would mean 'cheap labour' as well as 'cheap bread' failed to rally support among urban workers. True, Gambles shows that many protectionists saw free trade as a symptom of the distorted polity created by the Reform Act of 1832, and that they denounced the Repeal of the Corn Laws as another step on the nation's inexorable descent to democracy and revolution, but one is left to infer that such positions may have undermined their ability to construct a broad-based coalition in opposition to free trade. Similarly, because the study shuns the prosopographical techniques associated with the 'high political' school by focusing only on politicians' *public* utterances, it can tell us little about the factors that shaped Tory leaders' engagement with (and disengagement from) protectionism as a parliamentary and electoral strategy during this period. In short, Gambles' approach can offer a useful archaeology of the protectionist ideas circulating in public discourse, but it cannot tell us much about the reception of those ideas by different factions of the public (including that elite public, the 'politicians who really mattered'). Thus, while the book undoubtedly helps us to understand better both the depth of the ideological cleavage wrought by Repeal in 1846, and the intellectual antecedents of late nineteenth-century radical conservatism, its tight focus on the reconstruction of public discourse ultimately weakens its explanatory power.

10.2 Elections and popular politics

We must turn next to forms of political history that place greater emphasis on electoral politics and popular political culture (itself a highly contested term). Again, such history takes many forms and is often difficult to categorize. In this analysis I propose to examine two main traditions – the constituency politics tradition and the 'history from below' or social history tradition, mindful that the borderlands between the two traditions are not always as clear-cut as this typology might suggest. The constituency politics tradition has always been strongly influenced by political science methods, especially during the 1950s and 1960s when 'electoral sociology' – the sociological analysis of election data – was at the height of its influence among political historians.

During this period, modern British political history was largely rewritten through the frame of post-war pluralist/functionalist sociology and political science, with its emphasis on political parties and representative institutions as agencies for channelling and neutralizing social conflict.[5] Histories written under the influence of electoral sociology sought to analyse how political parties responded to the underlying processes of social change and class formation in the nineteenth and early twentieth centuries. For the most part they played down the impact of parties on these processes of change, and assumed that the key to understanding the course of political history lay in politicians' greater or lesser success in *adapting* to the social forces changing their world. Thus Hanham analysed how Liberal and Conservative politicians competed to mould the allegiance of the new urban voters created by the 1867 Reform Act (*Elections and Party Management*, 1959), James Cornford analysed how late nineteenth-century forces of suburbanization created the social basis for 'villa Toryism' ('Transformation of Conservatism', *Victorian Studies*, 1963), while Peter Clarke analysed how Liberals responded to this challenge by constructing a new, non-socialist programme of state 'welfare' that could appeal to working-class electors (*Lancashire and the New Liberalism*, 1971, discussed below). Today the linearity of these arguments – with their emphasis on supposedly inexorable forces of 'modernization' such as the rise of class, the decline of religion and the 'nationalization' of politics – has lost favour, partly thanks to changing intellectual fashions, but also because we now see the political realities of the post-Second World War era as a unique historical moment, rather than as the natural end point for democratic political development. It now seems curious than John Vincent should feel the need to detract from his brilliant analysis of the ideas and aspirations that sustained mid-Victorian popular Liberalism by presenting this as a pre-industrial form of 'class struggle' (according to Vincent, vertically integrated 'operational collectivities' fought over the structure of political and religious authority, but not over the distribution of things – supposedly the hallmark of 'modern', class-based politics).[6] Interestingly, we find the same emphasis on a shift from pre-modern ('status') politics to modern (class) politics in perhaps the most influential study stamped by the imprint of 'electoral sociology': Peter Clarke's *Lancashire and the New Liberalism* – our second case study.

Case study: *Lancashire and the New Liberalism*

It may seem odd to choose a work that is more than thirty years old as a case study of the constituency politics/electoral sociology tradition, but Peter Clarke's *Lancashire and the New Liberalism* (Cambridge, 1971; republished 1993) represents both the apotheosis of this approach to political history, and, like any truly great history, also the transcendence of the tradition within which it was conceived. As we have seen, it would be easy to dismiss the work as hopelessly dated since it starts from a set of assumptions about 'modernization' and the necessary transition from communal, status-based politics to materialist, class-based politics, which are now widely questioned (pp. 4–5, 393–407).[7] Indeed, historical fashions have changed so markedly that one recent self-consciously revisionist study argues that traditional religious and ethnic identities remained the dominant influence on Lancashire politics until at least the Second World War. In this analysis, Labour only prospered where it could tap into these older forms of political identity, rather than any supposed 'class-based' loyalties (Trevor Griffith, *Lancashire Working Classes*, 2001). But if Clarke overstates the rise of class-based forms of political identity, and therefore tends to overstate the impact of 'New Liberalism' on both voter allegiance and party ethos, there remains much to learn from this remarkably rich study. Perhaps its greatest strength is its determination to integrate the multiple dimensions of political history within a single study. The worlds of political ideas, elite strategies and popular politics are not just present, they are systematically combined throughout the book. Thus we see how new ideas about Liberalism as a movement for social reform coalesced during the 1890s, and how they won adherents among prominent politicians after the Boer War. We see how the growing band of professional politicians made it easier for champions of the new ideology to gain a foothold in constituencies, and how new techniques of communication (posters, mass leafleting, etc.) made it easier for them to proselytize the new politics. In outlining these arguments Clarke offers subtle readings of street politics and the role of the candidate in Edwardian electoral politics, which remain unsurpassed. Of course there are problems – the decline of localism is overdrawn, as is the class appeal of New Liberal social legislation, but there remains something compelling about Clarke's argument that politicians played an active part in the shift to a more class-centred politics in Britain. For this, it should be stressed, is no crudely reductionist analysis – Clarke's New Liberal politicians are not simply passive beneficiaries of class polarization in Edwardian Britain, they are the architects of a political strategy intended to undermine old-style popular Toryism, and thereby counteract the Liberal Party's damaging loss of support in suburbia. Thus Clarke argues that when old-style politics was 'overthrown in the early twentieth century, it was not because of a change in the economic infrastructure. It was a political initiative which precipitated the decisive class polarisation of the electorate' (p. 402).

Perhaps Clarke could have made more of Tory initiatives that tended in the same direction, for instance, the foregrounding of economic policy as the principal issue of political controversy by Tariff Reformers (E.H.H Green, *Crisis of Conservatism*, 1995), or the powerful cocktail of Protestantism, social reform and class rhetoric that Salvidge used to overthrow patrician control in Liverpool and reinvigorate Tory democracy in the city.[8] But for the breadth of its vision, and the subtlety of its interrogation of the relationship between politicians and 'the people', this remains a work of seminal importance.

Since the mid-1970s studies of constituency politics have relied less heavily on the methods and assumptions of the electoral sociology tradition, but they have continued to insist that historians place the relationship between politicians and the electorate centre stage, and that they pay attention to the local contexts within which national political struggles were so often waged. Champions of this approach, such as Stuart Ball and Duncan Tanner, are more interested in reconstructing the voices 'off-stage' than conventional 'high political' historians, and they assume that these voices played an important part in determining both the electoral fortune of parties and the freedom of manoeuvre available to elite politicians. Indeed Stuart Ball, whose own *Baldwin and the Conservative Party* (1988) has a strong Westminster focus, explicitly argues that the 'high political' approach is poorly suited to the analysis of twentieth-century politics because it exaggerates the extent to which politicians could remain insulated from outside pressures in an age of mass media and mass politics. Ball argues that by the late 1920s politicians were becoming increasingly sceptical of the press as a guide to public opinion, and consequently placed renewed emphasis on political meetings, and especially on internal party mechanisms for judging the mood both of the voters and of the party workers who remained so vital to electoral success.[9] Tanner also stresses the need to recognize 'the *interactive* nature of politics', and lays great stress on combining the techniques of social and political history at constituency level in order to understand the limited explanatory value of national studies that 'fail to identify the importance of a spatial or contextual perspective to electoral and political change'.[10]

Historians working within the 'constituency politics' tradition have generally been as interested in election processes as outcomes, and have therefore pioneered research into the franchise, electoral law, party organization and campaigning, in order better to understand how politicians sought to manage the development of the system that ultimately determined their destiny. Perhaps, sometimes, more could be done here to interrogate the gap between politicians' private thoughts and their public actions and pronouncements, but even when it has focused narrowly on the mechanics of electoral practice, such work has made an invaluable contribution to our understanding of political history. Conversely, the main weakness of this approach has undoubtedly been its tendency to focus too narrowly on organizational history – so that 'constituency politics' comes to mean the history of constituency parties when it should really be about the relationship between those parties and the wider electorate. This wider electorate has tended to be studied largely from the perspective of party activists, sometimes reinforced by the insights that can be gleaned from aggregate election data – but that, of course, simply brings us back to electoral sociology and its many sins.

Since the burgeoning of social history as a discipline in the 1960s, the study of elections and local politics has also been championed by historians whose primary interest is precisely the underlying attitudes and allegiances of voters themselves, rather than the fate of political candidates and their parties. Believing even more than the champions of electoral sociology in the *social bases of politics*, historians who have taken 'popular politics' as their core concern have tended to see politics as a prism through which to analyse social structure and (especially since the 'linguistic turn') popular culture. Consequently studies of 'popular politics' tend to foreground the analysis of social cleavages around class, gender and ethnicity, rather than conventional questions about party organization and techniques of voter mobilization. As part of the 'history from below' movement that flourished during the 1960s and 1970s this approach (like so much history of the era) often turned its back on questions of policy formation, and even on the impact of state policies within localities. In many respects, as Miles Taylor has pointed out, this reflected the fact that whilst E.P. Thompson's clarion call 'to rescue the poor stockinger . . . from the enormous condescension of posterity' may have inspired the move to write political history 'from below', non-Marxist influences that played down questions of ideology and governance exercised a more formative influence on the new social history, and tended to dilute the political imperatives of Thompson's project.[11] Indeed, it is important to remember that in the late 1970s and early 1980s it was Marxist historians who were to be found at the forefront of the critique of the insularity and de-politicization of social history and 'history from below'.[12]

10.3 New political histories

However, from the later 1970s social history was also facing a new *post*-Marxist challenge, which struck less at its neglect of the state and politics than at the reductionist assumptions underpinning its whole conception of 'the social'. Explanations positing simple, unmediated links between social class and political allegiance were the special target of this anti-reductionist critique, which perhaps explains why so many advocates of the 'new political history' thought that they were attacking Marxist heresies, when in truth there was precious little Marxist political history to attack, and even less that was unambiguously reductionist given the strong influence of E.P. Thompson on would-be Marxist historians, especially in Britain. In many a footnote, my own included, John Foster, Eric Hobsbawm and sometimes the Gramscian-influenced Robert Gray or the Althusserian Gareth Stedman Jones, had to stand in for the imagined army of orthodox Marxist historians. This critique of reductionism formed part of a broader 'shift to culture' or 'linguistic turn' in social history and hence in the history of popular politics. The origins of this growing emphasis on 'culture' lay in an engagement with cultural anthropology (especially through the work of Clifford Geertz), and with postmodern modes of thought more generally (notably through the work of Michel Foucault and Jacques Derrida). At its best such work has encouraged a more nuanced study of popular political culture broadly defined – i.e. the diverse political ideas and customs within society as a whole, rather than just within the closed world of professional politics. Since the reconstruction of meaning is the defining feature of this school, it has already greatly expanded our understanding of political culture – especially our understanding of what politics meant to contemporaries. In the British case the postmodernist emphasis on 'culture' has generated pioneering studies exploring the centrality of ideas about empire, race and gender to contemporary understandings of citizenship and the political nation.[13]

In many respects this 'new political history' strongly complements the high political tradition, or at least high political analysis that eschews cynical instrumentalist explanation, since both place a strong premium on the reconstruction of culture and on the importance of taking political rhetoric and political ideas seriously, rather than treating them merely as codes for more fundamental class or personal interests.[14] Somewhat surprisingly, this is not a point widely acknowledged by practising historians in either tradition, perhaps because each is always more anxious to assert the primacy of the political world in which they find it congenial to conduct their own historical excavations. Historians of 'popular politics' – including the new generation of postmodernists – like to mock 'high political' historians for their obsession with the closed, claustrophobic world of elite politics.[15] They argue that just because Lord Salisbury, or whoever, failed to understand 'villa Toryism,' let alone working-class Toryism, we are not absolved from trying to understand why 'villa' or working-class Tories thought that they understood and could trust Lord Salisbury (I know, I've done this myself).[16] Similarly, historians of 'high politics' like to mock popular politics for its naïve assumption that the beliefs and aspirations of political nobodies in Blackburn, Wolverhampton, or wherever, should be taken as seriously as the beliefs and aspirations of the political giants who controlled the destiny of a nation. The result is a fundamental bifurcation of political history into two almost wholly separate sub-disciplines – the one focusing on policy formation and elite intrigue within the state, the other on popular politics as a convenient window through which to study popular culture and the politics of everyday life. The big question, of course, is whether these approaches must *necessarily* be seen as discrete and antagonistic. Are the worlds of 'popular politics' and 'high politics' really separate worlds requiring ring-fenced academic endeavours, or is the distinction between them simply one of personal temperament rather than historical substance? In other words, can political history be reconceptualized so that it embraces questions both about popular mobilization *and* policy formation, popular beliefs *and* elite beliefs?

But before we explore the prospects for developing a reintegrated approach to political history we should perhaps confront the thorny question: 'What are we trying to do as political historians?' – or, to be more precise, 'What, if anything, are we trying to explain?' I say 'if anything' because it must be acknowledged that there has been a dramatic scaling-down of the explanatory ambition of political history in recent years, and a headlong flight from ideas of 'causation'. Moreover, this is not simply true of the 'new political history', where indebtedness to post-modernism has led both to an understandable scepticism about the exaggerated claims of the expert, and to a less helpful scepticism about the ultimate 'knowability' of the past. It is equally true of much 'high political' history written in recent years. Thus in his study of Salisbury's thought-world, Michael Bentley rejects the idea of political change 'as a process whose structural features can be identified and explained', and tells us that he will 'follow his [Salisbury's] mental processes rather than give them a coherence that eluded him'.[17] As with much recent postmodern political history, the result is a fascinating, almost anthropological, reconstruction of a political culture, but one that is defiantly indifferent to any broader claims to historical explanation. In this sense both 'new political history; and 'high political' history can be indicted for many of the same failings as the old, non-Marxist social history of the 1960s and 1970s. Not, of course, an indifference to politics per se, but rather a reluctance to focus directly on questions of policy formation and the structure of state power. Here exponents of 'high political' history come out better since their focus is at least the seat of power, even if they are generally uninterested in broader questions about the development of state power or the consequences of its deployment. By contrast, those reconstructing the rituals and languages of popular political culture need to demonstrate both the connections between popular culture and organized/elite politics, and the relationship between popular perceptions of power and the actual mechanisms for wielding power in any given society.[18]

Such arguments raise an important question: Is an interest in 'political culture' – or more precisely the cultural dimension of politics (whether elite or popular) – merely an interesting sideshow that can only hope to offer us 'thick description' of the mystifying rituals of politics, or can it become a crucial element within a more integrated, and genuinely explanatory, political history project? Here we inevitably wander into debates about the limits of historical knowledge, and the acceptability of eclecticism in historical method and theory. We must acknowledge the force of the postmodernist critique of the so-called 'totalizing ambition' in the social sciences, but also the cost that is paid if we abandon any attempt to view politics as an evolving system which demands, firstly, that we reconstruct the interconnectedness of politics; second, that we recognize the need to develop plausible explanations of change over time; and third, that we retain an analytical interest in 'structures' as well as 'cultures'. It is with an amplification of these points that I will conclude this essay.

10.4 Reintegrating political history?

Let us turn first to the claim that we should retain a strong interest in the structural context of politics. Economic and social structures are most obviously important for those focusing on popular politics, since here the potential for individual and group mobilization is likely to be directly related to the distribution of social, economic and cultural capital – that is to say to issues such as hours of work (and thus of free time), levels of residential stability, the relationship between wages and subsistence, ethnic homogeneity, literacy levels etc. Such factors will not magically explain the nature of popular politics, that was the old reductionist illusion, but they will tell us a great deal about the scope for popular political mobilization, and also about the everyday lives of the people that politicians sought to address through discourse. The freedom to weave new discourses about the social world, to conceptualize political identity and interest in new ways, may be considerable, but it is not infinite, and material 'reality' is one of the factors circumscribing the plausible languages for describing the social world in politics.[19]

But if professional politicians must be mindful of material realities as they polish their rhetorical flourishes, in other respects material constraints on their freedom of action are often much less pressing. Almost by definition, most possess the social, economic and cultural capital necessary to sustain political activism, though perhaps only a few could genuinely be said to have amassed such capital without accruing obligations that could compromise their freedom of political action. This was, after all, one of the great forces legitimating aristocratic rule in nineteenth-century Britain: Lord Salisbury and his ilk might be denounced as idle parasites, but at least they were their *own* idle parasites – they, at least, were definitely in no one's pocket. But of course even the greatest landed aristocrats experienced constraints on their freedom of action; perhaps not the crude constraints of material interest beloved of rational choice theorists, but certainly subtler constraints such as the preservation of 'social' capital among one's peers.

A second key point is that political history must adopt a diachronic as well as synchronic frame – that is to say it must be as concerned with charting and *explaining* change over time, as with describing the intricacies of politics at any given moment. We must not lose sight of the need to offer a 'thick description' of political culture – elite and popular alike – but we should ask not only what were the ideas and assumptions that informed political behaviour at any given moment, but also how did those ideas and assumptions become the orthodoxies of their day, and why did they ultimately lose their power to explain the social world. Of necessity this means that we should focus particular analytical attention on those moments when politics were most in flux – for instance on 1830–46, 1915–24, 1940–51 and 1973–83 in the case of modern Britain, though not to the exclusion of broader studies that can encompass both stability and change.

Third, and perhaps most importantly, we need to take seriously the injunction to focus critical attention on the interrelationships between the worlds of 'elite' and 'popular' politics. One starting point for such a reintegrated political history would be to foreground specific *sites* where the two worlds are routinely brought together. The political meeting is an obvious example, and one I have studied at length myself, but there are many others, including individual lobbying of MPs, collective petitioning of Parliament, constituency correspondence, and the myriad internal party gatherings where activists and leaders are brought together. At the same time we should also focus attention on politicians' contrasting actions and arguments within different political sites – exploring tensions between their private writings and public utterances, but also between their actions in Parliament and their explanations of those actions to constituents.

As James Vernon has argued, in some respects politics became less participatory as they became more democratic. Many of the symbolic rituals of political inclusion associated with eighteenth- and early nineteenth-century elections, most notably the hustings, were abolished in the name of 'rational reform', although this process was undoubtedly a slow and uneven one (*Politics and the People*, 1993). Even in the early twentieth century there were still instances of victorious politicians being 'chaired' through their constituencies by joyous supporters, and it was only with the rise of television in the late twentieth century that politicians finally felt able to save themselves from the indignity of facing genuine public meetings during elections (as opposed to showpiece gatherings of the party faithful). Moreover, if in some respects politics became less participatory with democratization, there is little doubt that politicians felt an increasing need to speak to (and for) the people with each successive extension of the franchise, and each advance in the means of communication. The need to shape popular opinion, and to mobilize it for partisan purposes, had become a central factor in political life by the 1870s. Most of the time this could be done at arm's length (much the most congenial method for most politicians): newspapers carried lengthy reports of parliamentary debates and set-piece speeches 'out of doors', while the messy business of street politics could mostly be delegated to constituency party workers and professional party speakers, who toured the country embroiling themselves in the unseemly controversies that most politicians sought to avoid. But at election times, and at other times of great political excitement, the public demanded – and generally got – much more direct contact with their political 'masters'. Moreover, there is considerable evidence that, down to the 1930s at least, politicians continued to tolerate the forced indignities of elections as a test of temperament and character. In 1937 Churchill wrote that

[n]o part of the education of a politician is more indispensable than the fighting of elections … Dignity may suffer, the superfine gloss is soon worn away; … much has to be accepted with a shrug, a sigh or a smile; but at any rate in the end one knows a good deal about what happens and why.

These comments were prompted by recollections of Lord Rosebery's failed attempt to present himself as a man of the people at the turn of the century. According to Churchill, '[h]e would not go through the laborious, vexatious and at times humiliating processes necessary under modern conditions . He would not stoop; he did not conquer'.[20]

Here we see another aspect of an integrated political history: an emphasis on shifting perceptions of 'mass' and 'elite' in British politics. We need to trace much more carefully shifting perceptions of 'the masses' among elite politicians and, no less importantly, shifting perceptions of politicians among the bulk of the population. For instance, we know that politicians increasingly used meetings to make direct appeals to the public in the later nineteenth century, and that old customs limiting public speaking to one's own constituency gradually fell into abeyance, but we still have only the shakiest sense of how politicians perceived their new mass audience, and what they thought it wanted from politics. Similarly, we know surprisingly little about changing public perceptions of politicians and Parliament. We have a general sense that the financial and administrative reforms of the first half of the nineteenth century helped boost the perceived legitimacy of the British state, and that this in turn helped establish the context for the flourishing of mid-Victorian popular Liberalism, but popular beliefs about good and bad governance remain hazy at best.[21] The general assumption seems to be that elite efforts to rein back the bloated 'fiscal-military state' of the eighteenth century harmonized with residual plebeian suspicion of the state as an engine of extortion and class rule to create a new consensus around a minimal, liberal state in the mid-Victorian era. However, this argument sits awkwardly both with claims that the Whig interventionist legislation of 1835–41 and 1846–52 played an important part in diffusing the radical critique of the state as indifferent to the plight of the unenfranchised masses, and with claims that grass-roots Liberalism was largely sustained by the continued force of popular opposition to symbols of the old order in State and Church.[22] But until we know more about changing patterns of public engagement with Parliament, for instance through lobbying and petitioning activity, changing expectations of the role of a constituency MP, involvement in the Victorian 'Local Parliaments' movement and changing ideas about the proper functions of local government, we will remain unclear whether the mid-nineteenth-century liberal state rested on the popular legitimacy bestowed by fiscal and administrative reform, or on the skilful exclusion of a still volatile and 'untamed' populace from all influence on government.[23]

In recent years we have seen a welcome trend towards taking the language of politics seriously, and recognizing the extent to which politicians' discursive strategies have played a part in the construction of popular political identities. Perhaps the focus has too often been on the construction of discourse, rather than on its reception – so that the effectiveness of a particular strategy is inferred rather than demonstrated – but this emphasis on reconstructing the meaning and 'purchase' of contemporary political discourse remains an important advance on approaches that assumed voter interests and identities to be predetermined. However, in taking the 'linguistic turn' in our pursuit of a fuller understanding of the complex relationship between politicians and 'the people', we must not forget that actions often speak louder than words. If political rhetoric can play its part in shaping political identities, so too can state legislation. Sometimes this is done explicitly, as with the 1870 Education Act, which allowed authorities to waive school fees on grounds of 'poverty', which it distinguished from 'pauperism' under the Poor Law, or the 1915 legislation that froze rents on 'working class' housing. But even when legislation does not play an active part in defining a social and political constituency, it frequently transforms the terrain of politics, creating new issues around which politicians can seek to mobilize support. Thus ad hoc legislative responses to the challenge of war between 1914 and 1920, including rent controls and the granting of comprehensive unemployment benefits, created material gains for many workers that Labour politicians subsequently felt obliged to defend against the threat of political retrenchment even though they bore little resemblance to their party's historic vision of a new politics of 'welfare'.

In short, in our rush to explore the subtle powers of language to constitute meaning and identity, we must not lose sight of that cry from the 1980s to 'bring the state back in'.[24] State power matters, not just as an end in itself (as the spoils of the party game), but as a force for transforming social structures and for redefining perceptions of social identity. In Britain, 'revolutions from above' have generally been much more subtle than in, say, Stalinist Russia, but changing practices of taxation and expenditure, and changing official definitions of citizenship and entitlement have done much to shape political expectations and aspirations. Despite the rhetoric of disinterested governance, politicians have frequently sought to wield state power in accordance with their vision of the 'good' society and polity – bolstering or curtailing the state Church, extending or reducing entitlements to state benefits, increasing or reducing the burden of taxation on different groups. Certainly, their freedom of action has usually been constrained by concerns to preserve 'legitimacy' – rhetoric about 'fairness', 'justice' and 'equity' had genuine popular appeal – but the mysteries of state power could nonetheless provide considerable insulation from such popular pressures. While high political histories often exaggerate this isolation from external pressures, pretending that the world of elite politics is all but hermetically sealed from demotic influences, histories of popular politics too often make the opposite mistake – assuming that state power is of no matter, and that the discursive and legislative strategies of 'elite' politicians played little part in shaping plebeian political traditions. Needless to say, both perspectives are inimical to the more integrated approach to political history advocated in this essay. To end with an old cliché, they are the twin dragons we must slay if political history is to overcome its schizophrenic mind-set – if it is to transcend the unhelpful dichotomies of 'high' and 'low', 'centre' and 'periphery' or 'elite' and 'popular' in favour of a systematic exploration of the interconnectedness of politics.

Guide to further reading

Michael Bentley, 'Party, Doctrine and Thought', in Bentley, *High and Low Politics in Modern Britain: Ten Studies* (Oxford, 1983), pp. 123–53.

Peter Clarke, 'Electoral Sociology of Modern Britain', *History* 57 (1972), pp. 31–55.

Maurice Cowling, *The Impact of Labour: the Beginning of Modern British Politics* (Cambridge, 1971).

Ronald P. Formisano, 'The Concept of Political Culture', *Journal of Interdisciplinary History* 31(3) (2001), pp. 393–426.

Catherine Hall, Keith McClelland and Jane Rendall, *Defining the Victorian Nation: Class, Race and Gender and the Reform Act of 1867* (Cambridge, 2000).

H.J. Hanham, *Elections and Party Management: Politics in the Time of Disraeli and Gladstone* (London, 1959).

Gareth Stedman Jones, *Languages of Class* (Cambridge, 1983).

Jon Lawrence and Miles Taylor (eds), *Party, State and Society: Electoral Behaviour in Britain Since 1820* (Aldershot, 1997).

Susan Pedersen, 'What is Political History Now?', in David Cannadine (ed.), *What is History Now?* (Basingstoke, 2002), pp. 36–56.

Philip Williamson, *Stanley Baldwin: Conservative Leadership and National Values* (Cambridge, 1999).

Kathleen Wilson, *The Sense of the People: Politics, Culture and Imperialism in England, 1715–1785* (Cambridge, 1995).

Notes

1 See Linda Colley, *Lewis Namier* (London, 1989), especially pp. 24–31.
2 Maurice Cowling, *The Impact of Labour: the Beginning of Modern British Politics* (Cambridge, 1971), p. 3.
3 Ibid., pp. 3–4.
4 Michael Bentley, 'Party, Doctrine and Thought', in Bentley, *High and Low Politics in Modern Britain: Ten Studies* (Oxford, 1983), pp. 123–53 and Maurice Cowling, *Religion and Public Doctrine in Modern England*, 3 vols (Cambridge, 1980–2001).
5 Jon Lawrence and Miles Taylor (eds), *Party, State and Society: Electoral Behaviour in Britain Since 1820* (Aldershot, 1997), pp. 1–27.
6 John Vincent, *Pollbooks: How Victorians Voted* (Cambridge, 1967), pp. 24–8, 31.
7 Also Peter Clarke, 'Electoral Sociology of Modern Britain' *History* 57 (1972), pp. 31–55.
8 Sandra O'Leary, 'Rethinking Popular Conservatism in Liverpool: Democracy and Reform' in M. Turner (ed.), *Reform and Reformers in Nineteenth Century Britain*, (forthcoming, Sunderland, 2003).
9 Stuart Ball, *Baldwin and the Conservative Party: the Crisis of 1929–1931* (New Haven, 1988), pp. xiv–xv.
10 Duncan Tanner, *Political Change and the Labour Party, 1900–1918* (Cambridge, 1990), especially pp. 12–15.
11 E.P.Thompson, *The Making of the English Working Class* (London, 1980), p. 12 and Miles Taylor, 'The Beginnings of Modern British Social History', *History Workshop Journal* 43 (1997), pp. 155–76.
12 Tony Judt, 'A Clown in Regal Purple: Social History and the Historians', *History Workshop Journal* 7 (1979), pp. 66–94 and Geoff Eley and Keith

Nield, 'Why Does Social History Ignore Politics?' *Social History* 5 (1980), pp. 249–71.

13 For instance, Kathleen Wilson, *The Sense of the People: Politics, Culture and Imperialism in England, 1715–1785* (Cambridge, 1995); Catherine Hall, Keith McClelland and Jane Rendall, *Defining the Victorian Nation: Class, Race and Gender and the Reform Act of 1867* (Cambridge, 2000); Catherine Hall, *Civilising Subjects: Metropole and Colony in the English Imagination, 1830–1867* (Cambridge, 2002); James Vernon, *Politics and the People: a Study in English Political Culture, c.1815–1867* (Cambridge, 1993). See also the special issue of *Journal of British Studies* 41(3) (July 2002), 'New Directions in Political History'.

14 Susan Pedersen, 'What is Political History Now?', in David Cannadine (ed.), *What is History Now?* (Basingstoke, 2002), pp. 36–56.

15 Vernon, 'Politics and the People', p. 8.

16 Jon Lawrence, 'Class and Gender in the Making of Urban Toryism, 1880–1914', *English Historical Review* CVIII, 428 (July 1993), pp. 629–52 and Jon Lawrence and Jane Elliott, 'Parliamentary Election Results Reconsidered: an Analysis of Borough Elections, 1885–1910', *Parliamentary History* 16(1) (1997), pp. 18–29.

17 Michael Bentley, *Lord Salisbury's World: Conservative Environments in Late-Victorian Britain* (Cambridge, 2001), p. 3.

18 For a helpful discussion of these issues see Ronald P. Formisano, 'The Concept of Political Culture', *Journal of Interdisciplinary History* 31(3) (2001), pp. 393–426.

19 Jon Lawrence, *Speaking for the People: Party, Language and Popular Politics in England, 1867–1914,* (Cambridge, 1998), esp. Chapter 3.

20 Winston S. Churchill, *Great Contemporaries* (London, 1937), pp. 17–19; see also Jon Lawrence, 'Fascist Violence and the Politics of Public Order in Inter-war Britain: the Olympia Debate Revisited' (forthcoming) *Historical Research* (2003).

21 Boyd Hilton, *The Age of Atonement: the Influence of Evangelicalism on Social and Economic Thought, 1795–1865* (Oxford, 1988); Philip Harling, *The Waning of 'Old Corruption'. The Politics of Economical Reform in Britain, 1779–1846* (Oxford, 1996); Miles Taylor, *The Decline of British Radicalism, 1847–1860* (Oxford, 1995); Martin Daunton, *Trusting Leviathan: The Politics of Taxation in Britain, 1799–1914* (Cambridge, 2001).

22 Peter Mandler, *Aristocratic Government in the Age of Reform: Whigs and Liberals, 1830–1852* (Oxford, 1990); Gareth Stedman Jones, *Languages of Class* (Cambridge, 1983), pp. 166–7, 176; John Vincent, *The Formation of the Liberal Party, 1857–1868* (London, 1966) and Vincent, *Pollbooks*; Eugenio Biagini, *Liberty, Retrenchment and Reform: Popular Liberalism in the Age of Gladstone, 1860–1880* (Cambridge, 1992).

23 See especially Taylor, *Decline of British Radicalism*; also J.P. Parry, *The Rise and Fall of Liberal Government in Victorian Britain* (London and New Haven, 1993).
24 Peter B. Evans, Dietrich Rueschemeyer and Theda Skocpol (eds), *Bringing the State Back In* (Cambridge, 1985).

11

> Identify approach/es. 01/02/21
> ↳ explain & critique.
> What are the theoretical influences
> on this piece of writing?
> How does welskop use methods/theory
> What are the strengths/weaknesses of
> the way that theory is used here?

Social history

Thomas Welskopp

For Eric Hobsbawm, 1971 was 'a good moment to be a social historian'. In a triumphant assessment of achievement and in anticipation of things to come, he predicted synthesis of a centrifugal field. In a decade, social history had immensely broadened historians' views of the past. Yet close inspection revealed a fragmented picture. Writing from an unorthodox Marxist perspective, Hobsbawm called for a move from 'social history to the history of society'. This entailed a socio-economic interpretation of societies as structured entities, which would bring together the history of the 'many' with that of the powerful, and provide a more profound understanding of politics, which would be rooted in the material life of the people.[1] This anti-idealistic and anti-individualistic view of politics nevertheless retained the political sphere as the proper site of synthesis. Furthermore, Hobsbawm revived a notion of history as a coherent and continuous process with an inherent meaning that could be traced back to Leopold von Ranke's historism. — *Rankeanism.*

Hobsbawm carefully avoided the determinist inclinations of orthodox Marxism. Yet he deemed 'history of society' capable of grasping the totality of a society's past in a coherent narrative intended to describe and explain change over time, and he hoped to produce a 'metanarrative' fusing recognizably Marxian contours with the richness and contingencies of historical experiences. He expected this new metanarrative to challenge – and ultimately displace – the conventional political history of 'great men' privileged by historism and conventional political history. *Criticising Hobs*

Eight years later, social history had profoundly reshaped the landscape of the historical profession in the West. Yet in his stocktaking essay of 1979, Tony Judt cunningly opened with the remark that '[t]his [was] a bad time to be a social historian'. He called social history a pretentious 'clown in regal purple'. It was allegedly near to losing 'touch with the study of the past' altogether, had severed its links with chronology, and had ignored the historical importance of ideas.

Social history needs a Marxist perspective.

Despite claims to the contrary, it lacked proper 'theory', which for Judt meant that it lacked a Marxist perspective. Instead, social history had collapsed theory into method, and method into statistical techniques. Its borrowings from sociology and the political sciences had resulted in self-induced dependency. This in turn permitted uncritical reception of abstract 'models' like 'modernization'. These had produced a metanarrative quite unlike Hobsbawm's vision:

> [R]eceived ideas and stereotyped models too often take the place of theoretical insight or careful research ... Thus a term such as 'modernization' or some 'model' of progress is applied to a historical situation, which in its circular turn becomes source and justification for claims made on behalf of the word or concept in question.

For Judt, social history had no story of its own to tell and that which it did tell was no longer history proper.[2]

In 1995 and 1996, Geoff Eley and Keith Nield revisited the debate. The picture they draw of social history is one of existential crisis. They seem engaged in a two-front battle. In one direction they struggle hard to sensitize their structural realist and materialist colleagues to the challenges of postmodernism. In the other, they simultaneously try to fend off Patrick Joyce's proclamation of an 'end of social history' altogether, reclaiming the latter's indispensable potential to critique capitalism and class structures in an age of globalization. In their attempt to historicize social history, it remains unclear whether they still consider the field more than a politically correct tradition while the future would lie in a Foucauldian and poststructuralist discursive history of 'the social' and 'society', or if they, as Joyce contends, 'look to the past of social history as a way of looking to the future'.[3]

These views tell us much about social history's achievements and shortcomings. They reflect the continuing inability of protagonists and antagonists alike to move beyond the polarized terms of the debate. Social history has indeed opened up the historical discipline to new topics and methods. It has democratized history. It has turned the study of the past into an instrument of social critique.[4] Yet it has not provided a convincing synthesis beyond the Scylla of specialized empiricism and the Charybdis of modernization theory (including its Marxist variant). Paradoxically, therefore, social history has been the junior partner to various lead-disciplines, while retaining a surprisingly conventional notion of what history is.

11.1 A genealogy of pendulum swings

Social history originated in the Enlightenment. In the nineteenth century, social-historical approaches developed under the disciplinary umbrellas of the 'historical school' of political economics, nascent sociology (Max Weber and others) and

Marxist philosophy – particularly in Germany.[5] In Great Britain and – much more so – in the USA, a pluralist historiographical landscape provided room for positivist studies that today would be seen as social history. In the early twentieth century the British 'Fabian' socialists, American 'New Historians' and French *Annalistes* all produced genuine social history.[6] In German historiography, which lacked a positivist tradition and remained bound to the strict disciplinary rule of 'late historism', social historical approaches remained marginalized until well after 1945. *– Social hist*

Despite these older traditions, social history experienced its breakthrough only *varies* after the Second World War. There was enough common ground between *from* national trajectories of this ascendancy to call it a transnational project. Social historians studied human collectivities and movements in the past, as well as social *place* structure and change. They analysed demographic, economic and social processes, *to* and the ways they interacted. World-views, mentalities and 'cultures', *place.* standard of living and everyday life, the family, associations and other social groupings became objects of inquiry. Yet to define social history as a discipline devoted to the past of the 'social', the realm between the economy and the state, would not grasp its global aspirations. The interchange between capitalist economy and the 'social' has always figured large in social historical research. Particularly in Germany this combination of 'social and economic history' still marks a double opposition to the history of political ideas and events, and an increasingly ahistorical economic science. Furthermore, only in certain specialized sub-fields has social history ever resembled Trevelyan's 1942 notion of 'the history of a people with the politics left out'.[7] Social history owed too much to its Marxist roots ever to consider politics irrelevant. Social protest, conflict and revolutions became major fields of interest. Social history initiated the study of classes – especially the working class – as an emancipatory project. At the same time it confronted political history, with its emphasis on ideas and great men, with a potentially deeper and more adequate mode of explaining the political past. Hobsbawm's history of society examined the impact of social structures and processes upon polities, politics and policies.[8]

arg

Social historians everywhere encountered common theoretical problems. The relationship between 'structure' and 'agency' remains a controversial issue. How should the historian capture 'impersonal' socio-economic forces or collectivities like 'social classes'? What was the role of the historical subjects – now conceived as the 'ordinary people' rather than great men – within or against these forces and collectivities? How could one link the different dimensions of analysis in a convincing narrative? What causal weight should be attributed to 'structures' and 'meaningfully acting subjects', or 'social factors' and 'culture', in historical explanation?

Yet these common orientations did not produce a truly *international* social history. The discipline was largely confined by national boundaries. History of society developed no feasible working concept of society, instead retaining the nation-state as its focus. Most 'national' social histories thereby differed markedly from Anglo-American historical sociology, with its universalist modernization model and its preference for macro-sociological comparisons.[9] This 'nationalization' of social histories derived from both the peculiarities of the discipline in each nation and from the national histories they were part of and helped shape. Social history has never resolved the tensions between a universalist political perspective and a desire to narrate a coherent national history superior to traditional political histories. Universalist concepts – class, capitalism, modernization – were incorporated into individualized national histories. Despite its systematic approach and international ambition, social history merely generated national exceptionalisms. Theory, method and national metanarratives became difficult to disentangle.

British social history developed in the context of a lively pluralistic – and contentious – Marxism. It set out to explain the Industrial Revolution, the ascent of class society and the rather British conundrum that these processes produced a highly organized labour movement, but not the class consciousness predicted by Marxist theory. After 1945, Marxist social history fragmented into conflicting wings. One was spearheaded by Hobsbawm, Perry Anderson, Edward P. Thompson, Gareth Stedman Jones and the *History Workshop Journal* (1976–). The latter became a centre for 'history from below' and later for women's history, thus fostering many theoretical and methodological innovations. These British social historians rejected the determinist Marxist orthodoxy associated with Stalinism. New social history set out to overcome the paralysis of the standard-of-living debate of the 1950s by rejecting the debate's economist perspective and its preoccupation with 'nominal' and 'real' wages. Meanwhile, the Soviet invasion of Hungary in 1956 encouraged social historians to revitalize British Marxism. Theoretical issues and political imperatives combined to make a strong anti-structuralist case in favour of 'agency'. 'Experience' and 'hegemony' became buzzwords in labour history, respectively from below or above.[10] In Britain, therefore, social history reaffirmed the old dualism of structure and agency, and pushed the pendulum towards the latter.

US social history emerged in a more diverse landscape. Marxist influence was weaker, and it competed with a strong positivist tradition, drawing on Talcott Parson's structural functionalism and modernization theory. The latter profoundly shaped the national metanarrative generated by the 'new social history'. This relegated Marxism to a variant of the mainstream or an oppositional minority. Diversification spread further because American social history had more than one story to tell. Colonial society, the American Revolution, slavery, the Civil War, the Frontier, and ethnic diversity imposed themselves as topics alongside the history of the Industrial Revolution and class society. Furthermore, non-class social differences, characteristic of a nation of immigrants, often appeared to cross class lines.[11] American social history leaped at the apparently limitless opportunities created by the computer, and quantitative urban history, historical demography and family history, sophisticated sub-fields in Britain, France and Scandinavia, flourished. American 'new social history' was largely quantitative history.

Unlike the British variant, 1960s American social history was markedly *structuralist*. This predilection resulted from methodological preference rather than politics, although 'modernization' concepts added legitimacy. Statistical analysis of demographic data, migration and social mobility became the mediating element between economic, social and political aspects of social history. The discovery of a geographically and socially mobile population in nineteenth- and early twentieth-century America was interpreted as evidence of the interaction of structure and agency. Most social history monographs were studies of single cities, and this permitted the combination of demographic, urban, ethnic and working-class history.[12] Analysis of local economic and demographic change was intended to lay the structural groundwork for an account of social mobility patterns, and then to provide the link between economic base (structure), and social and political associations (agency) – with an emphasis on the importance of ethnicity as part of the political sphere. Agency was virtually collapsed into structure.

Social mobility studies attracted considerable criticism. Monographs were methodologically sophisticated to the point of statistical 'overkill', but seldom conclusive. Social mobility data was just as likely to confirm widening class cleavages as increasing upward mobility due to 'progress'. The explanatory deficit of social-mobility studies rested in their inability to decide whether mobility patterns resulted from structural conditions or individual preferences.

American 'new labour history' defined itself against an 'old labour history' that had concentrated on trades union organization and labour leaders, and had glorified the American tradition of conformist 'bread-and-butter-unionism'.[13] New labour history originally developed as part of 'new social history', but soon branched off in a Marxist direction. A first cohort of practitioners endeavoured to use quantitative methods to grasp the ordinary workers neglected by the 'old' labour history. They produced local monographs similar to the aforementioned studies, but with a leftist political punch.[14] They sought to recover a labour radicalism hitherto neglected in the historical record. The first radicals were said to have been immigrant workers excluded from white Anglo-Saxon trades unionism. Yet since statistical evidence for this radicalism was elusive, the 'new' labour history increasingly sought confirmation in qualitative material on symbols and rituals. Others pointed to hegemonic 'ruling ideologies' as an explanation for the absence of radicalism.

In this 'cultural turn' of the late 1970s optimistic and pessimistic accounts of American labour history emerged. Optimists stressed the agency displayed in workplace militancy during the nineteenth century, and tried to link it with later radical manifestations. They wrote an optimistic story of a repeatedly crushed, but ever resurgent, labour activism.[15] The pessimists, adopting neo-Marxism, saw American workers as victims of capitalist 'hegemony'. They too emphasized nineteenth-century militancy, but incorporated it into a tragedy of long-range defeat. They interpreted the late nineteenth and early twentieth century as a period in which managers used Taylorism and Fordism to wrestle technical knowledge from the workers, deskill labour and subordinate it to capitalism. Ethnic diversity played into the hands of management and ensured the lasting fragmentation of the workforce.[16]

Thus in the late 1970s and early 1980s, American 'new labour history' witnessed a cultural turn towards agency and hegemony, with the concept of experience mediating between the two. Since experience could be linked to identity so easily, American social history was even more open to poststructuralist ideas of difference and symbolic representation than its British counterpart. The swing of the pendulum started with quantitative structuralism, passed grass-roots experience, Antonio Gramsci and Clifford Geertz's anthropology, on its way, and eventually arrived at Foucault and Derrida.

In Germany, social history entered the historical discipline under peculiar circumstances. On the one hand, it had to struggle against a still hegemonic late historism, with its anachronistic emphasis on great men and politics. On the other it had to avoid identification with Marxist-Leninist historiography in the GDR. Thus it began as a non-Marxist, even anti-Marxist, endeavour. Social history was launched by historians like Werner Conze and Theodor Schieder, who had been prominent in the pro-Nazi *Volksgeschichte* of the 1930s. Revoking contaminated *völkisch* jargon after 1945, Conze and Schieder incorporated essential elements of historism into a 'history of structures' (*Strukturgeschichte*). This transformed anti-modernist *Volksgeschichte* into a social history able to face the realities of the 'technical-industrial era'. Conze still avoided the concept of society because of its Marxist connotations.[17] *Strukturgeschichte* was therefore rather elusive, for 'society' was never defined. Rather, structure served as an abstract substitute for politically suspect terms like relations of production and class. Critics argued that since structures were everywhere, the history of modern society would remain imprecise without a more specific socio-economic vocabulary.

Conze and Schieder replaced the organic community once represented by the *Volk* with a neo-humanist concept of the 'autonomous subject' derived from nineteenth-century historism. Drawing on the 'German sociologist' Hans Freyer, they combined a structuralist analysis of contemporary cultures with re-assertion of the role of great personalities. *Strukturgeschichte* dug into the histories of industrialization, workers, urban cultures and social vocabulary (*Begriffsgeschichte*) to uncover continuities beyond the ruptures apparently caused by the Industrial Revolution and democratization. *Strukturgeschichte* thus took issue with the Marxist preoccupation with class conflict. It sought to write the epic of the eternal confrontations between structures, and 'great personalities' capable of resisting and shaping them.[18] Conze and Schieder's synthesis aimed to amalgamate these confrontations into a sequence of 'individualities' in which even structural configurations assumed an individual quality.

Because *Strukturgeschichte* never produced this synthesis, and because it separated into a score of loosely linked sub-fields, its influence during the 1960s and 1970s has often been underestimated. Economic, urban, labour, demographic, agricultural and settlement histories have all been inspired by its programme, as has the history of social semantics. *Strukturgeschichte* therefore deserves credit for having established social history on the fortified territory of the German historical profession. It is noteworthy that this social history openly rejected Marxism. It sought to reconcile an outright 'structuralist' notion of the social (originating in Freyer's sociology and Fernand Braudel) with a concept of 'agency' as inherited from historism. This meant that 'agency' was reserved for 'great men' whose intentions the historian tried to 'understand' by a hermeneutic reading of the sources (that is, to uncover the *intentions* of historical actors). *Strukturgeschichte* placed structure and agency side by side, without accounting for the relationship between them.

The sudden emergence of a new generation of social historians in Germany in the late 1960s was responsible for *Strukturgeschichte*'s lack of recognition. Most of the new generation had actually been trained by Conze and Schieder (Gerhard A. Ritter, a student of Ernst Fraenkel, provided another major recruitment centre). Yet the new generation claimed for itself a rather different genealogy in which émigrés and interdisciplinary contacts – especially with sociology – were stressed. Marx was reintroduced, in an unorthodox adaptation indebted to Max Weber, Hans Rosenberg and Eckart Kehr. This self-proclaimed critical social history preached 'history as a social science'. It discarded *Strukturgeschichte* as inconsequential, empiricist or – worse – historicist, and reduced it to a mere staging post on the way to the true paradigm shift of the late 1960s.[19] A relatively coherent group of young historians around Hans-Ulrich Wehler and Jürgen Kocka, the newly founded Bielefeld University and the influential journal *Geschichte und Gesellschaft* (1975–), swiftly surpassed their social history predecessors.

Critical social history developed a radical *structuralism*. It re-established a causal chain between economic, social and political dimensions of historical analysis. A vaguely Marxian materialist conception of 'base' and 'superstructure' re-entered the field. Social history in Germany thus embraced a structuralist paradigm very different to the cultural emphasis found in Britain, and later the US.

German social history took this turn in reaction against historism and *Strukturgeschichte* alike. Epistemologically speaking, ideological criticism replaced hermeneutics. First, this meant that critical social historians rejected the notion that the past could be understood by exploring the intentions of historical subjects, for the latter were said to lack full insight into the structural constraints upon their own actions. Instead, these constraints became the focus of inquiry.[20] Second, social historians denounced historiographical approaches – particularly historism – that used hermeneutic methods to understand the past through the intentions of the personalities involved.[21] They discounted these approaches as methodologically naïve apologetics for the ruling class. Only structural analysis would free the real past from ideological distortion.

German 'social-science history' explicitly applied theory. In this 'quest for theory' (Reinhart Koselleck) it borrowed 'middle-range concepts' from economics, sociology and political science. The inventor of the 'middle-range concept', the American sociologist Robert K. Merton, saw it as a form of social theory that allowed for close empirical analysis. German social historians converted this into a means to understand limited historical periods. Thus models like 'imperialism', 'organized capitalism' or 'class formation' informed interpretations of very specific periods of history. Ultimately this limited the concepts' theoretical value. Social historians did not worry, however, because they considered theory purely 'instrumental', as if historical narratives were coloured, but not deeply affected, by choice of theory. Kocka, for instance, defined the historical 'story' as the sequence of divergences between the chosen model – the normal path – and past 'reality'.[22] 'Social-science history' openly professed a cheerful eclecticism. Yet all its concepts were firmly embedded in modernization theory.

Social-science history, despite its proclaimed departure from *Strukturgeschichte*, retained a similar concept of 'structure' for a different purpose. Koselleck's 'theory of historical time' defined a specifically modern type of 'experience'; historical time, he suggested, had accelerated so much in modernity that even 'structural moments' could be experienced as events. Kocka drew from this contention the opposite conclusion, that 'structure' was almost entirely beyond the grasp of human understanding. Consequently, a comprehensive explanation required a structural analysis of the conditions of and restraints upon 'agency'. 'Agency' – except as interest and conformity to 'structure' – moved to the margins of the historical account.[23]

'Social-science history' pushed for synthesis more energetically than its predecessor. Wehler developed *Gesellschaftsgeschichte* ('history of society') in pursuit of this ambition. *Gesellschaftsgeschichte* came to mean systematic analysis of the four key dimensions of modern society (the economic, social, political and cultural sphere interlinked by systems of social inequality) in order, ultimately, to explain the political process. This 'political social history' resonated with the concerns of a generation socialized in post-war Germany to expose the origins of Nazism. Whereas *Strukturgeschichte* had stressed long continuities that lessened the significance of this 'crime against civilization', and had transferred its investigation to an isolated sub-field called *Zeitgeschichte* ('contemporary history'), *Gesellschaftsgeschichte* sought long-range causes of Nazism back in the nineteenth century. Wehler and others designed a 'metanarrative' of a failed German modernization.[24]

Take Wehler's *German Empire* as an example.[25] In his polemical introduction, Wehler demanded a 'critical' history of the German Empire of 1871–1918 able to expose its responsibility for Nazism. His history proper starts by portraying the 'constellation of 1871' as a highly explosive coincidence of modernizing and anti-modern forces, foreshadowing the contradictions of the Reich up to 1914. The 'Agrarian Revolution' had commercialized agriculture and buttressed the dominance of the reactionary landed elites, especially in the eastern provinces of Prussia. Compared to the 'West' – Great Britain and America – Germany was a late industrializer. Yet because it began only in the 1850s, industrialization was all the more rapid, and created severe social strains. Consequently, the German bourgeoisie, especially the leaders of heavy industry, rejected liberalism in favour of a lasting political alliance with the conservative high bureaucracy and aristocracy. The failure of liberalism weakened civil society, while the repressive Bismarck regime stifled democratization, and crippled parliamentary government and social reform with a pseudo-populist 'revolution from above'.

Wehler's chapter on industrialization further develops his picture of rapid economic modernization and the consequent pressures on the political system. Ironically, these twenty pages contain the only truly social-historical considerations in the book. The remainder – nearly five-sixths – deals with politics. Wehler summarily dismisses the political parties as impotent forces in a political process dominated by traditional elites and the newly organized heavy industrial interests. He sees Bismarck's government as a flexible power broker juggling informal elite coalitions forced together by shared interests, ideological integration and hostility to 'Reich enemies' like the Social Democrats. The regime – even more under Wilhelm II – controlled society by manipulation. Integrating and stereotyping ideologies like anti-socialism, anti-Semitism and anti-Catholicism were propagated. Wehler presents the family, schools, universities and military as agents of authoritarian socialization. Class justice reinforced the authoritarian mentality in the upper half of German society, and that increased submissiveness to the monarch, the state and the elites.

The politics of manipulation kept the old order in place but did not create stability. On the contrary, it fostered tensions and alienated potential allies. State politics became a reactive crisis management, and the regime resorted to an increasingly aggressive nationalism in order to maintain loyalty. German imperialism, for instance, was a strategy designed to divert attention from internal conflict and channel aggression into international relations. German *Weltpolitik* thus was really a manipulative domestic policy. Germany became the driving force in the European arms race, building a fleet intended to contest British naval hegemony. These foreign-policy adventures provoked anti-German coalitions and ultimately international isolation. Militarism in German society made war inevitable. For Wehler, the German invasion of France and Russia in 1914 represented a last-ditch attempt to save the moribund Wilhelmine system. Yet Germany's defeat brought about the very social revolution the war had been supposed to prevent. Elite adversity to the democratic institutions of the Weimar Republic then helped Nazism to power during the Great Depression.

Wehler's strongly argued book has been immensely controversial, not least because it combines ascetic brevity with pointed judgements and blunt commentary. Each chapter draws on its own theoretical concept, so that theory often appears as a short-cut interpretation of a past 'reality', illustrated by a few historical details. Social history proper enters the picture surprisingly little. It is evident largely in a broadening of the 'political' to include organized interest groups and social institutions. Whereas almost no historical actors figure in the depiction of economic and social structures, the arena of politics is populated with stunningly personal stories of 'great men' and events. 'Manipulation' has to bear the whole burden of Wehler's attempt to bring society and politics together – great men seek to manipulate social processes. This metanarrative of a 'German divergence from the West' (*deutscher Sonderweg*) became influential because it fused modernization theory, structuralism, ideological critique and a morally accentuated interpretation of a crucial period into a 'critical' national history.[26]

11.2 Theoretical cornerstones of 'traditional' social history

In order to reunite national trends for more systematic discussion, I want to discuss some essentials of 'traditional' social history. A field representative of the discipline at large shall serve as an example: the approach to labour history as set forth in the 'working class formation paradigm' of the 1970s and 1980s. For most of the 1960s and 1970s, social history had been almost synonymous with labour history or, more generally, of ordinary men (literally 'men'). The concept of 'working class formation' represented an attempt to combine the history of workers in workplaces, neighbourhoods, families, bars and leisure associations, with labour movement history – strikes and class conflict, trades unions and party organization, ideology and 'class consciousness'. E.P. Thompson's *Making of the*

English Working Class (1963) triggered the development of a series of models of 'working class formation'.[27]

Their common approach was to turn a core concept of an 'economic base' determining an 'ideological superstructure' into a sequence of levels causally linked to each other and representing a progression from the advent of capitalism to the founding of socialist parties. Another commonality was the use of models of singular linear processes in history, against which 'histories proper' would be measured. Such theories promoted an idealized historical path to a morally defined end (liberal democracy or socialism) and were in vogue in contemporary economics (e.g. the 'long waves' approach) and sociology (modernization, Marxism).[28] It is not hard to discern the desire to reconcile theory with the old idea that history is a *unitary process*.

Kocka's essay on 'working class formation' in Germany (1800–75) is a case in point.[29] He starts by outlining a theoretical model distinguishing 'four analytical dimensions'. First, the overarching processes that transformed the Ancien Régime into modern 'class society', most notably the rise of capitalism, state building and the demographic transition. Second, he depicts the concomitant spread of wage work in centralized production facilities as the motor for homogenization of workers' class positions. Third, workers will hypothetically develop – on this basis – a collective identity, expressed in language, family structures, marriage patterns, residual segregation and culture. Finally,

> under certain conditions those who share a common class position and become a social class ... may, on the same basis, act collectively and perhaps organize [in trades unions and socialist parties], in conflict with other classes and perhaps the state.[30]

Kocka then describes in detail the 'lower classes' around 1800. As always, he brilliantly synthesizes a vast literature into a 'class' interpretation. He follows up with a minute account of the legal, economic and demographic changes outlined in level one of his model, drawing on legal decisions and much statistical data. The next chapter shows that servants, agricultural and casual workers, the largest occupational groups, were largely unaffected by wage work, and remained embedded in older production settings and legal restraints. Workers in 'domestic industries', in contrast, were increasingly dependent on merchant capital, but were not yet employed in a capitalist factory system. Journeymen had largely turned into wage workers, while their masters were on the brink of becoming petty employers. Yet guild traditions still lingered in collective organization along trade lines. Finally, factory workers almost matched Kocka's prototypical 'pure wage worker'. In this chapter Kocka relies largely on 'structural' analysis, but he does speculate on the 'typical experiences' of the groups in question. He does so in order to deal with the rather puzzling observation that some domestic workers and many journeymen 'contributed' to the early German labour movement, while factory workers held aloof.

Kocka's final section covers levels three and four of his model. He first points to unifying tendencies in the language of 'work' and 'class', social mobility and marriage patterns, and social protest – most notably the rapidly growing frequency of strikes in the late 1860s and early 1870s. Kocka then traces the emergence of trades unions and the rise of the Social Democratic parties. The former first appeared in certain artisan trades, a fact that does not confirm the prediction in the model that they should be developed first by factory workers. Kocka explains artisan unionism as a belated product of class conflict between masters and journeymen back in the revolution of 1848. Another development rather specific for Germany was the 'premature' appearance of independent labour parties. Kocka attributes this to the receptiveness of many journeymen for socialist ideologies and the inability of German liberalism to maintain political hegemony – in contrast to Britain. Kocka concludes that whereas a working class was present on levels one and two of his model, 'class formation' remained limited on the higher levels, in spite of progress between 1800 and 1875. 'Class formation' did result from the extension of capitalism and wage work, but it only translated into 'class consciousness' and collective action where a 'supplementary' 'conflict between tradition and modernization' entered the picture.[31]

It is interesting to note how Kocka deals with 'structure' and 'agency' in the causal architecture of his argument. Levels one and two provide mainly structural analyses. On level two he invokes typical 'experiences' but does not back them up empirically. Instead, the largely structural phenomena on level three sustain his earlier assumptions about 'experiences'. Instead of developing each level out of the preceding one, he implicitly reverses the causal order. Kocka also fails to convincingly explain the timing and the forms of German labour organization, for he actually has recourse to variables *external* to his model (socialist ideologies, weakness of liberalism). Finally, the role of 'traditions' in his argument is unclear. While the model should regard traditions as retarding labour organization, they sneak into the explanation as a 'sufficient cause' for the 'early' organization of artisan trades.

Kocka's model, like all concepts of 'class formation', attributes different qualities of 'structure' and 'agency' to each dimension of 'historical reality'.[32] Whereas all formulations of the model distinguish between demographic/economic, social and political/ideological levels of 'class formation', with Katznelson inserting a fourth, cultural, level in between the social and the political, they differ largely in the degree they allow for the historical subjects to be 'meaningful agents'. Zwahr's account of spreading kinship relations among 'born proletarians' is structural and leaves agency out entirely. For Katznelson and Kocka, industrialization and wage work provided homogenizing 'experiences', which workers had *passively* and which were *then* translated into 'agency' at the cultural and political levels. Agency exists only on the higher level, and is constrained by the lower. Thompson's 'reintroduction of the subject into history', by contrast, led him to define 'experience' *as* 'agency'. In Thompson's eyes, 'class' had to be 'experienced' – *actively made* and transformed into cultural and political 'class consciousness'. Yet, on closer examination, Thompson's seemingly totalizing concept of 'experience' is deceiving, since material 'relations of production' ('structures') determine what 'experiences' can be made in the first place. The novelty of Thompson is that he takes account of new forms of 'experience' (like the tradition of the 'freeborn Englishman'). These help shape particular *expressions* of working-class 'agency', but they do not alter the assumption that experiences must converge in *class* experiences.[33]

The 'working class formation paradigm' is a prime example of 'classic' social history's inability to bring structure and agency together. This structure generally meant causal primacy for structure and the de-centring of agency. 'Structure' was most salient ('hard' is a frequently used adjective) in economic institutions and relations of production. Although historians of the working class recognized that there were 'structures' in culture and organization, too, these seemed much less rigid. William H. Sewell has criticized this as 'misplaced materialism'.[34] For it is not the *degree of structuration* that distinguishes between segments of society, but their *specific structural properties*. Finally, social history's de-centring of the 'agent' has resulted in a tendency to make *collectivities* the unquestioned units of analysis, to the extent that they almost appeared capable of acting like people. 'Traditional' social history took group formation for granted, so it was almost impossible to think of social identity in terms of 'difference'. Yet 'difference' became the banner under which the new 'cultural history' assailed social history in the early 1980s.[35]

11.3 'Social history' under attack

Some say that social history first experienced 'crisis' in the late 1970s. In Britain and America this meant the disintegration of what had never really been a coherent field. Social history became a loosely circumscribed territory with room for numerous approaches, even if some seemed mutually exclusive.

Labour history was the first area where a 'history of experience' – *how* people experienced the past – strove to emancipate itself from Thompsonian patronage. This was evident in a new 'micro-history from below' and in claims for the relative autonomy of culture and rejection of economic determinism. History of experience, even when adopting a watered-down 'thick description' derived from Geertz's anthropology, largely remained within the social history perimeter. It combined minute analyses of symbolic systems with rather conventional descriptions of context.[36] Nevertheless, it initiated a shift in focus from sociology to social (or cultural) anthropology as a theoretical reference point. 'New cultural history' also sought to reverse the traditional privileging of economic causation.[37] Yet this revisionism retained the conceptual framework of materialist social history. Cultural representations still figured as internalizations – if symbolic – of material reality.[38]

Gareth Stedman Jones' view that language decisively shapes past reality was more radical, and opened the way for postmodernism and the 'linguistic turn'.[39] Likewise gender history attacked not only social historians' neglect of sexual difference, but the materialist character of their basic categories. Feminists denounced as 'essentialist' social historians' assumption that the proletariat was male.[40] Michel Foucault's discourse theory influenced most of these revisionists. His linkage of knowledge and power disturbed social historians by distracting attention from economic institutions, social conflict and 'real people'. Social history could deal neither with the alleged centrality of language nor the view that culture was a symbolic system independent of 'real' people. Social historians' representations of the past, their very notion of 'historical reality' and their 'scientific' approach all seemed at stake.

The above critiques all share the view that social categories should be understood in terms of difference. Even in their most conventional understanding, which considers 'difference' central to 'social identity', this poses a momentous challenge to a social history preoccupied with collectivities. For 'difference' is foremost an individual property of acting subjects. Acceptance of this proposition would mean a fundamental rethinking of how collectivities are formed. In the USA, the impact of 'difference' quickly led to expansion of social historical vocabulary, especially in the focus on the trinity of 'class, race and gender'. This did not in itself extend the horizons of social history, but made its stories more complicated.[41] More critical was that this 'deconstruction' of collectivities threatened the unitary notion of history still favoured, as we have seen, by many social historians. Hence social history's hostility to gender and micro-history.

Only Germany has seen a polarized debate between social and cultural history. On one side is a disciplinary establishment loyal to social history; confronting it are cultural historians, who, if not without disagreements, possess a common sense of purpose. This polarization is due to the unusually strong position acquired by 'social-science history' in the 1970s and early 1980s. Although it does not represent a majority in the historical discipline, and not even all social historians, 'social-science history' had temporarily exerted a sort of discursive hegemony over the field. In other countries, new approaches added breadth to an already pluralized field, but in Germany innovators had to fight an uphill battle against a 'new orthodoxy'. In the course of this struggle, German social history became identified with economic determinism, analysis of social structure, anti-hermeneutic structuralism, macro-causal explanations, political social history and the *Sonderweg* synthesis typified by Wehler. In the 1980s 'social-science history' rejected all challengers – whether *Alltagsgeschichte* or women's history. The intention was to taint these leftist threats with the odour of right-wing historism.

'Social-science history' has nevertheless changed and expanded during the last 30 years. Social historians finally started to heed the call for historical comparisons, which had been demanded during the *Sonderweg* debate. These studies transcended national histories, subverted the nationally centred *Sonderweg* model and undermined social history's categories of analysis. In labour history, this led to a critique of the 'working class formation paradigm'.[42] Social-science history's own large-scale project on the history of the bourgeoisie, launched in the mid-1980s, broadened the object of analysis to include culture, gender relations, value systems and discourses. The German 'bourgeoisie' increasingly appeared as a cultural formation rather than a socio-economic class.

Some proponents of new cultural history still define themselves against a narrowly conceived social history. The manner in which cultural historians bring together concepts usually considered incompatible is a peculiarly German phenomenon, as is the attempt to bring some coherence into cultural history by returning to turn-of-the-century German theories of culture.[43] And whereas social-science history continues to produce one monumental synthesis of national history after another, cultural historians struggle to present an alternative meta-narrative, pitting a story of 'radicalized modernity' against the *Sonderweg* thesis. Thus they remain confined to national history after all.[44] Some cultural historians even demand replacement of 'society' with 'culture' as a more comprehensive focus for synthesis.[45] Playing society off against culture represents another German *Sonderweg* inevitably leading to another dead end.[46]

11.4 What future?

Social history did have its merits. It was social history, after all, that brought up the question of social inequality in the study of the past, and introduced the workers and the underprivileged masses to the historical record. It explained the process of industrialization, and of social change and conflict in a broad sense. It pioneered the integration of economic, social and political analysis into the history of entire societies. Social history also became a fertile ground of theoretical debate. Current discussions of various theoretical 'turns' are still capitalizing on this pioneering work.

Yet revisionist challenges have exposed the whole historical discipline's weaknesses, social history included. I have pointed to social history's inability to reconcile structure and agency, to the weaknesses of its 'materialist' conception of the economy and collectivities, its neglect of culture as symbolic practice, and to its intransigent rejection of the notion of the historical construction of difference. The solutions offered by the linguistic turn to the problems of the agency of historical subjects, the cultural meanings of their interaction and the power relations intrinsic to economic, social and political institutions, are only partly convincing. Yet cultural historians have posed the right questions. A renewed social history must take on board a whole range of key insights derived from recent debates. Some historians speak of an imminent 'social turn' in the history of culture and society. This must not be a turn *back* to the 'old' structuralist social history, but a step 'beyond the cultural turn'.[47]

We might now be attaining a social history that pays full credit to language, symbols and discourse, but moves on by embedding these in 'social practice'. 'Practice theory' – as associated, for instance, with Pierre Bourdieu and Anthony Giddens – is capable of grasping interaction both as structured by rules and resources, and as acted out by the agency of subjects. Starting from the premise that agents interpret their environment in the process of making 'experiences', it can cope with the constructed nature of (historical) reality and multiple identities of actors. I can envisage in the near future a social history that combines the analysis of economic, social, cultural and political institutions from the perspective of the social subjects meaningfully interacting with one another. Collectivities will not be taken for granted, but will be explained in terms of social and cultural practice. This approach might breathe fresh life into research areas largely deserted since the linguistic turn. The histories of work, business enterprises and marketplaces, of social inequality, social movements and political culture, all conceived of as complex fields of interaction, stand out as potentially innovative research areas in an age of globalization.[48] This will be a self-reflexive social history, beyond the cultural turn, but conscious of its achievements.

Guide to further reading

Michael Bentley, *Modern Historiography. An Introduction* (London, 1999).

Victoria E. Bonnell and Lynn Hunt (eds), *Beyond the Cultural Turn. New Directions in the Study of Society and Culture* (Berkeley, 1999).

Christoph Conrad, 'Social History', in Neil J. Smelser and Peter B. Baltes (eds), *International Encyclopaedia of the Social and Behavioural Sciences*, Vol. 21 (Oxford, 2001), pp. 14299–306.

Geoff Eley and Keith Nield, 'Starting Over: The Present, the Postmodern and the Moment of Social History', in Keith Jenkins (ed.), *The Postmodern History Reader*, 3rd edn (London, 2001), pp. 366–79.

Anna Green and Kathleen Troup (eds), *The Houses of History. A Critical Reader in Twentieth-Century History and Theory* (Manchester, 1999).

Peter N. Stearns (ed.), *Encyclopedia of European Social History* (New York, 2001).

Notes

1   Eric J. Hobsbawm, 'From Social History to the History of Society', *Daedalus* 100 (1971), pp. 20–45, esp. 43.
2   Tony Judt, 'A Clown in Regal Purple: Social History and the Historians', *History Workshop Journal* 7 (1979), pp. 66–94, esp. 66, 67, 89.
3   Geoff Eley and Keith Nield, 'Starting Over: The Present, the Postmodern and the Moment of Social History', in Keith Jenkins (ed.), *The Postmodern History Reader*, 3rd edn (London, 2001), pp. 366–79 and Geoff Eley, 'Is All the World a Text? From Social History to the History of Society Two Decades Later', in Terrence J. McDonald (ed.), *The Historic Turn in the Human Sciences* (Ann Arbor, MI, 1996), pp. 193–243, esp. 216–23.
4   Stefan Berger, 'The Rise and Fall of "Critical" Historiography', *European Review of History* 3 (1996), pp. 213–32.
5   The German journal *Vierteljahrschrift für Sozial- und Wirtschaftsgeschichte* was first published in 1893.
6   Lucien Febvre and Marc Bloch founded the *Annales d'histoire économique et sociale* in Strasbourg in 1929. Cf. Chapter 6 in this volume, on the *Annales*, for further details and elaboration.
7   George Macaulay Trevelyan, *Illustrated English Social History* (London, 1942).
8   Cf. Jürgen Kocka, *Sozialgeschichte. Begriff – Entwicklung – Probleme*, 2nd edn (Göttingen, 1986), pp. 48–111.
9   Charles Tilly, *Big Structures, Large Processes, Huge Comparisons* (New York, 1984).
10   Geoff Eley, 'Edward Thompson, Social History and Political Culture: The Making of a Working-Class Public, 1780–1850', in Harvey J. Kaye and Keith McClelland (eds), *E.P. Thompson. Critical Perspectives* (Philadelphia, 1990), pp. 12–49.
11   Michael Kammen (ed.), *The Past Before Us* (Ithaca, 1980).
12   Stephen Thernstorm, *Poverty and Progress. Social Mobility in a Nineteenth-Century City* (Cambridge, MA, 1964) and Thernstorm, *The Other Bostonians. Poverty and Progress in the American Metropolis, 1880–1970* (Cambridge, MA, 1973).

13 The benchmark synthesis of the 'old' labour history was John R. Commons *et al.*, *History of Labor in the United States*, 4 vols (New York, 1918–35).

14 A good example is Alan Dawley, *Class and Community. The Industrial Revolution in Lynn* (Cambridge, MA, 1976).

15 The seminal study is David Montgomery, *The Fall of the House of Labor. The Workplace, the State, and American Labor Activism 1865–1925* (New York, 1987).

16 Harry Braverman, *Labor and Monopoly Capitalism. The Degradation of Work in the Twentieth Century* (New York and London, 1974); Richard C. Edwards, *Contested Terrain. The Transformation of the Workplace in the Twentieth Century* (New York, 1979); David M. Gordon, Richard C. Edwards and Michael Reich, *Segmented Work, Divided Workers. The Historical Transformation of Labor in the United States* (Cambridge, MA, 1982).

17 Werner Conze, *Die Strukturgeschichte des technisch-industriellen Zeitalters als Aufgabe für Forschung und Unterricht* (Köln, 1957).

18 Theodor Schieder, *Geschichte als Wissenschaft. Eine Einführung*, 2nd edn (München, 1968), pp. 18–20, 157–94.

19 Hans-Ulrich Wehler, *Geschichte als Historische Sozialwissenschaft* (Frankfurt am Main, 1973).

20 Kocka, *Sozialgeschichte*, p. 73.

21 Thomas Welskopp, 'Die Sozialgeschichte der Väter. Grenzen und Perspektiven der Historischen Sozialwissenschaft', *Geschichte und Gesellschaft* 24 (1998), pp. 169–94.

22 Jürgen Kocka, *Facing Total War. German Society 1914–1918* (Leamington Spa, 1984).

23 Kocka, *Sozialgeschichte,* p. 76f. For Koselleck's notion of structure see Reinhart Koselleck, 'Darstellung, Ereignis, Struktur', in Reinhart Koselleck, *Vergangene Zukunft. Zur Semantik geschichtlicher Zeiten* (Frankfurt am Main, 1989), pp. 144–57.

24 Stefan Berger, *The Search for Normality: National Identity and Historical Consciousness in Germany Since 1800* (Oxford, 1997).

25 Hans-Ulrich Wehler, *The German Empire 1871–1918* (Leamington Spa, 1985).

26 See his monumental *Deutsche Gesellschaftsgeschichte*, 3 vols published to date (München, 1987–95). A critical analysis is provided by Thomas Welskopp, 'Westbindung auf dem "Sonderweg". Die deutsche Sozialgeschichte vom Appendix der Wirtschaftsgeschichte zur Historischen Sozialwissenschaft', in Wolfgang Küttler, Jörn Rüsen and Ernst Schulin (eds), *Geschichtsdiskurs*, Vol. 5 (Frankfurt am Main, 1999), pp. 191–237.

27 Hartmut Zwahr, *Zur Konstituierung des Proletariats als Klasse. Strukturuntersuchung des Leipziger Proletariats während der industriellen Revolution* (Berlin (GDR), 1978) and Ira Katznelson, 'Working-Class

Formation: Constructing Cases and Comparisons', in Ira Katznelson and Aristide R. Zolberg (eds), *Working-Class Formation: Nineteenth Century Patterns in Western Europe and the United States* (Princeton, 1986), pp. 3–43.

28 Hansjörg Siegenthaler, 'Geschichte und Ökonomie nach der kulturalistischen Wende', *Geschichte und Gesellschaft* 25 (1999), pp. 276–301, esp. 280.

29 Jürgen Kocka, 'Problems of Working-Class Formation in Germany: The Early Years, 1800–1875', in Katznelson, Zolberg (eds), *Working-Class Formation*, pp. 279–351 and Jürgen Kocka, *Lohnarbeit und Klassenbildung. Arbeiter und Arbeiterbewegung in Deutschland 1800–1875* (Berlin, 1983).

30 Ibid., p. 283.

31 Ibid., p. 351.

32 Thomas Welskopp, 'Class Structures and the Firm: The Interplay of Workplace and Industrial Relations in Large Capitalist Enterprises', in Paul L. Robertson (ed.), *Authority and Control in Modern Industry. Theoretical and Empirical Perspectives* (London, 1999), pp. 73–119.

33 William H. Sewell, Jr, 'How Classes are Made: Critical Reflections on E.P. Thompson's Theory of Working-Class Formation', in Kaye, McClelland (eds), *E.P. Thompson*, pp. 50–77, esp 59–66.

34 William H. Sewell, Jr, 'Toward a Post-materialist Rhetoric for Labour History', in Lenard R. Berlanstein (ed.), *Rethinking Labor History. Essays on Discourse and Class Analysis* (Urbana, Chicago, 1993), pp. 16–38.

35 The zenith of German social history can be located around the turn to the 1980s. Cf. the triumphant tone in Wehler's stocktaking essay: Hans-Ulrich Wehler, 'Geschichtswissenschaft heute', in Jürgen Habermas (ed.), *Stichworte zur 'Geistigen Situation der Zeit'*, Vol. 2: *Politik und Kultur* (Frankfurt am Main, 1979), pp. 709–53.

36 For example, Sean Wilentz, *Chants Democratic. New York City and the Rise of the American Working Class, 1788–1850* (New York, 1984).

37 Lynn Hunt, *Politics, Culture, and Class in the French Revolution* (Berkeley, 1986); William H. Sewell, Jr, *Work and Revolution in France: The Language of Labour from the Old Regime to 1848* (Cambridge, 1980); Lynn Hunt (ed.), *The New Cultural History* (Berkeley, LA, 1989).

38 Miguel A. Cabrera, 'On Language, Culture, and Social Action', *History and Theory* 40 (2001), pp. 82–100, esp. 84–6.

39 Gareth Stedman Jones, *Languages of Class: Studies in English Working-Class History, 1832–1982* (Cambridge, 1983); Patrick Joyce (ed.), *The Historical Meanings of Work* (Cambridge, 1987); Patrick Joyce, *Democratic Subjects. The Self and the Social in Nineteenth-Century England* (New York, 1994).

40 Joan W. Scott, *Gender and the Politics of History* (New York, 1988) and Joan W. Scott, 'The Evidence of Experience', in James Chandler, Arnold I.

Davidson and Harry Harootunian (eds), *Questions of Evidence. Proof, Practice, and Persuasion across the Disciplines* (Chicago, London, 1994), pp. 363–87.

41 Kathleen Canning, 'Gender and the Politics of Class Formation: Rethinking German Labor History', *American Historical Review* 97 (1992), pp. 736–68.

42 Thomas Welskopp, *Arbeit und Macht im Hüttenwerk. Arbeits- und industrielle Beziehungen in der deutschen und amerikanischen Eisen- und Stahlindustrie von den 1860er bis zu den1930er Jahren* (Bonn, 1994).

43 Ute Daniel, *Kompendium Kulturgeschichte. Theorien, Praxis, Schlüsselwörter* (Frankfurt am Main, 2001).

44 Geoff Eley (ed.), *Society, Culture, and the State in Germany 1870–1930* (Ann Arbor, MI, 1996).

45 Rudolf Vierhaus, 'Die Rekonstruktion historischer Lebenswelten. Probleme moderner Kulturgeschichtsschreibung', in Hartmut Lehmann (ed.), *Wege zu einer neuen Kulturgeschichte* (Göttingen, 1995), pp. 6–28 and Ute Daniel, '"Kultur" und "Gesellschaft". Überlegungen zum Gegenstandsbereich der Sozialgeschichte', *Geschichte und Gesellschaft* 19 (1993), pp. 69–99.

46 Stefan Berger, 'Social History vs Cultural History', *Theory, Culture and Society* 18 (2001), pp. 145–53.

47 Victoria E. Bonnell and Lynn Hunt (eds), *Beyond the Cultural Turn. New Directions in the Study of Society and Culture* (Berkeley, 1999).

48 Anna Clark, *The Struggle for the Breeches. Gender and the Making of the British Working Class* (Berkeley, 1995); Kathleen Canning, *Languages of Labor and Gender: Female Factory Work in Germany, 1850–1914* (Ithaca, 1996); James Vernon, *Politics and the People. A Study in English Political Culture, c. 1815–1867* (Cambridge, 1993); Robert E. Weir, *Beyond Labor's Veil. The Culture of the Knights of Labor* (University Park, PA, 1996); Margaret L. Anderson, *Practicing Democracy. Elections and Political Culture in Imperial Germany* (Princeton, 2000); Thomas Welskopp, *Das Banner der Brüderlichkeit. Die deutsche Sozialdemokratie vom Vormärz bis zum Sozialistengesetz* (Bonn, 2000).

- SH breakthrough after WW?.
- Politics = always relevant.

12

Economic history

Pat Hudson

Economic history is distinctive in terms of subject matter and approach. It is concerned with the material underpinnings of human existence: how people make their livings, how food and goods are produced and distributed, and the sorts of societies, ways of life and institutions that different regimes of production and consumption support or encourage. Thus the best economic history is concerned with political, social and cultural as well as economic life. In terms of approach, economic history most often combines the historian's craft and training with the interests, theories and methods of social science, in particular economics. Employing social science concepts and theories in historical research and writing can be enlightening, but problems often arise because most social science of the last century has been geared to contemporary issues. The social sciences in general, and economics in particular, are largely present-centred and policy oriented. They incorporate many assumptions that are only applicable (and even then not always easily applicable) to modern, commercial, capitalistic, usually western, societies. They have a temporal and cultural bias. The dangers of using economics, or any other social science, in history are thus anachronism and ethnocentrism. Economic historians must think carefully about the social, cultural and economic environment of different periods and parts of the globe, and may need to adapt economic and social theory to their purposes, or even rethink aspects of economic and social science for themselves, to make them more appropriate to the historian's needs.

When asked to define economic history some years ago, Donald Coleman emphasized two aspects that differentiate it from both history and economics. First, economic history seeks to identify and measure forces normally outside the control of single individual actors. This causes problems for the many historians who reject the idea that forces can be identified as agents that create or condition historical events. Second, Coleman restated the truism that economic phenomena have no existence independent of the social, political, religious and physical environment in which they occur.[1] The embeddedness of economic activity within the social, cultural and personal fabric of everyday life means that the economic historian needs to take a holistic and interdisciplinary approach.

Despite its distinctiveness in these ways, it is the case that the nature and popularity of economic history have always been tied to developments in the parent disciplines of history and social science, particularly economics. In the 1960s and 1970s, for example, there was a widespread appreciation and uptake of social science approaches in history, and a concern for economic structures. This went along with the expansion of social science in universities and the popularity of Marxian ideas that placed emphasis upon the role of the economy in influencing social, cultural and political structures. Furthermore, the social sciences generally, and economics in particular, were more open than is the case today to evidence from the past as well as the present. Today, priorities in history, where they are not focused upon military and political narrative, have turned to cultural phenomena and to the use of literary and dramatic metaphors and methods of analysis rather than using the mechanical or causative reasoning that economists and economic historians generally employ. Textual sources have been increasingly privileged over the quantitative data that was traditionally favoured by economic historians. Some would say that these trends, taken together, have left economic history stranded. But economic history is not just a set of concerns passively waiting around for the right environment in which to flourish. It is able significantly to critique the narrow purview of much contemporary economic theory and also to ambush the many cultural historians who appear to have forgotten what the economy is and why causal analysis is important. Thus, economic history is currently faced with growing opportunities as well as some problems, and perhaps more of the former than the latter.

This chapter considers the ways in which the economy has figured in the work of historians, and at the way various approaches to economics have been used by historians to throw light on the past. It does this by outlining the history of economic history, relating it to broader trends in the development of history and social science. Stress is placed throughout upon different ways of conceptualizing the economic sphere and economic motivation, and in questioning the boundaries between economic actions and other forms of social and cultural behaviour.

12.1 Economic theory and history: two sorts of approaches

There are two very different ways in which the use of economic theory in history has come about. The first involves seeing the economy as fundamentally important within an overall explanation of history, underpinning a metanarrative. It involves acceptance that the nature of the economy has a primary role in conditioning all aspects of society, culture, politics. In its various forms the Marxian approach to history adopts this position, as do some forms of modernization theory. Marxian studies of social, cultural, legal or other aspects of life in the past inevitably involve relating the nature of their subject, and change in their subject over time, to the nature of the economy and shifts in the economic base of society. For example, E.P. Thompson in his classic, *The Making of the English Working Class* (1963), focused on the rise of class solidarity and social protest in the early nineteenth century, but shifts in technology, manufacturing, competition, work relations and trading are shown to be the forces underlying social change, in the face of which people came together and began to act, and to see themselves, in class terms. John Foster, in his *Class Struggle in the Industrial Revolution* (1974) used the Marxian base/superstructure model to compare the nature of class consciousness in three English towns in the nineteenth century. By these means he not only explained the revolutionary threat in Oldham in the 1840s, but also the more peaceable nature of the later nineteenth century, which, he argued (along Marxist-Leninist lines), was brought about by the economic stability of a more mature capitalism resting on the gains from imperialism. Although the Marxian model reached a peak of influence upon western history between the 1940s and the 1970s, and is now very consciously rejected by most historians and social theorists, its influence upon social science runs deep. It is impossible (even if thought desirable) entirely to escape its influence. We are all Marxian now in the sense that non-Marxist and post-Marxist works of history and social science often retain a strong commitment to considering the role of the economy as a major variable (if not a determining one) in analysing aspects of society and culture, past and present.

The second way in which an economic approach to history and the use of economic theory in history occurs is by using a variety of 'middle range' economic theories (which are not metanarratives in any sense) and various concepts and explanatory devices drawn from economic theory. The toolbox is varied. Historians have drawn upon many different strands of economic theory and have used diverse concepts from economic sociology, and from economic and social anthropology as well as from economics. Much can be gained by using first principles of economics, particularly supply and demand theory, to think through the impact of, for example, food shortages or population expansion during periods for which firm evidence is lacking. M.M. Postan's argument about the decline of feudal relations in England rested on economic reasoning about the impact of the Black Death upon the prices of land, labour and agricultural produce.[2] The dominant paradigm in economics during the last century, and particularly since the 1950s, has rested upon formal and mechanical models frequently represented in algebraic or graphical terms, and underpinned by the assumption that human beings, in satisfying their material needs, are driven by 'rational' profit-maximizing motives. This neo-classical approach has been very influential in economic history, but its use has varied over time. Such variations are best understood by considering the history of the subject.

12.2 The history of economic history: origins

For most of the eighteenth and nineteenth centuries, English, Scottish, French and German political economists, and the founding fathers of western social science (figures as diverse as Adam Smith, David Ricardo, John Stuart Mill, Karl Marx, Max Weber, Emile Durkheim and Ferdinand Tonnies), all drew from historical evidence when analysing society. In this sense economic history has a long lineage central to the emergence of social science in Europe. However, it arose more specifically as an academic concern of historians and economists at the end of the nineteenth century and in the early twentieth century. This came as part of a wider rejection of 'drum and trumpet' history – the history of elites, diplomacy and wars – in favour of the history of the mass of the population and of agriculture, industry and trading. This move to study non-elite and 'non-political' history was also the aim of the founders of the *Annales* School in France. It was a history favoured by socialists and social reformers who were addressing the problems arising from industrialization. This encouraged an economic history that looked to the past in order to understand the causes of social dislocation and for evidence of government regulation in the interests of the masses. In England, this approach was exemplified by the work of Sidney and Beatrice Webb, founders of the London School of Economics (LSE), by Arnold Toynbee, Barbara and John Hammond, Charles Beard and many of the first generation of academic writers in economic history. William Ashley was the first British historian to adopt a periodization not derived from political history, an important step in freeing history from the rule of political events.

Economic history also evolved as an academic subject, from the later nineteenth century, as a branch of economics. Indeed the so-called Historical School represented the dominant approach in economics in the early and mid-nineteenth century. It was highly empirical, statistically orientated and historically attuned. It placed emphasis upon fact gathering (from the past and the present) and induction (the idea that general patterns would emerge, if at all, once all the data had been assembled). Much early economic history was of this kind. Further enthusiastic recruits to economic history as a discipline came from the reaction of many economists against new developments taking place in economics in the 1880s and 1890s (the so-called marginalist or neo-classical revolution). These developments made economics more present-centred, more formal (mechanical, mathematical and graphical) in its methods and more deductive (depending upon the predictive ability of generalizations and statistical inference). This development was not only perceived as a major threat to the older Historical School, which eventually became a minority tradition, but economic history, allied to historical economics, was viewed as an attempt to find an alternative methodology to the growing mainstream in economics, one that would better take account of different time periods and cultures. William Cunningham, who published the first English economic history text in 1882, objected to the idea, dominant in neo-classical economics, of 'economic man' as a rational calculating and maximizing individual whose behaviour could be seen as deriving from an immutable human nature, present in all societies. He favoured the study of societies in their own time, and with their own special social and cultural attitudes and motivations.[3] These views came out in his controversies with Alfred Marshall, the leading exponent of the marginalist revolution in Britain. Although Marshall himself saw economics as 'the study of man in the ordinary business of life', the method he helped to establish encouraged economists to specialize in abstract generalized theorizing. Similar debates between the historical school and formal, neo-classical economists were going on in Europe and particularly in Germany where the *Methodenstreit* (debates upon method) in economics was most vociferous, partly because of the strength of the Historical School there.

From the outset, economic history as a distinctive academic discipline also included those who wished to take the deductive, formalist approach becoming dominant in economics and apply what was seen as rigorous 'scientific' method to studies of the past and to historical data. This was a very minor strand in economic history before the mid-twentieth century. Its attraction as a method was the application of those universalist assumptions about economic behaviour that Cunningham, among others, had been so keen to reject. This conflict, together with the commitment to economic history from socialists and reformers, made for keen debates within economic history about purpose and method from the outset.

12.3 The history of economic history: expansion and diversity

The subject expanded in the USA and Europe in the 1920s, in Britain with the foundation of the Economic History Society and the *Economic History Review*, and with a growing number of university appointments and courses in the subject. Much research appeared that used hitherto untouched historical documents for the first time: for example, the censuses of population and production, overseas trade figures, local municipal records, parliamentary reports and commissions, business archives. This broke new ground because the sources and the concerns that economic and social historians tackled had not traditionally been regarded as a priority for historians or even as a legitimate sphere of their interests. There was also a strong internationalist flavour to many of these early works: a preoccupation with international trade and with the nature of economic development in various parts of the globe. Economic history, in Britain at least, was also noted in this period for the relatively high proportion of female historians who had been attracted to the subject, including Eileen Power, E.M. Carus Wilson, Ivy Pinchbeck and Lilian Knowles. Their research interests helped to shape the scope and preoccupations of the subject, in particular its emphasis upon internationalism, the social impact of change and the experiences of families, women and children as well as men.[4]

Two very different strains were apparent in economic history in Britain by the early twentieth century. These spawned further creative tension.[5] The first can be termed the political or moral tradition represented in the work of R.H. Tawney, Barbara and John Hammond, Sidney and Beatrice Webb and G.D.H. Cole. These writers were influenced by varieties of socialist thought (either Christian socialism, Fabianism or Marxism). They sought connections with other developing fields of the social sciences, and attempted to answer big questions of causality such as the causes of the English Revolution or the Industrial Revolution. They also sought answers to contemporary moral and political questions through interrogating the past. Tawney argued against piling up statistics and facts, advocating the need to consider the moral questions and relationships that underlay economic activity. Tawney held the first chair in Economic History at LSE (from 1931). His best-known work *Religion and the Rise of Capitalism* (1926) challenged the Weber thesis that the rise of capitalism in western Europe was spurred by the social and economic values of Calvinism. Tawney argued that Calvinism provided a religious rationale for capitalism, and that both Puritanism and capitalism were perversions of Christian values that favoured social obligation over individualism. Tawney wore his moral position on his sleeve, and his interpretation of the capitalist ethic and other subjects was the focus of intense debate over many decades.

A second strain within economic history at this time might be termed the empirical and conservative: characterized by an economic focus, underdeveloped cultural or political context and a disinterest in formulating theories or laws about cause or effect. The approach was marked by an interest in newly excavated empirical detail and quantitative data. In different ways the works of Sir John Clapham, Herbert Heaton, A.P. Wadsworth and J. de L. Mann fall into this tradition. Clapham produced a three-volume *Economic History of Modern Britain* (1926–38), which used a range of evidence to study sectors of the economy in detail. He rejected the term 'industrial revolution' because he uncovered just how gradual and partial change was at the time. He also challenged the socialist and moral tradition by suggesting that, with the exception of a few dying trades, living conditions improved for the masses during industrialization.

The early twentieth-century expansion of economic history took place at a time when sociology and anthropology were joining economics in becoming less concerned with historical study, and focusing more upon contemporary studies and fieldwork. Economic history expanded to fill the void left by the increasingly present-centred nature of the other social sciences. The subject at this time was generally conceived as a broadly based branch of historical enquiry that took in social as well as strictly economic events and conditions, and had a broad definition of the economic sphere. This was also true of the subject in France and Germany, and because of this it had a wide appeal, not just as a university subject, but among a lay readership. In Britain it was popular in university extension studies classes and in courses run by the Workers Educational Association. Most economic historians wrote accessible books and pamphlets in a non-technical style and for a popular as well as an academic audience. *Religion and the Rise of Capitalism* had total sales running into six figures and was translated into several languages.

12.4 The history of economic history: the 1950s and 1960s

By the 1950s economic history as an identifiable academic discipline had largely fallen into the hands of the Clapham tradition marked most obviously, and perhaps surprisingly, by the succession of T.S. Ashton to Tawney's chair at LSE. Ashton was a conservative, not a socialist. His work nevertheless remained accessible and widely read. His best-seller *The Industrial Revolution* (1948) was written for a general readership in the *Oxford Home Library of Knowledge* series. However, the subject was changing in the 1940s and 1950s to incorporate more theoretical insight from contemporary economics, especially economic development and trade cycle theory. This resulted in some classic studies of trade cycles (following a pattern set by N.D. Kondratieff and Joseph Schumpeter in the 1920s and 1930s) and of the composition of GNP in different phases of economic growth (seen most obviously in Britain in the work of Phyllis Deane and W.A. Cole).[6] In addition, many worthy studies of particular industries or sectors of the economy appeared, such as Peter Mathias on brewing and Donald Coleman on paper.[7] There was a growing tendency at this time to see the experiences of western, and specifically British, industrialization as a model that could throw light upon solutions to third-world development problems, illustrated most clearly in the work of W.W. Rostow.[8] The 1950s onwards also saw the development of 'business history'. Large firms commissioned historians to write their histories, and classic works appeared such as Charles Wilson on Unilever, Donald Coleman on

Courtaulds, and Theo Barker on Pilkingtons.[9] This development created a bias in research in favour of successful and wealthy firms and, because the firms themselves had often financed the research, it tended to encourage interpretations favourable to big business.

The moral and socialist tradition also continued strongly, however. The British Marxist historians were at this time writing a parallel theoretically informed set of socio-economic histories seen in the work of Maurice Dobb, Eric Hobsbawm, Christopher Hill, Rodney Hilton, Edward Thompson, Victor Kiernon and others. Work of great interest and excitement was produced in the 1960s and 1970s, its popularity bolstered by the political climate and youth culture. Many of these books sold thousands of copies outside the realm of academe and they were internationally very important. A succession of books by Eric Hobsbawm about international economic change have sold in their hundreds of thousands across the globe since the 1960s.[10] Stress upon the pivotal role of the economy in impelling change, however strongly mediated by social and cultural factors and by human agency, made the work of Hilton, Hill, Hobsbawm and Thompson required reading on all undergraduate economic history courses. Political cleavages in the subject during these decades created acrimonious and lively debate in the pages of learned academic journals on topics such as the rise of the gentry and the rise of capitalism (debates carried over from Tawney's writings), the standard of living and the threat of political insurrection during the industrial revolution, and the causes and impact of imperialism. This led many young scholars, myself included, to believe that they had chosen the most exciting subject possible. Partly because of the influence of Marxist social historians, such as E.P. Thompson, but also because of the general expansion of social science in these years, much economic history, Marxian or not, incorporated a great deal of social history and some cultural history, particularly where this had a materialist basis. This was seen particularly in histories of social protest, labour and social conditions, trades unions and class. Much of it was written 'from below' – that is, from the perspective of working people rather than the elites.

12.5 The 'new economic history'

A major turning point in economic history came with the so-called 'New Economic History' of the 1960s and 1970s, also referred to as econometric history. Economic history had always had a strong quantitative bent but this became more sophisticated, using not just tables, graphs and figures better to display the character of data, but also employing statistical analysis to consider trends and the relationship between the movements of different variables. The big change occurred as more historians became convinced of the gains to be delivered by marrying the statistical approach with the formal deductive methods of neo-classical economics, and applying these to economic circumstances and choices in the past. This arose first in the United States, where economic history had always retained very close connections with economics, having developed as a university subject largely within economics departments. Economics at this time was becoming more confident and assertive in formal model building, and statistical inference as its cutting-edge method of choice, and many economic historians were infected by this enthusiasm. The most vigorous exponents of econometric history claimed it would eventually provide definitive answers to many of the most fundamental questions asked by economic historians. The implication was that this would put history back upon the objective or scientific path from which it had mistakenly wandered.

The 'new economic history', and quantitative history more generally, was aided by increasing use of computer technology. This not only facilitated the production of graphs, tables and statistical breakdowns, but also enabled more advanced model building, interpolations and simulations such as back projection, and counter-factual developments. 'Model building' refers to the construction of a simplified and abstracted set of economic relationships intended to represent the functioning of an economy or a sector of the economy. Such models have been used many times in the study of the British and American economies in the nineteenth and twentieth centuries and in studies of sectors such as railways and cotton. 'Back projection' is the estimation of what growth rates or other measures might have been for periods where figures do not exist by extrapolating on the basis of later periods where figures do exist. For example, Wrigley and Schofield's study of English population growth projected population figures from the 1851 Census back into the eighteenth century to calculate the shortfall in parish registrations.[11] Although counter-factual propositions are implicit in many historical arguments, 'counter-factual history' is the most controversial technique in econometric history. It involves calculation of the advantages of a historical innovation by comparing economic growth in the presence of the innovation with economic growth in the absence of the innovation (the latter estimated by building up a counter-factual model of the economy in the absence of the innovation). The groundbreaking work here was R.W. Fogel's *Railways and American Economic growth* (1964). In this, Fogel constructed a model of what the US economy might have looked like in 1890 if railways had never existed. By comparing this with the actual economy in that year, he demonstrated that the role of railways in American economic growth had been grossly overstated.

12.6 Achievements and problems of econometric history

The major achievements of econometric history in the 1960s and 1970s lay in highlighting new lines of enquiry, creating new data sets and growth indices, and in disturbing old impressionistically based assumptions. But there were many problems. The new economic history was usually highly reductive, numerical and laden with jargon, making it difficult for non-specialists to read or understand. This resulted in a group of econometricians writing largely for each other and with little regard for the rest of the historical establishment, a strong contrast with the accessible and popular nature of most branches of economic history in earlier decades.

The first wave of econometric history also frequently failed to be sufficiently critical of the reliability of the quantitative evidence that it used. Historians often got carried away with enthusiasm for the techniques and forgot to pay sufficient attention to the shortcomings of their sources. An additional problem lay in the fact that the models and methods of econometrics involve efforts to quantify (and reduce to a monetary value) things for which this is difficult, if not impossible – for example, changes in opportunities, social conditions and intellectual horizons, the quality of goods, the advantages of increased leisure. This brought much criticism from conventional historians, as did the fact that much of the new economic history made historically dubious assumptions about human behaviour on the basis of the universalist claims of neo-classical economics. Neo-classical models assume that people will always act to optimize their economic position (the so-called rationality postulate) and that prices have the power to convert individual choices into an efficient productive system. But the rationality postulate is impossible to apply to all societies in all times. The possibilities of individual rational choice are affected by many circumstances: by power relationships as well as by the degree of information to which economic agents have access (hence their expectations) and by their cognitive ability in processing such information. Rational choice theory will always be prone to challenge, particularly in analysing societies with poor information flows, devolved power structures, forceful customary arrangements, and low levels of literacy and education. In past societies, it may have been more rational for individuals to act to maximize the economic position of the village, the estate or the extended family than the individual or nuclear family, or not to maximize at all. Sufficiency may be more important in cultures and contexts where mortality is high and disease rife and/or where there are few consumer goods available. In such circumstances leisure rather than wealth is likely to be the prized possession.

Furthermore, the efficiency of the price system depends upon a competitive environment and upon the efficient flow of capital, labour, raw materials, finished goods and information. Competitive regimes of production and exchange, and the efficient flow of factors, goods and services are much less prevalent in earlier societies and in non-western cultures than they are today in Britain and the United States. The new economic history often erred in applying concepts and models anachronistically and without due regard for different cultural contexts. Furthermore, the econometric models that were constructed in this era were often derisively simplistic and easy to criticize. They depended upon a limited number of variables in relatively straightforward combinations: the first wave of econometric history was insufficiently self-critical and too ambitious to recognize the technical limits of the tools available at the time.

Econometric history was never the dominant approach in Britain, and certainly not in Europe or elsewhere in the world outside of the United States. It did, however, capture the high ground of economic history in the latter, and its proponents were forceful and influential in exporting their product to Europe. They also produced some thought-provoking and controversial work influencing the subject beyond the boundaries of their own techniques. Probably fewer than one in ten British economic historians were directly involved with econometrics (even fewer in Europe) but the association of economic history with such positivistic and frequently flawed scientific method contributed to a decline in the popularity of the subject. It was responsible for associating economic history with a much narrower set of methods and sphere of interest than had been the case earlier, and a disinterest in broader social, cultural and political issues.

12.7 Economic history since the 1980s: the rejection of Marxian analysis and the challenge of postmodernism and poststructuralism

In the 1970s and 1980s specialized areas of research within social and economic history emerged, or were consolidated, such as urban history, agricultural history, transport history, labour history, business history, medical history and demographic history. This sub-disciplinary specialization produced important results. In business history, for example, the subject broadened out to include work using insurance records, bankruptcy hearings, and oral evidence and other sources to look at smaller more typical firms. But specialization was also accompanied by a damaging compartmentalization that hindered understanding of historical processes in the round.[12] The separation of business history from labour history created obstacles to understanding, while urban history and agricultural history encouraged individual case studies rather than attempts to understand overall economic development. In the field of demography, groundbreaking work appeared using many new techniques, but demography is generally defined to exclude discussion of sexual behaviour, sexuality or sexual desire. With one or two key exceptions, the need to understand long-term change in a holistic way slipped largely from the agenda and this left economic history vulnerable to criticism.

While the identification of economic history with econometric history had weakened potential interest in the subject, fragmentation into specialized fields undermined the identity of economic history and its integrative role. More importantly, the rejection of Marxian analysis as an underpinning intellectual force in the social sciences and in history also reduced the attraction of studying the economy. Concern to avoid any charge of economic or technological determinism, or any association with what popular opinion now sees as a discredited body of theory, contributed to a general and damaging disinterest in the relationship between the economy and the rest of society.

A further factor in the declining popularity of economic history since the 1980s is the influence of postmodernism, and general scepticism about positivistic historical and social-science explanations. This has been strong in the last two or three decades. The argument that academic disciplines, including history and economics, which purport to explain reality, should be viewed as discursive formations that promote some ideas and also constrain what is written and thought, has naturally undermined respect for approaches that do not much question their own concepts and language or their basic assumptions about an anterior reality. Economics and economic history can be seen as particularly vulnerable to these charges. The rejection of positivism, alongside the related expansion of new forms of cultural history, has involved a growing preference for literary, dramatic, symbolic and linguistic analyses and understandings over the mechanical analogies and structural models that lie at the heart of traditional social science and especially of economics. Linking phenomena to their causes and understanding their impact upon broader systems has been increasingly supplanted by the desire to relate actions to their sense and to study representations rather than 'reality'. Traditional forms of economics and of economic history have little obvious role to play in the new dispensation. But the subject is undergoing change, following innovations in economic theory, rediscovering some of its earlier, holistic preoccupations with society and culture, and responding to the intellectual environment of the twenty-first century in rigorous ways.

12.8 Economics and history in the twenty-first century

The relationship between economic history and economic theory is shifting because economics is undergoing changes that make it potentially much more useful in historical applications. First, it is becoming a great deal more sophisticated in its assumptions about human motivations and the efficiency of markets, and in modelling the complex and differing circumstances that occur in the 'real world'. These developments are generally referred to as the new institutional economics.[13] Second, and much more radically, there are growing challenges to neo-classical formalism and rational choice theory arising from evolutionary approaches and a revival of the hermeneutic tradition. The preoccupations of economists are thus now more in line than they have been for many decades with those of economic historians. Such concerns include the varieties of market and non-market forms of exchange; gender relations in the formation of household decisions; 'irrational' behaviour; variation in the performance of firms and economies under similar sets of conditions; the structure of trade; the role of trust and reputation, custom and habit; economic horizons in risk-taking and decision-making; and issues concerning quality of life as a measure of economic growth.

The importance of institutions and their impact upon contracts and transaction costs is now much more fully recognized than in the past. Institutions are sets of rules and understandings that parties in business and commerce observe in order to act more efficiently. Transaction costs are the expenses incurred in doing business, negotiating a deal and making sure that it is carried out. Historians have long been acutely aware of the importance of these elements, particularly when studying imperfect markets, and the importance of customary and inflexible influences upon the adjustment of wages and prices. More attention is also now paid to asymmetric information where one party in a transaction knows more than the other. Such asymmetries are likely to have been more important in the past, especially in trade and in financial transactions. Reinforcing theories of asymmetric information is an acknowledgement of agency problems. Agency theory is concerned with how people get others to do what they want where there is asymmetric information, and where incentives and monitoring will be required: such circumstances characterize economic relationships particularly in earlier times.[14]

The technical limits of economics have also been greatly extended, particularly in time-series analysis and general equilibrium modelling. This allows formal models to cope with many more variables and with more complex interactions. Multiple equilibria models and a much greater use of game theory characterize economic theorizing. Game theory explains the structure and logic of inter-personal inter-reactions and is fast becoming the mainstay of modern economic theory, particularly in relation to contracting and bargaining, and in analysing institutions that develop in response to information asymmetries between parties to an exchange. This, together with the greater sophistication of rationality assumptions and the ability to allow for changing tastes and conventions, opens up the possibility of many new uses for economic theory in historical applications.

12.9 Economic history and economics: the challenge of alternative economics

Despite these developments, economists generally start with interests of a profit-maximizing or 'rational' kind, and then move to take institutions and social behaviour into account, while sociologists, anthropologists and others generally start with society, culture and institutions, explaining how economic behaviour (oriented towards interests or utilities) is 'embedded', and can only be understood, within them. These approaches involve different understandings of human nature as well as different methodologies, and this limits the potential for integration. It is not just a question of deduction versus induction but also of formal mechanical analogies and instrumental reasoning versus hermeneutic understanding. Hermeneutics is the method of the cultural sciences, a method of interpreting human action in a similar way to studying the authenticity of a text. It is based on a dialogical (two-way, reciprocal) process of shared understandings between creator and interpreter. Important minority traditions in economics have always sought to engage with hermeneutics and there is currently a growing revival of alternative economics adopting evolutionary, institutional and cultural approaches, and seeking entirely to reform the purview of economics from within. Unlike the neo-classical paradigm (even in its most sophisticated forms) these alternatives place emphasis upon interpretative understanding of human behaviour and motivations, not upon the predictive success of formal logical models.

Evolutionary economics is very different from neo-classical economics because it sees economic systems to be in constant disequilibrium. This is much more applicable to most historical contexts than the neo-classical idea of economies and markets tending towards equilibrium. Evolutionary theory takes its cue from biological rather than mechanical analogies, and the economic, the social and the cultural are regarded as inseparable elements in an environment that is constantly changing. Evolutionary theory stresses the importance of habits and routines, analogous to memes in socio-biology. These evolve slowly as both the result and the cause of change in the environment. Routines are behaviours (including language) that are conducted with little explicit thought. They create an institutional structure based upon continuous feedback from experience, which is rarely articulated. Such structures include the complex of socially learned and shared values, norms, beliefs, meanings, symbols, customs and standards that delineate the range of expected and accepted behaviour in a particular context.

Various hermeneutic approaches to economics take this emphasis upon institutions further to suggest that the economic behaviour of individuals cannot be adequately understood (as in conventional economics) as a kind of automatic reaction to objective stimuli; it must instead be understood in terms of an individual's *read-*

ing of prices, opportunities, relative costs, and so on. In other words priority must be given to the social environment and to the inter-subjective ways in which people make sense of the world and its stimuli, and communicate that sense one to another. This approach has the potential to revolutionize economics by suggesting that what really counts in economic explanation is not empirical verification or falsification (the traditional approach) but narrative and hermeneutic acceptability. Such an approach to economics gives history a new set of tools that are compatible with the cultural and linguistic turn. Stress upon the importance of the habitual, the everyday and unconscious routines in the material life of individuals, families and communities, is becoming a stronger current in socio-historical research. The habits of mind that are stressed, as well as routines, social arrangements and organizations, make the 'economic' workable, invest it with meanings, rules and sanctions, and give it both durability and a capacity for change.

12.10 Economic history: contrasting examples and a conclusion

I will, finally, consider two books that illustrate the enormous contrast in style and method characteristic of economic history and of the shifting approach to the subject over time. *Time on the Cross: The Economics of American Negro Slavery*, by Robert Fogel and Stanley Engerman, appeared in 1974 at the height of the econometric revolution. It is the best-known example of the new economic history of the period. The work appeared in two volumes, the second given over entirely to statistical evidence and methods.[15] Unlike Fogel's earlier book on the railroads, *Time on the Cross* is not a counter-factual study but employs neo-classical models and statistical analysis to demonstrate that slavery was more successful and efficient than the contemporary agricultural system based on free labour. Fogel and Engerman argue that, as a result, slavery provided a high standard of living for all southerners, including slaves. They argue that planters in the mid-nineteenth century were a rational and humane group, and that slaves were fairly prosperous and generally well treated. Slaves had both the capacity and the drive for upward social and economic mobility. They worked harder and more efficiently than free farm labourers and adopted a work ethic and style of family life similar to their capitalist employers. Slaves learned to respond to a range of economic incentives, to seek extra income, leisure and occupational advance through cooperation and identification with the economic interests of their masters. Fogel and Engerman call this 'the record of black achievement under adversity'. They also 'prove' that slavery had not ceased to be profitable to owners at the time of the US Civil War as several historians had previously argued. Their main sources are quantitative: plantation records of trade, slave output, profit and loss, coupled with census schedules for demographic evidence, and probate data.

The main claim made by Fogel and Engerman is that traditional historians of slavery had had to rely upon the unsystematic use of fragmentary literary sources. The bulk of quantifiable data was beyond their reach because they had lacked the assistance of computers, and the mathematical and statistical training for quantitative analysis. The fact that quantitative data is frequently as unsystematic and fragmentary as any other sort of evidence is swept under the carpet. This point is neatly illustrated in the debate between Fogel and Engerman and their critics on the subject of the whipping of slaves. Fogel and Engerman have a sophisticated argument about the role of punishments vis-à-vis incentives in slave labour discipline, but it is largely based upon quantitative data from just one set of plantation records, which cover a two-year period. Their source is almost certainly unrepresentative but, more importantly, their conclusions ignore the deterrent and fear elements of physical punishments, which are difficult, if not impossible, to quantify. This is symptomatic of a wider problem of privileging the importance of quantifiable over non-quantifiable evidence. They also confuse what is from what ought to be, assuming society operated on market principles, and arguing backwards from the outcomes of social and market processes in order to comment upon the motives and actions of individuals who participated in them, whether masters or slaves. There is no place in their analysis for masters who raped or partnered slave women at the risk of upsetting labour discipline, who owned more slaves than they could employ efficiently and who behaved irrationally in other ways such as by abusing slaves for racist rather than efficiency reasons. The most fundamental assumption of the work and the one that remains a weakness at the heart of the analysis is whether an economic system that had slavery at its core can justifiably be analysed in the same way as a capitalist economy using free labour. Are concepts such as 'economic exploitation' and 'economic efficiency' appropriate? Can neo-classical analysis really be applied to systems of involuntary servitude? Critics suggested that prejudice had resulted in the selective use of evidence, and that the resulting positive view of slavery and the motives of slave owners arose from the desire to make everything fit into a neo-classical model in which 'each and every slave owner regarded slaves solely as productive instruments and used them for a single transcendent purpose: the maximisation of pecuniary gain'.[16] *Time on the Cross* did, however, provoke extensive debate, stimulated new research that considerably advanced our knowledge of slavery, and forced later historians to be much more explicit about theoretical and ideological assumptions, as well as about the nature and use of sources.

Craig Muldrew's *The Economy of Obligation: The Culture of Credit and Social Relations in Early Modern England* (1998) is an example of recent economic history in which the economic, the social and the cultural meld together. Muldrew's aim is to write a social history of the market, arguing that markets have not been interpreted culturally because of the dominant influence of anachronistic neo-classical economic analysis:

> the relationship between economic theory and history needs to be reversed, so that a thickly researched historiography of the complex motivations and practices of agents – together with an understanding of how they themselves interpreted such actions – [can] inform future theory, rather than the other way round.[17]

Muldrew combines the sources and methods of community history used by social and economic historians with the practices of intellectual history, which look closely at the interactions and interpretations of contemporary texts. His sources include instructional pamphlets on the use of credit, letters, diaries and autobiographies, as well as court records and a range of account books, tax, probate and other evidence, which enables him to describe the trading activities and social structure of Kings Lynn (the focus of his research) in some detail. He examines the cultural meaning of credit and how this changed under the impact of the expanding economy of the later sixteenth century. He places emphasis upon trust and household reputation, and the importance of sociability and neighbourliness in understanding the nature of 'economic' transactions. He is interested in the cultural representation of trust and credit in the literature of the period, as well as in social practices. His concern is to examine economic motivation in the terms that contemporaries understood it.

Muldrew analyses the cultural changes that accompanied the expansion of the market, and the proliferation of credit based upon personal trust and the reputation of individuals and families. Households became more dependent on one another through complex networks of exchange, credit and obligation. The combination of competition and dependence this involved meant that families and neighbourhoods increasingly had to try to find a balance between hospitality, reciprocity and charity on the one hand, and thrift and profit on the other. Both were needed to keep the economy expanding and thus to ensure the financial security of both households and the wider society. Muldrew demonstrates that the practice of litigation in debt cases reflected the equality embodied in contemporary social theories of bargaining and market exchange. The book concludes by considering the impact of subsequent economic change in altering the way in which the ethics of marketing are now understood. By extending his thoughts to the present and by uncovering a complex economy very different from our own, Muldrew raises questions about our contemporary perceptions of the economy. The entire analysis is innovative in considering representations and understandings as well as actions, in combining cultural and economic history, and in using the skills and sources of literary analysis and intellectual history, as well as more conventional economic history. It is no accident that Muldrew did not train as an economic historian but as a social and cultural historian with an interest in economic activity and behaviour. This frees him from the tendency to seek conventional neo-classical explanations. While Fogel and Engerman's work was groundbreaking in showing the limits as well as the possibilities of the application of neo-classical models to historical debates, Muldrew's analysis resonates with the broader approach to the economy and with the moral commitment of an earlier generation of historians. His work reflects the current move among a wider array of historians to study the economy in diverse and innovative ways.

The future for economic history looks bright because it is able to draw upon a wider and more sophisticated range of economy theory and method than in the past, and because it is redefining the economic sphere in broader terms and for its own purposes, eschewing the disciplinary boundaries erected by modernism. It is placing new stress upon the cultural, social and institutional framework of economic activity, and it is drawing increasingly upon the tools of anthropology, ethnography and cultural history, alongside economics, to analyse those aspects of material life that conventional economists have rarely reached.

Guide to further reading

D.C. Coleman, *History and the Economic Past: An Account of the Rise and Decline of Economic History in Britain* (London, 1987).

N.F.R. Crafts, 'Cliometrics 1971–86: A Survey', *Journal of Applied Econometrics* 2(2) (1987), pp. 171–92.

S. Cullenberg, J. Ameriglio and D.F. Ruccio (eds), *Postmodernism, Economics and Knowledge* (London, 2001).

G. Hodgson, *Economics and Evolution: Bringing Life Back into Economics* (London, 1993).

G. Hodgson, *How Economics Forgot History: The Problem of Historical Specificity in Social Science* (London, 2001).

Pat Hudson, *History by Numbers* (London, 2000), Chapter 8.

Alon Kadish, *Historians, Economists and Economic History* (London, 1989).

Harvey J. Kaye, *The British Marxist Historians* (London, 1984).

Don Lavoie (ed.), *Economics and Hermeneutics* (London, 1990).

J. Maloney, *What's New in Economics?* (Manchester, 1992).

M. Rutherford, *Institutions in Economics* (Cambridge, 1994).

Notes

1 D.C. Coleman, in *History Today* xxxv (February 1985).
2 M.M. Postan, *The Medieval Economy and Society* (London, 1972).
3 W. Cunningham, *The Growth of English Industry and Commerce* (Cambridge, 1882).
4 M. Berg, 'The First Women Economic Historians', *Economic History Review* 45(2) (1992), pp. 308–29.
5 D.C. Coleman analyses these distinctive strains in a slightly different way in *History and the Economic Past: An Account of the Rise and Decline of Economic History in Britain* (Oxford, 1987).
6 P. Deane and W.A. Cole, *British Economic Growth, 1688–1959* (London, 1969).
7 P. Mathias, *The Brewing Industry in England, 1700–1830* (Cambridge, 1959); D.C. Coleman, *The British Paper Industry 1495–1860: A Study in Industrial Growth* (Oxford, 1958).
8 W.W. Rostow, *The Stages of Economic Growth* (Cambridge, 1960).
9 C. Wilson, *The History of Unilever: a Study of Economic Growth and Social Change* (London, 1954); D.C. Coleman, *Courtaulds: An Economic and Social History*, 3 vols (Oxford, 1969); T.C. Barker, *Pilkington Brothers and the Glass Industry* (London, 1960).
10 Starting with *The Age of Revolution, 1789–1848* (New York, 1962), the sequence includes *Industry and Empire* (London, 1968), *The Age of Capital, 1848–1875* (London, 1975), *The Age of Empire, 1875–1914* (New York, 1989) and *The Age of Extremes: The Short Twentieth Century, 1914–1991* (New York, 1994).
11 E.A. Wrigley and R. Schofield, *The Population History of England, 1541–1871* (Cambridge, 1981).
12 For critiques of this specialization see Keith Wrightson, 'The Enclosure of English Social History', in A. Wilson (ed.), *Rethinking Social History* (Manchester, 1993); J.D. Marshall, *The Tyranny of the Discrete* (Aldershot, 1997).
13 See O. Williamson, *The Economic Institutions of Capitalism* (New York, 1985). For an example of the potential of some institutional perspectives when applied to long-term economic change see D.C. North, *Institutional Change and Economic Performance* (Cambridge, 1990); for indications of their impact upon micro theory in relation to historical applications see Avner Grief, 'Micro-theory and Recent Developments in the Study of

Economic Institutions through Economic History', in M. Kreps and K.F. Wallis (eds), *Advances in Econometrics and Economics: Theory and Applications*, Vol. 2 (Cambridge, 1997), pp. 79–113.

14 For examples of historical work employing informational asymmetry and agency theory see A. Carlos and S. Nicholas, 'Agency Problems in Early Chartered Companies: The Case of the Hudson's Bay Company' *Journal of Economic History* 50(4) (1990), pp. 853–75; D. Sunderland, 'Principals and Agents: The Activities of the Crown Agents for the Colonies, 1880–1914', *Economic History Review* 52(2) (1999), pp. 284–306.

15 A second major work was published by Fogel in 1989, partly in response to the wave of criticism that followed *Time on the Cross*. This was accompanied by three companion volumes of technical papers written by various collaborators who had been working with Fogel since 1985.

16 Paul A. David *et al.*, *Reckoning with Slavery. A Critical Study of the Quantitative History of American Negro Slavery* (New York, 1976) p. 341.

17 Craig Muldrew, *The Economy of Obligation: The Culture of Credit and Social Relations in Early Modern England* (London, 1998), pp. 7–8.

13

Intellectual history/history of ideas

Beverley Southgate

13.1 Introduction

The terms 'intellectual history' and 'history of ideas' are here used interchange-ably[1] Either way, the concept is elusive – potentially all-embracing, but perenni-ally in danger of falling between any number of academic stools. Its all-embracing nature derives from its subject matter as the history of thought. This can include the history of philosophy, of science, of religious, political, economic or aesthetic ideas, and indeed the history of anything at all that has ever emerged from the human intellect. But such wide-ranging terrain can prove hazardous: it is hard to confine and locate neatly within the conventional departmental boundaries of academia, or even the regimented shelves of libraries and bookshops. The subject and its practitioners defy the constraints of disciplinary structures.

That defiance is not always approved by those academic frontier guards who strive to keep their sanitized domains free from external intrusions, but it can claim a thoroughly respectable pedigree. Able to trace its ancestry back at least as far as Aristotle, the subject quite properly exemplifies the Ancient Greek ideal of universality. For Aristotle himself, philosophy comprised science, politics, ethics, aesthetics, rhetoric, poetry, history – in fact anything to do with 'wisdom', or any-thing that might excite our 'wonder'; and historians of ideas can be seen as Aristotle's intellectual heirs in the breadth of their concerns.

Indeed, for the intellectually adventurous, the subject's academic promiscuity can constitute a major attraction, for while retaining its core concern with history and the historical, it is necessarily involved with many other areas, on which it draws both for procedures and for evidence. Literature, for example, whether poetry or prose, provides some of the most important source material for the study of ideas: one cannot study the thought of classical antiquity without grew, she reminds us of our indebtedness to brave individuals in the past, and alerts us to the tenuousness of our own hold on what we may all too often assume are the naturally given 'rights' of a liberal tradition. Writing of John Locke, she pointedly asks, 'And what of our own prospects for toleration?' (*Early Modern Liberalism*, p. 250). She is concerned, that is, through her history to inspire self-conscious liberally orientated action in the future, and she thus provides a very positive model for postmodern historical study.

13.7 Conclusion: the future

History of ideas shares the position of history more generally at the beginning of the twenty-first century: some sense has to be made of the subject in the context of postmodern challenges. This implies, first, that historians of ideas are bound to proceed in the manner ascribed above to Mersenne – aware of their inability to reach any ultimate 'truth' about the past, but able nonetheless pragmatically to make some headway in practical respects. It is those practical respects with which the second main implication of postmodernism is concerned: just what is the point of it all? And, as we have suggested above, that is not hard to answer. By trying to understand intellectual developments and transformations in the past – the ways that one set of ideas is gradually or more suddenly replaced by another, both at a personal and public level – we may gain some insight into our own thought processes, presuppositions, sometimes inconsistent beliefs, and motivations now. By studying other people at other times and in other cultures, we are confronted by alternatives, and by those who have struggled to assimilate ideas that initially seemed alien. We may, thus, further come to see their (and our own) historicity and contingency, and so be empowered to take some action for the future; and that future will almost certainly require an openness to ideas long since jettisoned from the western intellectual tradition. Annabel Patterson has written (*Early Modern Liberalism*, p. 215) of the need for 'the combined acts of memory and imagination, thinking backwards in order to think forwards'; and that might well set the agenda for historical study in postmodernity.

In that context, we might return to Geoffrey Elton, who described historians of ideas as 'a vociferous minority'. That was not intended as a compliment by a man who readily conceded that 'Good historians are not primarily men of ideas'.[18] But it may suggest a fitting aspiration for intellectual historians in the twenty-first century?

Guide to further reading

Iain Hampsher-Monk, *A History of Modern Political Thought: Major Political Thinkers from Hobbes to Marx* (Oxford, 1992).

David Harvey, *The Condition of Postmodernity: An Enquiry into the Origins of Cultural Change* (Oxford, 1989).

John Henry, *The Scientific Revolution and the Origins of Modern Science*, 2nd edn (Basingstoke, 2002).

Arthur Koestler, *The Sleepwalkers* (Harmondsworth, 1964).

Carolyn Merchant, *The Death of Nature: Women, Ecology, and the Scientific Revolution* (San Francisco, 1980).

Annabel Patterson, *Early Modern Liberalism* (Cambridge, 1997).

Richard H. Popkin, *A History of Scepticism from Erasmus to Spinoza* (Berkeley and Los Angeles, 1979).

Roy Porter, *The Enlightenment*, 2nd edn (Basingstoke, 2001).

Quentin Skinner, *Liberty Before Liberalism* (Cambridge, 1998).

James Tully (ed.), *Meaning and Context: Quentin Skinner and his Critics* (Cambridge, 1988).

Notes

Many thanks to John Ibbett for helpful conversations and constructive comments on an earlier draft.

1 Justification is provided by the fact that the leading academic *Journal of the History of Ideas* has as its sub-title 'an interdisciplinary journal devoted to intellectual history'. For discussion of such terminology, see Maurice Mandelbaum, 'The History of Ideas, Intellectual History, and the History of Philosophy', *History & Theory* 5 (1965), pp. 33–66.
2 Geoffrey Elton, *Return to Essentials* (Cambridge, 1991), p. 27.
3 Aristotle, *Metaphysics* I, 984a.
4 Leslie Stephen, *History of English Thought in the Eighteenth Century*, 2 vols (London, 1876), Vol. 1, p. 3.
5 Milan Kundera, *Immortality* (London, 1992), p. 136.
6 Francis Bacon, *The New Organon* ed. F.H. Anderson (Indianapolis, 1960), p. 75.

7   J.W. Draper, *A History of the Intellectual Development of Europe*, 2 vols (London, 1875), Vol. 1, p. 142; Vol. 2, p. 400.

8   J.T. Merz, *A History of European Thought in the Nineteenth Century*, 4 vols (Edinburgh and London, 1896–1914), Vol. 1, pp. 14, 61, 76.

9   Merz, *History*, Vol. 1, p. 7.

10 Mark Bevir, *The Logic of the History of Ideas* (Cambridge, 1999), p. 178 (my emphasis); cf. p. 190.

11 Quentin Skinner, 'Motives, Intentions and Interpretations', reprinted in James Tully (ed.), *Meaning and Context: Quentin Skinner and his Critics* (Cambridge, 1988), p. 76 (my emphasis added to 'meant' and 'intentions', and removed from 'is').

12 Conrad Russell in Juliet Gardiner (ed.), *The History Debate* (London, 1990), p. 48.

13 For Wittgenstein's example, as for much else in this chapter, I am indebted to Quentin Skinner, whose writings on both the theory and practice of history of ideas has been of the first importance during the last four decades. For Stevie Smith, 'Not Waving but Drowning', see James MacGibbon (ed.), *The Collected Poems of Stevie Smith* (London, 1985), p. 303.

14 Pierre Bayle, *Dictionary*, art. 'Pyrrhon', cited by Richard H. Popkin, *The History of Scepticism from Erasmus to Spinoza* (Berkeley and Los Angeles, 1979), p. 252, n. 3; Henry Buckle, *History of Civilizations in England*, 2 vols (London, 1858), Vol. 1, pp. 317, 328; Stephen, *History*, Vol. 1, p. 43.

15 R.H. Popkin, 'Berkeley and Pyrrhonism' (1951), reprinted in Myles Burnyeat (ed.), *The Skeptical Tradition* (Berkeley and Los Angeles, 1983), p. 394, n. 21.

16 Popkin, *History*, p. xxi; Richard A. Watson and James E. Force (eds), *The High Road to Pyrrhonism* (San Diego, 1980), pp. 29, 37, 53.

17 David Hume and John Leland, quoted by Popkin, *High Road*, pp. 57–8, 206.

18 Elton, *Essentials*, p. 29; *The Practice of History* (London, 1969), p. 192.

14

From women's history to gender history

Laura Lee Downs

On 18 March 1920, Virginia Woolf reminded readers of the venerable *Times Literary Supplement* that despite the existence of isolated works on the history of women (one of which she had reviewed that day), the lives and condition of women in history remained shrouded in profound obscurity: 'It has been common knowledge for ages that women exist, bear children, have no beards, and seldom go bald,' wrote Woolf with acerbic wit, 'but save in these respects, and in others where they are said to be identical with men, we know little of them and have little sound evidence upon which to base our conclusions. Moreover, we are seldom dispassionate.'[1] And indeed, aside from the work of a few maverick pioneers, to whom the history of women offered fresh and challenging terrain – Mary Beard, Ivy Pinchbeck, Léon Abensour, Alice Clark, Olive Schreiner – women's history continued to languish in the shadows of which Woolf had complained until the 1960s, when the first stirrings of renewed political activism (feminism's much-vaunted 'second wave') turned the sustained attention of historians and activists toward the recovery and analysis of those who remained 'hidden from history'.

The history of women has come a long way since Woolf underscored our astonishing ignorance on the subject, for with the revival of feminist militancy in the late 1960s came a vast outpouring of research on women in both Europe and the United States. Much has already been written on this initial phase of 'primitive accumulation', where scholars and activists devoted themselves to demonstrating in amplitude that women did indeed have a history, and that, moreover, recovering this rich and varied past had the potential to reshape the contours of official, 'male' history. This article will therefore focus on the evolution of historical writing about women since the mid-1980s. It opens with a brief survey of developments across the period 1975–2000, focusing in particular on the emergence of gender history from women's history, and on the way that the poststructuralist challenge has progressively reshaped both the methods and objects of research in the field since the late 1980s. It then turns to a more detailed analysis of two works – Leonore Davidoff and Catherine Hall's *Family Fortunes: Men and Women of the English Middle Class, 1780–1850* and Lyndal Roper's *Oedipus and the Devil: Witchcraft, Sexuality and Religion in Early Modern Europe* – in order to illustrate some of the ways that feminist historians have deployed the concept of gender so as to open out entirely new research domains, while developing new perspectives on existing fields of research.

In the early 1970s, feminist scholars and activists founded the first women's studies courses in universities and adult education programmes across the United States and Europe. '1973: the first course on women at Jussieu,' recalls Michelle Perrot.

> On the 7th of November, Andrée Michel opened fire with a lecture on 'Women and the family in developed societies.' The lecture hall was packed, the atmosphere over-heated by the hostility of leftist (male) students for whom the study of women was but a distraction from the real work of revolution.[2]

But such resistance merely fuelled feminist scholars' determination to recover their own history, a history that had been unjustly banished from view, a history that could serve to reinforce feminist politics by offering a historically grounded account of women's identity as a group distinct from men. As publications accumulated, feminist historians moved from their initial, hesitant question, 'Is it possible to write a history of women?' (and what might it look like?) toward the more confident formulation that to write a history *without* women was a fool-hardy endeavour indeed, for it would be to tell barely half the story. Fired by an enthusiasm that was at once political and intellectual, feminist scholars, students and activists engaged in individual and collective projects of research and teaching whose accumulated, and sometimes unexpected, results did not always fit smoothly into the existing narratives of history. The problem of integrating the 'women's story' soon prompted feminist scholars to challenge the traditional contours of their discipline by posing a new and difficult question: 'Is women's history merely an "innocuous supplement" to existing narratives, or does the integration of these new stories and perspectives demand that the analytic structures themselves be reshaped?' For if, as the growing body of scholarship on women suggested, gender identity was not a biological given but a social and historical creation, then the task of the historian was no longer merely adding women to an existing narrative whose outlines were familiar. Rather, her task was now to excavate the precise meanings that femininity and masculinity have carried in the past, to demonstrate the evolution of those meanings over time, and so to reveal the historically constructed nature of these concepts in our present world.

From early on, then, feminist scholars were committed not merely to adding new material to the historical record; but to changing the analytic structures of historical practice. Crucial to this ambition was the distinction drawn between biological sex, understood as the material and unchanging ground of one's identity, and the infinitely malleable carapace of gender, a socially constructed series of behaviours that code one as male or female, but that vary across time and space in such a way as to reveal their constructed nature. Women (and men, for that matter) were thus made and not born, and much productive research proceeded on the ground of the sex/gender distinction, as feminist historians smoked out the various ways that gender, understood as a socially constructed system of difference, had operated to shape social relations and understandings of self in societies past.

Women's history was fast transforming itself into a broader history of gender relations, though not without protest from scholars who feared that the turn to gender signalled the abandonment of women's history as a feminist political project.[3] And yet the very move by which women's historians had underscored the constructed nature of male and female roles in society had already destabilized the notion of identity as an essential, natural property. In this sense, gender history was immanent in the very development of women's history, and feminist scholars moved increasingly toward the study of gender as a way to locate the experiences of women in a broader context, while arguing for the gendered nature of all human experience, and not simply that of women.

The shift from women's history to gender history over the course of the 1980s thus had several important consequences, not the least of which was to contribute to the development of an entirely new arena of research: that of masculinity and 'men's' studies, a field that was to expand and develop rapidly during the 1990s. But de-essentializing maleness and femaleness by underscoring their historical construction also met a vital intellectual need of the young sub-discipline, by taking these categories out of the timeless realm of eternal verities, where male dominance and women's subordination were written into the very order of things, and returning them to the stream of history. By the same token, the de-essentializing of the category 'woman' served an equally important political goal, underscoring the historical, and hence changeable, non-necessary content of the category 'woman' as it is deployed in contemporary politics and social policy.

Finally, it was argued that the turn to gender would give feminist scholarship greater impact on the shape of historical discipline itself. For by the mid-1980s, it was clear that women's history on its own had failed to transform the epistemological bases of the historical discipline, despite the conviction of many feminist historians that the integration of the women's story rendered such transformation inevitable. Rather, women's history was being researched and taught alongside the standard narratives of 'real' history without affecting those narratives in any fundamental way. The only way to break out of this intellectual ghetto, it was argued, was to cease focusing exclusively on women and follow instead the mutual construction of masculinities and feminini-ties as they have evolved over time. Drawing heavily on the anthropologist's tool-kit, historians of gender sought to render the study of sexual division an instrument of his-torical analysis by arguing that such divisions are rooted in a more global sexual div-ision of social, symbolic and political space. Any history worth the name would henceforth have to abandon the pretext that the masculine represents a neutral and universal history of the species, while the feminine remains the particular object of a revendicative identity politics. Rather, historians of any subject, whether military, social, political or diplomatic, would henceforth have to identify the gendered consti-tution of their object of analysis, to demonstrate how it had been coded masculine or feminine, and then explain what the consequences of that gendering have been for its evolution in time. For gender (unlike women) was everywhere, or so the theory went.

Feminist scholars' desire to render women visible in history thus resulted ulti-mately in a broader conceptual vision of the social distinction of the sexes; a less militantly woman-centred concept, perhaps, but one that has nonetheless altered historical practice, not only among feminist scholars but among many of their male colleagues as well. Feminist politics and the demands of scholarship thus remained tightly intertwined in the intellectual history of the discipline, even as its practitioners moved outwards from the particulars of women's history to a more universal history of gender, understood as a fundamental aspect of social being and social order.

Throughout this initial phase of its development, women's history had been riding the people's history wave, which, fed by a number of streams (notably the *Annales* School and the 'new' social history movement) peaked in the 1960s and early 1970s. In this, the golden age of social history, where scholars strove to restore the voices of common people to history, women found their place as a prime example of the generally unheard-from in standard history textbooks. In addition, the link to social history gave women's history a strong orientation toward labour history, an orientation that was reinforced by the conviction, common to 1970s feminists in Europe and the United States, that one key to women's liberation from the patriarchal domination of fathers and husbands lay in their finding paid employment outside the home.

Social and labour history would continue to dominate the emerging fields of women's and gender history until the late 1980s, by which point historians in general, and women's and gender historians in particular, began turning away from social history, with its basis in macro-structural forms of analysis (social and economic structures as determinants of individual behaviour), toward more cultural and discursive forms of analysis, often grounded in more micro-histori-cal contexts. Thanks to their long-standing recourse to the notion of social con-struction in the study of masculinities and femininities past, feminist historians found themselves on the cutting edge of this larger poststructuralist movement in historical analysis. For at the very moment that feminist critiques of an essential-izing women's history were driving the growth and elaboration of gender history, the entire discipline of social history was engaged as a whole in the search for more nuanced ways of addressing the relationships among the social, material and cultural aspects of history. Frustrated by the limits of earlier, social science-driven and/or Marxist perspectives, scholars across the discipline placed increasing stress on the importance of the play between representation and social reality. Here, the use of the notion of social construction (in this case of sex/gender) became a way to navigate between the two.

At a time when the discipline of social history was pushing up against the limits of earlier models and conceptualizations, then, feminist historians carved out an avant-garde role for themselves as theoretical and methodological innovators, developing fruitful new approaches that were grounded in psychoanalytic under-standings of gender identity-formation, and in the insights of radical feminist consciousness-raising groups into the inherently political nature of domestic gender relations, which are, after all, relations of power. The feminist challenge to stable social categories like male and female, achieved through the historical study of gender relations as they have shifted in time, thus preceded the arrival of poststructuralist theory in departments of history, which arrived bearing the chic banner of 'French theory'. Although such theory had blossomed in departments of language and literature since the late 1970s, the message came to history rather late in the day, borne notably by Joan Wallach Scott in her famous essay 'Gender: A Useful Category of Historical Analysis', first published in the *American Historical Review* in 1986.

Feminist historians would thus play a leading role in the theoretical and meth-odological debates that shook the discipline from the late 1980s through the mid-1990s. As we will see, these debates would upset the epistemological certitudes on which history had confidently rested, notably the idea that textual sources give us a direct window onto the past. At the same time, they challenged the original syn-thesis of scholarship and politics that had characterized women's and gender his-tory, by casting doubt on the notion that at the core of each individual subject lies a stable and coherent identity. In order to explore more concretely what the turn from women's to gender history, and the subsequent engagement with post-structuralism have meant for the practice of women's and gender history, the next section of this chapter focuses on the evolution of the field in England. I choose to explore this case more closely in part because it provides the specific historio-graphical context for an analysis of Davidoff and Hall's magisterial study of gender in the making of the English middle class, a key text in the development and deployment of gender as a tool of historical analysis. But I also use this specific case study to demonstrate in detail that the shift from social to cultural history, from the analysis of experience to the analysis of discourse and the construction of social categories, has had important consequences for the shape of the field as a whole, shifting attention from histories based in women's experiences (notably of work) to analyses of the gendered construction of the basic categories that have shaped our perceptions of civil and political life. Of course, this shift had its parallels in the United States, France and Germany, where from about 1990 on, numerous historians turned increasingly away from macro-structural analysis toward more cultural and micro-level studies. But it is only by exploring the particularities of a single historiographical tradition that one can document precisely the effects that the turn from social to cultural and discursive forms of analysis has had on the forms and objects of historical analysis in general, and feminist historical analysis in particular. The chapter then closes with a brief discussion of Lyndal Roper's deeply searching essays on gender, witchcraft and religious reform in sixteenth-century Augsburg. Though written in the early 1990s, when the stormy debate around poststructuralism was at its height, these essays look beyond that moment and set forth a challenging agenda for gender historians that, in my view, has yet to be met.

14.1 Feminist historians and the 'new' social history

The field of women's history in England first took shape within the great tradition of social, and socialist, history of working-class life and labour. It was an intellectually and politically vibrant tradition, one that had given rise by the mid-1960s to a 'new' social history that stressed the agency of working-class people in making their own history. The epistemological base of this 'new' social history rested on Edward Thompson's famous articulation between agency and structure, between experiences (of exploitation), social identity (class consciousness) and politics. Class was thus understood as a dynamic process set in motion by individual agents as much as by material conditions. For the new social historians, then, individual experience played a vital role in forming collective identities, which, in turn, formed the indispensable ground of all political and revolutionary action.

But if the chain binding experience, social identity and politics constituted the epistemological ground of early feminist scholarship, it was the vast, if poorly paid, domain of popular and adult education that gave the first generation of feminist historians a precarious institutional anchor. Working outside the four walls of traditional universities, in programmes that were often located in working-class neighbourhoods, socialist historians of both sexes offered courses on the lives and labour of British workers. In so doing, they sought to bind socialist intellectuals more closely to the working-class movement by returning to the people the history of their own class. It was here, in this politically alive if institutionally somewhat marginalized atmosphere, that feminist scholars of the 1960s and 1970s first began to research and teach the history of women and work as an integral aspect of people's history.

English women's history thus put down its first institutional and epistemological roots in the socialist movement for a people's history, organized around a new social history that, while methodologically innovative on a number of fronts, remained largely a history of men. Dominated by images of barrel-chested miners shouldering their axes, or sooty metalworkers hammering away like devils before the roaring flames of the forge, the initial narratives produced by the new social historians seem to have forgotten that the nation's first industrial proletariat, called to work in the weaving sheds of early nineteenth-century Lancashire, was predominantly female. Only with the flourishing of feminist-socialist scholarship after 1968 would this picture slowly begin to change, as the figures of women, bent over in the fields or standing at the loom, were gradually restored to view.

Over the next ten years or so, the majority of feminist scholars in Britain would continue to work on the margins of the university, teaching history in adult education or neighbourhood women's centres while participating in a flourishing array of autonomous associations that sprang up around the history of women: The Women's Research and Resources Centre in London (which later became the Feminist Library), the Feminist Archive (Bath), the Lesbian Archive (Manchester), numerous informal feminist history groups that met in London, Bristol, Brighton and Manchester (to name but a few), and the Virago Press, dedicated to publishing new work in women's history while reissuing handsome editions of out-of-print works as well. 'The margins can be a very productive terrain,' wrote Catherine Hall in 1992, 'a space from which both to challenge establishments and develop our own perspectives, build our own organizations, confirm our own collectivities'.[4] For feminist scholars of the 1970s, this marginality also served to remind them of the overarching political purpose of women's history: to restore women's voices to history while using these discoveries to transform present-day gender relations.

During the 1980s, feminist scholars moved gradually from adult education into the universities. In part, this movement was involuntary, for the severe budget slashing of the Thatcher years forced major cuts in adult education. At the same time, the first interdisciplinary programmes in women's studies appeared in certain of the 'new universities', including Bradford, Essex, Kent, Warwick and York. The need to create interdisciplinary programmes gave rise to fruitful exchanges among feminist scholars across the disciplines, breaking their isolation from one another inside separate departments (where they were often the lone exponents of women's studies) while reinforcing the cross-disciplinary nature of women's and gender history. And yet very few of the participants in these first women's studies programmes were historians, for until the end of the 1980s, the English historical discipline as a whole proved reluctant to concede that women's and gender history might be legitimate fields of research.[5] Numerous key works were thus produced by scholars in sociology (Leonore Davidoff), social policy (Pat Thane), education (Penny Summerfield, Carol Dyehouse) or social science administration (Jane Lewis) – scholars in the social sciences who found that adopting a historical approach was crucial to the success of their enterprise.

A look at two classic works from this period illustrates the shape that feminist historians' overarching preoccupation with the world of labour, and with the often tense relation between socialist feminists and their male comrades, assumed in the guise of history. Jill Liddington and Jill Norris's *One Hand Tied Behind Us* thus recounts the hitherto untold story of the radical suffrage movement among women textile workers in turn-of-the-century Lancashire.[6] Both authors were teaching in adult education in Manchester at the time (1978), and their book is the fruit of an enormous labour of research conducted in local archives and through interviews with the surviving daughters and granddaughters of such local activists as Selina Cooper and Doris Chew. Burdened by a double load of domestic and factory labour, these women sought the vote not merely as an end in itself, but as a means to the larger end of improving the conditions of life and labour for working-class men, women and children. Lancashire's radical suffragists thus fought equally hard to gain those social and economic rights that they judged every bit as important as the simple right to vote: equal pay, better educational opportunities, birth control, child allowances and the right to work on an equal footing with men. In order to piece together the tale of this all-but-forgotten movement, Liddington and Norris had to write against the conventional tale of exclusively middle-class heroics first propagated by middle-class and London-based activists such as Sylvia Pankhurst and Rachel Strachey, militant suffragists for whom the social and political activism of women workers was but a distant echo of their own, more narrowly vote-based struggle.[7] Inspired by the convictions of 1970s socialist-feminism, and sustained by the structures of popular education in a region that was heavily populated by retired textile workers, Liddington and Norris used their contacts in the milieu to recover the unwritten tale of a political movement, led by the women workers themselves, in which feminist politics and class struggle were inextricably linked.

Barbara Taylor's *Eve and the New Jerusalem: Socialism and Feminism in the Nineteenth Century* explores the encounter between feminism and Owenite socialism in early nineteenth-century England in what is, ultimately, a sustained meditation on the often fraught relationship of feminism to socialism. Taylor's richly documented study shows how Owen's moral critique of gender inequality within the family constituted an essential pillar of so-called 'utopian' socialism in the 1820s, 1830s and 1840s. Unlike the 'scientific' socialists of the later nineteenth century, for whom the struggle for gender equality was always subordinated to class struggle, Owenite socialists placed women's liberation at the heart of their political project to liberate all of humanity from all forms of oppression and inequality, be they class or gender based. Once again, one can read the preoccupations, and discontents, of 1970s socialist-feminists in the study of a long-since marginalized movement in which the liberation of women formed an integral part of the larger struggle, and not just a coda, left to the tender (and studiously vague) mercies of 'after the revolution'.

Feminist historians of the 1970s and early 1980s thus privileged working-class history and the study of women's work, sometimes adapting terms and categories of Marxist analysis – 'sex-class', 'sex struggle' and 'patriarchal mode of production' – in order to extend a materialist analysis of women's exploitation from the factory to the family, and so unmask the material basis of male domination. In some instances, patriarchy travelled alone in its relentless exploitation of women's domestic and reproductive labour.[8] More often, however, socialist-feminists analysed patriarchy in its unholy alliance with capitalism, a 'dual system' whose elements had to be analysed simultaneously in order to explain women's double burden of labour (and exploitation) – in the factory, to be sure, but also in the home. The tension that this first generation felt between feminism and socialism, between gender versus class as the privileged category of analysis, expressed itself above all in the long debate over whether patriarchy (understood as a system of relations that is generated entirely outside the workplace) or capitalism should be regarded as the prime source of working women's oppression. While much important work was produced under the sign of this 'dual systems theory', its underlying hermeneutic, in which patriarchy and capitalism are treated as autonomously functioning structures of oppression, would remain unchallenged until the early 1990s, when the history of women's experiences of work was broadened to embrace the study of gender divisions inside the workplace itself. The workplace then revealed itself to be a world in which notions of masculinity and femininity have always played a central role in shaping divisions of labour and hierarchies of authority, a world in which the two structures (patriarchy and capitalism) are in fact inextricably bound together in a single, gendered order of production. The adoption of gender as a central category of analysis would thus resolve certain of the epistemological difficulties that had dogged women's history from its origins – not, however, without raising several new epistemological problems of its own.

14.2 From women's history to gender history

The publication, in 1987, of Leonore Davidoff and Catherine Hall's highly influential book, *Family Fortunes: Men and Women of the English Middle Class, 1780–1850*, marked a decisive moment in the turn to gender history in England, and in gender's diffusion outward into historical practice more broadly. The product of nearly ten years' collaboration between the historian (Hall) and the sociologist (Davidoff), *Family Fortunes* recounts in detail the formation of the provincial middle classes in turn-of-the-nineteenth-century England, a process whose roots lie, the authors argue, in the progressive separation of public (male) space from the private and female-dominated realm of the middle-class home. At the heart of the book lies the ambition to analyse the construction of gendered identities within a particular society, with identity conceived as the link between individual psychology and the larger collectivity. In this sense, *Family Fortunes* contributed mightily not only to the broader diffusion of gender as a tool of historical analysis, but also to the turn in the late 1980s toward subjectivity as an object of historical study. ← important

Of course the idea of separate male and female spheres was far from new in 1987, for feminist scholars across Europe and the United States had long deployed the model as a description of middle-class social organization – or at least, of an *ideal* of middle-class social organization – in modern western societies. What was new was Hall and Davidoff's ambition to lay bare and analyse the gendered foundations of large social processes like class formation:

> We wanted not just to put the women back into a history from which they had been left out, but to rewrite that history so that proper recognition would be given to the ways in which gender, as a key axis of power in society, provides a crucial understanding of how any society is structured and organized.

wrote Catherine Hall some five years after the publication of *Family Fortunes*.

> What was the specific relation of women to class structures and how should women's class position be defined? How was class gendered . . .? Do men and women have different class identities? Are their forms of class consciousness and class solidarity the same? . . . D[o] women have an identity as women which cut[s] across forms of class belonging? [9]

The result is a book that speaks of both men and women, and of the formation of the middle classes during the Industrial Revolution on the basis of a gendered distinction in social space and social function.

This gendered distinction between the moral world of the home, where acts are reciprocal and performed for love, not money, and the competitive, amoral world of business and politics, is one that the authors trace back to the texts and practices of Protestant evangelical religion. To my mind, the exploration of the religious sources of gender distinction constitutes one of the most original aspects of Hall and Davidoff's argument. Among other things, it allows the authors to document in some detail the very particular visions of masculinity and femininity that emerged in this world of middle-class evangelicals; visions that were not necessarily (indeed, hardly at all) congruent with those of the landed aristocracy, on the one hand, or of the labouring poor on the other. Evangelical religion thus gave a specific moral meaning to the strict and gendered segregation of space and activity, to the productive activity of men in the world, and to the economic dependence of women, who remained close to the hearth and held aloft the pure flame of domesticity. Here, the pious husband would always find a morally uplifting retreat from the unavoidable sullying of hands and spirit that his implication in the competitive and treacherous worlds of business and politics entailed. Across the decades that *Family Fortunes* covers, gender and class are perpetually constructed and reconstructed in relation to one another and in the context of the gendered separation of public and private. And this, in turn, implies that the class consciousness of both men and women must, of necessity, take gendered forms.

With its uncanny capacity to reveal and analyse the gendered underpinnings of such fundamental social processes as class formation, Hall and Davidoff's book became something of a classic almost overnight. It was widely taught in university courses from the late 1980s onward, and not only in women's studies but in general history classes as well. Yet *Family Fortunes* also drew substantial criticism, often from feminist historians who criticized the separate spheres model for its functionalist logic, as well as for its proximity to the world-view of the very bourgeois whom it purports to analyse. And indeed, there is something deeply disturbing in the peaceful harmony with which the tale of the complementary division of public and private unfolds. It is a tale in which all hint of male domination as a political problem fades behind the comfortable harmonies of gender complementarity. It is a tale that, as Carolyn Steedman astutely observed:

> repeats the imperative of the Bildungsroman, which, in its many forms, typically symbolizes the process of socialization, and makes its characters and its readers really want to do what it is that they have to do anyway (be married, have children, clean the stairs ...)[10]

Yet the separate spheres model was seductive, a structure of binary classification that allowed feminist researchers to move beyond social history and to integrate women and gender into more political histories as well as, notably, into studies of the gendered contours of social and political citizenship. Studies of male–female relations, and of the construction of gendered identities in a wide range of social contexts, began to multiply rapidly, and the history of women and work inexorably lost its privileged position in feminist research.

14.3 Gender history and poststructuralism

The arrival of gender as a tool of historical analysis thus contributed to the displacement of feminist history's attention away from women's experiences (especially of work) and toward the construction of masculine and feminine identities across the social spectrum. This shift in object – from experience to the social construction of gendered identities – would be confirmed and extended by the arrival of poststructuralist theory in departments of women's studies and history all across Britain at the turn of the 1990s. Poststructuralist thinkers (with feminist poststructuralists often leading the way) thus mounted a powerful critique of historical practice, focusing in particular on historians' reliance on written texts ('primary sources') as a guide to events and experiences past. Borrowing various techniques of deconstruction from literary critics, poststructuralist historians analysed historical documents as literary artefacts, placing at the heart of their work an exploration of the internal structure of these texts and the construction of the categories on which their internal logic is based.

Rather than seeking to reconstruct the past 'as it really was', poststructuralist historians preached the analysis of discourses, of representations, and of the (often gendered) construction of social categories. If nothing else, this had the salutary effect of renewing and expanding techniques for the critical reading of sources. But in asking that historians turn their attention to the textual construction of social categories, poststructuralists also called into question the very epistemological base of the new social history, namely the logical chain that bound experience to identity, and from there moved to politics. The relationship between structure and agency that had animated so much of the new social history, including women's and gender history, was thus supplanted by a new concern with the relationship between culture and politics, and the ways that language serves to mediate that relationship. Those scholars who remained faithful to the project of social history would henceforth try to marry their narratives of social and economic structures with new stories of the 'cultures' of work – that is, of the representations and discourses that surround work, and notions of production and the economy more generally. But historians in general and feminist historians in particular would continue to move away from the world of labour, so cherished by the new social history, and toward a newly renovated cultural and political history that focused on such things as the gendered and

Masc & Fem.

raced construction of categories like citizenship, and of representations of nation and empire.

Feminist historians in England became acquainted with poststructuralist thought through a variety of tribunes, notably the American historian Joan Wallach Scott and the British philosopher and poet Denise Riley, whose widely read works disseminated to a broader public the sustained reflections of poststructuralist feminists on the constructed nature of such fundamental categories as 'woman/women' and 'gender.'[11] As a part of this reflection, poststructuralist feminists took up once again the question of power, though this time (following Michel Foucault on the power/knowledge nexus) the focus was less on the micropolitics of power in the household than on gender as a metaphor for social and political power. Hence, to borrow from Joan Scott's oft-quoted formulation, relations between the sexes constitute a 'primary aspect of social organization' (and not simply of class formation), for 'the differences between the sexes constitute and are constituted by hierarchical social structures'.[12] Gender thus becomes a 'primary way of signifying relationships of power ... one of the recurrent references by which political power has been conceived, legitimated and criticized'. Moreover, 'gender both refers to and establishes the meaning of the male/female opposition'.[13]

In light of these reflections, 'gender' in its social-historical incarnation (social relations of the sexes, the sexual division of labour) would undergo serious conceptual transformation as poststructuralist feminists displaced the accent from the social to the discursive construction of categories, including gender identities and the category of 'women' as a self-evident collectivity. Henceforth, the goal of gender history would no longer be that of recovering or reconstructing the experiences of women in the past, but rather that of tracing the process by which discourses about masculinity and femininity have been produced over time. The category of experience, on which reposed the narratives of social and gender history, was thus dismissed as part and parcel of a worn-out and positivist social history that had (since 1989) been deprived of all Marxist legitimation. Indeed, for some of the more radical partisans of poststructuralist feminism, experience does not really exist as such. Rather, the notions of experience, and of subjectivity itself, are themselves products of discursive processes that position individuals in relation to discursive formations, and so produce both their experiences and their sense of possessing a 'true' inner self. The real objects of historical research are therefore constituted by the discourses that organize experiences, and not by the experiences themselves.[14]

The turn toward cultural history and discursive modes of analysis met with a sharply divided reaction in the history departments of early 1990s England: on the one hand, a defensive rejection of what was perceived by some to be a perverse deconstruction of the entire historical enterprise; on the other, considerable enthusiasm from those historians who, since the late 1970s, had been living uneasily with the growing 'crisis' of social history.[15] This crisis was an epistemological one, rooted in historians' increasing discomfort with the determinist vision of the individual-experience-to-social-identity link on which so many narratives of social history rested. After all, it is by no means clear that a particular experience will inevitably give rise in individual consciousness to one social identity and not another. Indeed, once one relinquishes all notion of a fully determined relation between the two, then a troubling explanatory gap opens up between individual self-perception and the 'objective' structures of society and economy. So long as scholars were prepared to presume that the move from inner cognitive process to outward social identification was a fully determined one, no such gap was visible. By the late 1970s, however, historians were no longer so sure, as debates over problems such as 'false consciousness' (a way to account for those workers who, in an apparent failure to grasp the political consequences of their class position, vote Conservative) led scholars increasingly to question the determinist nature of the epistemological chain binding individual consciousness to larger collective identities.

Well before the arrival of poststructuralist theory, then, social historians already entertained serious doubts about the explanatory power of categories like 'experience'. Small wonder that the poststructuralist message found receptive ears in English history departments. Indeed, for some (ex-)social historians, the study of discourse became the sole possible way to do history, a history that focused on the 'discursive aspects of experience', and on analysing the discursive logic within which individual identities were produced.[16]

Feminist historians in England were likewise divided in the face of the poststructuralist onslaught on the certitudes of experience. Thus, poststructuralists' 'refusal of the real' presented genuine, practical problems for scholars (feminist and non-feminist alike) who had been raised inside the empiricist traditions that have long shaped English historical research. In addition, many feminist scholars were frankly suspicious of the claim that our understanding of the intersection between gender and power had arisen exclusively from poststructuralist thought. After all, hadn't feminist consciousness-raising groups, with their stress on the personal as political, generated just as much insight into the power/knowledge couplet as had the rarefied debates of poststructuralism? But in the end, it was the profound anti-humanism of poststructuralism's most extreme claims that stirred the sharpest reaction from feminist historians, for whom an approach that preached the analysis of discourse rather than of human activity and consciousness was deeply off-putting. Though powerfully drawn by the prospect of the broadening of gender's analytic reach to include gendered analyses of the foundations of social and political organization, many feminist scholars remained ambivalent before poststructuralists' radical demand for a complete abandonment of the study of social phenomena and experiences in favour of a kind of cultural history that seemed utterly turned in on itself, circularly self-referential and absorbed by linguistic word play.[17]

Despite these reservations, however, poststructuralism and the crisis around England's own 'linguistic turn' have left durable traces in the methods and objects of historical research, placing the analysis of representations and discourses firmly on the agenda while turning historians' eyes from the analysis of social experience *tout court* toward more cultural histories of political and national identity, of citizenship, and of the multiple (and sometimes competing) forces of race, class and gender in shaping those identities. In the wake of the often violent debates around poststructuralism, feminist historians are thus working on a differently constituted range of subjects, and are drawing their techniques from an increasingly eclectic tool-kit. For if the basic epistemological differences between poststructuralists and anti-poststructuralists have found no real resolution (nor could they, being grounded in fundamentally opposed ontologies), the sound and fury that attended these debates over the period 1988–94 has since abated, leaving historians to continue their work as they may.

Yet even in this more theoretically heterodox era, some of the issues that divided poststructuralist feminists from their non- (or anti-) poststructuralist colleagues continue to find expression, though in less polemical and more historically grounded terms. Hence, those historians of gender who would like to take the more purely constructivist route continue to face some very real epistemological difficulties, notably the fact that gender, understood as a purely discursive construct, cannot in and of itself explain change. If, for example sexual identities are understood to be produced solely through discursive processes, then how are we to account for changes in said identities over time? Without some way of linking discursive process to social experience, historians cannot account for the changing meanings of masculine and feminine. This is doubtless the most serious problem that the radically constructivist posture (Scott, Butler) has left to historians of gender. For while endless performativity and subjectivities that are the pure product of discursive positioning pose no a priori problem for literary analysis, they are of limited use to historians, who need tools that will allow them to account for change in time. Some scholars have sought to resolve this problem by hooking gender to another, more dynamic category that can explain change (class being the obvious example here). Lyndal Roper proposes a rather different solution, suggesting that we look for some way to understand gender as both discursively constructed *and* as real bodily/psychic experience.

I would therefore like to close with a brief look at Lyndal Roper's work, focusing in particular on her *Oedipus and the Devil* (1994); a most suggestive set of essays that play off many of the debates around poststructuralism without ever really becoming entangled in their philosophical snares. Rather, Roper hews closely to her historical object, and uses to great effect a broad range of theoretical insights in order to develop fruitful and imaginative approaches to the very new questions that she poses of her material. In so doing, she raises some searching questions about the capacity of gender, in its purely constructivist incarnation, to serve as a tool of historical analysis.

14.4 Gender and history in a post-poststructuralist world

Oedipus and the Devil brings together a series of essays on witchcraft, religion and sexuality in early-modern Germany, written over the period 1988–92. When read together, these essays offer a sustained meditation on the role of the irrational and the unconscious in history, on the importance of the body, and on the relation of these two to sexual difference. They do so through a series of case studies drawn from Reformation and Counter-Reformation Augsburg that involve motherhood, witchcraft, possession, masculinity and sexuality – 'all fields in which gender is at issue, and where the relation of psyche and the body are at stake'.[18] Roper thus proposes no less than a cultural history of that age-old conundrum – the mind–body conjunction, as it was experienced and understood by early-modern Germans – but viewed from a startlingly new perspective, one in which gender is not simply an additional line of analysis, but rather lies at the heart of the matter. For as Roper points out, sexual difference, as physiological and psychological fact, and as social construction, is a central and constitutive aspect of human culture. Issues of sexual difference must therefore stand at the heart of cultural history.

Roper's ambition is to grasp the subjectivities of early-modern women and men across the period of the Reformation, subjectivities that, in her words, are 'recognizable, evincing patterns with which we are familiar'.[19] Through a series of precise investigations, based on specific kinds of archives that the cultural revolution of religious reform produced in abundance (witchcraft trials, ordinances of discipline), she seeks to illuminate such questions as: how did early modern understandings of the body shift in the context of struggles between a Catholic theology of the body as a vessel of divine (or diabolic) possession and a Protestant theology that sundered the link between the physical and the spiritual? How did the magical capacities associated with female bodies differ from those associated with male bodies? How did the dilemmas surrounding the psychic identity of womanhood express themselves in accusations of witchcraft? Gender and matters of sexual difference weave themselves through the fabric of the stories she tells, of the deep antagonisms among women that emerged in the trial (1669), of a lying-in maid accused by her (female) clients of harming their young infants through sorcery, or of the generational conflicts among men that expressed themselves in ordinances of discipline intended to control the drunken brawling of village youth. In each case, the dark side of subjectivity comes to the fore: the powerful enmities that can arise when a young mother, anxious about her child's fate and her own ability to nourish it, projects her anxieties onto the person of the older, postmenopausal lying-in maid trusted with its care, when the infant in question fails to thrive; or the political threat that the raw fighting energy of rowdy young men could present to a stable, patriarchal village order. On the one hand, such brute energy, properly channelled, provided the military force necessary to defend the city. But when young (and sometimes not-so-young) men went marauding through tavern and street, beating one another (and at times their own wives) to within an inch of their lives, the village council was forced to intervene in order to control the disruptive impact of such excesses of virility. In the end, Roper concludes that 'Sixteenth-century masculinity drew its psychic strength not from the dignity of the men but from the rumbustious energy which such discipline was supposedly designed to check.'[20] The uncivilized wildness of 'manly' men was thus the product of civilized society's carefully structured rules.

Throughout these essays, Roper strives to maintain a tension between certain universal aspects of human psychic process, evoked in her working assumption that early-modern subjectivities are 'recognizable' to us, and attention to that which changes in time, namely the particular content with which the categories 'masculine' and 'feminine' are invested. She thus invites us to see gendered subjectivities as the product of a dialectic relationship between those more labile, socially constructed elements and some notion of an essential self that is located in the fact of having a sexed body:

> Sexual identity can never be satisfactorily understood if we conceive it as a set of discourses about masculinity or femininity. Nor can the individual subject be adequately understood as a container of discourse – a conception which evacuates subjectivity of psychology.[21]

On the one hand, therefore, sexuality comprises elements that run deep and are difficult to change. At another level, we find that 'glittering profusion of sexual identities' that historians have discerned in discourse. In between the two, notes Roper, lies the realm of individual subjectivity, a meeting ground for the social and the psychic that lies at the core of each individual. In order to explore the realm of the psychic, however, historians need a theory of subjectivity that will allow them to account for the tenacious hold of sexual stereotypes (in the present or the past), while explaining the attraction of 'particular rhetorics of gender' at a given historical moment. Moreover, historians need to specify the kinds of connections that arise between social and psychic phenomena, so that they can distinguish that which is historical about our gendered subjectivities from their transhistorical psychic elements. For so long as it lacks an account of the links between the social and the psychic, gender cannot adequately conceptualize change. By linking gender to the social via individual subjectivity, Roper proposes to endow gender with a historical dimension that it necessarily lacks when it is understood as a discursive creation alone.

Roper thus takes her distance from a long-established article of feminist faith, namely the radical constructivist conviction that gender is the pure product of social, cultural and linguistic practices, asserting, rather, that 'sexual difference has its own physiological and psychological reality, and that recognition of this fact must affect the way we write history'.[22] Hence, she astutely identifies one of the fundamental difficulties with both social and linguistic constructionism, namely that each 'short-circuits' the realm between language and subjectivity, as if there were no space there to be bridged. In the constructivist universe, language, by means of its social character, simply 'impresses a social construction of gender upon the wax of the individual psyche'. But bodies are not the mere creations of discourse. And if we already have plenty of histories of discourses about the body, what is sorely lacking is a history that can problematize the relationship between the psychic and the physical (since bodily experience must of necessity be connected with mental life).

Roper attributes the determined constructivism of feminist historians to their long-standing tendency to 'deny' the importance of the body.[23] Though deeply sympathetic to the desire to escape the snares of femininity by fleeing from their bodies and retreating to the 'rational reaches of discourse', Roper is nonetheless convinced that the costs of such flight are too high. After all,

> sexual difference is not purely discursive nor merely social. It is also physical. The cost of the flight from the body and from sexual difference is evident in what much feminist historical writing has found it impossible to speak about; or indeed, in the passionate tone of the theoretical work which insists on the radically constructed nature of sexual difference ... We need an understanding of sexual difference which will incorporate, not fight against, the corporeal.[24]

So experience seems to be entering into the equation once again, though this time through the rather different door of bodily and psychic phenomena.

Roper thus asks us to consider how it is we might link discursive constructs like gender to social and psychic experience. It is a question that was hardly posed in the thick of theory wars (which instead tossed experience out with the bathwater). But the epistemological difficulties that a purely constructivist concept of gender present (namely, that gender, conceived as a purely discursive construct, cannot in and of itself explain change) force us to consider this question very seriously. Here, Roper joins Barbara Taylor and Sally Alexander in what Colin Jones and Dror Wahrman have called an 'anticonstructionist backlash: wondering ... whether historians have overemphasized the cultural construction of subjectivity to the preclusion of deep historical mechanisms that are a precondition to becoming human'.[25] For both Taylor and Roper, psychoanalysis is one obvious place to look for a way forward through this dilemma, allowing gender historians to come to terms with that which changes in time (the content of what constitutes fantasies of maleness and femaleness) and that which, perhaps, does not (the basic psychic process, 'those mechanisms of fantasy formation, particularly identification, that are the precondition of having any sexed subjectivity at all').[26] One may have reservations about a solution that rests on positing a continuity in the underlying structures of the human psyche across time. But the questions that Roper raises about the role of subjectivity and experience in the shaping of gender identity are precisely the questions that need exploring, for it is this kind of inquiry that poststructuralists pushed to one side in their haste to demonstrate the discursive construction of both subjectivity and experience.[27]

Oedipus and the Devil thus offers a searching and sustained engagement with certain of the epistemological questions that the poststructuralist turn to pure constructivism left hanging in the balance, notably the status of gender as a tool of historical analysis, but also the question of whether gender, on its own, acts as a motor for historical change. These are questions that have no clear answers, as yet, and are more likely to be resolved by history's practitioners than by those who merely speculate about how history can and cannot be written.

Guide to further reading

Alison Assiter, *Enlightened Women: Modernist Feminism in a Postmodern Age* (London, 1995).

Lynn Hunt, 'The Challenge of Gender', in Hans Medick and Anne-Charlotte Trepp (eds), *Geschlectergeschichte und Allgemeine Geschichte* (Goettingen, 1998), pp. 59–97.

Joan Kelly, *Women, History and Theory: The Essays of Joan Kelly* (Chicago, 1984).

David Morgan, 'Men Made Manifest: Histories and Masculinities', *Gender and History* 1 (1989).

Linda Nicholson (ed.), *Feminism/Postmodernism* (London, 1990).

Joan W. Scott (ed.), *Feminism and History* (Oxford, 1996).

Notes

1   Virginia Woolf, review of Léonie Villard, *La Femme anglaise au XIXe siècle et son évolution d'après le roman anglais contemporain* (Henry Didier, 1920), first published in the *Times Literary Supplement,* 18 March 1920, cited in Rachel Bowlby (ed.), *Virginia Woolf: A Woman's Essays* (London, 1992), p. 18.

2   Michelle Perrot, *Les Femmes ou les silences de l'histoire* (Paris, 1998), pp. xi–xii.

3   Judith Bennett, 'Feminism and History', *Gender and History* 1(3) (Autumn 1989), pp. 251–71; Joan Hoff, 'Gender as a Postmodern Category of Paralysis', *Women's History Review* 3(2) (1994), pp. 149–68; Jane Rendall, 'Women's History: Beyond the Cage?', *History* 75 (1990), pp. 63–72.

4   Catherine Hall, *White, Male and Middle Class: Explorations in Feminism and History* (Oxford, 1992), p. 34.

5   A survey of 53 history departments in 1991 Britain revealed that despite the fact that nearly half the students were women, only 17 per cent of lecturing jobs were held by women, while only 12.7 per cent of senior lecturers, 6.6 per cent of readers and three out of 134 professors were women. *Times Literary Supplement*, 7 June 1991, cited in Hall, *White, Male and Middle Class*, p. 34.

6   Jill Liddington and Jill Norris, *'One Hand Tied Behind Us': The Rise of the Women's Suffrage Movement* (London, 1978).

7   Sylvia Pankhurst, *The Suffragette* (New York, 1911) and Rachel Strachey, *The Cause* (London, 1978; first published 1928).

8   Christine Delphy, 'L'ennemi principale', *Partisans* (1970), pp. 54–5.

9   Hall, *White, Male and Middle Class*, pp. 12–13.

10 Carolyn Steedman, 'Bimbos from Hell', *Social History* 19(1) (January, 1994), pp. 57–66, esp. 65. Also, Steedman, '"Public" and "Private" in Women's Lives', *Journal of Historical Sociology* 3(3) (1990). For an elegant critique of the separate spheres concept, see Amanda Vickery, 'Golden Age to Separate Spheres? A Review of the Categories and Chronology of English Women's History', *Historical Journal* 36(2) (1993), pp. 383–414. For an intelligent and extremely useful exploration of the ways that the widely variable range of individual character and experience constantly threatens to destabilize the binary constructs (such as public and private) that underpin ideologies of gender difference, see Mary Poovey, *Uneven Developments: The Ideological Work of Gender in Mid-Victorian England* (Chicago, 1988).

11 Joan Scott, *Gender and the Politics of History* (New York, 1988) and Denise Riley, *Am I that Name? Feminism and the Category of Women in History* (Minneapolis, 1988).

12 Scott, *Gender and the Politics of History*, p. 25.

13 Ibid., pp. 48–9.

14 In other words, recourse to 'experience' as a category of analysis presupposes the system of signification that must itself be analysed. Scott, 'The Evidence of Experience', *Critical Inquiry* 17(4) (1991), pp. 773–97.

15 See Richard Evans, *In Defense of History* (London, 1997) for a detailed summary of the opposition to poststructuralist 'nihilists'.

16 Patrick Joyce, 'History and Postmodernism', *Past and Present* 133 (November 1991) and Joyce, 'The End of Social History?', *Social History* 20 (1995).

17 See Hall, *White, Male and Middle Class*, p. 15.

18 Roper, *Oedipus and the Devil* (London and New York, 1994), p. 3.

19 Roper, *Oedipus and the Devil,* p. 227.

20 Roper, *Oedipus and the Devil,* pp. 119–20.

21 Roper, *Oedipus and the Devil,* p. 26.

22 Roper, *Oedipus and the Devil,* p. 3.

23 Here I think Roper overstates her claim, leaving to one side the work of such feminist historians as Carolyn Bynum, whose groundbreaking book *Holy Feast and Holy Fast: The Religious Significance of Food to Medieval Women* (Berkeley, 1987) explores the intersections between religious expression, female subjectivity and constructions of masculine and feminine in thirteenth- and fourteenth-century Europe.

24 Roper, *Oedipus and the Devil,* pp. 17, 18.

25 Colin Jones and Dror Wahrman (eds), *The Age of Cultural Revolutions: Britain and France, 1750–1820* (Berkeley, 2002), p. 14.

26 Barbara Taylor, 'Misogyny and Feminism: The Case of Mary Wollstonecraft', in Jones and Wahrman, *Age of Cultural Revolutions,* pp. 203–17 and Roper, *Oedipus and the Devil,* p. 13.

27 Roper herself admits that psychoanalysis must be deployed alongside other forms of analysis, that the full range of human behaviour cannot be reduced to basic psychic mechanisms. The analysis offered in each of her essays is thus multi-causal, with historical circumstances and contingency playing at least as great a role as psychic conflict. In the end, and to the great benefit of history, Roper's actual historical essays do not grant psychoanalytic explanation the kind of primacy that she preaches in her introductory essay. For a lucid analysis of the issues at stake in historians' adoption of psychoanalytic approaches, see Garthine Walker's contribution to this volume (Chapter 8).

15

Race, ethnicity and history

Milla Rosenberg

Although theories of race have a long trajectory, the ways in which historians have approached race began to shift rapidly in the nineteenth century. While scholars of the past had long drawn upon geographic conceptions of peoples, historians increasingly viewed cultures as hierarchical – that is, they ranked peoples with a set of classifications provided by new scientific disciplines. The turn to science served in extending hierarchies of racial difference.

This consideration of the making of race in history requires us to be sceptical of such systems of classification yet aware of the *effects* they have had on the lives, experiences and cultures of people across the world. In other words, we must distinguish the use of *racist* categories to explain history, from the analysis of the ways in which race has been used by historical actors, whether racist, non-, or anti-racist, to make sense of the world. In the former case, race is taken as a self-evident scientific or biological fact that explains the ways in which people see the world and act in it; in the latter, it is a culturally and historically constructed category, and racial attributes are *ascribed* to people. The concept of race in this latter sense is worth studying, as it has pervaded numerous historical texts that sought to render cultural groups different from the writer's own. As a conceptual category, most late nineteenth-century historians used race to assign fixed quanta of cultural worth; thus, race has served to distribute benefits to those judged 'naturally' well born. Yet, these inequalities have met with resistance across all cultures, from political struggle, to scientific counter-research, to academic scholarship and legal contestation.

In this chapter, I look at historical writing from the late nineteenth century as a way of understanding how racialized theories informed some of the most prominent works of history. Then, I will explore how new theories, and particularly forms of cultural history, have shaped historical works until the present.

15.1 Race, racism and anti-racism in historical explanation before 1920

The revolutions of the eighteenth century held out promise for colonized peoples – as revolution erupted in the United States, France and then the continent, some revolutionaries advocated the abolition of slavery and the recognition of equality for all peoples. Haiti established independence from France in 1799 – the first time an oppressed people threw off a colonial power. Yet, the coming to power of Napoleon in 1801, the speeding up of trade and industrialization and a renewed imperialism led to the resurgence of strategies of domination.

One of these strategies was the application of new sciences to assert hierarchies, which positioned people of colour as inferior and white peoples as superior. With roots in the Enlightenment, scientists sought to generate a system of classification that would place all human 'species' on a measurable scale. In the early nineteenth century, the founder of comparative anatomy, Georges Cuvier, forcibly removed a South African woman and took her to France. After she fell ill and died, he and his colleague Henri de Blainville dissected her and put her genitalia on display as a way to prove Africans' 'primitive' status.

At mid-century, Charles Darwin's *On the Origin of Species* outlined the forces of natural selection. As historian Jennifer Terry notes, this theory emphasized 'the dynamics of mating, reproduction, and survival'.[1] As such, it lent itself to 'Social-Darwinism', whereby evolutionists extended these theories to take political positions on issues surrounding immigration and reproduction. In 1883, British scientist Francis Galton, a cousin of Charles Darwin, coined the term 'eugenics', which he defined as 'the science of improvement of the human race germ plasm through better breeding'. That is, eugenics appealed to the language of science as a means to limit the births of those deemed 'unfit' (including blacks, Jews, gays, deaf people and the 'feeble-minded') and increase the births of the wealthiest classes. Eugenics became such a powerful system that it traversed national borders – the First International Congress of Eugenics was held in London in 1912, the Second and Third, in 1921 and 1932, respectively, were convened in New York City, drawing participants from Norway, Czechoslovakia, Japan, Venezuela, India and New Zealand.

These assertions of progress through the 'management' of races would shape social policy, anthropology and history. This is clear in the work of Houston Stewart Chamberlain.

Chamberlain, an English-born son of an admiral, travelled to Geneva, where he studied botany, astronomy, anatomy and physiology. After strains on his health, he moved to Dresden and focused his studies on Wagnerian music and philosophy (he would later marry Wagner's daughter). While his first book was a work of art criticism, he shifted back to natural science; after relocating to

Vienna, he published a highly regarded botanical study, a treatise on Wagner's dramas, and then, finally, the controversial *Grundlagen des Neunzehnten Jahrhunderts* (*Foundations of the Nineteenth Century*) in 1899.

The *Foundations* was, in an immediate sense, a response to Assyriology, a discipline that had flourished in the universities of Germany. The work addresses a professor Delitzsch, who had recently found evidence of worship of one God among 'the Semitic tribes of Canaan which at the time of Khammurabi, two thousand years before the birth of Christ, flooded Assyria, were worshippers of one God, and that the name of that God was Jahve (Jehovah)'.[2] At issue here was the degree to which scholars could discuss Near Eastern origins or religious commonalities in Germany, a nation experiencing an increasing nationalism in the late nineteenth century. This nationalist fervour was buttressed by several currents in the academy. As George Mosse has noted, disciplines such as anthropology, ethnology and linguistics, the latter which Frederich Schlegel helped to develop, attempted to draw a line between European and supposed 'lesser' cultures. Schlegel legitimated the notion that India was the foundation for all European languages. While he did not explicitly claim European superiority, he disparaged languages derived from Chinese (including Native American and Slavonic) as random and weak. Through his theory of 'noble' and 'ignoble' languages, Schlegel popularized the concept of 'Aryan' origins.

Chamberlain instead set out to provide a complex account of the rise of Indo-European civilization, the story of what he called 'Der Germane'. Within this appellation, Chamberlain attempted to subsume all Celts, Germans, Slavs and 'all those races of northern Europe', including the white peoples of the United States. While he excluded the French, he claimed Louis XIV as a 'genuine Germane' for having challenged the Papacy. Using this classification, Chamberlain asserted a racial discourse of history.

Chamberlain outlined a sweeping narrative of 'critical knowledge' of the past, a past 'which is still living'. From research on the first eighteen centuries of the 'Christian era', with reference to the ancients, the nineteenth century would emerge 'clearly shaped', not in encyclopaedic form, 'but as a living "corporeal' thing' (Chamberlain, *Foundations of the Nineteenth Century*, p. xii). This corporeal history represented a scientific conception of the past.

Foundations was very well received, garnering praise in Germany, Britain and America. Kaiser Wilhelm II thanked Chamberlain by letter:

> Our stifled youth needed a liberator like yourself, one who revealed to us the Indo-German origins which no one knew about. And so it was only at the cost of a hard struggle that the original Germanic Aryanism (das Uranische-Germanische) which slumbered in the depths of my soul was able to assert itself.[3]

Chamberlain's writings assumed that race was *the* underlying category that explained the course of history, determined (or should determine) the behaviour of individuals and groups, and set out Germany's mission in the world. His vision impacted not only historians, but also legislators, scientists and commentators, who saw race as a *problem* to be regulated.

15.2 Race, empires and progress

In the 1930s, historians began to use several theories to explicate the meanings of race. When historians like Chamberlain asserted that their race was superior, they rewrote the ancient past to trace the grand development of a European people. Theirs was a story of progress through the history of race. Ancient cultures have benefited from new readings, including social science research on 'race relations' and histories of ancient languages, to best understand commonalities across cultural difference.

The concept of 'race' is entangled with the notion of 'civilization'. Historians have long seen 'world history' as a successive study of *empires* and the formation of new political identities. Much nineteenth-century historical writing – from English Whig history to German historism – was concerned with the rise of empires and states, and aimed to legitimate them historically. Some of these assumptions about necessary historical development survived in social scientific theories such as modernization theory. As such, students of history have considered interactions between different empires; given the West's tendency to locate its origins in Greco-Roman culture, were the encounters between Greco-Roman and African civilizations reciprocally influential? The works considered in this section represent critiques of certain explicitly or tacitly racist ideas of progress – including some versions of the notion of 'modernization'.

Frank Snowden has written two defining works on the links among Mediterranean, Egyptian and Ethiopian civilizations. In *Blacks in Antiquity* (1970), Snowden explored Africans' experiences in Greco-Roman culture from the time of Homer through the rule of Justinian. His task is to trace Greco-Roman views of Ethiopians using diverse evidence: 'literary, epigraphical, papyrological, numismatic, and archaeological' (*Blacks in Antiquity*, p. viii). He demonstrates the African origins of western 'civilization'. Yet, Snowden's use of 'Ethiopian' follows Greek and Roman usage. Both cultures homogenized all African peoples regardless of place under this term. In parallel to the way 'Negro' performs an erasure of African and Caribbean cultural variation, Snowden renders classical depictions of Africans.

His aim in *Before Colour Prejudice* (1983) was to provide a 'comprehensive study of *the image of blacks in the minds of Mediterranean whites* who opposed them in battle or lived with them in peace during the period from the Pharaohs to the Caesars' (*Before Colour Prejudice*, p. vii; my emphasis). Snowden's method is twofold: first, he closely examines the meanings of artists' conceptions of black-ness. Second, he draws upon social science research on the origin of colour preju-dice – while the ancients accepted slavery as an institution and sometimes made ethnocentric judgements of *other* societies, 'nothing comparable to the virulent colour prejudice of modern times existed in the ancient world' (*Before Colour Prejudice*, p. 63). Blackness was viewed neither as a sign of inferiority nor as a bar to integration. While one finds pejorative statements about blackness, the ancients were aware of varying conceptions of beauty; thus, 'it is questionable whether indi-viduals should be called "racist" because they accept prevailing aesthetic canons in the country' (*Before Colour Prejudice*, p. 63). Still, we must ask about the individ-ual's status, and whether their texts defined social norms, enacted legislation or were symptomatic of the dominant views of the empire.

The interaction between classical and African cultures is also central to Martin Bernal's two-volume *Black Athena*. This sweeping study tracks the influence of Egypt on Greek culture. Written by a scholar of Chinese studies, Bernal became interested in ancient Jewish history. Around this time, he began to study the Hebrew language and noted many parallels between Hebrew and Greek. Within four years, Bernal had recognized that nearly 90 per cent of the Greek language was comprised of Indo-European, Egyptian and Semitic roots.

Bernal sets out two models of scholarship on the Near East: the 'Ancient' model and the 'Aryan' model. In the former, the dominant view in Greek cul-ture, Greece had arisen from Phoenician origins around 2100 BCE. In contrast, the Aryan model held that an invasion from the north overtook pre-Hellenic Greece and gave it a fundamentally Indo-European civilization. Drawing upon the work of the historian of science Thomas Kuhn, Bernal points out that this *paradigm* emerged in the last 150 years in the context of European neo-colonial-ism and anti-Jewish discourse.

Bernal then traces how the ancient model was gradually displaced in the eigh-teenth century by aristocrats, influenced by the Enlightenment, who turned to science for the 'origins' of man. Informed by Romanticism, European scholars from Johann Gottfried von Herder, who fostered the discipline of linguistics, to Johann Winkelman, the founder of art history as a discipline, posited Greece as the foundation of European civilization. These writers would figure 'Egypt' as increasingly backward, and Europe became redefined as the site of 'progress'. While both volumes deal with how racism shaped accounts of European origins, the terms *race* and *racism* are only briefly treated; for Bernal, after 1650, racism is 'greatly intensified by the increased colonization of North America, with its twin policies of extermination of the Native Americans and enslavement of Africans' (*Black Athena*, pp. 201–2). In sum, Bernal criticizes the kind of history written by open racists like Chamberlain and the subtly racist implications of certain recent stories of progress.

15.3 Critiquing whiteness: the grammars of race

The texts in this section, informed by currents in literary theory, seek to unravel the 'grammars' of race. Grammars here refer to codes, both linguistic and social, denoting stereotypes, terms or 'small acts', that mark racial hierarchy, difference and contestation.

David Roediger's work marks an important departure in the uses of theory to compose histories of race. Drawing upon writers of colour, especially novelist and literary theorist Toni Morrison, he critiques race as not simply a 'Negro problem', but rather a problem of whites, showing 'working-class "whiteness" and white supremacy as creations, in part, of the white working class itself' (*Wages of Whiteness*, p. 9). In *The Wages of Whiteness* (1991), Roediger tracks the formation of the 'white worker' in Antebellum America. His goal is to find how labourers came to see themselves as white in relation to systems of slavery and the movement for Reconstruction. He explores how Irish immigrants, many of whom had built alliances with African-Americans in unions as well as in social settings, were divided through racist stereotypes. Irish politicians, turning to the Democratic Party, crudely dismissed its opposition through the grammar of race: 'Democratic politicians charged that Republicans and abolitionists had "nigger on the brain"' (*Wages of Whiteness*, p. 154).

While Roediger's work may seem indebted to poststructuralism, it is actually more closely allied with Mikhail Bakhtin's theory of language. Roediger critiques poststructuralism for neglecting interactions between the 'individual' and the 'text', and its assumption that

> each generation finds its own different meanings in texts. Bakhtin on the other hand, holds that 'at any given moment ... language is stratified not only into linguistic dialects ... but also – and for us this is the essential point – into languages which are socio-ideological'.[4]

In other words, Roediger seeks to render the complex production of racial 'grammar' without losing the role of class in language itself. The *Wages of Whiteness* is thus an innovative social history of race and labour.

Examining blackface minstrelsy, Roediger usefully points out that many performers were artisans, mechanics, and working-class tradesmen; in sex-segregated spaces, white workers caroused and played out fantasies of racial difference. Interestingly, one can locate a degree of oppositional culture within blackface – masters were often ridiculed, yet many shows supported white supremacist views, and mocked civil and women's rights.

While this oppositional element of blackface is significant, it cannot replace histories of raced *experience*. Although the literature on race thus far had sought out every text complicit in the production of *racism*, few had traced either the felt sense or the challenges of race or ethnicity, as told by those resisting racism.

Ronald Takaki's *A Different Mirror* (1993) explores the cross-currents of migration and the contributions of Native Americans, Mexicans, Chinese, Irish, Japanese, Jews and African-Americans to debates about race. Writing in the wake of the Los Angeles riots and demographic projections that white Americans would soon become a minority, Takaki takes as a point of departure the debates over 'multi-culturalism' by tracing America's diversity since the first settlement at Jamestown in 1607.

Takaki uses Shakespeare's *The Tempest*, with its monstrous character Caliban, as a parable of colonists' racist conceptions of native peoples and the effects of racism in the New World. Drawing on retheorizations of *The Tempest* by Shakespeare scholar Stephen Greenblatt, Takaki shows how the play illuminated the politics of colonization. The play's title referenced a real incident – in 1609, a ship on its way to 'Virginia' had shipwrecked in Bermuda. Shakespeare knew some of the voyagers and set his play in 'Bermoothes'. Creating 'Caliban' from the word 'Carib', the name for an Indian tribe, Carib became a metonym for New World racist fantasies – it was believed that Caliban could be acculturated; yet, he came from a 'vile race'. His mother, 'Sycorax', was a witch from Africa, giving him dangerous connotations; yet, he was a 'deformed slave'. For Takaki, race is socially constructed, and these constructions considerably affected conditions for minorities in America.

Takaki takes a comparative approach to 'the varied experiences of different racial and ethnic groups . . . within shared contexts' (*Different Mirror*, p. 10). In tracing Chinese migration, Takaki relocates the formation of 'immigrant' identity to the West Coast, away from the dominant saga of New York's Ellis Island. After Reconstruction, many southerners sought to use Chinese labour on plantations. Soon, they were demonized in ways similar to blacks, as 'heathen, morally inferior, childlike, and lustful' (*Different Mirror*, p. 205). This transfer of racism was perniciously inscribed into law. During the murder trial of Ling Sing in 1854, the California Supreme Court declared that the 'the words "Indian, Negro, Black, and White" were generic terms, designating races', and that therefore 'Chinese and other people not white could not testify against whites' (*Different Mirror*, p. 206). This became the prelude to the federal Chinese Exclusion Act, which closed America's borders in 1882 and, in 1902, was extended indefinitely. Still, despite overwhelming odds, the Chinese formed vibrant communities in California and the north-west.

In *Race Rebels*, Robin D.G. Kelley (1994) gives a history of working-class blacks from 'way, way down below'. Informed by W.E.B. DuBois's *Black Reconstruction* (1935) and C.L.R. James's *Black Jacobins* (1938) on the overthrow of French colonialism in Haiti, as well as new work in British cultural studies,

Kelley traces the small acts of resistance by black labourers and the ways they maintained 'a sense of racial identity and solidarity' (*Race Rebels*, p. 5). While Kelley acknowledges the mid-1960s writings of E.P.Thompson and Eugene Genovese, he draws upon those earlier 'majestic histories of revolution, resistance, and the making of new working classes out of the destruction of slavery [which] anticipated the "new" social historians' efforts to write "history from below"' (*Race Rebels*, p. 5).

Breaking from both labour histories that focused solely on white workers and African-American historiography that posited a generalized 'black community', Kelley tracks the *hidden transcripts*, a concept developed by anthropologist James Scott, of black working-class lives at the margins. From the songs and poems of African-Americans in the Communist Party, to the black volunteers who fought fascism in the Spanish Civil War, to the politics of 'hipness' in the life of young Malcolm X, the politics of black cultural production, vis-à-vis, but not dependent upon, racism becomes visible. Kelley's work, informed by Marxism and by the 'history from below' movement, but not reducible to it, captures the making of radical African-American culture.

15.4 Cultivating race: the poststructuralist and postcolonial turn

Historians have addressed race as not simply the product of individual actors, but as a kind of constantly retold grand fable. Mosse anticipated this method, that of poststructuralism, in his discussion of myth. He wrote:

> Racism substituted myth for reality; and the world that it created, with its stereotypes, virtues, and vices, was a fairy-tale world, which dangled a utopia before the eyes of those who longed for a way out of the confusion of modernity and the rush of time.

In other words, race was constructed as a myth (akin to Foucault's 'discourse'), which, Mosse noted, became a 'foundation for national policy' of the Nazis. Mosse traced this myth through racial iconography, in what appears to be the first anti-racist study to include and critique paintings, political cartoons and propaganda.

Thus, race is not static or fixed – systems of racial classification were profoundly shaped by political dynamics, scientific priorities and the increasing demands of mercantile trade. But race and politics were mutually affected in another way – that of racial 'cultivation'. Racial *cultivation* refers to ways in which social classes figured 'race' as a means to elevate or maintain their status. In the early modern era, aristocrats spoke of race increasingly in terms of primary, 'authentic' stock. Countering royal genealogies asserted by monarchy, aristocratic commentators such as Sir Edward Coke and Boulainvilliers confronted the realities of *sanguinity* – marriages for the purposes of wider political rule – with a 'racial' discourse of aristocratic privilege. Drawing upon poststructuralism, we understand from Foucault that meanings are constructed through language. His *genealogy* in *The History of Sexuality* briefly noted a historical shift from this *deployment of alliance* (that is, the use of marriage alliances to further diplomacy) to the concept of *biopower* (in other words the role that sciences had in extending power over human life). Foucault asserts that the interchange between these two points is the model of *confession*, which is extended in and through medicine and psychiatry. Whereas confession had been confined to the Church, doctors and psychiatrists increasingly adopted it as a means to secure professional authority. What is more ambiguous is how this shift played out, especially in colonial contexts.

Ann Laura Stoler's *Race and the Education of Desire* is a detailed study of racial cultivation. Stoler opens with a careful reading of the 1976 Collège de France lectures of Michel Foucault. Drawing upon archival research, Stoler fills in a major gap in Foucault's work: an engagement with racism. While Foucault had provided stunning critiques of prisons, sexuality,[5] and medicine, many Foucauldian scholars who sought to confront race were at a loss. While studies of peasant revolts under colonialism had benefited from structuralism,[6] only a few works combined a tenable critique of imperialism with a nuanced analysis of the forces that gave rise to it. Edward Said's *Orientalism* critiqued European conceptions of a racially homogenous 'Oriental' – whether Arabic, Asian or Indian, travel writers and novelists rendered the 'Oriental' as incompetent and inferior.[7]

Stoler is interested in how Foucault's chronologies have bracketed certain possibilities for colonial studies. She writes (in *Race and the Education of Desire*, pp. 5–6):

> What is striking is how consistently Foucault's own framing of the European bourgeois order has been exempt from the very sorts of criticism that his insistence on the fused regimes of knowledge/power would seem to encourage and allow. Why have we been so willing to accept his story of a nineteenth-century sexual order that systematically excludes and/or subsumes the fact of colonialism within it?

In other words, what analytical tools are needed to examine colonial regimes outside of the terms of western discourse?

Stoler renders Foucault's 7 January 1976 lecture as an 'analytic repositioning' of his earlier work. In subsequent weeks, Foucault would trace a 'war of races'. This discourse saw the formation of law as 'the consequence of massacres, conquests, and domination, not as the embodiment of natural rights' (*Race and the Education of Desire*, p. 65). For Foucault, this discourse did not detach itself from 'rights' – truth is still linked to 'the rights of a family (to property), of a class (to privilege), of a race (to rule)' (*Race and the Education of Desire*, p. 65). As aristocrats challenged royal genealogies, this 'war of races' became one of 'an upper-race and lower-race', with the latter representing the 'reappearance of its own past' (*Race and the Education of Desire*, p. 66). The latter quote may seem cryptic, but means that aristocrats both acknowledged the king's power and vigorously defended themselves as the 'pure' stock and leaders of the realm.

One of Stoler's critical insights is that 'Nineteenth-century science may have legitimated racial classifications as many have claimed, but it [did] so by drawing on an earlier lexicon, on that of the struggle of races' (*Race and the Education of Desire*, p. 68). In other words, sciences like craniology depended upon earlier racial grammars. Modern racism has its roots in a discourse on 'races', which would become singularly rendered as *race*.

Drawing together a range of analyses, Ruth Roach Pierson and Nupur Chaudhuri's *Nation, Empire, Colony* serves as a key starting point for understanding the histories of women under colonialism and within nation-states. The Introduction builds upon insights of feminists of colour to explore the asymmetries of race and class in the experiences of women. Yet, this analysis does not assume that the categories 'gender' and 'women' are synonymous. Pierson and Chaudhuri note that 'the ways one becomes a woman or a man are much more complex than in simple opposition to members of the other sex' (*Nation, Empire, Colony*, p. 2). Thus, the authors recognize that gender can be 'raced'; put more broadly, social categories are linked within a network of power relations.

This set of essays emerged from a 1995 meeting of the International Federation for Research in Women's History. The Federation advocated international women's history without 'global' pretensions, a term associated with neo-imperialism. In dialogue with Stoler's work, the authors bring research on both the 'metropole' and 'colony' together, 'to dismantle the barriers separating the imperialists' history from that of the imperialized, the colonists' from that of the colonized, the narrative of the nation's core from that of its excluded margins' (*Nation, Empire, Colony*, p. 3).

Rosalyn Terborg-Penn considers the links between the US suffrage movement and parallel activism in the Caribbean. She shows how American women's political work was inflected by neo-Victorian conceptions of womanhood, which figured Caribbean women as 'Other'. Her writing shows that 'successful twentieth-century woman suffrage movements appeared first in western nations, which controlled colonies in other areas of the globe, and in white-dominated or white-colonized colonies'. Working against the assumption that women of colour had no involvement in the early movement, the author shows how Caribbean women, working-class and well-to-do, lobbied for the right to vote as early as the century's turn. Often, feminist victories in the USA sparked new efforts by working-class Puerto Rican and St Thomian women for suffrage. Combining readings of new work in colonial women's history and her own preliminary research, Terborg-Penn traces how white American suffragettes often expressed racist views of black women.

Gabriela Cano's essay 'The *Porfiriato* and the Mexican Revolution' shows how the Mexican Revolution of the 1890s would affect representations of Mexican identity. In dialogue with work on Indians in Mexico, Cano illuminates the stakes of nationalism. Cano combines two approaches: an analysis of images of the 'Mexican woman' at the turn of the century, and a critique of liberal republicanism, which viewed indigenous peoples as a block to progress. Many writers, influenced by the Social-Darwinism of Auguste Comte and Herbert Spencer, claimed that Mexican women were naturally sentimental, given to domesticity and 'discreet'. Women, nevertheless, gradually called for equality and the proper governing of Mexico. Still, women had to contend with definitions of Mexican femininity as racially impure. Statements from prominent figures like novelist Julio Sesto 'implied that the "Mexican woman" is *mestiza*, that is, a mixture of Spanish and Indian blood in which European physical traits, such as whiteness, have predominated and diluted Indian ones'.

After civil war in 1911 broke the power of the *Porfiriato* (the dictatorship of Porfirio Díaz), fears about women's power subsided somewhat in more radical circles and in post-revolutionary governments. Within five years, the military government of the Yucatan was supporting feminist congresses, which challenged the power of Catholicism in Mexico. Thus, women's movements, in their official recognition, were often part of a larger strategy of nationalism and modernization.

In 'Men, Women, and the Community Borders', Sayoko Yoneda portrays the Japanese military 'comfort women' that forced Korean women into prostitution during the Second World War. In an impressive essay that calls attention to a pressing problem of historical memory, Yoneda draws upon recent newspaper accounts of comfort women to excavate how this system depended upon both sexism *and* racism. She notes that in the 1930s, when Japan began to invade China, Japanese prostitutes travelled with soldiers and served in the 'comfort' system – this afforded women a sense of patriotism and allowed them to escape a more haphazard, unregulated system at home. But as the war escalated, the number of Japanese prostitutes was 'insufficient'. At this time, the government began to look toward Korea, which was under Japanese control.

The Japanese government would, in addition, extract women from the Philippines, Singapore and Indonesia in the early 1940s. Yoneda also connects the rise of prostitution to the 'sex tours' that many businessmen, from Japan and the West, conduct today in the Philippines and Thailand – notably, Thai and Filipina women have been taken to Japan against their will. The Japanese government has continued to deny its involvement in this system or express any remorse to these women.

It is fair to say that poststructuralism is open to the charge of constructing the oppressed as the negative term – the 'Other' – of a binary opposition. Thus, we ought to explore histories of race that show the contestedness of theories of race.

15.5 Race as a contested discourse

Recent histories of slavery, informed by new theoretical developments, have reinvigorated the field. So many pioneering studies of the Atlantic slave trade were written during and after the Civil Rights Movement, when the methods of psychohistory and social history predominated. Yet, in the 1980s, many historians began to situate their work in relation to several disciplines, including semiotics and cultural anthropology. Sue Peabody's *There Are No Slaves in France*, located at the intersection of legal history and cultural history, looks at legal cases, edicts and registers to understand the experience of slaves in France and the political culture of the Ancien Régime.

Benefiting from the groundbreaking work of Robert Darnton, the author places lawyers, masters, slaves and royal officials within their historical and legal contexts to give a *micro-history* of eighteenth-century France. Treating race here in a way that implicitly challenges the narrative of modernization that Mosse had asserted, Peabody tracks the role of the Church in the regulation and potential 'liberation' of slaves within France. For example, baptism, while inscribed into the *Code Noir* (1685) as solely a precondition for slaves upon entering France, actually served as one path to freedom. Some French masters, along with their English counterparts, would 'recognize baptism as a formal act of manumission' (*There Are No Slaves*, p. 80).

Second, Peabody excavates a critical concept in histories of race in France: the 'Freedom Principle', according to which once a slave touched French soil, they were free. While in practice, the French kept servants as early as the 1570s, the phrase 'There are no slaves in France' resonated in the streets of Paris. This principle would be the basis for many legal challenges to enslavement and detainment of African slaves.

For authors influenced by structuralism, such as George Stocking, 'race' is largely the product of declarations by scientists, policy-makers and legislators – they construct a *dominant discourse* of the 'Other', an object of scientific, legal and political knowledges. With Peabody, race is *refigured* – dominant discourses by the king, ministers and police are contested by both accounts of free blacks as well as those who *spoke back* to the law in the courts.

Lawyers who defended escaped slaves drew upon legal arguments grounded in the view that early Christianity had helped to undo Roman slavery. Peabody writes of the case of Jean Boucaux vs Bernard Verdelin – Boucaux was the son of two slaves owned by the governor of the French colony Saint Domingue. When the governor died, his widow married Monsieur Verdelin, and they soon travelled to the island to make arrangements on the estate. In 1728, they returned with two slaves, including Boucaux, who served as Verdelin's cook for nine years. Near the end of that period, Boucaux married a French woman. From then on, Boucaux became the object of Verdelin's hatred; the enmity became so strong that in 1738, 'Verdelin had Boucaux arrested "because he suspected Boucaux of planning an escape and he was afraid to lose him"' (*There Are No Slaves*, p. 25). Boucaux prevailed, providing an important precedent for future legal decisions in the French Admiralty Court.

Students interested in how both racism and anti-slavery discourse shaped law will find much insight here. Peabody traces how the *Code Noir* (literally 'Black Code') of 1685 met increasing legal challenges throughout the eighteenth century. Notably, the grammar of the *Code Noir* appeared 150 years later in the United States, where 'black codes' enforced common law segregation throughout the United States. This critical point demands further research. How did racial discourses travel? What forces allowed racism to move within and across specific geographic domains? In order to confront this issue, we must consider how race has operated through *political* spheres. As we further explore the history of colonized subjects under slavery, we begin to find the traffic of regulations between 'home' country and colony.

Matthew Frye Jacobson's book, *Whiteness of a Different Colour* (1998) is attentive to the ways in which language serves in the fabrication of race. He opens with a 'Note on Usage' that discusses the author's decision not to put the word race in undermining quotation marks. A stylistic and practical move, Jacobson found that nearly every sentence would have been rife with quotation marks. Still, he included the word 'race', as well as 'Teutons', 'Nordics', 'Hebrews', and other appellations in quotation marks when an author actually used this punctuation.

First, Jacobson's decision is incisive: to understand historical meanings around race, we must consider not only how critical theories shape current writing, but also how authors of the past problematized or deployed race. Sometimes, authors did so strategically to challenge dominant conceptions of race; at others, those dedicated to segregation used scare quotes to further a white supremacist agenda.

Second, this is a rare opportunity to meditate upon the composing of scholarship on race. While he originally tended to put words such as 'Anglo-Saxon' and 'racial' in quotes, terms such as 'white' or 'black' received less consideration. Bidding the reader to consider their own linguistic desires, he writes:

I wonder about the unexamined racial certainty that this denotes, too. All these designations belong on the same epistemological footing, and so they appear before you now without any stylistic marker to separate archaic fabrications from current ones. If you are inclined to supply your own as you go, I only invite you, too, to note the patterns of your own choices. A principled consistency on this score is rendered very difficult by the culture within which we operate. (*Whiteness of a Different Colour*, p. x, my emphasis)

Jacobson makes a claim here that must be unpacked. If all classifications of race are *equally* problematic, then what does it mean for cultural groups to redefine insults or reclaim domains from which blacks were historically marginalized? For example, hip-hop artists sometimes speak of 'droppin' science'; artists depend on and *transvalue* the *power* of science to establish the 'truth' of their rhymes. Thus, over time, certain terms are reappropriated by sub-cultures to create very different epistemologies. We need new histories that consider the *specific* valences each racial concept carries.

The construction of whiteness is a central theme in Jacobson's work. Combining archival research in immigration law, demography and stunningly perceptive readings of literature, Jacobson carefully traces the racialized landscape for European immigrants to America. Rather than assume that race has a fixed meaning, he critiques works that confuse race with colour.

In other words, Jacobson's goal is

to map the significance of the racial designations that have framed the history of European immigration – white and Caucasian on the one hand, and narrower distinctions such as Anglo-Saxon, Celt, Hebrew, Slav, Mediterranean, or Nordic on the other – in order to make sense of pervasive racial articulations that scholars have too conveniently passed over simply as misuses of the word 'race'. (Whiteness of a Different Colour, p. 6)

The historical, experiential specificity of *race* is crucial here. Some African-American scholars, such as W.E.B. DuBois, were not ready to simply discard the term 'race', as they understood its significance *within* black culture. For Jewish, Irish, Mediterranean and Slavic emigrants, the ways in which one became 'white' were not given – their transmutation into 'Caucasians' was a complex, non linear process. Jacobson periodizes this gradual shift into three eras: 1790 to 1840, 1840 to 1924, and 1924 to 1965. The first era was marked by the rise of the designation 'free white male inhabitants' in several state constitutions. Concomitantly, legislators rendered specific restrictions against blacks, who were defined as 'dependants'. This highlighted a paternalist racism – blacks held the same political status as women and children.

While Jacobson acknowledges Roediger's work, he differs with Roediger's focus upon class formation. If white workers solely benefited from what W.E.B. DuBois called the 'public and psychological wage' of esteem from political institutions, then how do we explain nativist stereotypes directed at Celtic, Slavic and Italian peoples? How is it possible that Irish people were once viewed as 'savages'?

Between 1840 and 1924, America was rapidly transformed by the second wave of industrialization with mines, chemical plants and steel mills. Thus, the Republican ideology of 'independence' confronted the reality of emigrants who sought religious freedoms and new opportunities. Republicanism, Jacobson shows, was marked by the shifting boundaries of racism. He notes that while before the 1840s, 'whiteness' depended upon its opposition to 'non-whiteness', the latter half of the century witnessed the construction of scientific hierarchies of racial difference.

Readers seeking to understand the rise of American eugenics will find much wisdom here. Jacobson critiques assumptions of the most prominent, conservative commentators of this era, including Harry Laughlin and Madison Grant. Also useful are examples of the ways in which writers, both emigrant and non-emigrant, offered snapshots of racial meanings. From the works of Hugh Henry Brackenridge, to the turn-of-the-century writings of Charles Chestnutt, to Arthur Miller's politically acute novel *Focus* (1945), Jacobson intersperses how authors understood the boundaries of race. This is not so much a recuperative effort as a theorization – Jacobson outlines how scientific theories of race infused literary texts, and what they articulated about the politics of race.

Racial assumptions of difference underwrote even anti-racist efforts in the 1930s and 1940s. The liberal focus on the 'Negro question' would posit new dichotomies (white/coloured, white/Negro), erasing Asians and Latinos from public discourse. Anthropologists only bolstered these notions, asserting the 'three great divisions of mankind': 'Caucasian', 'Mongoloid' and 'Negroid'. Jacobson captures how 'ethnic' writers negotiated these systems.

15.6 Conclusion

Historians are in a unique position to subvert dominant debates about the meanings of race. Recently, after an interminable silence on race from the profession, historians have begun to apply knowledges in the public sphere. For example, Eric Foner called upon the state of New York to recognize its participation in the slave system. Encouraging projects that would educate citizens, he identified corporations that benefited from slavery.[8]

Given the legacy of discrimination, histories of race can open up dialogue and initiate the process of redressing the violences that racism has wrought. The need for cultural understanding, across all (supposed) racial and ethnic boundaries, will lead to promising futures.

Guide to further reading

Martin Bernal, *Black Athena: the Afroasiatic Roots of Classical Civilization*, 2 vols (London, 1987; New Brunswick, 1991).

N. Chaudhuri and R.R. Pierson (eds), *Nation, Empire, Colony: Historicizing Race and Gender* (Bloomington, 1998).

Matthew Frye Jacobson, *Whiteness of a Different Colour: European Immigrants and the Alchemy of Race* (Cambridge, MA, 1998).

Robin D.G. Kelley, *Race Rebels: Culture, Politics, and the Black Working Class* (New York, 1994).

Sue Peabody, *'There Are No Slaves in France': The Political Culture of Race and Slavery in the Ancien Régime* (New York, 1996).

David Roediger, *The Wages of Whiteness: Race and the Making of the American Working Class* (London, 1991).

Frank M. Snowden, Jr, *Blacks in Antiquity: Ethiopians in the Greco-Roman Experience* (Cambridge, MA, 1970).

Frank M. Snowden, Jr, *Before Colour Prejudice: The Ancient View of Blacks* (Cambridge, MA, 1983).

George W. Stocking, Jr, *Race, Culture, and Evolution: Essays in the History of Anthropology* (New York, 1968). ·

Ann Laura Stoler, *Race and the Education of Desire: Foucault's History of Sexuality and the Colonial Order of Things* (Durham, NC, 1995).

Notes

I would like to thank Jennifer Terry, David Horn, C.L. Cole, Dale Van Kley, and Melissa Orlie for dialoguing with me and fostering my interests across the disciplinary terrain covered here. Much appreciation goes to Kevin Passmore for his encouragement and careful reading of this essay.

1   Jennifer Terry, *An American Obsession: Science, Medicine, and Homosexuality in Modern Society* (Chicago, 1999), pp. 36–7.

2   John Lees 'Introduction', in Houston Stewart Chamberlain, *Foundations of the Nineteenth Century*, trans. John Lees (New York, 1914; first published 1901), p. ix.

3   Léon Poliakov, *The Aryan Myth: A History of Racist and Nationalist Ideas in Europe*, trans. Edmund Howard (New York, 1974; first published 1971), p. 319.

4   Quoted in David Roediger, *The Wages of Whiteness: Race and the Making of the American Working Class* (London, 1991), p. 15.

5   For the ways in which scientific discourses of race shaped homosexuality consult Jennifer Terry, *An American Obsession: Science, Medicine, and Homosexuality in Modern Society* (Chicago, 1999). For racism and figurations of gay sexuality in late nineteenth-century film and literature, see Siobhan B. Somerville, *Queering the Colour Line: Race and the Invention of Homosexuality in American Culture* (Durham, North Carolina, 2000).

6   Ranajit Guha (ed.), *Subaltern Studies: Writings on South Asian History and Society* (Delhi, 1982).

7   Edward W. Said, *Orientalism* (New York, 1979). Although Oriental studies, as a discipline, once took aim at both Muslims and Jews, Said shows that the Israeli military and rightist parties have demonized Palestinians as 'irrational' and incapable of self-government.

8   'Slavery's Fellow Travelers', *New York Times,* 14 July 2000. Foner notes that in the nineteenth century, New York's merchant class controlled the South's cotton trade, thereby challenging the still persistent notion that the North was somehow 'less' racist.

16

Voices from below: doing people's history in Cardiff Docklands

Glenn Jordan

History, in the hands of the professional historian, is apt to present itself as an esoteric form of knowledge. It fetishizes archive-based research, as it has done since the Rankean revolution – or counter-revolution – in scholarship. When matters of interpretation are in dispute, disagreement may turn on such apparently arcane questions as the wordings of a coronation oath, the dating of a royal portrait or the correlation of harvest yields with fluctuations in peasant nuptuality. Argument is embedded in dense thickets of footnotage, and lay readers who attempt to unravel it find themselves enmeshed in a cabbala of acronyms, abbreviations and signs . . .

Popular memory is on the face of it the very antithesis of written history.

Raphael Samuel [1]

Who produces history? Whose side is history on? What is the relationship between history and cultural democracy? One of the most interesting developments in the practice of academic and public history since the early or mid-twentieth century (depending on where one wishes to assign the point of 'origins') has been the 'recovery' of marginalized memories, voices and experiences – of the working classes, women, black people and other subordinate groups. Whether based in academic institutions or in community settings, 'people's history' has transformed the practice of history writing in a range of contexts, from books to exhibitions to media programmes. When it has been rooted in cultural democracy – i.e. in practices that ensure the active involvement of a broad public, including marginalized groups – 'people's history' has sometimes transformed people's lives.

This chapter is a case study of one attempt to practise cultural democracy, including people's history, community education and community art, over a period of some fifteen years in one of Britain's oldest multi-ethnic, working-class communities. It reflects on that practice and seeks to relate it to larger issues having to do with unofficial knowledge, engaged intellectual work and the project of history from below. The organization is Butetown History & Arts Centre; the location is Cardiff docklands, specifically the famous, often maligned, community known as Butetown, or 'Tiger Bay'.

16.1 The context

From the mid-1800s to the 1990s, Butetown linked the port of Cardiff with the city centre. From the 1840s to the redevelopment of the 1960s, this small, mile-long district housed one of Britain's largest immigrant and minority communities. It was home to people from more than 50 nations, from virtually all over the world: Welsh, Irish, English and Scots; Greeks, Turks and Cypriots; Spanish, Italians, Portuguese and Maltese; Cape Verdeans and other colonial Portuguese; Yemeni, Egyptians and Somalis; Nigerians, Sierra Leoneans and other West Africans; West Indians; French and Colonial French; Chinese and Malays; Indians (i.e. people from what is now India, Pakistan and Bangladesh); Poles, Ukranians and eastern European Jews; Estonians, Latvians and Lithuanians; Germans, Norwegians, Finns and Danes; North, South and Central Americans; and a few more.

Most of the immigrants in Cardiff docklands were Merchant Navy men, who transported Welsh coal around the world. Most of the women with whom they formed relationships and married were local, resulting in the development of the community as not only multi-ethnic but as thoroughly racially and culturally mixed. (Given this legacy, the history that Butetown History & Arts Centre produces – whether in our exhibitions and books or our bottle openers and key chains – problematizes any notion of Welshness or Britishness that is mono-cultural or White.)

For a century, beginning in the 1850s, Butetown included a thriving commercial sector and part of a notorious 'Sailor Town' – with prostitution, gambling, and numerous legal and illegal drinking establishments. Its 'dens of vice' were the frequent target of Victorian moralist campaigns; its alleged activities inspired a series of moral panics – over TB, venereal disease and mixed-race relationships.[2] Throughout most of its history, the area was physically isolated – an 'island' bounded by (now filled-in) canals, railway tracks and the sea, whose geographical separateness helped to naturalize its Otherness.[3]

Today, Butetown sits surrounded by a massive docklands regeneration scheme involving some 2700 acres and featuring a huge artificial lake, leisure complexes, luxury hotels, restaurants, galleries and other attractions catering primarily for tourists and the middle classes. The scheme is billed as EUROPE'S MOST EXCITING WATERFRONT DEVELOPMENT.

This chapter explores the work of an initiative – Butetown Community History Project, and its successor, Butetown History & Arts Centre – that is positioned in the heart of this development. The discussion weaves between the particular and the general, locating our case in a broader context of (a) the politics of history writing, (b) people's history and (c) cultural democracy.

The chapter makes considerable use of dialogue with three individuals who have been associated with this initiative over a long period of time: Glenn Jordan, the Centre's co-founder and Director; Marcia Brahim Barry, co-founder and long-term member of Centre's board of directors; and Professor Chris Weedon, who has served as Chair of the organization since the mid-1990s.[4] The interviews with Marcia and Chris were conducted in 1996 by Karen Gerhke, an Erasmus student from Germany, for an undergraduate dissertation (supervised by Glenn Jordan) at the University of Glamorgan.[5]

16.2 'History from below'

What is the role of historical knowledge in society? Does it play in favour of, or against, the existing social order? Is it an elitist product that descends from the specialists to the 'consumers' of history by way of books, television and tourism? Or is it rooted, from the outset, in a collective need, an active relationship to the past …?

Jean Chesneaux [6]

Oral history … can be a means for transforming both the content and the purpose of history.

Paul Thompson [7]

Grassroots history, history seen from below or the history of the common people … no longer needs commercials.

Eric Hobsbawn [8]

Movements towards the development of *people's history* – i.e. history grounded in radical politics that explores and celebrates the lives and struggles of working-class and marginalized groups – have a long history. Determining origins is usually, if not always, fraught with difficulties. As far as 'people's history' – or 'history from below' is concerned, one can locate the starting point in many different contexts, depending on the country concerned and one's criteria for defining 'people's history'. For example, to take the case of the USA, one could say that it began in the 1930s with the Federal Writers' Project interviews of ex-slaves or more recently in the public history and oral history movements.[9] Whatever birth date one wishes to assign, it is the case that 'people's history', like many other radical cultural initiatives, has become especially significant after '1968'.

One of the most useful periodizations is provided in a seminal intervention by members of the Centre for Contemporary Cultural Studies (CCCS) at the University of Birmingham.[10] They identified six different phases or traditions in the development of people's history (in Britain): (1) the early work of John and Barbara Hammond, two radical liberals, on working-class culture;[11] (2) the Communist Party Historians' Group of the early post-war period, which included a number of people who later became leading historians – such as Christopher Hill, Rodney Hilton, Eric Hobsbawn, Dorothy Thompson, E.P. Thompson and George Rudé; (3) the historical research and political practice of E.P. Thompson, especially his *The Making of the English Working Class* (1968);[12] (4) the more recent oral history or 'popular memory' movement, which began in the 1970s and has now achieved considerable international success;[13] (5) radical community history, which often involves 'the people' not just as the object of history but as researchers, writers and publishers of history;[14] and (6) feminist history writing from the 1970s onwards.

As will become apparent from the following discussion, the work of Butetown History & Arts Centre, since its inception in 1987/88, resonates with the core concerns of movements for people's history and cultural democracy – both in Britain and elsewhere in the world.

16.3 Butetown History & Arts Centre

So history is a political battleground. The sanction of the past is sought by those committed to upholding authority and by those intent on subverting it, and both are assured of finding plenty of ammunition.

John Tosh [15]

Oral history . . . makes a much fairer trial possible: witnesses can now also be called from the under-classes, the unprivileged, and the defeated . . .

Paul Thompson [16]

Butetown History & Arts Centre (www.bhac.org) currently occupies some 2500 square feet of ground-floor space in the heart of Cardiff docklands. The Centre includes an image and sound archive, two gallery spaces, an educational resources office, a classroom/meeting room and a small shop. Our current budget is about £150,000 ($230,000) per year. Most of our income comes from grants, usually project grants lasting from one to three years – from sources such as the Home Office, the Arts Council of Wales, the Community Fund (formerly the Charities Lottery), Cardiff County Council and foundations. We also currently generate about £25,000 ($40,000) per year from the selling of books, photographs, cards and other products in our gallery shop; from the educational services that we offer to school groups; and by providing television and other media companies with images from our archive.

In partnership with local people, we collect, preserve and utilize oral histories, old photographs and other documents. We are a multi-ethnic, multi-racial team, including full-time workers, part-time workers and volunteers. At the time of writing, our paid staff occupy the equivalent of five or six full-time posts: the Centre Director, an Administrator, an Archivist/Picture Researcher, an Exhibitions Officer, an Education Officer (whose specialities include history, geography and the National Curriculum), an Arts Education Officer (whose background is in storytelling, theatre and world music), two Community Outreach Officers/Community Historians (one of whom works specifically with the Somali and other refugee communities) and a Marketing Officer (who doubles as our Graphic Designer). Our dozen or so volunteers include gallery workers, typists and research assistants. The participation of volunteers precedes that of paid staff and has always been central to our success.

Ours is history with a social purpose, a conscious attempt to link *historical knowledge to social practices*, including critical, interventionist practices. Our work transgresses the boundaries between *social history*, the study of social relations, institutions and practices, and *cultural history*, the study of meanings and values.[17] The *problem of representation* – of past and present relations among dominant, subordinate, marginal and contested *images* and *narratives* – lies at the core of our engagements.

Our goals are: to ensure that the social and cultural history of Cardiff docklands is carefully collected and preserved for posterity with the active involvement of local residents; to offer opportunities for all members of the local community – across the broadest spectrum of social backgrounds, cultural backgrounds and age ranges – to engage in creative practice; to produce educational materials, exhibitions, performances and other cultural products grounded in local history and experience; and to facilitate understanding and respect between people of different class, racial and cultural backgrounds. Our long-term aim is to create a Bay People's Museum & Arts Centre – with a major archive, permanent galleries, changing exhibitions, classrooms, a performance space, a café and a gift shop. The challenge is to realize this goal while remaining true to our founding principles and ethos.

16.4 Groundings

If history was thought of as an activity rather than a profession, then the number of its practitioners would be legion.

Raphael Samuel [18]

But history is far too important a matter to be left to the historians!

Jean Chesneaux [19]

Founded in 1987/88 by a black American anthropologist and half a dozen local residents, Butetown History & Arts Centre is an intervention on the terrain of culture and power. It began as a serious attempt to develop a group of locally based indigenous researchers – working-class, *organic intellectuals* – and to create a space for the production of *alternative histories, identities and representations* of life in Cardiff docklands. Our work, especially in the early phases, shares the ethos of other emancipatory intellectual projects – such as feminist history, as Catherine Hall explains:

Feminist history as first conceptualized in the early 1970s was about the recovery of women's history. We needed to fill out the enormous gaps in our historical knowledge which were a direct result of the male domination of historical work.[20]

And British labour and working-class history – as John Tosh explains:

The purpose of much labour history written by politically committed historians is to sharpen the social awareness of the workers, to confirm their commitment to political action, and to reassure them that history is 'on their side'. . . . In Britain this approach is reflected in the History Workshop movement . . . which began in the late 1960s; for them, the historical reconstruction of working people's experience serves as 'a source of inspiration and understanding' – to use a phrase from the first editorial in the History Workshop Journal.[21]

'*Recovering*' marginalized experience, '*filling in the gaps*' and *subverting dominant constructions*, using history as a means of *sharpening social awareness, increasing understanding* and i*nspiring action* – all of this is consistent with the practice of Butetown History & Arts Centre. Listen to Marcia Brahim Barry, a founder member of the project:

We knew that we had a unique history but we hadn't realized how unique it was until someone [a Black American anthropologist called Glenn Jordan] came in and said, 'You are history and if we don't do something about it, it will be lost.' So in a way, for me, it became a crusade ... I suddenly realised that everything around us was changing – we could actually see it – and that the elderly people were dying and lots of residents had moved away through the 'slum clearance' of the 1950s and 1960s, so the community had depleted and from I believe about 5000 in the 1950s, we're now down to two and a half thousand ... We realised that we had to start to do something about it.[22]

The anthropologist/oral historian, an activist-intellectual who had largely abandoned the ivory towers of the academy, confirmed what the Butetown community already knew but the dominant culture seemed constantly to deny. Whatever his intentions, one of the effects of his intervention was to affirm the importance of their history, to validate key aspects of locally based *popular memory* and *unofficial knowledge*. Through dialogue with an Other, their *self-recognition* was facilitated.

For people in the Butetown community (i.e. in 'Tiger Bay' and 'The Docks'), Butetown Community History Project offered a space in which they could contribute to an oppositional history, to a culturally democratic practice of research and writing that sought to challenge and subvert hegemonic constructions. For generations, people in and from this community have encountered images and stories about themselves in newspapers[23] and magazines, in fiction and autobiographical books, in academic studies, in the common-sense rhetoric of everyday conversation. For some 150 years, since the 1850s, their community has been recurrently represented in negative terms – as dirty, violent, diseased and immoral; and in romantic terms – as primitive, exotic and fascinating. As one local resident explains:

Whatever the origin of the name [i.e. 'Tiger Bay'], ever since the dawn of its people, a negative mythology has surrounded it. Disparaging second-hand hearsay remarks – such as 'You wouldn't walk down the streets in Tiger Bay!', 'It was dangerous there!', 'Harm would come to you there!', 'They carry knives and all kinds of weapons down the Bay!', 'It was a terrible place. People gambled openly in the street!', etc. – can still be heard today from people who, on the whole, never set foot in Tiger Bay.[24]

The most famous representation is that produced by Howard Spring (1889–1965), the Welsh popular writer, in his autobiography:

[T]here was a fascination in the walk through Tiger Bay. Chinks and Dagos, Lascars and Levantines, slippered about the faintly evil by-ways that ran off

from Bute Street ... Children of the strangest colours, fruit of frightful misal-
liances, staggered half-naked about the streets; and the shop windows were dec-
orated with names that were the epitome of all the clans and classes under the
sun ... It was a dirty, rotten and romantic district, an offence and an inspi-
ration, and I loved it.[25]

People from this community are deeply offended by such constructions.

When Butetown Community History Project was born, it was necessarily always-already positioned within a long-established field of representations.[26] The ethnographer/oral historian who co-founded the project was partially aware of this fact; local people were fully aware of it. Thus, for them, at least as much as for him, this initiative was, from the very beginning, a dialogic, cultural-political intervention. It was not so much a matter of finding out about a community that had been 'hidden from history' (to use the phrase made famous by Sheila Rowbotham).[27] Rather, it was that of studying a community that was hyper-visible in the sense that they are always-already written about, yet simultaneously invisible in that key dimensions of their experience have been hidden – mostly because those who represented them rarely bothered to ask them for their stories or points of view.

Butetown Community History Project, certainly from the point of view of the anthropologist/oral historian, sought to achieve empowerment through practical education and demystification of the research process.[28] The following is from an interview in which Marcia Brahim Barry describes our practice in the early years of 1988–90. The activity being described is part of the work we did in our first community education initiative, a weekly course/workshop begun in February 1988. The interviewer, as before, is Karen Gehrke.

MB: I don't know whether you know the old library. Well ... Glenn wanted
us to start to learn to do research and we all went up there and it was the
summer holidays and so we did a few stints ... [with] people just looking in
old newspapers and things. It was quite fascinating because people were begin-
ning to learn to do research. And yet because we were all together, it wasn't like
doing some sort of painful task ... In fact, we got involved in looking up the
papers and found them really fascinating. And you could actually see what he
was trying to tell you ...

[H]e used to stress that we actually could write our own history, that we
could write the history that we saw, not the history that people thought was our
history, so that we actually had a voice ...[29]

The effort was not simply to get people to collect and tell their own stories but also to encourage them to engage with what had already been written and said about them: the project always involved an element of critical engagement with hegemonic discourses, e.g. local discourses of racial and cultural difference. To this end, we began by studying old newspapers. The intent was also to read accounts by social scientists and (other) fiction writers.

The course title was 'The Way We Were: Life Stories from Tiger Bay'. The first session attracted 42 people. This sort of turnout was unheard of: the local authority had been trying to get adult education classes going in Butetown for a few years with very little success.

In terms of funding and other material resources, we began our weekly sessions with virtually nothing. Our only possessions, purchased thanks to a small grant of £350 from the county Community Education Service, were minimal level broadcast-quality equipment – a Marantz CP430 cassette recorder and two good microphones – and a small supply of audiotapes. One consequence of the lack of resources was that it helped to bond the group together through collective responsibility:

> *MB: We didn't have any money so we had the Butetown Community Centre for nothing on Tuesday nights. . . . I used to bring the kettle from home. Molly and Rita or Olwen or any of us – we all pooled our money and we bought biscuits and tea and coffee.*[30]

The point of the sessions was twofold: for local residents to learn how to do oral history and for the group to begin systematically collecting life stories on audiotape. The idea was for the anthropologist/oral historian to mediate the process of knowledge acquisition, eventually making his presence unnecessary. The emphasis was not simply on training (practical demonstration of techniques in interviewing, use of the microphones, etc.) but on education (critical discussion of themes and issues in research, oral history and cultural democracy):

> *MB: The first half of the sessions would be for us to learn interviewing techniques, and so we used a book by Paul Thompson [The Voice of the Past] . . . Glenn got a stack of them. We were all supposed to pay him but I don't think anybody did. In the end he gave us all a book. So we used to talk about oral history and we used to think of questions and themes and we used to read passages out of the books . . . I don't think we realised what was happening to us, but we were actually developing [knowledge and] skills.*

The sessions were intended to run for 32 weeks, but ended up running for three years. About half of those who regularly attended those sessions are still actively involved in the Centre today. Obviously, our sessions had some significant, lasting effect. Alessandro Portelli has observed:

[W]hen the encounter takes place [on the basis] of equality, not only the observer, but also the 'observed', may be stimulated to think new thoughts about themselves. This throws a new light on an old problem: the observer's interference on the observed reality. The positivistic fetish of non-interference has developed outlandish techniques to bypass or remove this problem. I believe we ought to turn the question on its head, and consider the changes that our presence may cause as some of the most important results of our fieldwork.[31]

16.5 Keeping cultural democracy alive

Perhaps after reading the foregoing discussion about cultural democracy in our early years, the reader may imagine that it has been easy to maintain. Nothing could be further from the truth, as the following dialogue between Karen Gehrke and Chris Weedon makes clear:

KG: You mentioned once that an idea behind the Centre was also . . . to realise the idea of cultural democracy.

CW: Yes, . . . the whole project, even when it was in its early phases of a community history project, was an exercise in cultural democracy in the sense that rather than having someone from the outside come and do it, the idea was that people should collect their own history, should interview each other, collect their photographs, archive them and all the rest of it. And that every decision . . . and all the objectives should be discussed by the group. And it should be a collective thing that went forward, which everybody was involved in irrespective of their background, education or whatever . . .

Now obviously since those early days it's got bigger, but I think those principals are still important. It's just that it's more diverse now, so people choose to work in different areas. Everybody can't do everything because there are too many things going on, but certainly the idea that it should be people doing it for themselves and it should be empowering . . . is still there.

KG: So you think from your point of view it worked out so far?

CW: I wouldn't say it was a 100 per cent success, I think it's an ongoing battle. I think cultural democracy is very difficult because [it] rests on the notion that people really want to take responsibility and I think one of the things that this project has shown is often people don't actually want to take responsibility. I mean they want to feel like they're involved and they want to have a say but they don't always want to do all the other things that come beyond that, to actually realise it.

There are limits to how much they are willing to do, or what areas they are willing to get involved in . . . I think it's an ongoing struggle, cultural democracy.[32]

With regard to taking responsibility, it is still the case that almost all of the audio-taped life history interviews in our archive were done more than a decade ago by two volunteers (the anthropologist and Marcia Barry) in the first few years of our existence. Despite the community's deeply felt view that their history needs to be preserved, not many local people have been willing to go out and ensure that it is done – even though the necessary equipment and expertise is readily available to them.

16.6 What do we do with voices?[33]

Our oral history archive now includes about 800 hours of audio-recorded interviews and a dozen hours of video (the latter made in collaboration with two local video groups). We have not yet been able to make substantial use of this material. Because of the resources required, transforming audio-recorded interviews into a form that can be shared with a public audience of readers or listeners can pose serious difficulties for groups such as ours.

We have made use of oral testimony on radio. Our most notable achievement with the media was our central involvement in the production of *Bay People*, two half-hour programmes, narrated by Glenn Jordan and broadcast on BBC Radio Wales in October 2001. Most of the voices in the programmes are of people, from varying ethnic backgrounds, who we recommended; and many of the interviews were recorded in our centre. These developments suggest important shifts in the politics of representation.

Producing books from audiotapes is a long, laborious and costly business. From our early days we have intended to produce two volumes of life histories: *Women's Lives from Tiger Bay* and *Men's Lives from Tiger Bay*. More generally, we planned to produce publications, including children's books, that would make extensive use of oral history. To date, that has not happened; indeed, as it turns out, all of the life stories/community histories that we have published – except for short extracts for our exhibition panels or our (previously existing) newsletter – have been by people who have typed their texts onto computer, i.e. into a form that could be easily read, discussed and edited. This has ironic consequences: those whose voices are most marginalized within this community have yet to appear in print – despite our lofty, culturally democratic aims.

16.7 The people write back

This is not the story of my life. It is simply a record of memories of a childhood spent 'Down the Docks' in Cardiff. Some of the sights and sounds, the smells, the feelings.
Phyllis Grogan Chappell [34]

A number of community-based groups have produced and published working-class writing, including community histories and life stories. In the UK perhaps the most successful is Centreprise, based in the Hackney district of London.

> *Centreprise began publishing working-class writing in 1972 ... From its beginnings as a local history project, Centreprise publishing has expanded to include, alongside history, a wide range of other work by local people. Publications include: writing by young people; local autobiographies of working-class life; local history materials; writing by literacy students; Black writing; and the poetry and stories produced by the writers' workshops.*
>
> *In its first few years (1972–5) Centreprise produced 25 titles, each of which sold between 450 and 5,000 copies. Subsequently it continued to publish several titles each year and in 1992 had a list of 34 titles in print.*[35]

The publishing programme of Butetown History & Arts Centre has not been nearly as successful as Centreprise. Our efforts, however, are guided by similar principles and practices – except we do not place as much emphasis on work. To date, our publications include eight books (we co-produced one other) and two booklets.[36]

From the very beginning, we established a series entitled 'Life Stories from Tiger Bay' in which local people would be encouraged to publish. Thus far, four titles have been published in the series: Neil Sinclair, *The Tiger Bay Story* (140 pages, 1993); Phyllis Grogan Chappell, *A Tiger Bay Childhood: Growing Up in the 1930s* (80 pages, 1994); Harry 'Shipmate' Cooke, *How I Saw It: A Stroll thro' Old Cardiff Bay* (112 pages, 1995); and Neil Sinclair, *Endangered Tiger: A Community under Threat* (196 pages, 2003). We are currently working on a fifth title: Olwen Blackman Watkins, *A Family Affair: Three Generations in Tiger Bay*.

The books in our Life Stories series are user-friendly: the size is A5 (approximately 150 × 210 mm) and the length is usually considerably less than 200 pages. The shortest book, Phyllis Chappell's *A Tiger Bay Childhood*, is only 80 pages. I kept pushing her to write more until we had enough text to produce a book rather than a booklet. There is a serious point here, which has to do with the politics of visibility: if working-class writing is to be noticed, one needs to be able to see the title on the spine.

What is the motivation to write these books? Alessandro Portelli has observed, 'The telling of a story preserves the teller from oblivion.'[37] In the case of our writers from Tiger Bay, the desire seems more to proclaim 'WE WERE!' rather than affirm 'I AM!' These writers privilege family and, especially, community history – not autobiography.[38] The desire to tell their personal stories is superseded by a quest to write insider accounts about a maligned community that they know and, usually, love.

Their sources are not research reports or maps or census books. They are shared memories and stories preserved across generations through traditions of storytelling and in the interactions of daily life – the sort of memory and knowledge discussed in the following passage by the CCCS Popular Memory Group:

> *A knowledge of past and present is also produced in the course of everyday life ... Such knowledge may circulate, usually without amplification, in everyday talk and in personal ... narratives. It may even be recorded in certain intimate cultural forms: letters, diaries, photograph albums and collections of things with past associations. It may be encapsulated in anecdotes that acquire the force and generality of myth ... Usually this history is ... not only unrecorded, but actually silenced. It is not offered the occasion to speak.*[39]

Such memory is the object of much of our work.

It is sometimes said that oral history and life stories are inevitably *partial* – both in the sense that they are incomplete (i.e. they are often fragmented or bitty and do not provide a sufficiently broad-based account) and that they are partisan (i.e. they are not 'objective' or 'neutral' but take up a position, often that of defending their community and/or their past). The writers in our Life Stories from Tiger Bay series are well aware of this, and regard their moral stance as a positive one.

The role of the anthropologist/oral historian in the production of the books in the series is that of facilitator. Sometimes he has rearranged disparate bits of the text to form more coherent sections and chapters; edited sentences for grammatical reasons; or suggested names for chapters. However, his editing does not extend to matters of 'truth': he does not challenge 'the facts' that the locals present. He also tends to relinquish the power to name: most of the books' titles were chosen by their authors, sometimes over the editor's objections. The key concern in the editing process has been preserving the author's voice – such that local people who know the author could literally hear him or her speaking if they read the text. The mode of writing is popular, rather than academic.[40]

The merit of our Life Stories books does not simply lie in their motivations, sources and style. Perhaps their greatest contribution lies in the detailed accounts they provide – i.e. the specific information that can trigger local memories, and can also serve the student or scholar as a guide to further investigation.

Since 2000, our publishing programme has considerably increased, this time with the anthropologist/oral historian often assuming the role of 'author'. This does not signal an abandonment of our commitment to cultural democracy but a decision to produce a more diverse range of publications, including books that privilege visual imagery – in particular, photographs.

16.8 History, memory and the visual

Why photographs? Because of their power – to trigger emotions; to bring together individual and collective memory; to convince the viewer that what they see did indeed exist. Marita Sturken explains:

> *The photograph of personal value is a talisman ... It evokes both memory and loss, both a trace of life and the prospect of death ... [I]t is a mechanism through which the past can be constructed and situated within the present. Images have the capacity to create, interfere with, and trouble the memories we hold as individuals and as a culture. They lend shape to personal stories and truth claims, and function as technologies of memory, producing both memory and forgetting.*[41]

Our turn to photographs seems to have happened by accident. In 1989, Butetown Community History Project was commissioned by an organization called NewEmploy Wales to prepare a permanent exhibition for its new office in Cardiff Bay, which was to be a training centre for local young people.

The exhibition was co-curated by the anthropologist and Olwen Blackman Watkins, one of the most highly respected residents of Butetown and a recently retired schoolteacher. Using her large personal collection of family and community photographs as a starting point, we collected hundreds of photographs dating from near the turn of the century to the redevelopment (so-called 'slum clearance') of the area in the 1960s. The images were copied, enlarged and professionally framed. The exhibition consisted of some 90 images: most of them were 12 x 16, 16 x 20, or 20 x 24 inches; six or seven of them were very large, perhaps around 48 inches in width.

The exhibition opened on a hot Sunday afternoon in July 1989. The response was phenomenal: 400 people showed up. The building was literally jam-packed. As past and present residents of Butetown encountered the images, they seemed to not quite believe it. They pointed to people in the group photographs and argued over their names. They laughed and cried as they recognized themselves, their friends, their place. Some even went home and brought back some of their own photographs to share with the group. The joy of recognition, the validation of popular memory, the pain of loss – that is the experience many local people had upon seeing those images.

We knew that photographs were important, but we had not realized how important. From that moment, we resolved to collect photographic images. Unlike the museum, we have not especially sought to collect original photographs – we think people should keep their personal and family photographs – although sometimes such images have been donated to us for safe keeping. Our archive now includes nearly 5000 images.[42]

The exhibition at NewEmploy Wales remained in place for more than ten years, until that organization ceased to exist. Despite the fact that the pictures did not change, people still came to see them. The exhibition became a site of memory. Why? Because, to echo Roland Barthes, those photographs reminded local viewers that what they saw – their friends, their streets, their community, their selves – was no longer but 'has indeed been'.[43]

In 1997, after holding a few temporary exhibitions in other buildings in Cardiff docklands, Butetown History & Arts Centre developed its own gallery.[44] Our gallery is committed to cultural democracy – to producing and presenting images, text, sound and moving images that are accessible and meaningful to ordinary people. Most of our exhibitions engage with issues of local people's history, cultural politics and everyday life, exploring themes such as immigration, identity, community, popular culture, urban regeneration, and media representations of racial and cultural difference. Common sources for our self-generated exhibitions include photographs by street photographers, photographs from personal and family albums, and images from newspapers and other popular media.

Although we seek to reach 'non-traditional viewers' – i.e. people who rarely, if ever, attend museums or galleries – we do not assume that they are unintelligent or unsophisticated. We wish to produce exhibitions that are visually interesting and intellectually rigorous. Thus, for example, our exhibitions are becoming increasingly polyvocal: they may incorporate competing conceptions of the past or they may both praise and problematize the images they contain.[45]

To accompany our exhibitions, we now produce substantial exhibition catalogues, exploring issues such as the *poetics and politics of representation*[46] and usually designed so they can have a life after the exhibitions.[47]

As I write (December 2002), we are completing our fourth image-based book: *Fractured Horizon: A Landscape of Memory*.[48] This small, beautiful and disturbing book is the result of a project done in 2001 by Mathew Manning, then a student studying photography and media studies at the University of Glamorgan, and Patti Flynn, a singer-writer whose family has deep roots in that place that is now called Cardiff Bay. Together, through pictures and words, they confront the past and present of Cardiff docklands:

Over a period of several weeks, the writer and the photographer walk together around the shoreline of the area that is being reinvented as Cardiff Bay ... In order to guide the photographer, the narrator draws upon a personal and collective archive of stored impressions. To find what she remembers, to repossess fragments of her past, the narrator takes the photographer to the edges, the margins, the not-yet-completed spaces of the redevelopment. There, among the time-ravaged and the eroded, the used and the abandoned, she manages almost to be at home.

... These are photographs of the present, imprinted with traces of the past.[49]

Catherine Belsey has stated, 'The kind of cultural history I am putting forward is a history of representation.'[50] This is close to the project we pursue in our exhibitions and related activity. People's history, as we practise it, includes ways of seeing – i.e. an engagement with images that goes beyond any assumption that they simply provide 'evidence' or a 'window on to reality'.

Fractured Horizon, the exhibition and the book, signals an engagement with the visual that is very different from that usually practised by historians, including those producing 'people's history': image and text exist in a dialogic relationship in which neither is privileged. Raphael Samuel has perceptively observed:

'History from below' ... stopped short of any engagement with graphics. Caught up in the cultural revolution of the 1960s it nevertheless remained wedded to quite traditional forms of writing, teaching and research. E.P. Thompson's The Making of the English Working Class *(1963) has not a single print to leaven the 800 pages of narrative which covers some of the most brilliant years of English political caricature. Nor has Peter Laslett's* The World We Have Lost *(1965) ... 'New-wave' social history did take photographs on board ... but it was for their reality content rather their pictorial value or interest – in short because they were thought of as being of a piece of documentary truth.*

He continues:

It seems possible that history's new-found interest in 'representation', and its belated recognition of the deconstructive turn in contemporary thought, will allow for, and even force, a more central engagement with graphics ... Photographs, if in the spirit of postmodernism they are dissevered from any notion of the real, might be studied for the theatricality of social appearances, rather than as likenesses of everyday life.[51]

'Postmodernism' is a term rarely used at Butetown History & Arts Centre. Nonetheless, some of our practices are informed by mild doses of poststructuralist and postmodernist ideas.

16.9 Concluding reflections

This chapter has raised various issues having to do with people's history and cultural democracy through a discussion of a project that has existed for some fifteen years in the docklands area of Cardiff. It has explored how Butetown Community History Project began and the ethos and practices – of oral history, collaborative research, community-based education, community publishing and exhibiting – that it and its successor (Butetown History & Arts Centre) have sought to maintain. It has repeatedly demonstrated the centrality of history to cultural democracy and the persistence of community.

I would like to conclude by reflecting on two challenges – that of doing radical intellectual work and that of achieving cultural democracy. Consider the following statement from Stuart Hall, the cultural theorist and activist intellectual:

> *I come back to the deadly seriousness of intellectual work. It is a deadly serious matter. I come back to the critical distinction between intellectual work and academic work: they overlap, they abut with one another, they feed off one another, the one provides you with the means to the other. But they are not the same thing. I come back to the difficulty of instituting a genuine cultural and critical practice, which is intended to produce some kind of organic intellectual political work . . . I come back to theory and politics, the politics of theory. Not theory as the will to truth, but theory as a set of contested, localized, conjunctural knowledges, which have to be debated in a dialogical way. But also as a practice which always thinks about its intervention in a world in which it would make some difference, in which it would have some effect. Finally, a practice which understands the need for intellectual modesty.*[52]

From the perspective of Butetown History & Arts Centre, as for Stuart Hall, radical intellectual work is serious business, involving localized intervention and long-term engagement. It also implies a commitment to collective work and shared responsibility. However, this is not always easy to achieve: people have different skills and motivations and, as indicated earlier, they sometimes do not wish to take significant responsibility for ensuring that the organization succeeds.

Finally, in our view, doing radical intellectual work includes a commitment to writing in a form that is both intellectually rigorous and – in terms of vocabulary, syntax and mode of presentation – accessible to a broad audience, including people who have had no higher education. In the case of this essay, this position means that whatever is written here should, in principle, be accessible to members of our organization or the local community who might wish to read it.

Writing in this way poses real challenges. I do not claim to have always met them.

Guide to further reading

Stuart Hall, 'The Spectacle of the Other', in S. Hall (ed.), *Representation: Cultural Representations and Signifying Practices* (London, 1997), pp. 223–90.

Eric Hobsbawn, 'On History from Below', in *On History*, (London, 1997), pp. 201–16.

Glenn Jordan (ed.), *'Down the Bay': 'Picture Post', Humanist Photography and Images of 1950s Cardiff* (Cardiff, 2001).

Glenn Jordan and Chris Weedon, 'Whose History Is It? Class, Cultural Democracy and Constructions of the Past', in Jordan and Weedon, *Cultural Politics* (Oxford, 1995), pp. 112–73.

Robert Perks and Alistair Thomson (eds), *The Oral History Reader* (London, 1998).

Popular Memory Group, 'Popular Memory: Theory, Politics, Method', in Centre for Contemporary Cultural Studies, *Making Histories: Studies in History-writing and Politics* (London, 1982), pp. 205–52.

Alessandro Portelli, *The Death of Luigi Trastulli and Other Stories: Form and Meaning in Oral History* (Albany, 1991).

Peter Read, 'Presenting Voices in Different Media: Print, Radio and CD-ROM', in Robert Perks and Alistair Thomson, *The Oral History Reader* (London, 1998), pp. 414–20.

Marita Sturken, 'The Image as Memorial: Personal Photographs in Cultural Memory' in Marianne Hirsch (ed.), *The Familial Gaze* (Hanover and London, 1999), pp. 178–95.

Paul Thompson, *The Voice of the Past: Oral History* (Oxford, 1978).

Notes

Thanks to Chris Weedon, Stefan Berger, Teresa Rees, Radhika Mohanram and Heiko Feldner for their comments on this chapter.

1   Raphael Samuel, 'Unofficial Knowledge' in Vol. 1 of his *Theatres of Memory* (London, 1994), pp. 3, 6.

2   Not all of Cardiff's Sailor Town was in Tiger Bay and not all of Tiger Bay was in the Sailor Town. This fact is often overlooked.

3   On stereotyping and the racializing of 'Others', see Stuart Hall, 'The Spectacle of the Other' in Hall (ed.), *Representation* (London, 1997), pp. 223–90.

4   Chris Weedon is best known as a feminist cultural theorist. Her doctoral thesis, however, is on the cultural politics of British working-class writing; see Christine M. Weedon, *Aspects of the Politics of Literature and Working-class Writing in Interwar Britain* (PhD thesis, Centre for Contemporary Cultural Studies, University of Birmingham, 1984).

5   Karen Gehrke, *Struggling For Cultural Democracy: A Case Study of Butetown History & Arts Centre* (BA dissertation, Communication Studies, University of Glamorgan, 1996).

6   Jean Chesneaux, *Past and Futures: Or What Is History For?* (London, 1978), p. 1.

7   Paul Thompson, *The Voice of the Past: Oral History* (Oxford, 1978), p. 2.

8   Eric Hobsbawn, 'On History from Below', in Frederick Krantz (ed.), *History from Below: Studies in Popular Protest and Popular Ideology* (Oxford, 1988), pp. 13–28.

9   George P. Rawick (ed.), *The American Slave: A Composite Autobiography*, Vols 1–19 (Westport, CT, 1972)

10 Centre for Contemporary Cultural Studies, *Making Histories: Studies in History-writing and Politics* (London, 1982).

11 John and Barbara Hammond, *The Village Labourer* (London, 1911); *The Town Labourer* (London, 1917); and *The Skilled Labourer* (London, 1919).

12 E.P. Thompson, *The Making of the English Working Class* (London, 1968).

13 For an excellent introduction to developments in oral history see Robert Perks and Alistair Thomson (eds), *The Oral History Reader* (London, 1998). The 'classic text' in the field arguably remains Thompson's *Voice of the Past*.

14 This work tends to be published by small, local publishers, e.g. in Britain, by groups belonging to the Federation of Worker Writers and Community Publishers (FWWCP).

15 John Tosh, *The Pursuit of History* (London, 1984), p. 8.

16 Thompson, *Voice of the Past*, p. 5.

17 One might wonder why the two fields do not more often come together, since practices signify and meanings are reproduced in and through practices.

18 Samuel, 'Unofficial Knowledge', p. 17.

19 Chesneaux, *Past and Futures*, p. 9.

20 Catherine Hall, *White, Male and Middle Class: Explorations in Feminism and History* (Cambridge, 1992), p. 5.

21 Tosh, *The Pursuit of History*, p. 6.

22 Marcia Brahim Barry, Interview document; transcript of interview conducted by Karen Gerhke, 1 March 1996. All quotations from Marcia Barry are from this document.

23 There have been innumerable articles in local newspapers on 'Tiger Bay'. In the 1800s and early 1900s the *Cardiff Times* and *South Wales Daily News* regularly provided their readers with long, juicy accounts. In the 1920s and 1930s the *Western Mail* periodically launched viciously racist tirades against 'coloured seamen'. Since then, the *South Wales Echo* has provided many a romantic, mythological contribution.

24 Neil Sinclair, *The Tiger Bay Story* (Cardiff, 1993), p. 3.

25 Howard Spring, *Heaven Lies About Us: A Fragment of Infancy* (London, 1939), p. 33.

26 For an analysis of Spring's discourse see Glenn Jordan, 'Images of Tiger Bay: Did Howard Spring Tell the Truth?', *Llafur: Journal of the Society for Welsh Labour History* 5(1) (1988), pp. 53–9. The rhetoric of 'insider' accounts is explored in Glenn Jordan and Chris Weedon, 'When the Subaltern Speaks, What Do They Say?', in Paul Gilroy, Lawrence Grossberg and Angela McRobbie (eds), *Without Guarantees: In Honour of Stuart Hall* (London, 2000).

27 Sheila Rowbotham, *Hidden from History* (London, 1973). Often women's history is literally hidden. When we were working on our first exhibition we went through the local history collection in Cardiff Central Library in search of images of women at work. We found virtually nothing.

28 Over the decades, the area has literally become a social laboratory – without any consent from the community. Every year perhaps a few dozen students from Cardiff University descend on what is left of Tiger Bay. Local people, with very few exceptions, have grown very tired of them – so tired that they often send the students to us, i.e. to the official 'experts' on their community.

29 The anthropologist was already an experienced researcher – with an interesting connection to Butetown. As an undergraduate and graduate student at Stanford University in California (1970–76), he was a research assistant to Professor St Clair Drake, an African-American scholar who, like Kenneth Little, did anthropological fieldwork in Tiger Bay in the 1940s. See St Clair Drake, *Values, Social Structure and Race Relations in the British Isles* (PhD thesis, Department of Anthropology, University of Chicago, 1954).

30 Marcia Barry, interview document, 1 March 1996.

31 Alessandro Portelli, 'Research as an Experiment in Equality' in his *The Death of Luigi Trastulli and Other Stories: Form and Meaning in Oral History* (Albany, 1991), p. 43f.

32 Chris Weedon, interview document: transcript of interview conducted by Karen Gerhke, 2 March 1996.

33 For an excellent discussion of practical problems involved in making use of audiotaped oral history see Peter Read, 'Presenting Voices in Different

Media: Print, Radio and CD-ROM', in Perks and Thomson, *The Oral History Reader*, pp. 414–20.

34 Phyllis Grogan Chappell, Preface to *A Tiger Bay Childhood* (Cardiff, 1994), p. 1.

35 Glenn Jordan and Chris Weedon, *Cultural Politics* (Oxford, 1995), p. 133. Centreprise's 'People's Autobiography' project in the 1970s had an ethos very similar to ours: see, e.g. *A People's Autobiography of Hackney, Working Lives: Hackney, Volume One: 1900–1945* (London, 1977).

36 The two booklets are *Prejudice & Pride* (BHAC, 2001), which accompanied an exhibition on African-Caribbean people in post-war Britain; and *Windrush: A Sense of Belonging* (BHAC, 2001), a selection of poetry by children from a local Saturday school.

37 Portelli, '"The Time of My Life": Functions of Time in Oral History', in *The Death of Luigi Trastulli and Other Stories*, p. 59.

38 One of these books, Harry Cooke's *How I Saw It*, does not include family history. Harry grew up in Liverpool, not Cardiff.

39 Popular Memory Group, 'Popular Memory: Theory, Politics, Method', in *Making Histories*, p. 210.

40 That is, except on those occasions where the authors themselves, perhaps imagining their audience, shift into an assumed 'academic' register – as in parts of the Preface to Neil Sinclair's *The Tiger Bay Story*.

41 Marita Sturken, 'The Image as Memorial: Personal Photographs in Cultural Memory', in Marianne Hirsch (ed.), *The Familial Gaze* (Hanover, 1999), p. 178.

42 The development of our image archive has made an impact. Most recent television programmes made in Britain about old Cardiff docklands and/or about immigrants and minorities in Wales include images from our archive. A number of our photographs are on the BBC Wales website; now, unlike before, Wales appears as a multi-ethnic nation.

43 Roland Barthes, *Camera Lucida: Reflections on Photography* (London, 1984), p. 115.

44 Opening our gallery was made possible by a grant from the European Regional Development Fund (ERDF) to develop a 'visitor attraction', i.e. to facilitate economic and cultural development in the new Cardiff Bay.

45 This was the case for an exhibition held in May–July 2002. *One Island, Many Faiths: 100 Years of Diverse Religions in Tiger Bay* explored the competing discourses and practices of the many religious organizations that have sought to establish a foothold in Butetown. Baptists, Catholics, Church-in-Wales, Greek Orthodox, Lutheran, Methodists, Muslims, Quakers and the Salvation Army.

46 I borrow this term from Stuart Hall (ed.), *Representation* (London, 1997) and from James Clifford and George E. Marcus, *Writing Culture: The Poetics and Politics of Ethnography* (Berkeley, 1986).

47 The first of these new publications is Glenn Jordan (ed.), *'Down the Bay':*

'Picture Post', Humanist Photography and Images of 1950s Cardiff (Cardiff, 2001). The second is Glenn Jordan, *Tramp Steamers, Seamen & Sailor Town: Jack Sullivan's Paintings of Old Cardiff Docklands* (Cardiff, 2002).

48 BHAC received a publishing grant from the Arts Council of Wales to subsidize the publication of *Fractured Horizon*. I mention this fact because we have often had difficulties convincing the art establishment that we do *art* – as we may have difficulties convincing some readers that we do *history*.

49 Glenn Jordan, 'Tortured Journey: Cardiff Bay, Photography and the Landscape of Memory', Introduction to Patti Flynn, Mathew Manning and Glenn Jordan, *Fractured Horizon: A Landscape of Memory* (Cardiff, 2003).

50 Catherine Belsey, 'Reading Cultural History', in Tasmin Spargo (ed.), *Reading the Past* (Houndmills, 2000), p. 106.

51 Raphael Samuel, 'Unofficial Knowledge', in *Theatres of Memory*, pp. 38–9; emphasis added.

52 Stuart Hall, 'Cultural Studies and its Theoretical Legacies', in Lawrence Grossberg, Cary Nelson and Paula Treichler (eds), *Cultural Studies* (London, 1992), p. 286.

Glossary

This glossary is not exhaustive. It explains difficult terms that recur in several chapters. It does not explain words associated with particular theories, for that is the task of specific chapters.

Agency   The capacity of an individual or group to act consciously towards a particular end.

Determinism   In history refers usually to the notion that historical processes conform to certain patterns or laws that (a) are beyond our control and (b) make a particular course of events necessary or inevitable. The opposite belief is the notion of free will. *See also Agency and Teleology.*

Discourse   Used generally to refer to communication in speech or writing, or to a lengthy spoken or written treatment of a subject. Discourse is used in a special sense by poststructuralists, and refers to the relationship between language and its context   as a means of both producing and organizing meaning in social contexts. As such it is related to social power.

Empiricism   The doctrine that knowledge should be founded upon experience, observation and perhaps experiment.

Epistemology   The theory of knowledge, its validity and foundations.

Hegemony   A dominant group's rule by ideological consent (non-coercive means); the dominant group achieves power and control over other groups in society by successfully representing to them that the existing state of affairs is in their best interest.

Hermeneutic   In history usually means the interpretation of sources, often to uncover the intentions and ideas of their authors.

Heuristic   A concept or other device that serves to discover or learn something.

Historism   A historical doctrine associated particularly with Leopold von Ranke in which all actions, categories, truths and values, are explicable in terms of particular historical conditions, and in consequence can be understood only by examining particular historical contexts, in detachment from present-day attitudes. Historists often focus on political history and great men. The term 'historicism' is also used to designate this type of historiography, but we have preferred historism in this volume because historicism is also used to designate the doctrine that particular events can only be understood in terms of 'historical laws'. Historism as we have defined it rejects this contention on the grounds that historical events are always unique.

Metanarrative   A theory that purports to be comprehensive and to be able to explain all particular instances (Also known as grandnarrative, master narrative, grand theory.)

Metaphysical   Used generally to designate or abstract, perhaps speculative, reasoning. Used by Derrida – in a different sense – to designate the illusory quest for underlying realities.

Ontology   The study of the nature of being, of what it is to be in the world.

Positivism   A doctrine contending that sense perceptions are the only admissible basis of human knowledge and precise thought. Positivists hold that historical laws – if there are any – must be derived from observation. Positivists often attacked metaphysics as abstract speculation.

Relativism   the doctrine that knowledge is not absolute, but depends upon point of view.

Subject   Can designate the ability of an individual or a group to make sense of the world and choose a particular course of action (*see Agency*) or, in contrast, it can mean subjection to linguistic or social structures. Some theories attempt to reconcile these two meanings of the term.

Teleology   The notion that history moves towards a predetermined end – socialism, capitalism, the rule of God, the realization of the nation-state, for example.

Universalism/universalist   Concepts, ideas or theories that are considered to be generally applicable – not just to particular categories of people, nations or societies.

Index